What Einstein Kept Under His Hat

"Bob Wolke is that rare mix of lab-coat scientist and raconteur, as if Albert Einstein's mother had married Rodney Dangerfield's father. He's informed, amusing, and delivers clear answers as well as good, in-depth science." —Christopher Kimball, founder, publisher, and editor of *Cook's Illustrated* and *Cook's Country*

"Robert Wolke's scientific lore is more than entertaining—it's essential to making us better cooks, more savvy shoppers, and less phobic eaters." —James Peterson, author of *Splendid Soups* and *Glorious French Food*

"I may never need to know why baking soda turns red cabbage blue, but it's reassuring to know that I can find the answer, along with many others, in here." —Bill Yosses, author of *The Perfect Finish*

"Books like Robert L. Wolke's are showing cooks how to continue evolving at a time in which it would appear that gastronomy has stalled." —Ferran Adrià, chef and founder, El Bulli restaurant, Roses, Spain

"Bob Wolke writes about the hows and whys of cooking with clarity, humor, and passion. Who else can explain the science of braising or the mechanics of heat transfer and still make you chuckle?" —Jack Bishop, editorial director, *Cook's Illustrated*

"Wolke's explanations are so well written that they read like a witty novel, except it is all true." —Elinor Klivans, author of *Chocolate Cakes: 50 Great Cakes for Every Occasion*

"Infectious, informative, and even surprisingly useful."
—Mark Kurlansky, author of *Cod* and *The Story of Salt*

"Teaches cooks about chemistry, and chemists about food. If you love cooking, chemistry, and puns, this is for you!"
—Charles P. Casey, former president, American Chemical Society

"An engrossing, authoritative, witty, lucid, and insightful book that provides a host of answers to questions that you've probably always wondered about as well as those that you've never imagined."
—*Chemical Educator*

"Wolke . . . manages to combine the clarity of a good journalist with the nosiness of a good scientist. He doesn't just dissect food, he loves to cook and eat it too. He is . . . just the kind of scientist who would be vivacious at a dinner party." —Jean-Baptiste Sancey, chef and owner, The Railway gastropub, Honiton, UK

"Wolke knows his stuff; bridges the gap between laboratory and kitchen." —Rhonda Parkinson, author of *The Everything Stir-Fry Cookbook*

"This guy knows *lotsa* stuff!" —Howard Stern, radio personality and judge, *America's Got Talent* (NBC)

Also by Robert L. Wolke

TEXTBOOKS

Impact: Science on Society

Chemistry Explained

TRADE BOOKS

What Einstein Didn't Know:
Scientific Answers to Everyday Questions

What Einstein Told His Barber:
More Scientific Answers to Everyday Questions

What Einstein Told His Cook:
Kitchen Science Explained

W. W. NORTON & COMPANY

New York London

What
Einstein
Kept Under
His Hat

*Secrets of
Science in the
Kitchen*

ROBERT L. WOLKE

with recipes by
Marlene Parrish

For information about permission to reproduce selections from this book, write to Permissions, W. W. Norton & Company, Inc., 500 Fifth Avenue, New York, NY 10110

Manufacturing by Courier Westford
Book design by Barbara M. Bachman
Production manager: Louise Mattarelliano

ISBN 978-0-393-34165-2 pbk.

W. W. Norton & Company, Inc., 500 Fifth Avenue, New York, N.Y. 10110
www.wwnorton.com

W. W. Norton & Company Ltd., Castle House, 75/76 Wells Street, London W1T 3QT

1 2 3 4 5 6 7 8 9 0

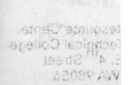

I dedicate this book, as I have my life, to my wife,

companion, motivator, and most loving critic,

Marlene Parrish, who characterizes

herself as Einstein's Cook.

CONTENTS

Why does iced tea turn cloudy? · How does green tea differ from other teas? · Are enzymes alive? · Can I make coffee and tea from the same kettle water? · Will coffee stay hotter if I put the cream in right away, or only when I'm ready to drink it? · What are alcohols? · What is a hop? · Why are there sulfites in wine? · What's so special about Sherry? · Does hanging a spoon handle in the neck of the bottle keep Champagne from going flat? · Why do Champagne corks have that funny shape? · What makes bourbon bourbon? · Why does a mint julep glass turn frosty? · What's the best way to cool a drink with ice without watering it down? · Is there a formula for telling when I'm getting dangerously drunk? · How can I get a red wine stain out of a tablecloth? . . . and more.

What ever happened to skim milk? · Why are there so many types of dairy cream? · Does yogurt contain live bacteria? · Why is soft-serve ice cream soft? · Does eating ice cream in hot weather really cool one off? · Why does ice cream shrink when it melts? · Why does all cream cheese come from Philadelphia? · What makes American cheese American? · Does all cheese need to be pasteurized? · Why is string cheese so stringy? · How does a "nut" of butter thicken a pan sauce? · How are eggs graded? · Are brown eggs better than white eggs? · Does a blood spot in an egg mean it's fertilized? · Would double-yolk eggs hatch twins? · How can I keep boiled eggs from cracking? · Why does a hard-cooked egg spin, but a raw egg won't? · Why do hard-cooked egg yolks turn green? · What makes an egg rotten? · Why do eggs have dimples? · Can pasteurized eggs be used the same as unpasteurized eggs? · Are thousand-year-old eggs for real? . . . and more.

What makes the vivid colors in vegetables? · Why do green vegetables turn drab when cooked? · How should fruits and vegetables be washed? · Why do some potatoes have gray patches? · Is rhubarb poisonous? · How do vegetables get their minerals? · Why do onions *really* make me cry? · Why are "sweet" onions sweet? · Why is my cucumber bitter? · Why does heated soy milk boil over? · How do they make tofu? · What is miso made of? · Why do beans and other legumes produce gas? · Must beans be soaked before cooking? . . . and more.

How can I speed up the ripening of fruits? · Why does a cut apple turn brown? · When a banana ripens and gets sweeter, does it contain more calories? · Why are some oils edible and others not? · Exactly what are trans fats? · Why do fats turn rancid? · What is a free radical? · Does light olive oil contain fewer calories? · What's "extra" about extra-virgin olive oil? · What is a fatty acid? · What's the difference between black and green olives? · How does osmosis work? · Why did my strawberry preserves turn out soupy? · Do all fruits float? · What's the difference between apple juice and apple cider? · Are "raw" cashews raw? . . . and more.

What are the different forms of carbohydrates? · What makes mashed potatoes gluey? · Why do leftover starchy foods turn hard in the refrigerator? · Is there an easy way to use chopsticks? · What is converted rice? · Why does unbleached flour cost more than bleached flour? · How does self-rising flour raise itself? · What kind of wheat is buckwheat? · How can I best match a pasta shape with a sauce? · Is the nutritional fiber destroyed when I liquefy fruit in a blender? · Which kinds of fiber contain calories and which don't? · What is "steel cut" corn meal? · Why do tortillas contain lime? · What are sugar alcohols? · What is stevia? · Why mustn't babies be fed honey? . . . and more.

Why are wild and farm-raised salmon different colors? · Why do they treat tuna with carbon monoxide? · Do they really make fake scallops by punching out skate wings? · How does lime juice "cook" ceviche? · What do I do with *bottarga*? · What kinds of mussels are there? · Are razor clams good to eat? · How do wet, dry, and diver scallops differ? · Why are shrimp different colors? · Why is shrimp scampi called that? . . . and more.

Is "mechanically separated meat" dangerous? · Why is my supermarket's hamburger meat red on the outside and brown on the
inside? · Does marinating work? · What is souse? · Why are there
rainbows on my roast beef? · Why are hot dogs pink?·· Are nitrites
dangerous? · Exactly what is braising? · What's the difference
between browning and caramelizing? · Why does food turn brown
when sautéed? · Why are there so many precautions about making a
stock? · Where does simmering end and boiling begin? · Does
adding lemon juice to a stock increase its calcium content? · Why do
we cook with wine? · Which is better for grilling, charcoal or gas? . .
. and more.

What's essential about an essential oil? · What makes spices spicy?
· Why is cooked garlic so different from raw garlic? · Is garlic powder an invention of the Devil? · Can garlic-infused oil be dangerous? · Should herbs be added near the beginning of cooking or near
the end? · How much dried herb shall I use instead of the fresh
herb? · What is the average shelf life of an herb or spice? · How do
pantry-pest bugs survive in a can of Cayenne pepper? · How do they
make liquid smoke? · Is wasabi real? · How can I keep grated horseradish "hot" in the refrigerator? · Why did grinding cloves destroy
my spice grinder? · How does a salt pig work? · Why is vanilla so
expensive? . . . and more.

Does a box of baking soda in the refrigerator kill odors? · Where
should I keep my butter? · Why do foods spoil? · Do airport X-rays

INTRODUCTION

THIS IS THE SECOND food-focused book, and the fourth book overall, in what has turned out to be my "Einstein series," a series I didn't anticipate when I started it. But then, I have never planned the courses of my careers. I simply followed the advice of Yogi Berra— whenever I came to a fork in the road, I took it. A succession of forks has led me from teaching and research in nuclear chemistry to text-book authorship, university administration, journalism, and trade book authorship, where you now find me. It was some years ago that I left my academic career to spend my full time writing, a love of mine equal to my loves of science and teaching. The "Einstein" books are one result.

But why would a chemistry professor write about food? For one thing, good food has intrigued me ever since I first encountered it— not at my mother's knee, but some twenty years later in graduate school. Cornell University's College of Home Economics (now the Division of Nutritional Sciences) operated a cafeteria in which the products of the students' cooking classes were sold at prices that a graduate assistant could afford. The menus included foods that I had never before seen, prepared with the care and dedication that only a prospective grade of A could inspire. It was perhaps predictable that I should one day marry my loves of science, teaching, writing, and food, and nestle them between the covers of books. The crowning stroke of fortune was my marriage to a fifth love (in order of chronology, not priority): Marlene Parrish, a restaurant reviewer and culinary journalist full of passion for . . . well, everything that I have passion for.

IN 1935, when Albert Einstein first walked into his kitchen at 112 Mercer Street in Princeton, New Jersey, he of course saw a stove. But in his mind he also saw an apparatus for transforming the chemical energy in wood or gas into thermal energy and for conveying that thermal energy into a chicken. None of which, of course, diminished his subsequent enjoyment of the chicken, but all of which probably added an extra bit of spice to his dinner, a spice undetected by less scientifically tuned intellects.

Science is a sort of intellectual spice that adds depth and allure to everyday things, not the least of which is food. Food, of course, gives us pleasure and nourishment. But *understanding* our food—where it came from, what it is made of, what happens when we cook it, all in the contexts of the many experiences and circumstances that make up the world of gastronomy—nourishes our minds and adds immensely to our enjoyment of cooking and eating.

The cliché has it that cooking is chemistry. True, but other sciences bear equally on what goes on in our kitchens. There is the physics of heat transmission, the mechanics of whipping and emulsifying, the microbiology of fermentation, the anatomy of meats, the engineering of utensils and equipment, and the technology of producing and packaging prepared foods—all preceded by the agronomy and animal husbandry that take place on our farms. Kitchen science is not the mere chemistry of cooking. It involves a lot of what I call thinking outside the pot.

This book, then, is a truth-seeking exploration of the farm, the market, and the kitchen by a scientist—not, most assuredly, an Einstein, but a scientist with a congenital curiosity about everything he sees and an urge to share the joy of knowing with others.

THE ENTHUSIASTIC RECEPTION accorded the first volume of *What Einstein Told His Cook*, together with the limitless number of opportunities for scientific scrutiny in the world of food, has inspired the present sequel. Unlike its predecessor, which focused mainly on specific foods such as sugar, salt, and fats, the present volume is organized into eight major food categories: beverages, dairy and eggs, vegetables, fruits, grains and carbohydrates, seafoods, meats, and herbs and spices. There is also a chapter on kitchen tools and equipment and a concluding chapter offering a handful of lagniappes to please not the diner's palate but the reader's inquiring mind.

As she did for the previous book, my wife, Marlene, has wrought and thoroughly tested (on me) about three dozen tempting and accessible recipes that put the scientific principles to work in the home "laboratory."

And as in the earlier volume, the questions come mainly from readers of my *Washington Post* column, "Food 101," and thus represent the concerns of real cooks and consumers, who are often bewildered by the products and labels vying for their attention in today's multifarious food markets. It is a rare privilege for an author to be in direct correspondence with a cross section of his readers, so that he can tailor his writing to their specific needs and concerns.

One of the most difficult decisions to be made in writing a popular science book is at what level to pitch the scientific explanations. Too high a level will of course lose the less scientifically sophisticated readers. But I see no corresponding danger in writing for those who have studied no science beyond the bare minimum required in most school curricula, and who will readily admit that even that much "didn't stick." I therefore write for the latter type of reader without apology, having been told by scientists, engineers, and chefs that even they have learned from my previous books. For that segment of my audience, I dig into my bag of teaching tricks to employ novel explanatory approaches that can generate fresh insights.

Teaching in a book (and that's what I'm doing) is different from teaching in a classroom. Each Q&A unit in this book, which can be read independently, launches a new issue requiring a new explanation. But science is a continuum; it doesn't come in discrete pieces, like M&M's. Hence, when explaining one concept I have often found it necessary to restate, very briefly, a closely related one that had been covered earlier. Otherwise, the unit would be incomplete and unsatisfying. So please note that I do this intentionally. It's one of my teaching tricks.

I have explained all concepts in nontechnical language, using similes and metaphors related to everyday life whenever possible. Nevertheless, I do present the pertinent scientific terminology in italics within parentheses, so that the reader can relate it to his or her other readings and, if desired, follow up on it in more technical references.

I believe that words, which of course are only symbols for concepts, are often more easily understood if their origins are known. For that reason I have included the etymologies (and occasionally the pronunciations) of some of the scientific terms that might otherwise intimidate the uninitiated.

The current volume is somewhat deeper and richer in science than the previous one, in recognition of the growing appetite for science among foodies, both avocational and professional. I have set aside the more technical details, however, in sections that I call "Sidebar Science," which each reader may choose to read or skip, depending on the depth of his or her scientific interests. Skipping them will not interrupt the continuity of the text, especially since the Q&A units are designed to be read independently, wherever one may chance to open the book.

If, as Miguel de Cervantes wrote in *Don Quijote de la Mancha*, hunger is the best sauce in the world, then humor is the best *digestif*.

In my opinion, there are few subjects or circumstances that cannot be made more palatable and digestible by being seasoned with humor. As food and cooking can be fun, so can—and should—science. In this vein I have not restrained myself (very much) from injecting a wry observation wherever I deemed it appropriate. At the risk of disaffecting pun haters, I have also scattered "Foodie's Fictionary" definitions throughout the book like truffles (or nettles?) in a forest.

After all, one cannot enjoy food without at times putting one's tongue in one's cheek.

NOTE: *This book is all-natural and has not been tested on animals.*

ACKNOWLEDGMENTS

To PARAPHRASE JOHN DONNE, no writer is an island; he has editors.

It may not be universally realized that every word in a book or newspaper has been scrutinized and checked by at least one, and often as many as a dozen, pairs of eyes, whose invisible fingerprints (to muddle a couple of metaphors) are all over it.

While writing this book and its predecessor, I have benefited greatly from the wisdom, advice, and good judgment of W. W. Norton's senior editor Maria Guarnaschelli, the personification of "tough love," who acted not as a mere after-the-fact editor, but as a fond collaborator from the project's inception to its completion. Without her guiding hand in the tasks of crafting and re-crafting its scope and organization, this book would not have been possible.

My gratitude has been earned also by Maria's sharp and most capable assistant, Erik Johnson, for coordinating the many elements that go into the publication of a book, including nagging the author about deadlines.

Among the skillful professionals at W. W. Norton who turned my manuscript into a book, led by president Drake McFeely, editor-in-chief Star Lawrence, and managing editor Nancy Palmquist, are designer Barbara Bachman, jacket artist John Fulbrook III, art director Georgia Liebman, publishing director Jeannie Luciano, director of manufacturing Andy Marasia, production manager Anna Oler, sales manager Bill Rusin, and project editor Susan Sanfrey. The illustrations are the products of talented freelance artists Alan Witschonke and Rodney Duran. I thank them all.

My special appreciation goes to ultrameticulous copy editor Katya Rice, whose sharp eye and linguistic expertise (who else would write me an entire paragraph to justify a changed comma?) kept the text either immaculately syntactic or syntactically immaculate, and who would incisively have pointed out the difference.

I remain grateful to my literary agent, Ethan Ellenberg, who long ago encouraged me to write the book that became the first in my "Einstein Series." The volume you are now holding is the fourth in what I had hoped might some day become a trilogy.

Until now, I have not availed myself of an opportunity to thank in print the people who over the years catalyzed my metamorphosis from chemist to writer.

For launching me on the very first step of my journalistic journey, I am grateful to Nancy Brown, editor of *The University Times*, the University of Pittsburgh's faculty and staff newspaper, who asked me to write a column when I didn't know I was capable of writing a column.

I am indebted to Mark Nordenberg, former dean of the School of Law and currently chancellor of the University of Pittsburgh, for perceiving enough of a writer in me to ask that I write profiles of distinguished alumni for the Law School's alumni magazine.

And I shall always remember the late chancellor of the University of Pittsburgh Wesley Posvar, for recognizing the morale-building value of humor in a university, and for encouraging my satirical monologues at the university's annual administrative conferences.

For the past seven-plus years, *Washington Post* food editors Nancy McKeown, Jeanne McManus, and Judy Havermann have granted me the privilege of writing for that august newspaper, the bright and curious readers of which have provided the grist for this book. I could never have imagined such an outcome while sitting in a one-semester journalism class at Fort Hamilton High School under the tutelage of the incomparable A. H. Lass.

A special hug goes to Paula Wolfert, who believed in me as a fledgling food writer, who encouraged me, and who gave me valuable advice.

And of course, my wife and coauthor, Marlene Parrish, deserves my admiration not only for the work she did on the recipes but also for enduring the deprivation of my company during my many months of slaving away at the computer.

What Einstein Kept Under His Hat

Chapter One

Something to Drink?

....

WHAT ARE THE FIRST TWO things a server says to you as soon as you've been seated in a restaurant? (1) "Hello, my name is Bruce/Aimee and I'll be your server." (2) "May I bring you something to drink?"

Thus far, I have been successful in repressing the replies: (1) "Glad to meet you. My name is Bob and I'll be your customer." Or (2) "Thanks, but I came here primarily to eat."

I concede that it would be useful to know the server's name if it were permissible to summon him/her in time of need by yelling across the room, "Hey, Bruce/Aimee, over here!" But that would be boorish.

(When I lived in Puerto Rico, I found that it is perfectly acceptable to summon a server with a brisk "Sssst!," which carries across the room but isn't unduly disturbing to other patrons. It is quite effective and not considered the least bit vulgar. I highly recommend that we obtain Miss Manners' permission to adopt that practice here in the States.)

I have often suspected that many people respond to the "Something to drink?" question by naming whatever liquid first comes to mind, from an apéritif or cocktail to iced tea and the ubiquitous Diet Coke, simply because they feel it's expected of them. Or maybe they're afraid to answer "Just water, please" because they dread the question that often follows, "Bottled or tap?," which demands to be answered in a way that wards off the label "cheapskate," like a priest brandishing a crucifix against a vampire.

When thinking about drinking, we must sidestep the all-too-common meaning of "a drink" in our society. "Let's have a drink" is rarely an invitation to share a glass of carrot juice; it strongly implies the consumption of an alcoholic beverage. And a person who is said to "drink too much" certainly isn't hooked on milkshakes. Drinking liquor has even captured its own verb, *imbibe*, which in reality has several other contexts that you'll virtually never hear.

Look. You don't need me to tell you the difference between eating and drinking, between solid food and liquid beverage. But let's lay it all out on the table for detached and objective scrutiny, as if we were aliens just off the saucer from a planet where all food is gaseous and consumed by inhalation.

Drinking is the mechanism by which we "eat" liquids, as opposed to solids and semisolids. We take solid food into our mouths by biting it off or shoveling it in, if you'll pardon the metaphor. On the other hand, we take liquids into our mouths by sucking—even from a glass. (Think about it.) Before solid food can be swallowed, it must be chewed and mixed with saliva to make it supple enough to slide "down the hatch." Liquids, however, can go directly down the hatch without any pretreatment.

When we talk about drinks, we are talking primarily about water. All beverages that we consume are about 90 percent water, the universal liquid on Earth without which we cannot live.

Coke and Pepsi are 89 percent water by weight; milk and orange juice are 88 percent water; coffee and tea, more than 99 percent. Wines average around 87 percent, while 80-proof whiskey, because of its significant content of another liquid, ethyl alcohol, comes in at only about 67 percent water.

How does our physiology handle the ingestion of all these liquids?

Just behind the mouth in a region called the pharynx lie the openings of two tubes: the trachea for breathing and the esophagus, or gullet, for eating and drinking. Thus, swallowing, whether liquids or semisolids, can be a bit of a risky business lest they go down "the wrong pipe" and choke off our air supply. Nature has therefore provided us with a complex series of muscular reflexes, with valves or sphincters that open and close to propel our food and drink down the esophagus to the stomach, rather than into the trachea or up into the nasal cavity (except when children burst into laughter while drinking milk).

Having thus belabored the obvious for the benefit of any visiting aliens, let us begin our shared literary repast with a variety of "somethings to drink."

NICE ICE

Someone in my household (I have my suspicions) put a half-empty plastic bottle of cola in the freezing compartment of the refrigerator. When I discovered it a couple of days later, I was surprised to see that it had frozen into lacy crystals of pure white ice against a background of unfrozen brown. Why wasn't the frozen cola brown, like the original liquid?

. . . .

Let's follow the fate of the soda from the time that rascal put it in the freezer, probably with the misguided intention of keeping it nice and fizzy till the next attack of thirst.

All liquids turn into solids—that is, they freeze—when they get cold enough. Pure water freezes at 32°F (0°C), but your soda isn't pure water. Far from it. It contains flavorings, phosphoric acid, coloring, and sweeteners—sugar, corn syrup, or artificial sweeteners.

Still, the vast majority of the molecules in the bottle are good old H_2O. And when they are cold enough to freeze, they join together into a rigid network—a geometrically regular, three-dimensional arrangement of H_2O molecules that we call ice. The molecules in ice are in fact so rigidly fixed in their places that they are hard to break apart from one another. Ice is therefore (surprise!) a much harder substance than liquid water.

With all those other non-H_2O molecules cluttering up the place, however, the water molecules have a harder time finding one another so they can join together and form ice crystals. So the soda had to be cooled down past its normal 32-degree temperature before it was able to freeze.

But freeze it eventually did. The water molecules eventually slowed down enough to settle comfortably into their places. As they did, they were able to elbow aside all those foreign molecules, so the ice they formed was relatively pure. That's the white ice you saw. All the "brown molecules" had been left behind.

Ice floes in the Arctic are made of relatively salt-free ice for the same reason, in spite of the fact that they were frozen from salty seawater.

MIST-TEA

When I make tea, it's always beautifully clear when freshly made. But when refrigerated, it often turns cloudy. What causes that, and can I prevent it from happening?

. . . .

Tea leaves contain tannins, a loose collection of chemicals that give tea much of its flavor and body, and especially that astringent, puckering effect in the mouth. They dissolve in water to form a clear solution, as long as the water isn't too cold or slightly alkaline.* Your

---

* In chemistry, the opposite of an acid is called a base. Acids and bases neutralize each other. But because *base* is a word with many common meanings (more than a

cloudiness occurs when some of the tannins in the hot tea fall out of solution (*precipitate*) as tiny solid particles when the tea is cooled. Cloudiness can also form when certain tannins react with the caffeine in the tea.

Tannins are present to some extent in most plant materials but are particularly abundant in oak galls (abnormal growths on oak trees); certain barks, woods, and roots; and nut shells.

All tannins are soluble in water, but how much of them can dissolve in a given amount of water (their *solubilities*) depends on the temperature of the water and upon its acidity or alkalinity. When hot water is used to make strong tea (the usual first step in making iced tea), it extracts most of the tannins from the leaves. Then, when the solution is cooled down with ice cubes, all those tannins cannot stay dissolved, and they fall back out as fine, suspended solid particles that give the tea a cloudy appearance.

Tannins are more soluble in acidic solutions, so that when an acid such as lemon juice is added to tea, any solid particles of tannin will dissolve and the cloudiness will clear up.

Also, if the tea is initially brewed with hard water—that is, with water containing dissolved calcium or magnesium salts—these minerals can react with the tannins to form relatively insoluble complex chemicals that show up as flotsam and jetsam.

If your water is hard, then, try adding a little lemon juice to clear up any cloudiness. Or switch to a different tea, because some teas, such as Assam and Darjeeling, are richer in tannins and thus more prone to cloudiness than others, such as Ceylon.

---

dozen each as noun and adjective), I use the words *alkali* and *alkaline* in this book instead of *base* and *basic*. Strictly speaking, however, the word *alkali* should be reserved for the very strong bases sodium hydroxide (lye) and potassium hydroxide.

Sidebar Science: *Well, tan my hide!*

THE WORDS *tannin* and *tannic acid* are often used inter-changeably, but not by chemists and other finicky types. *Tannic acid* is a specific chemical compound, a high-molecular-weight penta-m-digalloyl-glucose, a.k.a. gallotannic acid, with the formula $C_{76}H_{52}O_{46}$. On the other hand, the word *tannins* refers to a whole class of complex plant chemicals that just happens to include tannic acid. They are generically called tannins, not because of any particular chemical similarity (although they are mostly what are known as polyphenols), but because they have been used since prehistoric times for tanning hides: converting raw animal skins into leather in order to improve their durability and resistance to heat, water, bacteria, and fungi.

Tannin polyphenols turn hides into leather by reacting with proteins in the skins to form insoluble adhesive-like substances that bind the protein fibers tightly together. In this tight, dry form, the hide is much stronger and more durable than the raw skin.

Tanning your own hide is a completely different state of affairs. Soaking your body in strong tea or extract of boiled oak galls is not recommended, but exposure to sunlight will induce your skin to produce the dark pigment melanin. So-called self-tanning lotions (they don't tan themselves; they tan you) usu-ally contain dihydroxyacetone, or DHA, a colorless chemical that reacts with amino acids in the outermost cells of the epi-dermis (the *stratum corneum*) to produce a variety of dark reac-tion products.

My Chai

Chai (rhymes with "pie") is the word for tea in many parts of Asia, where the tea plant originated. Tea's use spread over Asia by land and ultimately conquered Europe (especially England) by sea.

When the ships of the Dutch East India Company brought tea from China to Europe in the seventeenth century, the Dutch changed the Chinese dialectical word *t'e* to *tee*. The English then changed the spelling to *tea*. Back in Asia, where tea was being transported by overland routes, some regions along the way called it *ch'a* (the Mandarin name) or *chai*. Today, if your ancestors first obtained their tea by overland trade, you probably call it chai; if it first arrived by sea, you call it tea. Or as Paul Revere might have put it: "Chai if by land and tea if by sea."

One Indian version of chai is a sweet and spicy milk tea that has become increasingly popular throughout the world. Chai is so mainstream in the United States today that it can be found not only on the menu at Starbucks but also in aseptic cartons in many supermarkets.

---

2 **cups water**

2 **teaspoons loose black tea or 2 tea bags**

1 **small cinnamon stick, about 2 inches long**

1 **cardamom pod, lightly crushed**

1 **small whole clove**

1 **slice fresh ginger, the size of a nickel, peeled**

2 **cups whole milk, soy milk, or rice milk**

Honey, to taste

---

1. Place all the ingredients except the honey in a saucepan and slowly bring to a boil. Swirl the mixture around for about 3 minutes, or until it reaches the desired strength and the spices release their aromas.

2. Strain into teacups and add honey to taste. Chai tastes best when very strong and very sweet. Some people prefer to add the milk after the tea has been strained and sweetened.

MAKES 4 SERVINGS

IT'S BETTER BEING GREEN

*There's a lot of talk about green tea these days.
But isn't all tea green to begin with? Are there
other tea plants with other-colored leaves, or are
other teas picked after the green is gone? I bought
some green tea the other day and it looks pretty
black to me, not green at all.*

. . . .

All tea comes from the same, one-and-only tea plant, *Camellia sinensis*, whose leaves certainly were chlorophyll-green on the living plant. But based upon how the leaves are processed, there are three types of tea: green, which is consumed mostly in the Far East; black, the favorite of the British and other Westerners; and oolong ("black dragon" in Chinese dialect), which is intermediate in flavor between the green and the black.

Beyond this, there are a bewildering number of names for dozens of kinds of tea based on their places of origin, the sizes of their leaves, or added flavorings such as jasmine, bergamot (in Earl Grey), and orange blossoms.

In all cases, the leaves are first plucked from the plant and encouraged to wither and lose moisture, usually by means of hot air or, more traditionally, by being exposed to the sun. After that, the green, black, and oolong teas take different paths.

Leaves destined to be sold as green tea are blasted with steam or roasted on iron pans in order to deactivate enzymes in the plant cells (see "What's an enzyme?" on p. 12) and prevent the so-called fermentation that black and oolong teas undergo. The leaves for green tea are dried until the moisture content is about 3 percent, and then are crushed or powdered.

In the case of black and oolong teas, the withered leaves are rolled in a large rolling machine that twists them and breaks open their cells, simultaneously exposing the insides to oxygen and releasing an enzyme (polyphenol oxidase) that oxidizes the polyphenol tannins in the leaves. Among the products of the oxidation reactions are orange, red, and yellow compounds called theaflavins and thearubigins, which give the tea briskness and color.

This oxidation process is almost universally but mistakenly referred to as fermentation, but yeasts and bacteria have nothing to do with it; it's purely a chemical, not a biological, process. The difference between oolong and black tea lies in how long the oxidation process is permitted to continue: a few hours for black tea and only about half as long for oolong. The time and temperature must be strictly controlled to produce a tea of superior flavor. The oxidation process is stopped by deactivating the enabling enzyme with hot air, as in making green tea. That's why green tea brews a lighter-colored beverage than black tea: fewer theaflavins and thearubigins.

The ultimate flavor properties of a tea will depend not only on how the leaves are processed but on how and where the bush grows, the local climate, the season during which the leaves are picked, and the position of the leaves on the plant.

By the way, if you expect me to expound on the reputed health benefits of drinking green tea, I must disappoint you. All I know is what I read, and my take on what I read is that the outlook is encouraging but that the jury has not yet come to a unanimous verdict. Presumably, any healthful benefits of green tea must have something to do with the fact that its polyphenols have not been oxidized, and polyphenols are antioxidants: they gobble up age- and illness-causing free radicals in the body.

I drink it every morning instead of coffee.

ENZYMES HAVE been misunderstood almost as much as instruction manuals for VCRs. Everyone know that enzymes play essential roles in all living things, but what exactly are they?

Are they alive, like bacteria? No. They're chemicals, almost all of them proteins, that accelerate the complex chemical reactions essential to living things, both plant and animal. In other words, they are *catalysts*, substances that help chemical reactions go faster but are not used up in the process. Without enzymes, the chemistry of life would be impossibly slow, if it proceeded at all.

An enzyme molecule does its catalyzing job when a specific part of it, called its *active site*, reacts with a specific chemical, called its *substrate*, enabling that substrate to take part in vital chemical processes thousands or millions of times faster than it ordinarily would. The molecules of each type of enzyme have a unique shape that can react with only one specific substrate, thereby catalyzing only one specific chemical reaction. There is a unique enzyme for each of the hundreds of chemical reactions essential to the lives of all plants and animals.

For example, the dissolving of waste carbon dioxide from our bodily tissues into our bloodstreams and the "undissolving" of it back to gas for exhalation from our lungs are absolutely essential life processes. But if it weren't for the enzyme *carbonic anhydrase*, these processes would take place so slowly that we couldn't survive. Carbonic anhydrase makes the processes happen ten million times faster. Each carbonic anhydrase molecule can perform its speed-up act on a million carbon dioxide molecules per second.

An enzyme is named by tacking the suffix *-ase* onto a brief description of what it does. The tea enzyme is named polyphenol oxidase because it oxidizes polyphenols. If there were such a thing as an enzyme that speeds up the glazing of pottery, it might be called a vase glazease.

LITMUS TEA

*Why does my tea turn a lighter color when I add
lemon? On the other hand, my grandmother used
to add a pinch of baking soda to her tea, and it
turned as dark as brandy. What did she know
that I don't know?*

. . . .

Are you sure it *wasn't* brandy? Might Granny perhaps have been engaging in a bit of teacup tippling?

But okay, I'll take her word for it. Here's what was going on in both your cups.

You've heard people talk about a "litmus test," to show whether a politician is on one side of an issue or the other? Well, litmus is a dye obtained from lichens; it is pink when in an acidic environment and blue when in an alkaline environment. Unlike politicians, litmus gives a straight yes or no answer: either acidic or not acidic (alkaline).

Litmus is what chemists call an *acid-base indicator*. Some of the tannins in tea are also acid-base indicators; they are one color in an acidic environment and another color in an alkaline environment. Your acidic lemon juice turns some of the tea's tannins yellow, and Granny's alkaline baking soda turns them reddish-brown.

Another example of an acid-base indicator is the pigment in red cabbage, one of the class of colored food chemicals called anthocyanins. Anthocyanins are responsible for the colors of many flowers and fruits, including apples, plums, and grapes.

The color of cabbage's main anthocyanin changes with the acidity or alkalinity of its surroundings. It ranges from red in a strongly acidic environment to purple in a neutral (neither acidic nor alkaline) environment and goes from blue to greenish-yellow in increasingly alkaline environments. Cabbage looks more appetizing when toward the reddish end of the spectrum, so it is often cooked with (acidic) apples, whose sweetness can be balanced by a little red-enhancing vinegar added before serving.

Sidebar Science: *A litmus quest*

WHAT MAKES acid-base indicators change color?

Tannic acid, as one example, is what chemists call a weak acid, meaning that it is, well, not a strong acid. (See how easy chemistry is?) A weak acid's molecules consist of two parts, a *hydrogen ion* (a positively charged hydrogen atom) and an *anion* (AN-eye-on), a negatively charged atom or group of atoms. We'll call the hydrogen ion H and the anion A; when they're together in the whole acid molecule, we'll call it HA.

It's the A part of the tannic acid molecule that is colored. When Grandma adds her alkaline baking soda, it gobbles up some of the acid's H's, leaving an excess of free A's and therefore a darker color. On the other hand, when you add your acidic lemon juice, it contributes lots of H's of its own, which combine with many of the A's, in effect tying them up and curtailing their effects. Hence, the color becomes weaker; the brown turns to yellow.

Tannins have historically been used as dyes, as I learned early in life from my grandfather, a Russian immigrant. He had a magnificent white beard, but his mustache was permanently stained yellow from his habit of drinking tea from a glass.

NO CAF-FIEND

*I'm a tea drinker, but I'm trying to cut down
on caffeine. What if I used smaller cups?
That is, what if I put one tea bag in a small
cup and another tea bag in a large cup, filled
them both with boiling water, and let them
steep for five minutes? Would the smaller
cup contain less caffeine?*

. . . .

Interesting thought, but no cigar.

Caffeine is very soluble in water; as much as 150 grams of caffeine could dissolve in a cup of boiling-hot water. But there isn't anywhere near that much caffeine in a tea bag. Typically, it's less than a thousandth of that.

What caffeine there is is extracted out of the tea bag almost completely in the first minute or so of steeping. So either way, big cup or small cup, all the bag's caffeine is in your tea. You might as well use the big cup and have a longer-lasting drink at no increase in caffeine.

TEA (AND COFFEE) FOR TWO

*I drink tea and my boyfriend drinks coffee. As
soon as the kettle begins to whistle, he wants to
take it off the burner and pour the water into his
filter. I want to leave the kettle on longer, because
I think water for tea should be hotter. But he says
it will never get any hotter, no matter how
long we leave it on. Who's right?*

. . . .

You're right about the tea and he's both right and wrong about the water. I think we can work it out without your having to resort to separate kettles.

Most connoisseurs agree with you that in order to extract the proper amount of flavor from black or oolong tea leaves, the water must be as hot as possible. But no matter how much you heat it, water will never get hotter than boiling: 212°F (100°C), minus a degree or two, depending on the altitude and weather. That's because water boils—turns to steam—when its molecules acquire just enough energy to overcome the atmosphere's pressure on the water's surface and break away into the air. If a molecule happens to acquire more than that amount of energy, it takes its excess energy along with it as it flies out. That extra energy is therefore lost from the water in the kettle and isn't available to raise its temperature. So your boyfriend scores a point on that one.

But whistling tea kettles can be deceptive. When your kettle emits its first weak peeps, only a few of the more robust bubbles will have succeeded in making it all the way to the surface to release their steam and make the whistle whistle. The water is not yet fully boiling. For your black or oolong tea, then, you have to keep heating until all the water is bubbling furiously, the whistle has been screaming at maximum pitch and volume for at least several seconds, and your kitchen is beginning to fill up with stray dogs.

Green tea, however, follows different rules. Experts say that it should be brewed at a lower temperature of about 165 to 180°F (74 to 82°C), presumably because higher temperatures could promote oxidation of its valuable polyphenols (see p. 11).

Coffee is an entirely different cup of tea, so to speak. Water that is boiling vigorously isn't desirable for making coffee because its steam would carry off too many of the volatile, aromatic flavor components, of which coffee has many more than tea. (Nobody has ever said, "Wake up and smell the tea.") That's why the crudest and most forthright method of making coffee—boiling the grounds in a pot of water—makes a brew better suited to the inside of an automobile battery than a breakfast cup.

The best ways to make coffee, in my opinion, are the filter method, in which hot water is poured over freshly ground beans in a filter-paper cone and drips through by gravity, and the French press or piston-and-cylinder method, in which hot water is poured over the grounds in the bottom of a tall vessel and allowed to steep for about three minutes, after which a perforated plunger is pushed down to press the "mud" to the bottom.

Whatever the method, water that isn't hot enough won't extract enough of the hundreds of chemical constituents that have been identified in coffee, all of which are sensitive to heat, air, and interactions with one another. Which ones and how much of each wind up in your cup depend on such things as the type of coffee, the relative amounts of coffee and water, the particle size of the grind, the mixing action in the brewing apparatus, the temperature of the water, and how long it is left in contact with the grounds. All in all, though, the optimum temperature for coffee water is around 190 to 200°F (88 to 93° C), or "just off the boil."

To settle your domestic dispute, then, I recommend that you get the water to a full, roaring boil, turn off the heat, and quickly pour some onto your tea leaves or bags in a preheated pot. Then count to ten, during which time the water will cool just enough, and hand the kettle to your boyfriend, who may then proceed with his coffee-making.

Could Solomon have done better?

YOU WANT CREAM IN THAT?

*I like my coffee with cream, but I also like it to be
as hot as possible when I drink it. I know that the
cream will cool it off, but when should I add it?
As soon as I pour the coffee, or only when
I'm ready to drink it? In which case will the
coffee be hotter at drinking time?
Or does it make any difference?*

. . . .

I doubt that the ancient Greek philosophers spent much time on this (especially since they didn't have coffee), but it's a challenging question, if not an earthshaking one.

You could settle it with an accurate thermometer, but you'd have to measure out exactly the same amounts of coffee and cream into exactly the same type of cup, all at precisely the same initial temperature, etc., etc. But doing a carefully controlled scientific experiment in a kitchen has its problems, so let's just think it out.

All other things being equal, you'd think that both methods would lead to the same temperature of the final mixture, because you're combining x calories of heat in the coffee with y calories of heat in the cream, for a total of $x + y$ calories in the mixture either way. (Regarding the use of the word *calorie*, see the box on p. 21.)

Unfortunately, according to Wolke's Law of Pervasive Perversity, all other things are never equal. Whether it's black coffee or creamed coffee, it must sit around until you're ready to drink it. Meanwhile, it has been cooling off, because the air is cooler than the liquid in the cup and heat is therefore flowing from the liquid into the air. Heat will always flow from a substance at a higher temperature to an adjoining substance that is at a lower temperature.

But there are two important differences between the creamed

coffee and the black coffee: (1) the cup of creamed coffee contains slightly more liquid because of the added volume of the cream, and (2) the creamed coffee is cooler than the black coffee.

Difference number 1 means that the creamed coffee with its larger volume will take more time to cool off. That is, more heat must be removed to lower its temperature by any given number of degrees. (A bathtub of water takes more time to cool than a bucket of bathwater of the same temperature.) Difference number 2 has the same result: the slightly cooler creamed coffee will cool off more slowly than the slightly hotter black coffee, because the smaller the temperature difference between a hot object and its surroundings, the slower will be its rate of cooling. So immediate creaming wins again.

My advice is to add the cream as soon as possible. The coffee will be hotter by as much as a degree or two at drinking time, and I'm sure your life will be much the better for it.

I'm pleased to report that this problem was the subject of a careful scientific experiment led by the college student Jonathan Afilalo and published in the spring 1999 issue of the *Dawson Research Journal of Experimental Science*. This is a most impressive journal that

Sidebar Science: *Cooling it*

THE HIGHER the temperature of an object, the faster it will lose its heat by radiation. That's the Stefan-Boltzmann Law. Also, the bigger the temperature difference between two objects in contact with each other (such as coffee and air, for example), the faster the hot one will lose its heat to the cooler one by conduction. That's Newton's Law of Cooling. There are precise mathematical formulas for both of these laws, but I see no reason to burden this page with them. I'll return to Newton's Law in Chapter 9.

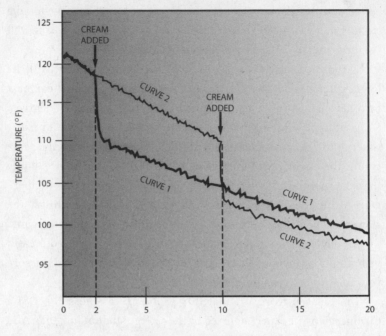

TIME AFTER POURING COFFEE (MINUTES)

The cooling of a cup of coffee when the cream is added two minutes after pouring (curve 1), and when the cream is added ten minutes after pouring (curve 2). Adding the cream earlier yields hotter coffee at drinking time.

publishes papers on original, professional-quality research by undergraduate students at Dawson College in Montreal, Quebec.

The students' experiment came to the same conclusion as I did, as shown by their measured cooling curves plotted in the graph above. In curve 1 the cream was added two minutes after the coffee had been poured, whereas in curve 2 it wasn't added until ten minutes after pouring. Note that thereafter the temperature in curve 1 remained about a degree and a half higher than in curve 2. Early addition of cream does keep the coffee hotter.

When a calorie is not a calorie

There is a difference between what a chemist calls a calorie and what a nutritionist calls a calorie. The chemist's calorie is the amount of heat energy required to raise the temperature of *one gram* of water by one degree Celsius, whereas the nutritionist's calorie, the calorie you see in diet books and on food labels, is the amount of heat energy required to raise the temperature of *one thousand grams* (a kilogram) of water by one degree Celsius. Obviously, then, a nutritionist's calorie is a thousand times bigger than a chemist's, and the chemist would call it a kilocalorie, or kcal.

In this book I find myself in the awkward position of being a chemist writing about food for an audience that spans both camps. For consistency in this book, and if my chemistry colleagues will forgive me, I will use the word *calorie* in the nutritionist's sense unless otherwise noted. In many cases, I use the word *calories* simply to mean an unspecified amount of heat energy, in which case the chemist/nutritionist dichotomy doesn't matter.

For those chemists who are not appeased, here is a supply of kilos to insert in front of the word *calorie* whenever you encounter it in the book: kilo kilo kilo kilo kilo kilo kilo kilo kilo kilo kilo kilo kilo kilo kilo kilo kilo kilo kilo kilo kilo kilo kilo kilo kilo kilo kilo kilo kilo kilo kilo kilo kilo kilo kilo kilo kilo kilo kilo kilo.

(Note to users of the International System of units: One nutritional kilocalorie, kcal, is equal to 4.19 kiloJoules or kJ.)

OUR ALCOHOLIC RELATIVES

*I know there is ethyl alcohol, methyl alcohol,
and rubbing alcohol. Which of those are edible—
or drinkable—and which are not? Are all alcohols
born the same before they undergo various
changes or additions?*

. . . .

No. Even though they are members of the same chemical family, there are vast and crucial differences among the alcohols, and it can be a matter of life and death to be aware of them.

Alcohols are a large family of organic (carbon-containing) chemicals that are related in two ways: their molecules contain one or more *hydroxyl groups* (OH), and they react with organic acids to form chemicals known as esters.

Scientists classify everything from animals to chemicals according to their shared characteristics—characteristics that may be of no practical interest, or even downright misleading, to nonmembers of the science guild. Fret not, therefore, that eggplant (*Solanum melongena*) and potatoes (*Solanum tuberosum*) are in the same botanical family as the poisonous deadly nightshade (*Solanum dulcamara*), or that lobsters and wood lice both belong to the family of Crustacea. But don't we all have strange relatives? Take my uncle Leon. Please. (Apologies to Henny Youngman.)

Similarly, alcohols include the highly poisonous methyl alcohol, CH_3OH, a.k.a. methanol or wood alcohol; the somewhat less toxic isopropyl alcohol, C_3H_7OH, a.k.a. isopropanol or rubbing alcohol; and the even less toxic—but still potent—ethyl alcohol, C_2H_5OH, a.k.a. ethanol or grain alcohol, the alcohol in beer, wine, and spirits. That's not to mention alcohols that we never think of as alcohols, such as cholesterol, $C_{27}H_{45}OH$, and glycerol or glycerin, $C_3H_5(OH)_3$. (As you have noticed, chemists name all alcohols with the suffix *-ol*.)

So, don't let the name "alcohol" fool you into thinking that a chemical is relatively harmless. Dead is a lot worse than drunk.

THE FOODIE'S FICTIONARY: Taste bud—a sip of beer

ALL HOPPED UP

*The label on my beer bottle says that it's made
from "the finest hops." What's a hop?*

. . . .

Hops are the dried flowers of the hop plant, known to botanists as *Humulus lupulus*. It's a tall, climbing vine of the hemp family, and its flowers impart that mellow bitterness to beers and ales, balancing the sweetness of the malt. They also contribute a grassy flavor note

Flower buds of the hop plant (*Humulus lupulus*).
Hops are an essential ingredient in beer.

and a pleasant aroma, depending on when in the brewing process they are added to the wort—the fermenting grain mixture.

In Belgium, the early spring shoots of the hop plant are a delicacy when cooked and served like asparagus.

There are some interesting sidelights to the story of the hop. For one thing, there are boy hops and girl hops. It's the mature female flowers, because of their unique resins, that have been used for about a thousand years to flavor brews and tonics. The female plants, incidentally, do very well with no males around; their flowers simply develop no seeds and will not reproduce. Most brewers prefer their hops without seeds, so the males aren't usually cultivated. (No aspersions intended on the males of other species.)

Practically every quality from sedative to diuretic to aphrodisiac has at one time or another been ascribed to the female hop, and it has historically been added to elixirs and concoctions intended for virtually every purpose. The bitter flavor of hops probably has a lot to do with the traditional belief that good medicine must taste bad.

Do the long-reputed sedative properties of hops have anything to do with the sleepiness that overtakes one after drinking beer? No one really knows. A gallon of beer is made with one or two ounces of hops, but it may contain four or five times as much alcohol, a well-known sedative. We'll never know the soporific role of the hops until someone carries out the appropriate experiments with alcoholic and non-alcoholic beers containing the same amount of hops. (Looking for a school science project?)

Hops are an essential ingredient in beer, and not only for their aroma and bitterness. They clarify the beer by precipitating the proteins in the wort, and they have antibiotic properties that help preserve the beer. Among the more than 150 chemical compounds that have been identified in their essential oil are chemicals (*terpenes*) called isohumulones, which are light-sensitive. When struck by either visible or ultraviolet light, they break down into very active free radicals (see p. 175) that react with sulfur in the beer's proteins to produce smelly compounds called skunky thiols, which the human senses of taste and smell are able to detect at levels of a few parts per trillion. They are chemically similar to the thiol compound in the glands of skunks that earns them their unsociable reputation.

Beer that has been exposed to light for as little as 20 minutes reputedly can develop a "skunky" taste. That's why beer is packaged either in cans or in light-proof brown bottles. To be safe, then, I recommend that you not leave your beer in the glass while "nursing" it. Drink it as fast as you can.

THE FOODIE'S FICTIONARY: Hops—neither skips nor jumps

Beer Batter Bread

So you think beer is just for drinking? Think again. This beer bread makes excellent toast and wonderful toasted cheese sandwiches. The flavor varies, depending on the beer you use. I tested this recipe with Pittsburgh's hearty local brew, Penn Pilsner Dark. The bread tastes best the day it is made.

---

3 cups self-rising flour

3 tablespoons sugar

1 can or bottle (12 ounces) of beer, preferably not light

---

1. Place an oven rack in the lower third of the oven. Preheat the oven to 350°F. Spray a 9-by-5-by-3-inch loaf pan with nonstick cooking spray.
2. In a large bowl, mix the flour and sugar thoroughly. Gradually add the beer while stirring with a wooden spoon until no patches of dry flour are visible. (Do not overbeat or the bread will toughen.) The batter will be sticky. Transfer it to the loaf pan and spread it into the corners.
3. Bake for 50 to 60 minutes, or until a skewer or cake tester plunged deep into the middle of the bread comes out clean. The top of the loaf will have a cobbled appearance.
4. Turn the bread out of the pan onto a wire rack and let it cool for at least an hour. Use a sharp, serrated knife to slice. The crust will be crunchy and the interior soft and moist.

MAKES 1 LOAF

THE FOODIE'S FICTIONARY: Sourdough—gambling losses

SUL-FIGHTS?

*Why do so many wine labels say "Contains
sulfites"? My husband has been told he's allergic
to them, but when we asked at the liquor store
we were told that all wine naturally contains
sulfites. Then why the warning? They don't
label coffee "Contains caffeine."*

. . . .

Sulfites—not to be confused with sulfates—are a family of chemical salts derived from sulfur dioxide (SO_2). They are formed during the fermentation of wine from sulfur compounds naturally present in the grapes, so a certain small amount is indeed natural and unavoidable.

In addition, sulfites (or sulfur dioxide gas from burning sulfur) have been added to wines for thousands of years to protect them against oxidation and discoloration. Moreover, sulfites can kill harmful bacteria and wild yeast cells in the grape pressings so that the "tame" fermenting organisms can get a biologically clean start. Without the preservative effect of added sulfites, wines would not be drinkable after one or two years, which may be little problem for a wine that is best drunk young, such as a Beaujolais, but would be a tragedy for a slow-aging Bordeaux.

About one person in a hundred is sensitive to sulfites, which can even bring on an asthma attack in asthmatics. Sensitive individuals should avoid foods that contain any of the following: sulfur dioxide, potassium bisulfite, potassium metabisulfite, sodium bisulfite, sodium metabisulfite, and sodium sulfite. Note that, except for sulfur dioxide itself, the tip-off is the suffix *-ite* in the chemical name.

As with all ingested substances, it's not a simple matter of good and bad. Any chemical is inherently neither "safe" nor "dangerous." It's all a matter of amount. The legal limit of sulfites in wine in the

United States is 350 parts per million (ppm), although most wines with added sulfites contain only 25 to 150 ppm. According to federal law, if a wine contains 10 ppm or more of sulfites, the label must state that it "contains sulfites."

With your wine storekeeper's assistance, look for an FDA-approved "No sulfites added" notice on the labels of some bottles. Your husband can then try them and see if the small amount of natural sulfite is enough to give him a reaction.

And by the way, anyone who says that something "smells like sulfur" probably never took a chemistry course. The solid element sulfur, known biblically as brimstone, is perfectly odorless, but many of its compounds are evil-smelling. Sulfur dioxide is the smell of burning sulfur.

VEDDY, VEDDY SHERRY

What's so special about Sherry that makes it a separate category of wine? Is it the grape, the region, the method of production?

. . . .

It's all three, but primarily the method of production.

There are some five thousand varieties of wine grapes that could be used in almost one hundred *appellations d'origine* in France alone, plus seventy-four appellations in California, not to mention Australia, Chile, and dozens of other wine-producing countries. Multiplied by perhaps ten years of vintages, that amounts to over 37 million possible bottles of decent wine—plus untold bottles of plonk. I often wonder how anyone can select the best wine to match a dinner course when faced with such a staggering range of choices lying in a make-believe cellar the size of Antartica.

But I do know something about Sherry, having visited the one place in the world where it is produced: in and around the town of Jerez de la Frontera, a couple of hours' drive south of Seville in Spain's province of Cádiz. There, I was figuratively and almost literally immersed in Sherry as I toured the headquarters of Williams & Humbert, producers of Dry Sack, Pando, Canasta Cream, and many other Sherries and brandies.

Why the non-Spanish names Williams and Humbert, you may ask? And whence the English word *Sherry*? Several of the Sherry companies in Jerez were founded in the nineteenth century by British entrepreneurs for the purpose of exporting Sherry to England, where the dry Sherries have always been favored as apéritifs and the sweet ones as dessert wines. The word *Sherry* came into English from the name *Jerez* (HER-eth), but throughout the Spanish-speaking world Sherry is still known as *vino de Jerez*.

So what's so special about Sherry?

The identity of Sherry is tightly controlled by a regulatory council. To earn the Denomination of Origin "Jerez-Xérès-Sherry," the grapes must be Palomino, or less commonly Pedro Ximénez or Muscat, and they must be grown within the triangle formed by the towns of Jerez de la Frontera, Sanlúcar de Barrameda, and El Puerto de Santa María. (The regulatory council most zealously excludes the American state of California.) This small region has a unique microclimate influenced by the Atlantic Ocean, the Guadalquivir and Guadalete rivers, and the moist, warm winds from nearby North Africa. Probably the most influential factor in developing the character of the grapes is the area's chalky, almost white *albariza* soil, which has an unusual capacity for absorbing and retaining air and water.

Of course, many great wines come from exceptional microclimates and soils. But what sets Sherries apart from all others is the unique process by which they are blended and aged.

After the grapes are pressed, the "must," as the pressings are called, is put into huge stainless-steel tanks to ferment for forty to fifty days at a controlled temperature, achieving an alcohol content of 11 to 13 percent. The young wine then goes into 130-gallon American white oak casks (butts), where the aging begins.

Then comes decision time, when each wine is classified as being suited for transformation into either a dry Fino or a sweeter Oloroso, the two broad categories of Sherry. Finos include Manzanillas and Amontillados, while Olorosos include Cortados and various blends of the very sweet Pedro Ximénez grape. Wines destined to be Finos are fortified (strengthened with added alcohol) to 15 percent alcohol, Olorosos to about 17 percent.

The reason for the difference is that the *flor* (literally, flower), a layer of local, naturally occurring yeasts that forms on the surface, cannot survive at an alcohol concentration higher than 15 percent, and all Finos must serve out their aging time under a layer of *flor* to develop their characteristic lightness and flavor. Olorosos are aged without a layer of *flor*, allowing air to oxidize them to a darker color, fuller body, and stronger nose. (*Oloroso* means fragrant.) Amontillados begin their aging under *flor* and finish after a *flor*-killing fortification to 17 percent alcohol.

During the aging, an intricate blending process unique to Sherries is carried out. Called *soleras y criaderas*, it consists of running the wine through a stack of butts containing wines of increasing ages. From the oldest, called the *solera*, one-third of the wine is drawn off for bottling. It is replenished from the next-oldest (the first *criadera*), which in turn is replenished from the next-oldest, (the second *criadera*), and so on, until the youngest wine butts at the top of the stack are "refreshed," or filled, with brand-new pressings. (*Criadera* comes from the Spanish word for nursery; the *criaderas* are the upper butts in which the younger wines are nurtured. *Solera* refers to the stone floor, where the bottom layer of butts holds the mature wine ready for bottling.)

The complete cycle takes years, with several months of aging time between successive *solera* bottlings. By this method, the young wines

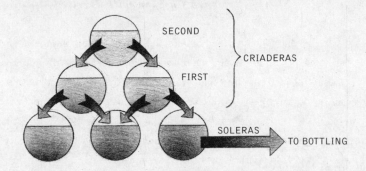

Part of the process for blending and ageing Sherry. Portions of the younger wines in the upper casks (*criaderas*) are drawn off into successively older, lower casks. Wine from the lowest and final cask (the *solera*) is bottled.

gradually take on the characteristics of the older ones, leading to a consistent product that can retain its unique characteristics over a period of decades.

And *that's* what's so special about Sherry.

THE FOODIE'S FICTIONARY: Amaretto—an opera by Verdi

Sherry-Browned Chicken with Garlic

When Bob and I visit a friend of ours, the cookbook author Janet Mendel, at her home in southern Spain, she makes this dish for us.

I use a 12-inch cast-iron skillet for browning the chicken and an Oloroso Seco Sherry, which is a medium Sherry. It makes a lustrous mahogany-colored glaze. Don't be afraid to use all the garlic called for. As it cooks, it mellows to a mild sweetness. Pour the ample juices—a flavorful sauce of olive oil, Sherry, and garlic—over the chicken pieces.

---

2 **pounds chicken thighs and legs (about 4 large thighs and 3 drumsticks will fit in a 12-inch skillet)**
Kosher salt and freshly ground pepper
1 **head garlic (about 15 large cloves)**
$^1/_3$ **cup extra-virgin olive oil, preferably Spanish**
$^1/_2$ **cup medium-dry Sherry, Amontillado or Oloroso Seco**
2 **tablespoons Spanish brandy or cognac, optional**

---

1. Rinse the chicken under cool water and pat dry with paper towels. Sprinkle both sides with salt and pepper.
2. Lightly smash the garlic cloves with the side of a large knife blade to split the skins. Set aside 8 of them, unpeeled. Peel the remaining cloves and slice them into relatively uniform slices.
3. Heat the olive oil in a heavy, deep skillet over medium heat. Add the garlic slices and sauté for 1 to 2 minutes, or just until golden. Skim them out with a slotted spoon, drain on a paper towel, and reserve.
4. Raise the heat to medium-high, add the chicken pieces, and fry (covering the skillet with a spatter shield, if you have one), turning as needed, for about 15 minutes, until browned on all sides.
5. Add the unpeeled garlic cloves, Sherry, and brandy. Continue cooking over medium-high heat, turning the pieces occasionally for 8 to 10 minutes, until the liquid is almost cooked away and the chicken begins to sizzle again.
6. Transfer the chicken and garlic cloves to a warmed serving dish, and pour the pan juices over all. Garnish the dish with the reserved fried garlic slices.

MAKES 4 SERVINGS

SPOONING WITH CHAMPAGNE

*My lady friend was recently visiting me from
England. We drank Champagne but didn't finish
the bottle. She suggested that I hang the handle of
a silver spoon down into the neck of the bottle
before putting it in the fridge. (She saw this on the
telly over there.) Believe it or not, the next day the
Champagne had not gone flat. How does this
work? Would a fork work as well?*

. . . .

Yes, a fork would work just as well. So would a railroad spike. Or a
magic wand, for that matter, because the spoon did absolutely nothing. The spoon dodge is pure bunk. Or, if your British friend prefers,
humbug and poppycock.

Champagne simply doesn't go flat as fast as beer and soda do. It
would have been just as fizzy the next day without the spoon. All that
really mattered is that you refrigerated it. That's important because
carbon dioxide, like all gases, dissolves and stays dissolved to a
greater extent in colder liquids.

In order for a dissolved gas to escape from a liquid, the gas molecules must have a microscopic speck of material (a *nucleation site*)
upon which to congregate until there are enough of them to form a
bubble. The main reason that true Champagne stays bubbly longer is
that it is extremely clear and speck-free. If it says *méthode champ-
enoise* on the label, it has been clarified by *dégorgement*—a process in
which all sediment is allowed to settle down into the neck of the
inverted bottle, after which the neck is frozen and the ice plug, along
with the trapped sediment, is removed. Beers are rarely clarified to
that extent and therefore lose their fizz more rapidly.

To save your leftover Champagne overnight, refrigerate the bottle with a tight stopper—not tableware—in its neck. You never know when you'll have even more to celebrate in the morning.

About that tight stopper: You can spend up to $20 for a fancy "Champagne stopper" in one of those shops that cater to winos—uh, I mean wine enthusiasts. It grips the lip of the bottle around which the wire had been wound, and then you screw its rubber disk down tightly against the bottle's mouth. It's just great at holding the pressure if you intend to shake up the bottle. But it's entirely unnecessary in less dire circumstances. The lip and the original wire cage were intended to hold the high pressure of gas produced during the in-the-bottle fermentation. That's what makes the bottle pop when you pull the cork. But after the bottle has been opened, there's no such pressure. Any cork or bottle stopper will preserve the residual gas in your leftover Champagne, provided that it is kept cold and unshaken.

(A footnote: Reportedly, a group of scientists at Stanford University in 1994 found that sparkling wine remained bubbly longer when the bottle was left open than when it was re-corked. But they had to do a lot of test-drinking during this prolonged experiment, and their observations may not have been, shall we say, sharply focused.)

Sidebar Science: *Put a cork in it*

WHY DO Champagne corks have that weird shape, like a mushroom wearing a dirndl skirt?

When planted in the bottle, they were just as cylindrical as
the corks used in still wine bottles, only bigger. A normal-sized
wine cork is 24 mm (about 0.94 in.) in diameter; it is compressed and inserted into an 18 mm (0.71 in.) bottle neck by a
"corker" machine. (Cork is quite compressible.) Champagne
corks, on the other hand, are 31 mm (1.22 in.) in diameter and
are squeezed into a 17.5 mm (0.69 in.) neck, with the top third
of the cork sticking out as a "head" that can be grasped for
opening. As soon as it is liberated from confinement, the bottom portion, which is soft and wet, expands back to its original
diameter. (Cork is also quite elastic.)

You can observe cork's compressibility and elasticity by
soaking a used Champagne cork in water for a few days to soften
it, whereupon it will expand back to its original cylindrical form
along its whole length. It will also revert to its original shape if
you soften it by simply microwaving it for a couple of minutes.

(Caution: Don't operate an empty or nearly empty microwave oven. Radiation that isn't absorbed by food or water can
bounce back into the wave generator—the *magnetron*—and damage it. Put a cup of water into the oven along with the cork.)

THE WAR BETWEEN THE STATES

I've always wondered about Kentucky bourbon
and Tennessee sour mash whiskey. No other
states seem to have a lock on their types of spirits.
What sets them apart, and why can't the same
products be made in other states?

. . . .

What sets them apart is largely local pride, but virtually identical whiskey can be made anywhere. They just can't use those state names if they were made, for example, in North Dakota.

First, what is it that makes bourbon bourbon? Bourbon is officially defined by the federal Alcohol and Tobacco Tax and Trade Bureau (TTB), which was split off from the ridiculously conceived Bureau of Alcohol, Tobacco and Firearms (ATF) by the Homeland Security Act of 2002. It is defined as a straight (unblended) whiskey produced at a maximum alcoholic strength of 80 percent by volume from a fermented mash containing at least 51 percent corn, and aged at a maximum alcoholic strength of 62.5 percent in charred, new oak containers. In practice, however, most bourbon whiskeys are distilled to around 60 percent alcohol, and bottled at 40 to 50 percent. And they are made from 65 to 75 percent corn, plus smaller amounts of other grains such as barley, rye, or wheat.

According to the TTB, the word *bourbon* may not be used to describe any distilled spirits produced outside the United States. But no names of states are mentioned in the regulations, except for the perfectly reasonable ruling that a bourbon may not be labeled "Kentucky Bourbon" unless it was made in Kentucky. There are approximately 162 distilleries producing genuine bourbon in the United States. Most of them, but by no means all, are located in Kentucky.

Now what about Jack Daniel's Tennessee Whiskey? Is it a bourbon? Strictly speaking (and I'd better speak strictly here because tempers run high on this topic), no. It fits all the legal definitions of bourbon—made primarily from corn; aged in charred, new oak barrels; and well within the strength specifications—except for one thing: It undergoes an additional step. After distillation and before aging, it is dripped through a ten-foot-thick layer of sugar-maple charcoal, a process billed by Jack Daniel's as "charcoal mellowing" but known officially as the Lincoln County Process. That's the only procedural difference between Jack Daniel's and most of the anointed and consecrated bourbons.

Jack Daniel's brags about being a sour mash whiskey, meaning that part of the mash used in the fermentation process consists of the exhausted remains of a previous fermentation. But the sour mash process is used in making almost all bourbons and other whiskeys today, so this fact alone has nothing to do with the Zen of being bourbon.

THE FOODIE'S FICTIONARY: Barley—scarcely

Jack Daniel's Rib-Ticklin' Barbecue Sauce

It would be a waste to limit a bottle of Jack's to simply sipping, when it can add a kick to this sauce. For 2 racks of baby back ribs, you will need about 1 cup of barbecue sauce. Save the other cup to slather over broiled chicken later in the week. You'll want to add this sauce to your collection of good BBQ recipes.

---

1 cup ketchup

$1/4$ cup Jack Daniel's black label whiskey

$1/4$ cup dark molasses

$1/4$ cup cider vinegar

1 tablespoon Worcestershire sauce

1 tablespoon freshly squeezed lemon juice

1 tablespoon soy sauce

$1/2$ teaspoon freshly ground pepper

$1/2$ teaspoon dry mustard

1 clove garlic, crushed

Mix all the ingredients together in a small saucepan. Place over medium-high heat, bring to a boil, and then reduce the heat to low and simmer for 10 minutes, stirring occasionally.

MAKES ABOUT 2 CUPS

. . . AND THEY'RE OFF!

*At a Kentucky Derby Day party, my friends
served mint juleps. I noticed that shortly after the
host mixed each drink, a coating of frost formed
on the outside of the glass. I know that a tall glass
of Tom Collins, for example, will get wet on the
outside, but I've never seen it get cold enough to
freeze. What's special about the mint julep?*

. . . .

Ask any dyed-in-the-cotton Southerner and the answer will be
"Plenty."

When sipped at the speed of a Southern drawl on a hot summer's
eve beneath a fragrant, blooming magnolia, few beverages are more
refreshing than a mint julep—or more insidiously intoxicating,
because its seductive sweetness masks the fact that it is virtually
straight bourbon. But also intoxicating (to some of us) is the science
behind the frosting.

Stripped to its mundane fundamentals, a mint julep is made by
mashing mint leaves with sugar in a metal mug or goblet, filling it
with crushed ice, and pouring a generous glug of bourbon in. Now, if
we were to add plain water instead of bourbon, the ice and the water
would soon come to the same temperature: a temperature at which
they could coexist without all the ice melting or all the water freezing.
(They would come to *equilibrium*.) That temperature, as you have
guessed, is the freezing point of H_2O, normally 32°F or 0°C.

But bourbon, bless its heart, contains alcohol as well as water.
The alcohol (helped by the sugar) lowers the freezing point, just as
antifreeze lowers the freezing point of the coolant in your car's radiator. Because the freezing point is now lower, so is the ice-and-water
coexistence temperature, which is the same. If the ice and liquid are
still to coexist, they must get down to this lower temperature by melt-

ing some of the ice, a process that absorbs heat and makes the mixture colder. It's the same phenomenon that makes an ice-and-salt mixture so cold that it can freeze cream in an old-fashioned ice cream freezer. The salt in this case lowers the freezing point, as the alcohol does in the julep.

The cooling of the goblet's contents by the bourbon's alcohol can be so great that on a humid day the moisture in the air will not only condense on the outside of the goblet but actually freeze there, forming a coating of frost. A Tom Collins won't get cold enough to freeze the moisture on the outside of its glass because it may contain only a few ice cubes and not enough alcohol to lower the freezing temperature very much. In a julep goblet, however, all that crushed ice has a huge surface area at which the ice/water equilibrium can play out its temperature-lowering game on a grand scale.

For the most spectacular presentation, mint juleps should be made and served in sterling silver—not silver-plated—goblets or cups, rather than in glasses. Glass is a very poor conductor of heat (and cold), whereas sterling silver is 92.5 percent silver, and silver is the best heat conductor of all metals.

A mere Yankee, I dare not venture to present here a recipe for a mint julep, inasmuch as part of the reason the South is warmer than the North is that Southerners are engaged in perpetual heated arguments about the best way to make one. Find a Kentucky colonel (no, not that one; he's no longer with us) and ask him.

SHAKE 'N' STIR

*I've been having a discussion with some friends
about chilling drinks by stirring or shaking
with ice cubes—how much ice to use and what
the dilution factor would be. One guy said that
he uses lots of ice to chill faster and get less
dilution. I countered that it may chill faster, but
the dilution factor would be the same: less water
from each cube, perhaps, but the total amount
of melted ice would be the same.
Any help greatly appreciated.*

. . . .

I'm with the other guy.

First, the colder the ice the better. Colder ice will cool the liquid faster, just as colder rocks would do. And melting is not necessary for cooling; cold rocks would do the job as well.

If two substances are in contact, heat will flow automatically from the warmer one into the cooler one. In this case, heat flows out of the liquid and into the ice. Or, if you will, ice sucks heat out of the liquid. The colder the ice starts out, the more calories of heat it can suck out of the liquid before it reaches its melting/freezing point of $32°F$ ($0°C$) and even begins to think about melting. So if the ice is cold enough—far enough below $32°F$—there need be little, if any, melting and consequent dilution.

Second, the more ice the better. Lots of ice in the container forces the liquid into crevices between the ice chunks, creating thin layers of liquid that make efficient thermal contact with the ice surfaces and cool faster than would thicker layers of liquid. Another way of putting this is that the more ice chunks there are, the more ice surface is available for heat exchange with the liquid. So again there's faster cooling and less, if any, melting—if you don't leave the ice in too long. The best cooling mantra then, is "Lots of ice, short time."

That's ice *cubes*, incidentally, not cracked ice. Cracked ice has so much surface area, and the heat exchange between it and the liquid is so efficient, that it will start melting and watering down your drink before you can say Jack Daniel's.

Unfortunately, most bartenders' ice isn't very cold. It has probably been sitting in the bin for hours, warming up to within a few degrees of its melting point, so it doesn't have much cooling capacity before it begins to melt and dilute your drink.

But luckily, ice doesn't melt as soon as it gets to its melting point. Each gram of ice needs to absorb another slug of calories—0.080 calories, its *heat of fusion*—in order to break down its solid structure and turn into a fluid. So even not-very-cold ice will still do a pretty good job of cooling, albeit accompanied by some melting and dilution. Just don't let the bartender stir or (heaven forbid) shake your martini too long.

Because we do want some melting to take place in a martini (the drink will be too harsh unless it contains about 10 percent added water), one must strike the proper balance among the amount of ice, its temperature, and the length of stirring. That's why so many people mess up martinis, which in principle should be the simplest drink in the world to make.

MIND YOUR CHEER

*I'm a moderate drinker. I have a glass of wine
with dinner, and in social situations I'll often
have one or two drinks. Really, that's all. But at
holiday-season parties it's easy to lose track while
nibbling and chatting, so on occasion I have
imbibed a bit too much for my own comfort and,
I fear, for the comfort of others as well. I know
everybody's different, but are there any guidelines
for figuring out what effects various amounts of
alcohol are likely to have on a person?*

. . . .

Having spent decades on a university campus (no, it didn't take
me that long to graduate; I was on the faculty), I have heard more than
a little about what the students call "hearty parties." Translation:
binge drinking.

But the college crowd doesn't have a monopoly on bingeing,
whether deliberate or accidental. For us in the postgraduate population, the occasional holiday-party overdose can be more sinister
because we can't just stagger back to the dorm. In most cases we have
to drive home. And while that thought is sobering, the drive, unfortunately, is not.

A 2000 study supported by the National Highway Traffic Safety
Administration found that driving performance begins to deteriorate at a blood alcohol concentration of only 0.02, one-fourth the
national standard of 0.08 for a Driving Under the Influence (DUI)
citation.

So how can we regulate our alcohol intake to reach intoxication
stage 1 (relaxation and congeniality) without overshooting to stages 2
(garrulity and diminished inhibition), 3 (poor physical coordination

and slurred speech), 4 (lack of control or restraint), 5 (lethargy and stupor), 6 (vertigo), 7 (coma), and 8 (death)?

The discouraging answer is that we can't. At least not reliably. There are just too many confounding factors. Among the many variables that determine one's reaction to a given amount of alcohol are genetics, metabolism rate (women's rates are generally higher than men's), body weight, and personal alcohol history (heavy drinkers can "hold" more). Overriding all of these factors is how a given amount of alcohol is consumed: whether it is diluted by a mixer, whether it is consumed with or without food, and over how long a period of time it is consumed. The more dilution, the more food, and the longer the imbibing time, the less effect the alcohol will have.

The foremost factor is the total amount of ethyl alcohol consumed. The proverbial plaint "But I only had two drinks" can mean almost anything. In the United Kingdom a standard "drink unit" is any beverage that contains 8 grams of pure alcohol. In the United States a "drink" is taken to mean 12 to 15 grams of pure alcohol, while in Japan it's 20 grams. But you'll never see "grams of alcohol" on a beer, wine, or liquor label.

What effects will these amounts of alcohol have on you personally? None, until they get into your bloodstream. That's why the accepted measure of intoxication level is the blood alcohol concentration, or BAC: the number of grams of alcohol per 100 milliliters of blood. The BAC isn't measured directly in the blood (except at the autopsy), but it can be measured in the breath because alcohol is transferred from the blood to the breath in the lungs. The concentration of alcohol in the blood has been found to be about 2,100 times its concentration in the breath, so breath testers can be calibrated to read directly in BAC's.

Ingested alcohol is absorbed uniformly into all water in the body; about 80 percent of the absorption takes place in the stomach and 20 percent in the small intestine. The BAC will therefore depend on how much water a person's body contains: the more of that water is in the form of blood, the lower the concentration of a given amount of alcohol and the lesser the physiological effects. Again, everybody's different, but on average, males are 58 percent water by weight and females are 49 percent, while blood is 80.6 percent water in both men and women.

Engaging in a bit of calculator calisthenics using these numbers and the fact that the density of blood is 1.06 grams per milliliter, I find that for each 10 grams of pure alcohol absorbed by a 170-pound male, his BAC will go up by 0.019. For a 120-pound female, ten grams of pure alcohol will raise her BAC by 0.032. That means that to reach the legal BAC of 0.080 for a DUI citation, a 170-pound male need drink 42 grams of pure alcohol and a 120 pound female need drink only 25 grams.

In round numbers, that translates to (name your poison):

- **80-proof spirits (40 percent alcohol):** 5 ounces for a 170-pound male and 3 ounces for a 120-pound female.
- **Wine (at 13 percent alcohol):** 14 ounces for a 170-pound male and 8 ounces for a 120-pound female.
- **Beer (at 5 percent alcohol):** 37 ounces for a 170-pound male and 22 ounces for a 120-pound female.

These estimates are very rough, not only because people differ so much but because the calculations assume prompt and complete absorption of the alcohol, without accounting for delayed absorption caused by eating while drinking, or for the liver's continuous processing of the alcohol, or for the elimination of alcohol in urine over the course of the party. It's all a rather complex input/output system. Nevertheless, for a very conservative, ballpark estimate, keep track of the number of ounces you consume, and take the amounts above, adjusted for body weight and food consumption, as your probable "drunk threshold."

Of course, you'll want to stop long before that. But admittedly it's hard to count ounces while singing "Auld Lang Syne" with a lamp-shade on your head. What you can do, however, whether you're male or female, big or small, a heavy or "social" drinker, is this: Every half-hour on the dot, conjure up a virtual out-of-body experience and observe your own behavior from an objective distance. The moment you see or hear yourself entering stage 2, or at most stage 3, cut yourself off at the bar, eat more food, and go home with your rep-utation intact.

A modest proposal

The blood alcohol concentration (BAC) numbers used by law enforcement agencies, the U.S. Department of Transportation (DOT), and the National Highway Traffic Safety Administration (NHTSA) are the numbers of grams of alcohol per 100 milliliters of blood. The numbers come out to be two-place decimals; for exam-ple, the maximum legal level for drivers is 0.08, or eight-hundredths of a gram per 100 mililiters. But many people have difficulty interpreting these small numbers, and they are in any case cumbersome. So instead of defining the BAC as *grams* of alcohol per 100 milliliters of blood, why not redefine it as *milligrams* of alcohol per 100 milliliters of blood? All the BAC's will then be whole numbers. The limit for drunk driving would be 80 instead of 0.08. Lesser alcohol concentrations would be 70, 60, 50, and so on.

Are you listening, DOT and NHTSA?

(Of course, there will always be the drunk who, upon being told his blood registers 100, will think he made a perfect score.)

POST-GASTRONOMIC STRESS SYNDROME

*I have heard about all sorts of treatments for
removing red wine stains from tablecloths and
clothing. The things I hear about most often
are club soda and salt, but I've tried both
without success. There must be a way that
really works. Do you know it?*

. . . .

Upon learning that I have a Ph.D. in chemistry, innumerable
acquaintances have asked my expert advice on profound scientific
questions such as yours. (For this I spent twenty years in school?)

But okay. I hereby abandon my role of writing about the food and
drink that go into our mouths in favor of addressing what misses our
mouths and winds up in parts unintended.

The moment a klutzy guest upsets a glass of red wine onto the
hostess's tablecloth, there inevitably arises a chorus of cries from all
assembled: "Get some club soda!" "Pour white wine on it!" "Get
vinegar!" "Cover it with salt!" All well-meaning but useless. As far as
salt is concerned, its only value is to soak up the excess liquid by capillary action, which sand would accomplish just as well. But there
shouldn't be any excess liquid anyway if you have blotted the stain
immediately, an essential first step in treating any stain.

As for the three touted liquids—club soda, white wine, and vinegar—the irony is that they are all acidic and may actually intensify the
stain. Here's why.

The pigments in grape skins, belonging to a family of food coloring chemicals known as anthocyanins, behave as acid-base indicators (see p. 13). That is, they are red in acidic media and pale purple
in alkaline media. Adding an acidic liquid to the already acidic wine
stain does nothing except perhaps to dilute the stain, which plain
water would do.

I have always been suspicious of the club soda remedy, which is touted more highly than any other. I just couldn't see any chemical reason for it to work, so I decided to test it. (The trouble with this world is that people go around telling other people what works for this or that, without anyone ever doing a careful experiment to see if it's true.)

First, I treated a fresh wine stain on white cotton with plain carbonated water, or seltzer, known to chemists as carbonic acid. Being acidic, it did nothing to diminish the red color of the wine stain.

Then I tried the legendary club soda, which is carbonated water with a small amount of added sodium bicarbonate (baking soda) and in some cases also a small amount of sodium citrate. Both of these chemicals reduce the acidity, but I found that the club soda was still slightly acidic and didn't change the red color. It did zilch. So much for the many members of the Club Soda Club.

Well, what does work? A few years ago, researchers at the University of California, Davis—professor of enology (wine chemistry) Andrew L. Waterhouse and his student Natalie Ramirez—tested a variety of formulations, both commercial and homemade. Several commercial "wine stain remover" products failed miserably. But depending on the type of fabric and the age of the stain, generally good results were obtained with a 50–50 mixture of 3 percent hydrogen peroxide and a certain brand of liquid dishwashing detergent.

There is no need to mix up such a concoction and keep it around for emergencies; it doesn't keep well anyway. But the hydrogen peroxide in the Davis tests gave me an important clue, because peroxides are bleaches, although much less potent than chlorine bleach, which might remove not only the stain but all the color in the fabric as well. Peroxides are what the detergent makers call "color-safe bleaches." They oxidize the colored chemicals to colorless forms.

I decided to test several new products containing sodium percarbonate, a so-called addition product of sodium carbonate (washing soda) with hydrogen peroxide, which have come onto the market since the Davis experiments were done. I found that they work miraculously well on red wine stains.

I tested three of the percarbonate products that were available in my supermarket: Oxi Clean, Clorox Oxygen Action, and Shout Oxy Power. I sprinkled them (they're all white powders) on wine-stained white cotton, sprayed them liberally with water to wet the powders and let them sit for about ten minutes.

As I watched, the highly alkaline sodium carbonate turned the stains blue, and then the hydrogen peroxide took over and bleached the blue color out almost completely. (Shout Oxy Power worked

Sidebar Science: *Electron kidnappers*

IN CHEMISTRY, "oxidation" refers to a much broader class of reactions than the simple interaction of a substance with oxygen. In the more general sense, it refers to any reaction in which electrons are lost by an atom or molecule. Hydrogen peroxide and other peroxides are oxidizing agents that can snatch electrons away from the molecules of many other chemical compounds.

Now, colored chemical compounds are colored because their electrons absorb certain specific wavelengths or colors of light out of the daylight (a mixture of all visible wavelengths) that falls upon them, while reflecting all the remaining wavelengths back to our eyes. What we see, then, is reflected light that is missing a couple of the incident colors. For example, a daffodil petal absorbs some of the blue wavelengths out of the daylight, so it reflects back to us light that is deficient in blue, which we perceive as yellow. We then say that the flower itself "is yellow." But if an oxidizing agent were to snatch away the blue-light-absorbing electrons, the yellow color would be gone. The flower would have been bleached.

somewhat faster than the others.) I then threw the fabrics into the washing machine, percarbonate and all, and washed them with detergent. Not a trace of stain was left in any of them!

So check the ingredient labels on cleaning products in the super-market. If you see "sodium percarbonate," buy it and keep it handy. It's good for many other stain-removal jobs.

Save the club soda for your scotch.

A craven disclaimer: Stain removal can be challenging and not always predictable, depending on the exact nature of the staining substance, the age of the stain, and the type and color of the fabric. My tests were done on fresh merlot stains on plain white cotton. Never use any stain-removal technique—including the one above—without first testing it on an incon-spicuous part of the tablecloth or garment.

How to remove a fresh red wine stain

Be prepared. Keep a cleaning product containing sodium percar-bonate in the kitchen—for example, Oxi Clean, Clorox Oxygen Action, or Shout Oxy Power. These are all white powders.

Follow these steps:

1. Pour wine. Serve dinner. Enjoy food, wine, and merriment.
2. Watch in silent horror as guest spills red wine on tablecloth.
3. Without delay, blot excess wine with paper towels while telling the culprit not to worry and imagining him burning in Hell.
4. Sprinkle white percarbonate powder onto stained area.
5. Spray liberally with water (from a mister) to make a paste.
6. Allow paste to stand for 10 minutes while making small talk and imagining culprit burning in Hell.
7. At first opportunity, take tablecloth to washing machine, percarbonate paste and all.
8. Launder tablecloth as usual with normal amount of detergent.
9. Go to confession for your wicked thoughts.

Chapter Two

Down on the Farm

....

THE FARM IS where it all begins. The earth. The land. The soil.
Some nine thousand years ago, when we humans began to supplement our hunting-and-gathering existence with animal domestication and agriculture, we planted the seeds (to use a fitting metaphor) of modern farming. Although we still hunt and gather on the seas (see Chapter 6), the main source of virtually all human food is agriculture, farming the Good Earth to raise both crop and stock.

There are many kinds of farms. The greatest number by far raise grain (see Chapter 5), such as the rice, corn, and wheat that sustain nearly all of the world's population. Others grow fruits (Chapter 4) and members of the catchall category we call vegetables (Chapter 3). Still others raise livestock for their meat (Chapter 7), their milk, or their eggs.

This chapter focuses on the last two: the products of dairy farms. There, the two fundamentals of animal existence, the life-initiating egg and the life-sustaining milk of mammals, are obtained from domesticated animals. We either consume them as is or transform them mechanically, chemically, or biologically into products such as butter and cheese and then incorporate them into hundreds of dishes throughout the world's cuisines.

You will not find here the answer to a mystery that has haunted me for years, because I haven't been able to find an answer: Why do we speak of dairy and eggs as if there were an obvious connection between them, as there is between fruits and vegetables or between meat and fish? A quick glance at the animals involved should convince even the most casual observer that cows and chickens really have little in common. The farmer has yet to be born who goes out in the morning to collect cow's eggs and to milk the chickens.

Nevertheless, I shall perpetuate the "dairy and egg" association by treating them both within the same chapter.

THE SKIM SCAM

I always used skim milk until recently, when
fat-free milk became more available. I didn't like
the fat-free milk as much, however, and my
visiting grandson wouldn't touch it. So I bought
some low-fat milk. That made me wonder:
What's the difference between these products? True
skim milk was blue-white, and the edge around
the glass was translucent. Why can't I have my
good old skim milk back again?

. . . .

When a billboard asks, "Got milk?," we may be tempted to reply, "Can you be more specific, please? Are you asking about raw milk, pasteurized milk, homogenized milk, aseptically packaged milk, whole milk, skim milk, 2 percent milk, 1 percent milk, fat-free milk, evaporated milk, condensed milk, or buttermilk?"

If cows ever knew how we humans monkey around with their God-given, natural product, they'd jump over the moon.

But first, do you think you know what milk *is*? According to the U.S. Code of Federal Regulations, Title 21, Volume 8, Chapter I, Part 1240, Subpart A, Section 1240.3(j), Release 13, milk is "the lacteal secretion obtained from one or more healthy milk-producing animals, e.g., cows, goats, sheep, and water buffalo, including, but not limited to, the following: lowfat milk, skim milk, cream, half and half, dry milk, nonfat dry milk, dry cream, condensed or concentrated milk products, cultured or acidified milk or milk products . . ." and on and on for eighty-eight more words.

(Bureaucracy? What bureaucracy?)

Now that we know what we're talking about—always a good idea— let's first tackle the fat problem. I'll stick to the "lacteal secretion" of cows (genus *Bos*) only, assuming that you know what they are without the help of a zoologist or the U.S. Code of Federal Regulations.

Our contemporary American society appears to have concluded that the 8 grams of fat in an 8-ounce glass of typical whole milk constitutes a serious threat to our survival as a civilization. Hence, our markets offer us a dizzying variety of milks with ever-diminishing fat contents.

In simpler times, one could obtain "skimmed milk" or "skim milk" by allowing most of the fat globules to rise to the top of a bottle of whole, un-homogenized milk and skimming off what we called "the cream," as if milk and cream were two distinct products with nothing in between. But today, both milk and cream come in a variety of fat contents.

Our supermarkets' dairy sections offer us a confusin' profusion of choices—a broad spectrum of fat contents in milk products produced, according to the U.S. Code of Federal Regulations, Title 21, Volume 8, etc., etc., "by modifying the chemical or physical characteristics of milk, cream, or whey by using enzymes, solvents, heat, pressure, cooling, vacuum, genetic engineering, fractionation, or other similar processes, [or] by the addition or subtraction of milk fat or the addition of safe and suitable optional ingredients for the protein, vitamin, or mineral fortification of the product." But you knew all that, right?

So what's a consumer to do?

Fortunately, what the dairy industry hath given, the government hath taken away. The U.S. Food and Drug Administration (FDA) has lumped the fat contents of milk and cream into only four categories of milk and six of cream, including two sour creams. Table 1 lists these products by the label names the FDA permits the manufacturers to use, as of a January 1998 regulation. The corresponding traditional names are shown in parentheses.

The numbers of fat grams and calories shown in the table are taken from the USDA's Nutrient Database for Standard Reference, a compilation of the average compositions of virtually all foods. Individual brands, however, will vary somewhat.

Note that even though there are 9 calories in a gram of fat, the number of calories in a given milk product is not necessarily nine times its number of grams of fat; there are calories also in its proteins and carbohydrates. Also, because the various kinds of milk differ in more ways than fat content, the number of calories per cup won't necessarily be additive or subtractive in line with the amount of fat.

From the table we see that eliminating virtually all the fat from whole milk reduces the number of calories per cup only from 149 to 86, saving you a mere 63 calories. On the other hand, substituting a cup of one kind of cream for another can make as much as a 500-calorie difference.

One cup of heavy whipping cream, incidentally, makes two cups of whipped cream, halving one's guilt-by-volume. The second cup is pure, no-calorie air.

We perpetrate even greater crimes on milk than relieving it of its fat-induced richness. For example, we remove about 60 percent of the water from whole milk, put it in cans, and call it evaporated milk (19.1 grams of fat and 338 calories per cup). All of the milk's fat is retained, except in the inevitable low-fat and no-fat versions of evaporated milk. For example, evaporated skimmed milk (or is it skimmed evaporated milk?) contains 0.5 gram of fat and 200 calo-

Table 1. Commercial milk and cream products

MILK	GRAMS OF FAT PER CUP	CALORIES PER CUP
Whole milk	8.15	149
Reduced fat, less fat (low-fat, 2 percent)	4.69	122
Low-fat (1 percent)	2.59	102
Nonfat, fat-free, skim, zero fat, no-fat (skim milk)	0.4	86
CREAM		
Heavy whipping cream (heavy cream)	88.1	821
Light whipping cream	73.9	698
Light cream, coffee cream, table cream	46.3	468
Half-and-half	27.8	315
CULTURED SOUR CREAM		
Regular	48.2	492
Reduced-fat	29.0	327

ries per cup. Sweetened condensed milk (26.6 grams of fat and 982 calories per cup) is evaporated milk mixed with about 45 percent sugar.

And so it goes. Your precious skim milk still exists, albeit hidden behind any one of several modern aliases.

LA CRÈME DE LA CRÈME

What's the difference between all the
kinds of cream I see in my grocer's dairy case:
heavy cream, whipping cream, light cream,
half-and-half, etc.?

. . . .

Cream is made from milk by boosting the percentage of milk fat (also called butterfat, because it is made into butter) beyond the percentage the cow put into it. That is, some of the watery, non-fatty part of the original milk (the "skim milk") is removed to increase its "richness": its smooth, unctuous mouth feel.

How? Well, gravity will do the job automatically if one lets whole, un-homogenized milk stand for a while. Since fat is lighter (less dense) than water, it will float to the top, and the fat-rich portion— the cream—can be poured off.

But dairies separate the globules of fat much more quickly and efficiently from the rest of the milk by using centrifuges or so-called cream separators—machines that spin the whole milk around at thousands of revolutions per minute as if it were laundry in the spin cycle of a washing machine gone berserk. The heavier (more dense), watery skim is forced outward more strongly than the fat and migrates toward the outer portions of the bowl-shaped container, while the less dense fat globules linger nearer the center. A stack of conical vanes collects products of various densities, that is, products with various percentages of fat.

The U.S. Department of Agriculture (USDA) regulates the labeling of creams of various fat contents. Heavy cream, sometimes called heavy whipping cream, is literally the *crème de la crème*, because it contains the highest percentage of butterfat: from 36 to 40 percent. Lighter whipping creams may contain from 30 to 36 percent butter-

A small, hand-cranked cream separator. The cream comes out
of one spout (at left) and the milk comes out of the other.
(Courtesy Hoegger Goat Supply.)

fat, but anything less than 30 percent won't whip. Light cream, some-times called coffee cream, contains 18 to 30 percent butterfat.

Half-and-half is supposedly half milk and half cream, but that's not to be taken literally; its butterfat content depends on how heavy or light the "cream" half is. Half-and-half can run from 10.5 to 18 percent butterfat.

Because the label wordings can still vary within the USDA regulations, just select your cream in the market by looking at the fat content printed on the container.

Pillowcase Sweets

This is an adaptation of a handwritten recipe by American painter Mary Cassatt (1844–1926). She made these soft caramels for company when she and the impressionist painter Edgar Degas entertained in Paris. Cassatt's recipe books have not survived, and this is the only recipe attributed to her. These homemade cocoa-covered caramels, each shaped like a tiny pillow, were placed on guests' bed pillows during turn-down service at the grand opening of the Renaissance Hotel in Pittsburgh. (Cassatt was born in Allegheny City, Pennsylvania, now part of Pittsburgh.)

Follow the recipe exactly. If the kitchen is too warm, the candies tend to soften and spread. In a cooler room, they keep their shape. If you like fudge, you'll love these pillows.

---

6 **ounces bittersweet chocolate**

1 $^1/_2$ **cups confectioners' sugar**

6 **tablespoons ($^3/_4$ stick) unsalted butter**

1 **cup honey**

1 **cup heavy cream**

$^1/_4$ **cup unsweetened cocoa powder for dusting**

---

1. Lightly oil a marble or granite surface or a cookie sheet. Do not use a Teflon or similarly coated cookie sheet. Set aside until needed.

2. On the large holes of a handheld grater, grate the chocolate into a medium bowl or pie tin.

3. Place the grated chocolate and all the remaining ingredients except the cocoa in a heavy, medium saucepan and mix them together with a wooden spoon.

4. Stirring occasionally, bring to a boil over medium-high heat and continue cooking until the mixture reaches 238°F on a candy thermometer. This will take about 10 minutes.

5. Carefully pour the hot mixture onto the oiled surface—do not spread it— and allow it to cool.

6. Using a bench scraper, gather the candy into 4 balls and dust them lightly

with some of the cocoa powder. Roll them into logs about 1 inch in diameter. Dust again with the cocoa powder, place on a cookie sheet, and cover with plastic wrap. Refrigerate for several hours until firm, or up to overnight.

7. Uncover the logs and slice them into 1-inch-wide pieces. As you slice, the knife blade will drag each piece into a pillow shape. Place candies flat in a tin or candy box and cover tightly.

8. Refrigerate until ready to serve. The candies will keep for about a week. To serve, lay pieces in individual candy papers or foil cups.

MAKES ABOUT 48 PIECES

GOOD BUG, BAD BUG

The label on a container of plain yogurt lists
pectin among the ingredients. If they add pectin to
thicken it, isn't it more like a jelly than a yogurt?

. . . .

In principle—and in many countries of the world—yogurt is very simple. It is made by adding certain strains of beneficial living bacteria to the milk from a cow, goat, or sheep. The bacteria feed on the lactose (milk sugar) in the milk, metabolizing it into lactic acid and other interestingly flavored chemicals, some of which (the acids among them) coagulate or curdle the milk's protein into a thick gel. But in the modern, mechanized American food industry, nothing is ever that simple.

Whole milk with all of its fat intact will produce a thick, rich yogurt. But there is a large consumer demand for low-fat yogurt. So to avoid a thin, runny product, manufacturers may add a thickener or stabilizer: milk solids, pectin (a water-soluble carbohydrate obtained mostly from fruits) or a small amount of gelatin.

Yogurt has been made for centuries in Eastern Europe and the Middle East, but only relatively recently has it taken hold in the United States, where it has a flaunted though unproven reputation for keeping us healthy, slim, and fit. Commercial yogurt manufacturers fight the calorie wars by making their products from low-fat or non-fat milk so that they can plaster those consumer-pleasing words across their labels. But because many Americans don't like the taste of plain yogurt, most of our yogurt products are doctored with sugar or fruit preserves, and up goes the calorie count anyway.

Does eating yogurt help you lose weight? Sure, if you eat it instead of stevedore-sized lunches and afternoon candy-bar snacks. But forget the come-hither adjectives on the containers and read the government-mandated Nutrition Facts chart; it gives the actual number of calories per serving.

Among the thousands of species of bacteria and molds there are bad guys and good guys, just as there were in the old westerns. The bad guys can make us sick, but we welcome the good guys and use them to produce a galaxy of wonderful foods, from yogurt to hundreds of cheeses, beers, and wines.

The first step in making yogurt is to kill off any pathogenic bacteria (the ones wearing very, very tiny black hats) that may be lurking in the milk. Ordinary pasteurization, which consists of heating the milk either to 161°F (72°C) for 15 seconds or to 145°F (63°C) for 30 minutes, would do the job, but yogurt makers generally use higher temperatures: 203°F (95°C) for 10 minutes or 185°F (85°C) for 30 minutes. The higher temperatures help to thicken the product's texture by coagulating some of the milk proteins. The pasteurized milk is then cooled to 109°F (43°C), a nice, comfortable temperature at which the good guys can flourish.

The white-hat bacteria used in making yogurt are *Lactobacillus bulgaricus* (LB) and *Streptococcus thermophilus* (ST), mixed in equal amounts. (Other bacteria, such as *Lactobacillus acidophilus*, may be added as well.) The LB and ST have a unique symbiotic relationship. While they dine together on the milk's lactose, the LB also breaks down proteins into amino acids (the building blocks of proteins) and peptides (two or more amino acids bound together) that the ST can eat. In turn, the ST produces carbon dioxide gas that stimulates the growth of the LB.

Among the main flavor chemicals these bacteria produce are lactic acid, acetic acid (the vinegar acid), and acetaldehyde, a tart, walnut- or green-apple-flavored compound also created during the fermentation of wine and beer. It's the lactic, acetic, and other acids that do the trick of thickening the milk into yogurt's creamy consistency.

In what must be the quintessence of ingratitude, as soon as the bacteria have done their job by producing just the right flavor and texture, most yogurt moguls kill them off with heat. In that case, the label will probably say "Heat-treated after culturing."

Some people believe that eating the live bacteria somehow makes them healthier, but there is no convincing scientific evidence of that. Nevertheless, if you prefer yogurt whose bacteria are still alive and kicking, look for something like "Contains active [or living] yogurt cultures" on the label. Better yet, look for the National Yogurt Association's LAC ("Live and Active Cultures") seal. That means that when manufactured, the product contained at least 10 million bacteria per gram, or over 2 billion in an 8-ounce cup. A sobering thought.

Don't be fooled by a yogurt label that says "Made with active cultures." *Of course* they were active originally, or they wouldn't have transformed the milk into yogurt. The question is whether they're still alive when you take the yogurt home and eat it.

It is possible that people who are mildly lactose-intolerant and have trouble digesting dairy products may be able to tolerate yogurt because the bacteria have already gobbled up most of the lactose. If the bacteria are ingested still alive, they may be able to survive our digestive processes and continue their lactose scavenging in our digestive tracts. But that supposition hasn't been sufficiently investigated.

THE FOODIE'S FICTIONARY: Peptide—a strong riptide

Sidebar Science: *Micelles, not your cells*

IN THE CONVERSION of milk into yogurt, the bacteria-produced acids act on the milk's protein, which is mostly casein, to make its tiny, widely dispersed globules (its *micelles*) come together into a solid mass. This happens when the bacteria have acted long enough to produce a certain level of acidity. For casein, that's a pH of 4.6, its so-called *isoelectric point*, at which the micelles (pronounced MY-cells) lose their mutually repulsive electric charges and can stick together. What one observes when that acidity level is reached is that the milk coagulates, or curdles into curds and whey. Down at the yogurt works, they then homogenize the curds, whey, and milk fat into a single, smooth texture.

Yogurt Cheese

If you like yogurt but prefer a thicker consistency, you can make cheese out of it by draining off the whey. Yogurt cheese can stand in for semisoft cheeses. It makes a good spread for bagels or bruschetta and takes to the added flavors of herbs. Serve it sweetened with honey as a dessert cheese with crackers.

---

2 cups plain whole-milk or low-fat (not nonfat) yogurt

---

1. Empty the yogurt into a fine-mesh strainer or into a colander lined with several layers of cheesecloth. Place the strainer or colander over a bowl.
2. Put the setup in the refrigerator and allow the yogurt to drip and drain for 2 to 24 hours. The longer the yogurt drains, the denser it will be. The liquid that accumulates is the whey. It may be discarded.
3. The semisoft yogurt cheese in the strainer or colander will be thick enough to spread, and the consistency will be somewhere between sour cream and fresh goat cheese.

MAKES 2 CUPS

DIY Sour Cream

You can make Do-It-Yourself sour cream using the "good bugs" in buttermilk: *Streptococcus lactis, S. cremoris,* and/or *S. diacetylactis,* with some *Leuconostoc* thrown in for good measure (and flavor). They'll feed on the cream's lactose, producing pleasantly sour lactic acid. While buttermilk is made from skim or partially skimmed milk, turning these bacteria loose on high-fat cream will produce a much richer product.

Unlike commercial sour cream, the homemade kind—provided you've made it with heavy cream—can be whipped. When whipping it, be careful not to overwhip, because it can turn suddenly to butter. Homemade sour cream, whipped or plain, makes a delicious topping for fruit tarts and for many chocolate desserts.

Old-fashioned pasteurized cream will thicken in 24 hours and will have a delicious tang. Ultrapasteurized cream will take a little longer to thicken and will have a softer texture. Both can be kept in the refrigerator for a whole month; the sour cream will get thicker and more flavorful.

---

2 cups heavy cream

5 teaspoons buttermilk

---

1. Combine the cream and buttermilk in a screw-top glass jar. Shake the jar for 1 minute.
2. Let the jar stand at room temperature for 24 hours while the liquid thickens to the consistency of sour cream. If the room is especially cool, you may need to let it stand an additional 12 to 24 hours.
3. Refrigerate for at least 24 hours, or preferably longer for better flavor and consistency, before using.

MAKES 2 CUPS

HOW SOFT IS SOFT-SERVE?

*I brought home a quart of Dairy Queen soft-serve
ice cream and put it in my freezer. To my surprise,
the next day it was just as hard as any ordinary
ice cream. I thought the soft serves, like Dairy
Queen and frozen yogurt, were special formulas
that always had that lovely, voluptuous mouth feel
that I like so much. What happened?*

. . . .

A (chocolate) Dairy Queen aficionado myself, I tried your experiment twice. Each time, as soon as I got the quart container into the car I measured its temperature by plunging a so-called instant-read thermometer into the middle and waiting for a couple of dozen "instants" until it reached its final reading. On the two occasions it measured 14 and 16°F (−10 and −9°C). Then, after a couple of days in my freezer, somewhat diminished in quantity by after-dinner "scientific tests," each quart measured 0°F (−18°C). My soft-serve, like yours, had become just as hard as ice cream.

Thus, Dairy Queen and the other soft-serves are nothing but ice cream at a warmer temperature. We love them not only because of their softer, smoother textures but because our palates are more sensitive to flavors at warmer temperatures.

The American Dairy Queen Corp. lists the ingredients of its vanilla product as milk fat and nonfat milk, sugar, corn syrup, whey, mono- and diglycerides, artificial flavor, guar gum, polysorbate-80, carrageenan (the last three are thickeners), and Vitamin A palmitate. Milk fat, the main ingredient, is of course butterfat, and butter is harder at lower temperatures because more of its fat is crystallized. (See p. 83.) The mono- and diglycerides behave similarly to the butterfat's whole fats (*triglycerides*), while the guar gum and carrageenan thickeners also tend to tighten up at lower temperatures. So it's no wonder that the Dairy Queen is soft when you buy it but hardens in the freezer.

At Dairy Queen, TCBY, Carvel, and many other franchised and independent stores, rivers of various soft ice cream products, including nonfat ice cream, low-fat ice milk (which perversely contains less milk than ice cream), frozen yogurt, and frozen custard, flow like lava from smug-looking machines that guzzle batches of packaged mixtures dumped into their maws. The machines mix and chill them, adjust their temperature and viscosity, and dispense them in a variety of flavors, even swirling two flavors together for irresolute customers who can't decide between chocolate and vanilla. (Can there be any question?)

Dairy Queen's product is a reduced-fat ice cream containing 5 percent fat. TCBY sells both nonfat and 4-percent-fat (billed as "96 percent fat-free") frozen yogurt. Frozen custard is the smoothest and creamiest of all, and as a consequence the fattiest. (There's no free lunch.) Typically it contains 10 percent butterfat and a minimum of 1.4 percent egg yolk solids.

Moving up the fat ladder, we come to "ordinary ice cream." Federal regulations require that ice creams without solid additives such as nuts or candy bits contain at least 10 percent butterfat. The leading fake-Swedish-named brand contains 16 percent butterfat.

THE FOODIE'S FICTIONARY:
Custard—the last stand in a food court

COOL, MAN!

Does eating ice cream in hot weather cool you off?

. . . .

People do seem to think so. At my local Dairy Queen there is always a long line of people seeking cool after-dinner desserts in the summer, but starting the day after Labor Day, the place is virtually "desserted."

The answer to your question is in fact, no. After all, we are warm-blooded creatures with thermostats set at 98.6°F (37°C), and eating something cold cannot change that. Our cooling mechanism is purely a surface phenomenon: the evaporation of perspiration from our skins, assisted, when we're lucky, by a breeze that hastens the process. Putting ice cream into one's mouth serves only to cool the mouth. You'd do much better by smearing the ice cream all over your body.

According to my calculations, melting a one-inch, 0°F (−18°C) ice cube in the mouth would absorb only 1.3 calories of heat. If distributed over the entire body, that amount of heat loss would lower the temperature of a 150-pound person by 0.007°F (0.004°C).

Dogs, however, do cool themselves through the mouth by sticking out their long, wet tongues and panting to evaporate the saliva. You might want to try that; it should be more effective than eating an ice cream cone.

THE FOODIE'S FICTIONARY:
Baked Alaska—the end result of global warming

IN CELEBRATION OF INFLATION

*I left about half a cup of unfinished ice cream out
of the refrigerator overnight and it melted down
into only about a quarter of a cup.
Why did it shrink so much?*

. . . .

It was half air.

Federal regulations specify that the amount of "overrun" in ice cream must be less than 100 percent. Overrun is the increase in volume between the product's ingredients and the final, air-whipped product. A doubling of volume, known as 100 percent overrun, means that the product is 50 percent air.

Oh, you didn't know that your ice cream may legally contain as much as 50 percent air? Yep. The amount varies widely among ice creams, but the practice is not considered cheating because air adds smoothness. Without beaten-in air, a brick of ice cream would be almost as hard as a frozen stick of butter. On the other hand, an ice cream containing much more than 50 percent air would strike you as watery and inferior.

Store-bought ice cream, whether soft-serve or regular, must legally weigh no less than 4.5 pounds per gallon, or 18 ounces per quart. Try weighing a quart of your favorite kind. If it weighs about 27 ounces, it contains roughly a 50 percent overrun, or 25 percent air. If it weighs less than 18 ounces, call the cops.

THE FOODIE'S FICTIONARY:
Sherbet—the correct spelling of "sherbert," dammit

PITTSBURGH CREAM CHEESE?

*Just for fun, I counted almost two dozen kinds of
cheese in the cheese section of my "gourmet"
market, and I'd guess there are hundreds more in
the world. But two old standbys from my
childhood seem to be different from all the others:
cream cheese and cottage cheese. When I was a kid
I didn't know anything else. What makes them so
different? Are they purely American?*

. . . .

Not purely American, but primarily so.

What cream cheese and cottage cheese have in common, along
with French Neufchâtel and a few others, is that they are not aged or
ripened. The milk or milk-and-cream mixture is curdled by an acid
(usually lactic acid), and the curds are ready to eat as soon as they are
separated from the whey.

Variations of cottage cheese, probably the simplest of all cheeses, are
made throughout the world, presumably in cottages, although no one
seems to know the origin of the name. It has been known as pot cheese,
farmer cheese, bonnyclabber (in Ireland), and *Schmierkase* ("spreading
cheese" in Pennsylvania Dutch), with several variations in spelling.

In the United States, where cottage cheese is most popular and
where it was first manufactured commercially early in the twentieth
century, it is made by adding a culture of *Streptococcus lactis* to pasteurized skim or low-fat milk. These bacteria feed on the milk sugar
and produce the coagulating lactic acid. Usually, another bacterial
culture, *Leuconostoc citrovorum*, which produces flavorful compounds but no acid, is also added. After a fermentation period of several hours, the curds are cooked and some of the water is drained off,
leaving loose, crumbly clumps of curd. That's cottage cheese. If even
more water is removed to make a drier product, the product may be

called pot cheese. Press the curds into a cake or loaf and it's called farmer's cheese.

Because cottage cheese is quite moist (up to 80 percent water), it is very perishable. As a good growth medium for any pathogenic bacteria that may alight upon it, it must be kept refrigerated.

One cup (226 grams) of 2-percent-fat cottage cheese contains 203 calories, while a cup of 1-percent-fat cottage cheese contains 163 calories. Both kinds have a protein content of 28 grams, or 12.4 percent. That's why cottage cheese has a reputation as a diet food: It's high in protein, low in fat and carbohydrate.

Cream cheese is quite a different story. It is indeed an American invention, as you might guess from the fact that there seems to be only one brand, named for the city of Philadelphia, Pennsylvania. According to Kraft Foods, which owns the brand, cream cheese originated in 1872 at a dairy in Chester, New York. In 1880 it was branded "Philadelphia" by a New York distributor because at the time Philadelphia had a reputation for high-quality food products. (Pittsburgh cream cheese apparently didn't make the cut.)

Today's cream cheese has a minimum fat content of 33 percent and a maximum moisture content of 55 percent. The Philadelphia brand is 34.9 percent fat and contains 810 calories per cup. Its unique creamy-gummy consistency doesn't happen automatically, however. It is produced by any of several additives, including algin, a thickener derived from seaweed; locust bean gum from the seeds of the carob tree; gum tragacanth, obtained from various Asian and Eastern European plants; and guar gum, derived from the seed of a leguminous shrub. Smoothness has its price.

Best Damn Cheesecake

This velvety, creamy cheesecake is a cinch to make and never cracks in the oven. Serve with fresh berries, Rhubarb Coulis (p. 121), or bottled fruit syrup. For best results, use regular Philadelphia brand cream cheese. Do not use a whipped or low-fat variety.

CRUST:

> **About 10 long graham crackers**
>
> 1 **tablespoon sugar**
>
> 2 **tablespoons ($^1/_4$ stick) unsalted butter, melted**

FILLING:

> 3 **packages (8 ounces each) regular cream cheese,**
> **at room temperature**
>
> 4 **large eggs, at room temperature**
>
> 1 **teaspoon vanilla extract**
>
> 1 **cup sugar**
>
> **Pinch of salt**

TOPPING:

> 2 **cups (16-ounce container) sour cream (not low-fat)**
>
> 1 **tablespoon sugar**
>
> 1 **teaspoon vanilla extract**

---

1. Place a rack in the middle of the oven. Preheat the oven to 375°F. Spray a 9-inch springform pan with nonstick cooking spray.

2. Make the crust: Place the graham crackers in a food processor or in a zipper-top plastic bag. Whirl to make crumbs, or finely crush with a rolling pin. Measure 1 cup crumbs and place in a small bowl. (Discard any remaining crumbs.) Add the sugar and butter and toss with a fork to mix and moisten the crumbs evenly.

3. Spread the crumbs evenly over the bottom and about $^1/_2$ inch up the sides of

a springform pan, pressing lightly with your fingertips. Refrigerate the crust while you prepare the filling.

4. Make the filling: In a large bowl, using an electric mixer on medium-high speed, beat the cheese for 1 minute. Add the eggs, vanilla, and sugar and continue beating for 2 minutes, or until the mixture is creamy.

5. Pour the batter into the crust-lined pan. Place the pan on a baking sheet or pizza pan for stability. Place in the oven and bake for 35 minutes.

6. Make the topping: In a medium bowl, mix together the sour cream, sugar, and vanilla with a rubber spatula until smooth.

7. Remove the cheesecake from the oven. It will be somewhat wobbly in the center. Using a tablespoon, drop portions of the topping over the surface of the cheesecake, working from the outer rim toward the center, until it is evenly distributed and covers the entire top. Return the cake to the oven and bake for 5 minutes.

8. Remove the cheesecake from the oven, and let it cool in the pan on a wire rack. Cover the pan with plastic wrap and refrigerate for at least 6 hours or up to overnight.

9. To serve, run a knife blade between the pan sides and the cake to loosen the edges, then unclasp and remove the pan sides. Cut the cheesecake into wedges.

MAKES 10 TO 12 SERVINGS

RE: BRIE

What does the "%" sign signify on the label of a
Brie cheese? I've frequently seen cheese for sale
marked, for example, "Brie—60%."

....

It is the percentage of fat in the cheese, but expressed on what a chemist would call a *dry weight basis*—the percentage of fat in what would remain after all the moisture were removed.

In your example, the famous and ancient (eighth-century) French soft cheese called Brie, after a region east of Paris, can be made from milk and cream mixtures of various butterfat contents, resulting in cheeses containing various percentages of fat. The fat content of most cheeses is detailed on the packaging as a percentage of butterfat in the dry matter of the cheese.

Cheeses contain differing amounts of moisture, even in different batches of the same cheese. So if we want to express the percentage of fat in a cheese—the number of grams of fat per 100 grams of cheese— what should we use as the 100 grams of cheese, moist cheese or dried cheese? Obviously, the result will be more accurate and meaningful if we eliminate the varying amounts of moisture and report the percentage of fat as a percentage of the dry material.

Thus, a sample of the cheese is heated in a laboratory oven to remove all moisture, leaving mostly dried protein and fat. Then the amount of fat is measured and expressed as a percentage of the dry matter. That number will be larger than the percentage of fat in the whole (un-dried) cheese.

For example, let's say that a whole, moist Brie is 20 percent water. A hundred grams of it would dry down to 80 grams of dry matter. If that 80 grams of dry matter were then found to contain 40 grams of fat, the cheese would be labeled "50% fat" (40/80). But that's 40 grams of fat in what was originally 100 grams of whole, un-dried cheese. So the whole, moist cheese is actually only 40 percent fat (40/100).

The fat-percent labeling isn't a dodge to make the cheese seem to have more butterfat than it does. Because the water content of all foods can vary so much from sample to sample, food scientists are in the habit of drying their samples first to eliminate the water and then expressing their composition on a dry weight basis. That's standard practice in expressing the compositions of many other materials that can have varying moisture content.

Mineral water?

Purveyors of certain "gourmet" (read expensive) sea salts boast that their product contains so many "healthful minerals" that it is only 85 percent sodium chloride. The dodge is that their salt hasn't been thoroughly dried and the other 15 percent is mostly water. On a dry weight basis, their salt would be more than 97 percent sodium chloride, just like all other salts approved for human consumption.

CHEESEMAKER, CHEESEMAKER, MAKE ME A CHEESE!

I am an apprentice cheese maker. When making Camembert we add Penicillium candidum *(or some other form of penicillin) to the milk or spray it on the outside. My mother is allergic to penicillin but has never had a reaction to my Camembert. Why? Also, U.S. regulations require that the milk in cheese be pasteurized or that the cheese be aged for at least sixty days. I know pasteurization gets rid of bad bacteria such as listeriosis or brucellosis (which my grandmother called undulant fever), but how does aging get rid of them?*

. . . .

First, we have to straighten out some terminology. You're confusing the bacteria with the diseases they cause, the drug with the mold, and the mold with the allergen—the substance that triggers allergic reactions in some people. Here's the straight scoop:

- *Penicillin* (not penicillium) is the name of the drug.
- *Penicillium* (not penicillin) is the genus of the mold that produces the drug.
- *Listeriosis* and *brucellosis* are diseases caused by bacteria, not the names of the bacteria themselves.

The drug. The oft-told story of the "wonder drug" penicillin goes back to 1928, when the Scottish physician-bacteriologist Alexander Fleming took a vacation from his work at St. Mary's Hospital in London. He returned weeks later to find that some spores of the mold *Penicillium notatum* had drifted into his laboratory and settled on one of his cultures of the pathogenic *Staphylococcus aureus* bacteria.

(Fleming reportedly ran a rather sloppy lab and habitually left uncovered culture dishes out in the open.)

He noticed that the bacteria refused to grow near where the mold colony was growing, and surmised that the *Penicillium* mold was releasing some kind of antibacterial substance. He named the substance "penicillin" and won a Nobel Prize for it in 1945. (Advice to aspiring Nobel laureates: Keep a sloppy lab and take long vacations.)

Today, penicillin is produced on a large scale by "farming" the mold spores of *Penicillium chrysogenum*, a more prolific penicillin producer than *P. notatum*, in steel tanks, feeding them on "corn steep," a carbohydrate- and nitrogen-rich waste product of the wet-grinding of corn in making cornstarch.

It's important to understand what your mother is and is not allergic to. She is allergic to the chemical penicillin itself (formula $R-C_9H_{11}N_2O_4S$, where R represents one of several atomic groupings), not the *P. chrysogenum* mold. The *Penicillium* molds used in cheese making do not generate penicillin, so they pose no problem for anyone who is allergic to the drug.

The molds. Molds are fungi that grow on moist, warm organic matter. As mycophiles (mushroom lovers) well know, there are good guys and bad guys among the fungi. Even some of the *Penicillium* species produce toxins that may make a food inedible or dangerous. For example, the bluish-green mold that makes your over-the-hill foods look like Chia Pets is a *Penicillium*. But penicillin it is not. So throw away all moldy food, along with any nearby food that may have been exposed to its airborne spores. Don't run your kitchen like Fleming ran his lab.

Several different *Penicillium* species are used in making cheese, either by injecting the mold culture into the cheese (interior-ripened cheese) or by coating the cheese rounds with the mold (surface-ripened cheese). The molds contribute good flavors and impart a soft "bloom" to the cheese surfaces. Among the species most commonly used are *P. camemberti* for Camembert; *P. glaucum* for Gorgonzola;

P. candidum for Brie, Coulommiers, and several French goat cheeses, and *P. roqueforti* for Roquefort, Danish blue, and Stilton.

The bacteria. Bacteria, of course, can also be good guys or bad guys. Among the common black-hat, pathogenic bacteria are *Listeria monocytogenes* and certain members of the genus *Brucella*. The symptoms of infection by these bacteria are called listeriosis and brucellosis, respectively. Brucellosis goes by several different names—Malta fever, Mediterranean fever, Cyprus fever, etc.—depending on the part of the world in which the various *Brucella* species have caused the most trouble. (The name undulant fever comes from the fact that the fever chart of a brucellosis sufferer undulates up and down as the days go by.)

Both the *Listeria* and the *Brucella* bacteria, along with other pathogenic villains such as *Campylobacter jejuni*, several species of *Salmonella*, and the ever-popular *Escherichia coli* O157:H7 can breed in the moist environments of dairies and cheese plants.

The cheese. For more than fifty-five years, the FDA has required that all cheeses sold in the United States, whether domestic or imported, meet any one of the following three conditions: (1) the milk it is made from has been pasteurized by being heated to 145°F (63°C) for 30 minutes or 161°F (72°C) for 15 seconds, (2) the cheese itself has been subjected to equivalent heating conditions, or (3) the cheese has been aged for at least sixty days at a temperature no lower than 35°F (1.7°C). Long aging to produce the harder cheeses such as Gruyere and Cheddar both increases the acidity of the curd and dries it out, and many bacteria cannot multiply under dry, acidic conditions. But soft cheeses, which are not aged as long, cannot be made with absolute safety from unpasteurized milk.

Over the past several years, the FDA has been making noises about lengthening or eliminating the sixty-day aging option, that is, forbidding the distribution of any cheese, aged or not, that was made from unpasteurized or "raw" milk, on the grounds that *Listeria* and *E. coli* bacteria have been known to survive a sixty-day aging period.

(The second option, pasteurizing the finished cheese, is in most cases quite impractical.)

Vociferous objections to this trial balloon have been raised in many quarters, including European cheese makers and exporters, who use raw milk for many of the products they're most proud of; American artisanal cheese makers; and just plain food lovers, many of whom believe that pasteurization damages flavor and that illness from *Listeria* contamination of cheese is very rare, anyway. (Of the few hundred annual listeriosis deaths in the United States, it is difficult to pin down how many may have been caused by cheese, because other foods, notably hot dogs, delicatessen meats, and chicken, are the major sources of *Listeria* contamination and many outbreaks have no identifiable source.)

So, can we still buy cheeses made from unpasteurized milk? Yes. As of this writing, they're sold quite legally in many markets. The labels will say they're made from "raw milk." Do some producers cheat by aging their raw-milk cheeses for less than sixty days? Indubitably. Will the FDA ever ban all unpasteurized cheese? If they do, it will be over the figurative dead bodies of thousands of cheese lovers.

Tune in tomorrow for the next episode of "As the Cheese Wheel Turns."

STRINGING ALONG

What gives string cheese its peculiar texture?
It pulls apart in strands.

. . . .

String cheese is a novelty form of mozzarella, a soft, white, elastic cheese.

American mozzarella, made from cow's milk, is a poor relation to the Italian mozzarella (*mozzarella di bufala*) from the region along the shinbone of the Italian boot. *Mozzarella di bufala* is made from milk of the Asian water buffalo, introduced into Italy in the seventh century—a totally different animal from the American plains "buffalo," which isn't a buffalo at all, but a bison. Italian *mozzarella di bufala* is infinitely more moist, creamy, and delicately flavored than the cow's-milk product whose native habitat in the United States is on top of a pizza.

In making mozzarella, the milk is coagulated and separated into Little Miss Muffett's proverbial curds (the protein and fat) and whey (the remaining watery liquid). The curds are then mixed with some hot whey and stretched and kneaded until the mixture becomes smooth and rubbery.

To make string cheese, the curd is melted and heated to 170°F (75°C), then pulled and stretched like taffy, but mainly in a single direction, so that the milk protein (casein) molecules line up and give the cheese a directional structure. The cheese is sold in the form of cigar-shaped rods that can be peeled like a banana into long, fibrous strands that look like, well, string.

Why on earth string cheese exists, I don't know, except that kids like to play with it. And it can be consumed as a hand held snack, like a vegetarian Slim Jim.

THE FOODIE'S FICTIONARY:
Whey—a contrary response to "No way!"

CAN YOU SAY "PROCESS"?

I see many kinds of "process cheese" convenience
foods in the supermarket. How are they related
to traditional cheeses like Cheddar, Swiss, and
so on? Do they all contain "real" cheese,
and if so, how much?

. . . .

In addition to the hundreds of classic cheeses developed over more than a thousand years in various parts of the world, we are blessed (?) today with many options for adding cheese flavor, be it natural or artificial, to our snacks and dishes. Dozens of cheesy (often in more ways than one) factory-produced concoctions beckon to us from the market's refrigerated cases. Almost all of them contain "real" cheese, but their ties to reality can be rather thin.

The primary virtue of these so-called "process" (not "processed") cheeses is that unlike many classic cheeses they are easily meltable and blendable. That's because they often contain emulsifying agents and/or have been beaten into smooth submission long before they reach your kitchen.

Classifying them, as you can imagine, can be quite a chore, but the FDA is up to it. Here are the FDA-defined categories in order of diminishing faithfulness to the historic and revered concept of cheese.

- **Pasteurized process cheese:** A mixture of two or more cheese varieties that have been heated and blended together with an emulsifier and optional ingredients such as water, salt, or coloring, into what the FDA appetizingly calls "a homogeneous plastic mass" with a minimum of 47 percent milk fat. These cheese products may contain added cream or fat, making them more easily meltable, but they must be at least 51 percent actual cheese. Example: Most American cheeses.

* **Pasteurized process cheese food (note: not a "cheese" but a "food"):** A pasteurized process cheese containing enough added ingredients such as cream, milk, skim milk, buttermilk, or whey to reduce the percentage of actual cheese in the product to below 51. May contain emulsifiers such as phosphates, citrates, or tartrates, but must contain at least 23 percent milk fat. Example: Land O'Lakes American Singles.
* **Pasteurized process cheese spread:** A pasteurized process cheese food that may contain a sweetener plus stabilizing and thickening gums such as xanthin or carrageenan. Must contain at least 20 percent milk fat. Example: Kraft Olive and Pimento Spread.
* **Pasteurized process cheese product:** Any process cheese product that contains less than 20 percent milk fat. Examples: Kraft Singles, Velveeta.
* **Imitation cheese:** Made from vegetable oil. Minimum milk fat: zero percent. In a glass by itself is Cheez Whiz Cheese Dip or Cheese Sauce. After whey, its most abundant ingredient is canola oil. Milk fat? Less than two percent.
* **Orange glop:** Not an official FDA classification, but the name I give to the stuff they pour over nachos, French fries, and hot dogs in places I wouldn't eat in.

. . . And consumers are supposed to think they're all simply "cheese"?

AMAZING DEGLAZING

When I make a sauce by deglazing the pan with wine or stock after sautéing meat, the result is usually too thin for my taste, even after I reduce it. So in accordance with French culinary custom, I "finish" the sauce by adding a "nut" of butter and whisking it in lightly, whereupon the sauce magically thickens. Adding any other fat, such as olive oil, doesn't do that. Why does butter do it?

. . . .

Calling butter a fat is like calling a truffle a mushroom. Butter's magic arises from its uniqueness, not only in its history and renowned flavor but in its composition. Butter contains a relatively large amount of water, and it's the water that gives butter its unfatlike properties, such as being able to bring a sauce together and frothing up when heated in a sauté pan. I'll get to these two phenomena later, but first, a little background.

Butter is a complex blend of fat (by law, at least 80 percent in the United States and 82 percent in the European Union) and water (16 to 18 percent), plus 1 or 2 percent protein (mostly casein) and, if salted, 1.5 to 3 percent salt, which both kicks up the flavor and wards off rancidity. A touch of a fat-soluble yellow-orange pigment is often added, especially in the winter, when cows of most breeds produce paler fat because their diets are devoid of carotene-rich, new-growth vegetation. The pigment, used also to color cheese, is annatto (*achiote* in Spanish), from the seeds of the South American tree *Bixa orellana*.

Fats and water won't ordinarily mix. But in butter, the milk's fatty part (the butterfat) and watery part (the buttermilk) are combined in what appears to be a homogeneous mass. On a microscopic scale, we would see that the water is in the form of tiny globules (measuring less than 0.0002 inch), dispersed uniformly throughout the sea of semi-liquid fat like so many poppy seeds in a Jell-O mold. Such a stable configuration of two liquids that won't ordinarily mix is called an emulsion. (See p. 378.) Butter is a water-in-oil emulsion.

Seemingly paradoxical is the fact that butter is made from cream, an emulsion with precisely the opposite structure. Cream consists of microscopic fat globules dispersed throughout a watery liquid: an oil-in-water emulsion. When cream is churned into butter, the mechanical action breaks open the surfaces of the tiny fat globules so that they can coalesce—first into rice-sized grains, and ultimately, after being squeezed and kneaded, into a continuous mass incorporating microscopic globules of water.

But, you say, butter is mostly solid fat, not a liquid oil. Actually, it is both. For one thing, in chemistry, the same word, *fat*, is used whether the substance happens to be solid or liquid at room temperature. Moreover, the milk fat in butter is partially in the form of a sea of soft, almost liquid "free fat" and partially in the form of solid crystals. Butters that have been churned at different temperatures and then cooled and tempered differently (much as a pastry chef tempers chocolate to control its fat crystals; see p. 435) wind up with different ratios of free fat to crystals, and hence with different degrees of firmness, ranging from soft spreaders to bread shredders.

Enter the wee little beasties. Several breeds of bacteria, some good for us and some bad, view milk sugar (lactose) as yummy victuals and will thrive in cream if we let them. The bad ones can be knocked off by pasteurization, while the good ones can be encouraged by warm temperatures to go ahead and nosh, generating some wonderfully flavorful by-products as they do. Both of these measures have important consequences for the butter.

In the United States, all cream used to make commercial butter must first be pasteurized by being held at 165°F (74°C) for 30 minutes, a process that connoisseurs insist imparts a slightly cooked, off flavor compared with down-on-the-farm, unpasteurized butter. In the best of all possible worlds, though regrettably not very often in our part of the world, the cream will then be cultured (or "ripened," "matured," or "soured") by the addition of bacteria, usually a mixture of *Lactococcus* and *Leuconostoc* strains, which produce lactic acid and diacetyl. Lactic acid adds a pleasant tang to butter, while diacetyl is the chemical that gives butter its most prominent characteristic flavor. Unfortunately, most American mass producers of butter (at up to 8,000 pounds per batch) skip the time-consuming culturing step.

By this time you have figured out that butter froths up in the sauté pan because its water turns to steam, which then bubbles its way out noisily. But in spite of its high water content, hot butter doesn't spatter in the pan as other hot fats do in the presence of water. Instead, the butter merely foams up around the food. That's because butter's water is in the form of individual, microscopic globules. They don't join together into droplets that, in contact with hot fat, would explode into relatively large bursts of steam, carrying spatters of hot fat along with them.

How, then, does butter homogenize and thicken a pan sauce? In two ways. First, butter's fat content can absorb the fat in the pan while its water content can absorb the wine or stock, thus bringing them into a sort of matrimonial harmony. But the marriage wouldn't last very long if the butter didn't contain a small amount (about 0.24 percent) of lecithin, an emulsifier. An emulsifier's molecules stabilize an emulsion by latching onto both fat molecules and water molecules at the same time, effectively keeping them together. (See p. 380.) When the entire contents of the pan have thus become a fat-and-water emulsion, the contents will obviously be thicker, glossier, and more unctuous than the watery wine or stock alone. French chefs ever since Escoffier have been finishing their pan sauces with *une noisette* of butter.

THE FOODIE'S FICTIONARY:
Acidophilus—the Escoffier of Greek cuisine

GOOD EGGS GET GOOD GRADES

There are so many kinds of eggs in my
supermarket, I don't know which to buy.
They all seem to be Grade A, which I suppose
is good, but what about size and freshness?

. . . .

The USDA grades eggs according to quality—not according to freshness—as AA, A, or B. To earn a grade of AA, an egg must have an air
cell within the wide end that is less than an eighth of an inch (3 millimeters) deep; a shell that is well shaped and clean, with very few
ridges or rough spots; and when the egg is broken onto a flat surface,
a yolk that stands up high and domelike in the center of a clear, thick,
and firm white.

Grades A and B fit these criteria slightly less rigorously. They may
not look as pretty when fried or poached, because the yolks may be a
bit flat and the whites a bit more runny, but they are perfectly fine for
uses in which they won't be served whole.

Submitting eggs for federal grading, however, is optional for the
producers (the human ones, that is, not the hens). Eggs sold in cartons without the USDA shield will have been graded according to
state laws, which vary all over the lot.

If you find some eggs in a carton that don't appear to be the same
size, curb your suspicions. The USDA determines their average size
by the weight of a whole dozen. The standard egg sizes are jumbo,
extra-large, large, medium, small, and peewee. By the dozen, they
weigh 30, 27, 24, 21, 18, and 15 ounces, respectively.

Unless they state otherwise, you can assume that all recipes,
including those in this book, have been tested using large eggs. But if
you have only mediums, here's how to substitute: If the recipe calls
for one, two, or three large eggs, use the same number of mediums.
For four, five, or six large eggs, add one medium. Have only extra-

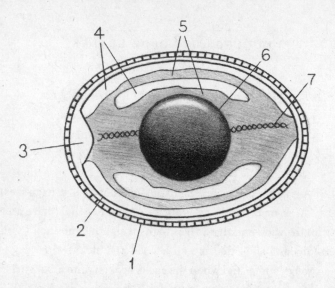

Simplified diagram of a hen's egg. (1) shell, (2) membrane, (3) air chamber, (4) thin albumen, (5) thick albumen, (6) yolk, (7) chalazae. (Redrawn by permission from Zdzisław E. Sikorski, ed., "Chemical and Functional Properties of Food Components," CRC Press, 2002.)

large eggs? For one, two, three, or four large eggs, use the same number of extra-large. For five or six large eggs, use one fewer extra-large. Or, just forget the whole thing and use ¼ cup of beaten egg for every egg specified in the recipe.

But are they fresh? Like so many other things we'd rather not think about, an egg's yolk tends to sag with age. Its white thins (like our hair) and grows cloudy (like our eyes), while its air cell increases in size (like . . . well, you know). But we don't know that until we've bought and broken the eggs.

Cartons of eggs from USDA-inspected plants and from most state-regulated plants must display the date on which the eggs were packed, which is almost always the same day they were laid. Although not required to by law, the packer or the supermarket chain may also choose to specify a "sell by" date, not to exceed thirty days from packing.

Eggs should be stored on an inside shelf of your refrigerator, not in those cute little depressions in the door rack. Refrigerator engineers apparently consider the rack an efficient use of space, but it's a poor preserver of eggs because of its higher and varying temperature. Refrigerated eggs will keep, with slightly deteriorating flavor and texture, for four to five weeks beyond the packing date. Keep them in their cartons to protect them from refrigerator odors; eggshells are porous and can absorb unpleasant smells. Most commercial eggs, however, have been coated with a thin film of oil to seal the pores and extend their shelf life by reducing moisture loss and preventing bacteria from invading the shell.

Fresh Orange Sponge Cake

One great thing about eggs is that you can separate the yolks from the whites and take advantage of their unique characteristics separately. In this cake, the yolks act as a binder and contribute fat, color, and rich flavor, while the whipped whites produce a light, foamy structure.

Delicate in texture and magnificent to behold, this cake is classic company fare. Sponge-type, also known as foam, cakes are springy and light. They include chiffon, angel food, and sponge cakes. All have one thing in common: stiffly beaten egg whites, on which their fluffiness depends.

Important: Never grease the cake pan for any foam-type cake. If it has been used before to bake a cake with shortening, scour it and dry it thoroughly before using. The batter needs a clean, dry wall to cling to.

The texture and flavor of sponge cakes are so delightful that the cakes are usually eaten without frosting, which can weigh them down. But a little lily-gilding—a shower of confectioners' sugar—does no harm.

This cake can be made in advance and stored at room temperature for 2 days, in the refrigerator for 5 days, or in the freezer for 2 months. But bring it back to room temperature for serving. Leftover cake? (You should be so lucky.) Serve slices, lightly toasted, for breakfast.

- 6 large egg whites
- 1^3/$_4$ cups all-purpose flour
- ^{1}/$_2$ teaspoon salt
- 1^1/$_2$ cups sugar
- 6 large egg yolks
- Orange oil, optional*
- 6 tablespoons freshly squeezed orange juice
- 1 tablespoon freshly grated orange zest
- Confectioners' sugar, for dusting, optional

---

1. In a medium bowl, allow the egg whites to warm to room temperature, about 1 hour.

2. Meanwhile, place a rack in the lower level of the oven. Preheat the oven to 350°F. Have ready a 10-inch tube pan.

3. Using a fine-mesh strainer or a sifter, sift together the flour and salt in a medium bowl. Set aside.

4. With an electric mixer on medium speed, beat the egg whites until foamy. Gradually add ½ cup of the sugar, beating after each addition. Continue beating until soft peaks form when the beater is slowly raised. Set aside.

5. In a large bowl, using the electric mixer with the same beaters on high speed, beat the egg yolks while gradually adding the remaining 1 cup of sugar until the mixture is thick and lemon colored. This will take 5 to 8 minutes in all. Add 1 or 2 drops orange oil, if using—a little goes a long way—and beat until combined.

6. Remove the beaters from the bowl, shake to free any adhering yolk, and continue with the recipe using a whisk and rubber spatula.

7. Add the orange juice and orange zest to the egg yolk mixture and whisk to combine. Add the flour mixture and whisk just until no white patches are visible.

8. With the whisk or spatula, and using an under-and-over motion, stir one-third of the egg whites into the yolk mixture to lighten it. Then fold in another half of the remaining egg whites. Finally, fold in the remaining egg whites just until blended.

9. Gently pour the fluffy batter into the tube pan. Bake for 35 to 40 minutes, or until the cake has risen to the top of the pan, the top is browned, and a cake tester inserted into the center of the cake comes out clean.

10. If your pan has feet, invert the pan over a wire rack. Alternatively, invert the pan over the neck of a bottle. Don't worry, it won't fall out. Let the cake hang for about 1 hour to cool completely.

11. Place the pan on a work surface. With a metal spatula, carefully loosen the cake from the pan and transfer to a platter. Serve plain or sift a dusting of confectioners' sugar over the top. Use a serrated knife to cut the cake.

MAKES 12 SERVINGS

*Orange oil is available in the baking areas of some supermarkets or at Williams-Sonoma or other cookware stores.

HOW NOW, BROWN EGG?

A well-known organic restaurant says it uses fertilized brown eggs, claiming that they are the "most nutritious eggs available." Are there any scientific facts to back this up?

. . . .

Unfortunately, no.

I hereby join forces with every other printed dissertation on eggs to assure you that no differences in flavor or nutrition have been found between brown eggs and white eggs. Just as brown-skinned people produce brown-skinned children, brown-feathered chickens lay brown-shelled eggs. Among the brown-egg layers are the Barred Plymouth Rock and the Red Rock Cross, while the white-feathered White Leghorn lays white eggs. The Columbian Rock, which sports both black and white feathers, is one of several exceptions. It must have flipped a genetic coin at some time in the past and decided to lay brown eggs.

The color of the yolk, incidentally, depends on the hen's diet; wheat-based diets produce lemon-yellow yolks, while alfalfa-based diets produce orange-yellow yolks.

Then why do brown eggs cost more? They are generally produced by species of larger hens that consume more feed and lay bigger eggs. One might also speculate that people who think brown eggs are superior are willing to pay more for them.

Some people believe that fertilized eggs are more healthful to eat because they contain a "life force" not present in "dead" foods. I shall not express my opinion of that idea because I am a very tolerant, open-minded, and nonjudgmental person who believes that people have the right to think whatever they choose.

No matter how absurd.

THE FOODIE'S FICTIONARY:
Egg roll—a Chinese Easter festival

VIRGIN HENS

While making breakfast the other day, I broke an
egg and found a red spot, looking like blood,
on the yolk. I threw it away, but was it okay
to eat? And what caused it?

It doesn't mean that the egg was fertilized, and it will not hatch no
matter how long you sit on it. Hens that lay eggs for commercial distribution have never even seen, much less "dated," a rooster. Layers
just aren't breeders.

The red spots are indeed blood, from the rupture of a blood vessel on the yolk's surface that occurred during formation of the egg, or
by a similar mishap in the wall of the oviduct. Less than one percent
of all eggs laid have blood spots.

The routine inspection process of candling—turning the eggs on
rollers in front of high-intensity lights (originally they were held up
to a candle) to reveal their interior qualities—catches most eggs with
blood spots, and they are removed. But a few inevitably sneak though
and reach the market. They are perfectly fit to eat, although Jewish
dietary law rejects them as not kosher.

Instant Vanilla Custard Sauce (Crème Anglaise)

Here's a trick I learned from Seattle chef Jerry Traunfeld of the Herbfarm. Early in his career, when he was a pastry chef at Stars, Jeremiah Towers' restaurant in San Francisco, Traunfeld had to make gallons and gallons of crème anglaise every day. It took way too much time, he said, when he'd rather be creating pastries. So he developed a reverse-cooking method for the sauce that is risk-free and speedy.

Instead of adding egg yolks to boiling milk, he adds boiling hot milk directly and quickly to slightly warmed egg yolks. The milk cooks them instantly with no risk of curdling. The custard immediately coats a spoon, which is the standard test for the finished sauce. It thickens further as it cools in the refrigerator. Hard to believe, until you try it.

Called by either its English or its French name, this sauce is wonderful warm or cold, served over apple dumplings or pie, strudel, chocolate cake, gingerbread, bread pudding, or even baked fruit. To dress it up for company, substitute 1 tablespoon Grand Marnier or Cointreau for the vanilla. And in season, transform it into eggnog by adding freshly grated nutmeg and rum.

---

  6 **large egg yolks, at room temperature**
$^1/_2$ **cup sugar**
$^1/_8$ **teaspoon salt**
  2 **cups whole milk**
$^3/_4$ **teaspoon vanilla extract**

FOR EGGNOG:
$^1/_4$ **teaspoon freshly grated nutmeg**
  1 **tablespoon rum, or more to taste**

---

1. Warm a medium bowl by rinsing it under hot tap water; dry. Place the egg yolks in the warmed bowl and place the bowl over barely warm water in a larger bowl. (You just want to take the chill off the yolks.)

2. Before proceeding to the next step, pick up the yolk bowl from the warming bowl and place it on a damp, flat washcloth. This will prevent the bowl from skidding on the counter when you start to whisk.

3. In a medium saucepan, combine the sugar, salt, and milk. Place over medium heat and stir constantly until the sugar has dissolved and the milk is coming to a boil.

4. As soon as the milk boils and as it rises in the pan, immediately remove the pan from the heat and quickly whisk the milk into the egg yolks, whisking briskly for the first 3 to 5 seconds and then switching to a slow stirring motion until all the milk is in (takes about 15 seconds). Continue to stir slowly and blend without any aeration for another 10 seconds. The yolks will cook without further heating.

5. Stir in the vanilla.

6. Pour the mixture through a fine-mesh strainer into a container to remove those thick, cordlike strands of egg white (chalazae) that anchor the yolk in the center of the egg. Refrigerate until ready to serve. The mixture will thicken as it cools.

MAKES 3 CUPS SAUCE, OR FOUR $^3/_4$ CUP SERVINGS OF EGGNOG.

A YOKE OF YOLKS

*How do double-yolk eggs form? Do the yolks
replace the space that would have been taken
by the white? Or is it a bigger egg?*

. . . .

In general, the yolks are smaller but the eggs overall are bigger.

About 3 to 5 percent of hens' eggs have two yolks. Some hens, driven by their genes and the conformation of their oviducts, seem to specialize in producing these twins. When you find a double-yolker in an otherwise normal dozen, it's a mistake—not of the hen, but of the inspectors at the egg farm, because all eggs are candled before being sold, and candling will show up any double-yolk eggs, which are put aside for special uses.

There's nothing wrong with eating a double-yolk egg when you come across one. In fact, double-yolkers are in demand for their novelty, and the supply can't keep up. When you do come across one, fry it sunny sides up.

A CRACK ATTACK

I recently read somewhere that adding salt to the water before boiling eggs prevents the eggshells from cracking. It has worked for me the three times I've done so. What is the chemical explanation for this effect?

. . . .

There is no chemical explanation because it's not true. Salt (sodium chloride) has no effect on eggshells (calcium carbonate), either chemically or physically.

An eggshell can crack when there is a sudden temperature difference between a cold shell and hot water. The heat makes the shell expand quickly but unevenly, because it has different thicknesses in different places. The uneven heating causes stresses that can fracture the shell at its weakest points. (Hold an egg up to a very bright light and you'll often see fine cracks in shells that look perfectly intact from the outside.) An egg may also crack if the air space inside the large end expands too quickly, before it can seep out slowly through the porous shell. A good precaution is to puncture the large end with a pushpin to let the air bubble out harmlessly as the egg heats.

To cook crack-free eggs, avoid plunging cold eggs into hot water. Instead, put them into a pot of cold water and then heat the pot until the water begins to boil. As soon as you see a few bubbles, turn down the heat to a simmer. Depending on how long you simmer them, the eggs will cook through the entire spectrum of doneness, from coddled in 1 or 2 minutes to hard-"boiled" in 12 to 15 minutes.

So how do we explain your experience? With all due respect, three trials do not a scientific experiment make. How do you know that the eggs would have cracked without the salt? Please repeat your experiment with six dozen eggs, half of them cooked with salt and half without. Record the number of cracks in each case and turn in your lab report to me by next Thursday.

But wait! There is indeed some wisdom in salting the egg water. Read on.

DUTCH BOY IN A BOTTLE

Several people have told me that adding a little vinegar to the water when boiling eggs prevents the shell from cracking. Does it? And how?

. . . .

It doesn't. And that gets me off the hook for your second question.

The acetic acid in vinegar will coagulate the protein in any albumen (egg white) leaking out of a shell that already has a crack in it. That's how acids in general act on proteins in general. But salt can have the same effect. Thus, adding vinegar, lemon juice (citric acid), or salt to the water is insurance for pessimists who expect their eggs to crack and want to stem the exodus of albumen. Acids and salt are leak stoppers, not leak preventers; they are fingers in the dike, so to speak.

THE EGG-SPINNING OLYMPICS

When I hard-boil eggs, why do the shells
sometimes peel off quite easily and at other times
they stick like crazy to the whites?

. . . .

When the eggs are done, cool them down quickly in cold running water. That shrinks the albumen away from the shell somewhat and makes an egg easier to peel. (It also keeps the yolks from turning green; see the following question.) Very fresh eggs are harder to peel because the albumen tends to stick to the membrane on the inside of the shell. But after several days the membrane retreats and the sticking tendency diminishes, so don't hard-cook your freshest ones.

By the way, after you hard-cook eggs, keep them refrigerated. It's easiest if you put them right back in the carton containing your uncooked eggs. But how do you tell the cooked ones from the raw? Easy. Put an egg on the counter and give it a spin. If it resists spinning, it's uncooked, but if it spins like a top, it's hard. The effect is most noticeable if you spin the eggs on their larger ends.

Or you could just pencil an *H* on the shell of each hard one, but where's the fun in that?

Sidebar Science: *Playing spin-the-egg*

THE YOLK and white in an uncooked egg are liquid and free to slosh around slightly inside the shell. When you twist the egg fast in an attempt to spin it, the contents resist moving. That is, the contents have *inertia*, a desire to stay motionless until pushed by some force or other. That's Newton's First Law of Motion: an egg yolk at rest will remain at rest until shoved by something harder than raw egg white. (Those weren't his exact words.) When you apply a twisting force to the outside of the egg, the force isn't transmitted effectively through the egg white; it's like trying to play pool with a liquid cue. The egg's contents try to stay motionless and lag behind. In effect, some of your twisting force is wasted and the egg won't spin as much as you might expect from how hard you twisted it. In a hard egg, on the other hand, the solid contents transmit your force to the whole egg mass, and the egg spins with the full amount of momentum you expect.

Want some more fun with egg physics? If you spin the egg on its wide end rather than on its side, it will spin faster. The reason is the same as for an ice skater who spins faster as soon as she pulls her arms and legs in closer to her body (closer to her *spin axis*). Her body's spin momentum (or *angular momentum*) is proportional to both her spin speed (her *angular velocity*) and the average distance of her body parts from the spin axis (her average *spin radius*). Her total momentum must remain constant (that is, *angular momentum is conserved*), so if she decreases her spin radius by pulling in her limbs, her spin velocity must go up. In the case of the egg, the spin radius is smaller when you spin it on its end rather than on its side, so it spins faster.

GREEN EGGS, NO HAM

*I've always stayed clear of hard-boiled eggs with
funny green or gray colors on the yolks. But I have
a four-year-old boy and we've read Dr. Seuss's*
Green Eggs and Ham *many times. Sam-I-Am's
eggs are sunny-side-up with green yolks.
Isn't that a bad lesson to teach kids?*

. . . .

On the cover of my copy, both the egg yolks and the ham are green,
so the good doctor must have intended the adjective *green* to modify
both nouns, *ham* as well as *eggs*. But I'd strongly advise you to stay
clear of green ham (but see p. 281) and will limit my comments to
the yolks.

What causes the greenish-black color of hard-cooked egg yolks?
This is an oft-asked and oft-answered question—but I don't mind
tackling it again.

First of all, the color is harmless. Even if the colored substance
were a toxic compound (it's not), it is present in only trace amounts.

As an egg ages, some of the sulfur-containing protein in the egg
white slowly decomposes, forming a small amount of evil-smelling
hydrogen sulfide gas, H_2S. Heat greatly accelerates this decomposition; at the temperature of boiling water, hydrogen sulfide will be
produced in an egg almost two hundred times as fast as at room temperature. The gas diffuses throughout the egg, and when it reaches
the yolk, which contains a small amount of iron, it reacts with the
iron to form iron sulfides, FeS and Fe_2S_3, known to chemists as ferrous sulfide and ferric sulfide, respectively. Ferrous sulfide happens
to be black-brown, while ferric sulfide is yellow-green. *Et voilà!* A
dirty-looking egg yolk. The exact color will depend on how much air
is available inside the egg, because in the presence of air the blackish

ferrous sulfide changes (it is *oxidized*) to the greenish ferric oxide. Because older eggs contain more air, their yolks tend to turn greener.

The longer an egg is heated and the more hydrogen sulfide gas is produced, the more it migrates to the surface of the yolk, and the greener and darker the yolk becomes. If hard-"boiled" eggs are made without actually being boiled, but simply by being left in a covered pan of water below the boiling point, the slightly lower temperature of the water will make a big difference in slowing the production and diffusion of hydrogen sulfide. As soon as the eggs are done, you should stop these ugly chemical reactions dead in their tracks by cooling the eggs in cold running water.

If your little boy wants an egg that's green enough to pass muster with Sam, try getting him a cassowary egg. A cassowary is a large, flightless Australian bird that lays eggs averaging about 3½ by 5½ inches and weighing about 1¼ pounds. The shells are quite green—although I confess I can't vouch for the contents.

Sidebar Science: *On rotten eggs*

THE ALBUMEN, or white, of an egg is 88 percent water and 11 percent a mixture of about a dozen different proteins. But most (54 percent) of the protein is ovalbumin, each of whose huge molecules contains more than three thousand atoms, including only six atoms of sulfur.

Nevertheless, that tiny amount of sulfur can cause quite a stink when converted into hydrogen sulfide, H_2S, a gas that is approximately as poisonous as the hydrogen cyanide gas, HCN, used in execution chambers. Fortunately, however, hydrogen sulfide is so incredibly smelly that people notice it long before it can build up to a harmful concentration in the air. It will empty a concert hall faster than a tone-deaf soprano.

Chemistry textbooks persist in telling us that hydrogen sulfide has the "familiar" smell of rotten eggs. But I'll wager that not one in ten thousand people, excepting really bad vaudeville performers, has ever smelled a rotten egg. If you ever do, though, you'll know that it's hydrogen sulfide. In fact, extremely tiny amounts of hydrogen sulfide are responsible for much of the aroma and flavor of even a cooked fresh egg.

How do eggs turn rotten? Contrary to common belief, it doesn't happen simply because an egg has attained geriatric status. Old eggs don't rot. Like old soldiers, they just fade away.

To test this notion, I kept an unopened egg on my desk at room temperature for about six months, half expecting at any time to be driven from my office by the stench of hydrogen sulfide. But that never happened. When I finally opened the egg, its contents had shrunk to a gelatinous mass occupying only about one-fifth of the space inside the shell. The rest of the space was filled with perfectly fresh air, with not a trace of hydrogen sulfide odor. The egg may have died of old age, but it did not turn rotten.

The rotting of an egg is like the rotting of any organic matter: It results from the action of decay-producing bacteria. There were no breaks in the shell through which bacteria could enter, so my egg had not been contaminated and no putrefaction occurred.

Even though eggshells are porous and therefore ostensibly vulnerable to invasion by bacteria, eggs have several defense mechanisms. First, freshly laid eggs are coated with a protective film called the *cuticle*. The two membranes just inside the shell are a second line of defense. Third, the albumen actually has antibacterial properties; among other things it contains the enzyme *lysozyme*, which fights bacteria by dissolving their cell walls. (Lysozyme in our tears also fights infection in our eyes.)

As soon as an egg is broken open, though, it's fiesta time for every microorganism in the neighborhood (can't you hear those tiny mariachis?) and it's all downhill from there.

One more non-rotten-egg story: Recently, I had the dubious privilege of examining a four-year-old hard-boiled and dyed Easter egg. It seems that for some cockamamie reason my dear wife, Marlene, had promised to save it for her four-year-old grandson, Oscar, until he went to college. He's eight now. Unbeknownst to me, the egg had been in our refrigerator all along. When Oscar visited us recently, he asked about his egg and Marlene produced it. Although I wouldn't want to eat it, it was still quite inoffensive, demonstrating once again that without bacteria and conditions conducive to their growth, an egg will not turn putrid. But we'll check it again during Oscar's freshman orientation program for the class of 2018.

ADORABLE EGGS

Why do some peeled hard-cooked eggs
have a big dimple in one end?

. . . .

A hen's egg contains a small air pocket just inside the shell at the broad end, the purpose of which is to let the chick breathe while pecking its way out on its birthday. Because the shells are porous and permeable to gases, outside air can diffuse in and exchange with the air inside. As an egg ages and its contents shrink away from the shell, more air comes in to fill the space and the air pocket grows larger. A really fresh egg will sink in water, but as it ages and the air pocket grows bigger, it will tend to turn its broad end up. Eventually, a stale egg will float entirely on the surface.

When you cook an egg, heat expands the air in the pocket and its pressure increases. As long as the white is still liquid, it can't flow into that air space because of the pressure. As the white cooks, it solidifies around the shape of the air pocket. Hence the dimple.

And by the way, those ropes of thick albumen that extend from the yolk to the membranes at both ends of the egg (see p. 86) and that hang on to the yolk when you're separating an egg are not the beginnings of an embryo. They're called *chalazae* (kuh-LAYZ-eye), a word inexplicably derived from the Greek meaning "hail." They serve to keep the yolk centered in the white. Chalazae are more prominent in very fresh eggs. There's no need to remove them, except perhaps if you are making a soufflé or a custard and want it to be as lump-free as possible.

Some hard-boiled advice

The American Egg Board recommends the following method for making hard-cooked eggs: "Place eggs in single layer in saucepan. Add enough tap water to come at least 1 inch above eggs. Cover. Quickly bring just to boiling. Turn off heat. If necessary, remove pan from burner to prevent further boiling. Let eggs stand, covered, in the hot water about 15 minutes for Large eggs (12 minutes for Medium, 18 for Extra Large)."

But take it with a grain of salt. As the nation's self-proclaimed eggsperts, the AEB must disseminate instructions that will work for the *average* cook. But one can drown in water that *averages* only six inches in depth.

Eggs may vary not only in size and freshness but also in their temperatures when placed in the saucepan, so they may not all reach boiling temperature as soon as the water boils. Also, different stoves and different pans will require different amounts of time to boil the water. And after the burner is turned off a heavy, porcelain-lined iron saucepan will keep its water hot longer and at a higher temperature than a thin aluminum one.

For these reasons, Marlene has not found the AEB's recommendations to be reliable. So what does she advise? Follow the AEB's instructions up until the water boils. But don't turn off the heat; turn it down to a bare simmer and begin your timing. Using the AEB values as a guide, base your timing on your own experience with your own stove and saucepan, your own usual-sized eggs, your own refrigerator, and the degree of hardness you prefer in your yolks.

It's worth sacrificing a few eggs to the gods of experimentation to find your "personal best." Jot down your chosen simmering time on a piece of paper and tape it to the inside of a kitchen cabinet door.

And may your eggs be forever perfect—for you.

THE QUEST FOR DIVINITY

Are pasteurized egg whites okay to use for making
Divinity? I tried them once, but not being a great
baker did not get a good result. I ended up with
little patches of sticky goo. I was wondering if the
pasteurization changed the egg whites enough
to make Divinity impossible.

. . . .

It may be difficult for any mortal to achieve divinity, but with patience you can do it.

Pasteurized-in-the-shell eggs are intended to eliminate the hazards of the food-poisoning bacteria *Salmonella enteritidis* and other salmonella species that can be found in poultry, meat and meat products, raw milk, and the yolks (usually not the whites) of raw eggs, among other places. Temperatures of 160°F (71°C) or above will kill the bacteria, but using raw egg yolks in such preparations as mayonnaise and Caesar salad can be risky.

If you had been able to get past the egg-white whipping stage, your Divinity would have been safe even with unpasteurized eggs, because for one thing you're using only the whites, and for another you're cooking them. The sticky goo was egg white that wasn't beaten enough, and that's the trouble with pasteurized eggs: the whites don't whip as well because the mild heating during the pasteurizing process partially denatures* or "cooks" the protein.

Eggs are pasteurized in the shell by being heated in warm water. A combination of time and water temperature heats them just enough

---

* When proteins are subjected to heat or acids, the structures of their long, twisted molecules change, usually by unraveling or "deconstructing" themselves and then shrinking or tightening up like knotted rubber bands. This molecular reconfiguration process is called *denaturing*. In this book, I will frequently refer to denaturing as a "reconfiguring" of the protein molecules.

to kill any salmonella without cooking the eggs. Nevertheless, pasteurized eggs will have a slightly thickened yolk and a slightly opaque white. They will cook in the same way as un-pasteurized eggs, but the whites won't whip as well because the proteins have been slightly denatured or reconfigured and won't form a good, stable foam as easily. While regular egg whites usually whip to the stiff peak stage in 1 to 3 minutes, pasteurized egg whites may take as long as 10 minutes.

So with one additional ingredient—more elbow grease—your Divinity will be truly divine. (Elbow grease adds no calories. In fact, it *uses up* calories.)

A SLIGHT EGGSAGGERATION

I always thought that thousand-year-old eggs were a myth until I saw some for sale in a Chinese market. How did people in the eleventh century know we'd want them in the twenty-first? And where have they been kept all that time?

. . . .

Okay, you're putting me on. *Touché!*

Thousand-year-old eggs, called *pidans* in Chinese, are a tongue-in-cheek eggsaggeration. Less lyrical Chinese may call them hundred-year-old eggs. Truth be told, however, they're only about a hundred *days* old, which may strike you as bad enough.

Here's how they're made.

Take a fresh duck egg in the shell, plaster it all over with a thick coating of a paste made of salt, lime (from a garden-supply store), pine ashes from your fireplace (or charcoal-grill ashes, if that's all you have), and strong brewed black tea, all thatched together with rice straw or even grass clippings. Now bury the thing in your garden for about three months. Dig it up, wash it off, remove the shell, and enjoy it with soy sauce and chopped ginger as an appetizer—despite the fact that it looks like a de-appetizer, with its dark green yolk and its blackish-amber "white."

I know whereof I speak. Several years ago, when I was sailing around the world on a Taiwanese ship, I was invited to the captain's quarters for dinner. He had his own private chef, who prepared a dazzling variety of unusual (to me) Chinese delicacies, including shark's-fin soup, sea cucumber (also known as sea slug), pigs' stomach linings and ovaries, and one of those eggs of uncertain age. It had a pungent, cheeselike flavor, the creamy texture of an avocado, a greenish-black yolk and a mottled blue, black, and amber-colored "white." It wasn't half bad, although I don't think I'd want one every day for breakfast.

Note that I have written this entire section with only one pun on the word *egg*, even though you may have eggspected me to take an eggstraordinarily eggcessive eggscursion into the realm of eggsotic and eggstremely eggsaggerated puns until you were completely eggsasperated and eggshausted.

But I hope you can take a yolk.

Sidebar Science: *Improving (?) with age*

THE CHANGES that take place in a "thousand-year-old egg" are caused primarily by the lime and the wood ashes, which are both rather strongly alkaline. (Lime is calcium oxide, CaO, and wood ashes contain potassium carbonate, K_2CO_3.) Over time, these alkaline substances infuse the tea, which seeps through the shell and acts on the proteins in the egg white, reconfiguring their molecules similarly to what cooking them would do. In the meantime, some of the normal chemical changes that take place in a, shall we say, "mature" egg yolk are also taking place, producing chemical products such as aldehydes and ketones, which are responsible for the sharpest of the flavors.

Chapter Three

Whatsoever a Man Soweth . . .

. . . .

. . . that shall he also reap.

Not to wax excessively biblical, but permit me to begin this chapter with a modernized version of Genesis.

In the beginning, there was one helluva Big Bang.

Exactly nine billion years later (I think it was on a Tuesday), God created the Earth. And the Earth was without form, and void.

And God said, Let the waters under the heaven be gathered together unto one place, and let the dry land appear; and it was so. And God called the dry land Earth.

But the dry land was not what we call dry land today. It was not soil. It was molten rock (magma), which after a couple of billion years more cooled and became solid rock. And not that there was anybody around to complain, but you can't grow crops in rock.

So when did soil appear on the surface of our planet, so that our ancestors could begin to sow, reap, and eat plants?

As the eons of seasons came and went, the rocks weathered and broke down from both physical and chemical causes. Physically, the rocks expanded in warm seasons and contracted in cold, causing cracks and fissures. Water that seeped into the cracks froze during the ensuing cold seasons and rended the rocks asunder by the powerful pressure of expansion when it froze. Moving glaciers scraped away at the surface rock, making rock dust, while the wind and running water contributed to the physical degradation of rocks into smaller and smaller fragments, from boulders to very fine grains.

Meanwhile, chemical reactions with groundwater and atmospheric carbon dioxide transformed the original rock minerals into new minerals, softer rocks, and soluble compounds that were transported by rivers and streams to other locations.

Eventually, God's "dry land" became small particles of mixed gravel, sand, silt, and clay, distributed wherever they could lodge over the face of the Earth. They were now soil.

When plants began to grow and die in this mineral-rich bedding, their decaying organic matter enriched the soil, making it even more fertile for humans to cultivate. And so was agriculture made possible in the most recent two-millionths of our planet's history.

The variety of foods we now raise in Earth's soil is limited only by climate and opportunity. In the preceding chapter we sampled the products of one kind of farm: the dairy farm. In subsequent chapters we focus individually on fruits and grains, which hold special places in the pantheon of human sustenance. But for now, we'll browse through the green fields, stopping here and there to examine a few of the hundreds of miscellaneous plant foods that we throw into the catchall category of "vegetables."

A PALETTE FOR THE PALATE

*Every time I pass the produce department of my
supermarket I'm impressed by the number of vivid
colors, especially greens, reds, oranges, and
yellows, among the fruits and vegetables. If it's not
too complex, what are all the chemicals that make
these colors, and what is their purpose?*

. . . .

The kaleidoscope of brightly colored fruits and vegetables—the red
tomatoes, watermelons, strawberries, and beets; the orange carrots,
sweet potatoes, pumpkins, apricots, and mangoes; the yellow lemons
and squashes; the bluish-purple grapes, plums, and cabbages; and all
the green beans and leafy vegetables—are due to a variety of phytochemicals that can be classified into three main groups, chlorophylls,
carotenoids, and flavonoids, the last of which includes anthocyanins
and anthoxanthins.

A *phytochemical*, from the Greek *phyton*, meaning "plant," is any
chemical compound produced by plants. But lately the term has been
appropriated by health-foodists to mean any plant chemical—beyond
the nutritious proteins, carbohydrates, fats, minerals, and vitamins—that may be deemed "good for you." That includes many of the
red, orange, yellow, green, and blue pigments in fruits and vegetables, which do indeed have known health benefits. But nicotine and
cocaine are also phytochemicals, are they not?

Chlorophyll needs no introduction. It is a green compound, each
of whose molecules contains a magnesium atom. But chlorophyll has
taught us that it's not easy *staying* green. When chlorophyll molecules
are reconfigured (*denatured*) by heat, their magnesium atoms are
released, converting the chlorophyll into pheophytin and pyropheo-
phytin, the dishearteningly olive-drab colors of overcooked green
vegetables. (See p. 111.)

Carotenoids range in color from yellow to orange and red. Orange beta carotene is converted into vitamin A in the body. Carotenoids beautify everything from carrots to corn, peaches, citrus fruits, squash, paprika, saffron, tomatoes, watermelons, and pink grapefruit. The last three, especially tomatoes, contain the fat-soluble carotenoid lycopene, an antioxidant that has been touted as a possible preventive of prostate cancer.

Anthocyanins are water-soluble pigments found in grapes, berries, plums, eggplant, cabbage, cherries, and autumn leaves. Purple or blue in alkaline environments, they turn red in acidic media.

With not too many exceptions, you can think of the carotenoids as the yellow, orange, and bright red colors in vegetables and the anthocyanins as the blue, purple, and dark red colors.

Among the less common food colors are *betalains*, the intensely red, water-soluble pigments in beets. When beets are sliced before cooking, much of their color dissolves out into the water. But when unpeeled and cooked whole, they remain as defiantly red as Fidel Castro.

And what is Nature's purpose in painting all these vegetables such pretty colors? It's not just for still-life painters. The bright colors attract animals, who eat the plants, to their mutual benefit. The animals benefit from the healthful antioxidant properties that Nature has built into many of the colored chemical compounds, while the plants benefit by the animals' pollinating their flowers and spreading their seeds.

THE FOODIE'S FICTIONARY:

Harvard beets—part of an unlikely sports headline

Sidebar Science: *Tomatoes are red, violets are blue*

THE CHARACTERISTIC red color of tomatoes, often attributed to lycopene, actually results from a combination of carotenoid pigments, of which lycopene is only the most abundant. The color of the fruit doesn't always correlate with the amount of carotenoids, much less with the amount of lycopene. So one can't draw valid conclusions about lycopene content from the redness of a tomato. Nevertheless, all tomatoes are pretty good sources of lycopene.

(To justify my heading, I am obliged to explain that the blue color of violets and the red color of roses are both due to an anthocyanin that is an acid-base indicator [see "A litmus quest," p. 14]. It is red in the slightly acidic rose petals and blue in the slightly alkaline violet petals.)

WHEN GREEN GROWS GRIM

Why do my green vegetables turn a drab color
when I cook them?

. . . .

The green color in plants and algae is a miraculous molecule called chlorophyll that can absorb the energy of sunlight and use it to convert carbon dioxide and water into glucose and oxygen gas. The plants then either use the glucose directly for their own growth energy or polymerize it (connect thousands of glucose molecules together) to form starches, which they store for future use. And because animals derive their vitality from eating those sugar and starch carbohydrates in plants, the chlorophyll molecule can be thought of as the source of most life on Earth.

But chlorophyll is a fickle friend to humans, the only species that cooks its plant foods to tenderize them. For when we do, the green color can become a dreary, unappetizing khaki. What happens is that the chlorophyll turns into chemicals called pheophytins.

A chlorophyll molecule consists of a conglomeration of carbon, hydrogen, oxygen, and nitrogen atoms called a *porphyrin* (POR-fer-in), with a magnesium atom buried in the center. But chlorophyll isn't a single chemical compound. There are two main types, which chemists, always eager to demonstrate their literacy, have named *chlorophyll a* and *chlorophyll b*. Chlorophyll a is blue-green, while chlorophyll b is a yellowish-green. Different ratios of *a*'s to *b*'s (most often two or three *a*'s to each *b*) determine the exact hues of various green plants.

When we cook our green beans, peas, Brussels sprouts, broccoli, or spinach, the heat first changes the shapes of the chlorophyll molecules (they *isomerize*), and if the vegetable is slightly acidic, as most vegetables are, the magnesium atoms may be ousted and replaced by a couple of the acid's many hydrogen atoms. This transforms the chlorophylls into chemicals called *pheophytins*. Chlorophyll a turns into a grayish-green pheophytin and chlorophyll b turns into an olive-green one. Because chlorophyll a is usually more prevalent and undergoes this change more rapidly than chlorophyll b, the grayish-green color is what we get.

The fact that acids initiate the chlorophyll-conversion reactions has on occasion tempted people to add a pinch of baking soda (sodium bicarbonate) to the cooking water to make it alkaline. But alkalinity attacks the complex carbohydrates that cement the vegetables' cells together, so one is merely trading ugliness for mushiness—with the dubious bonus of a soapy flavor from the bicarbonate.

Another chemical oddity in cooking green vegetables is that sodium, magnesium, and calcium salts inhibit the chlorophyll-conversion reactions, presumably by making it more difficult for the hydrogen atoms to get through the cell membranes and oust the magnesium atoms. Thus, salted cooking water (containing sodium chloride) and hard water (containing magnesium and calcium salts) help to retain the green color.

The practical message in all this is that the quicker a green vegetable is cooked, the less of its chlorophyll can change to muddy-colored pheophytins. In one study, broccoli lost 17.5 percent of its chlorophyll after being cooked for five minutes and 41.1 percent after ten minutes.

GERM WARFARE

What's the best way to wash my fruits, vegetables,
and produce to make sure there aren't any germs,
pesticides, and insecticides on them?

. . . .

Nothing personal, but haven't we become a bit of a paranoid society? Our drugstores and supermarkets cater to our fears (or do they encourage them?) by displaying dozens of antibacterial soaps, sprays, gels, lotions, hand washes, body washes, wipes, deodorants, and mouthwashes. Television commercials strike terror in our hearts by suggesting that there might be a germ or two lurking in our toilet bowls. (Well, for crying out loud, where are those poor little germs *supposed* to live?) I call it "bacteria hysteria."

What does this have to do with food? A search of my unanswered reader mail (forgive me; I try) reveals 130 communications bearing the words *germs* or *bacteria* and 195 bearing some form of the word *danger*, referring to food contamination. It sometimes seems as if there are more people who are afraid of their food today than people who are enjoying it. Are we becoming a nation of verminophobes, mysophobes, toxiphobes, and sitophobes? (See definitions below.)

I generally avoid writing about health issues because I'm not a microbiologist, nutritionist, or physician. But I will say a few words about possible pathogens and toxins in or on our foods—in particular, on our fruits and vegetables. After all, they have inevitably been in contact with microorganism-harboring soil, and have possibly been subjected to agricultural chemicals such as weed killers and insecticides, not to mention manure and other "natural" fertilizers used to raise organic foods.

There have been several products on the market intended for washing our lettuce, scallions, tomatoes, apples, and such, presumably to remove both bacteria and toxic chemicals. In the fall of 2000, Procter & Gamble introduced a product called Fit Produce Wash, but they soon discontinued it and sold the formula to HealthPro Brands. At $5 for an 8.5-ounce bottle (no wonder it didn't sell), it was a mixture of water, oleic acid, glycerol, ethyl alcohol, grapefruit oil, potassium hydroxide, baking soda, and citric acid.

Why these particular ingredients? The glycerol, alcohol, and oleic acid were presumably intended to dissolve and remove chemicals such as pesticides, which are generally insoluble in water. The potassium hydroxide attacked waxes, which are in any event approved by the FDA as harmless coatings for fruits such as cucumbers. As far as I can tell, the baking soda and citric acid were there only to react with each other to emit carbon dioxide gas, producing an Alka-Seltzer-like fizz to give the impression that the product was working hard.

Still on the market at this writing is Bi-O-Kleen Produce Wash, which "contains no animal ingredients" (should we have expected any?) and is "PETA approved" (but does it kill those poor little microorganisms?). It is made of "lime and lemon extracts, grapefruit seed extract, coconut surfactants, cold-pressed orange oil, and pure filtered water." I don't know if all those tutti-frutti ingredients do anything besides making the stuff sound yummy, but the "coconut surfactants" happen to be a synthetic (very unnatural) chemical called sodium cocoyl isethionate, a high-sudsing detergent used in soaps and shampoos.

Bi-O-Kleen has a couple of sister products. Veggie Wash claims to be "non-toxic, non-fuming, non-hazardous, non-caustic, and hypoallergenic" (and non-radioactive and non-explosive?). Organiclean contains "an anionic surfactant derived from coconuts"—very likely that same sodium cocoyl isethionate. All three products claim that they are more effective than plain water in cleaning fruits and vegetables.

Most experts, however, say that washing vigorously in running water is still the best bet. Running water will wash soil particles out of leafy greens, and that's where the harmful bacteria, if any, are most likely to be hiding. Water won't actually kill them, but neither will the produce-wash products, for that matter. If they did, they might leave residues of toxic (to humans) materials on the food. Moreover, if they claimed that they killed microorganisms, they would have to be tested for human safety and registered with the EPA as pesticides. (What irony!) So the produce washes sold to retail consumers are merely washes, not disinfectants. They're especially good at washing money out of your pocket.

For skin-enclosed fruits, such as apples, tomatoes, pears, peaches, cucumbers, lemons, and oranges, a few drops of liquid dishwashing detergent applied vigorously with a brush and rinsed off well will do a good job of removing any contaminants. That's an especially good idea for lemons and oranges if you intend to use their zest or peels in cooking.

One of the best defenses against bacteria on produce, which I employed when living in South America, is to wash the produce in a solution of about a teaspoon of chlorine bleach (a solution of sodium hypochlorite in water) per quart of water. Because the tapwater itself was suspect, I let the bleach solution stand for several hours before using it on the food, an unnecessary precaution here in the States.

Another safe and simple antibacterial treatment was devised in 1996 by food scientists at the University of Nebraska–Lincoln. It consists of spraying the produce with hydrogen peroxide solution (the 3 percent strength sold in drugstores as a disinfectant) and then with white vinegar, or vice versa. The two liquids mix on the food and react to release germ-killing oxygen gas. Any residual hydrogen peroxide on your lettuce will decompose quickly and is, in any event, tasteless, while any residual vinegar will give you a head start on the salad dressing.

Both the chlorine bleach method and the vinegar-and-peroxide method will also disinfect cutting boards and other food-preparation surfaces, especially after a scrub with detergent and a brush. If your cutting board reeks of chlorine after you use the bleach, a vinegar rinse will kill the smell.

While we're on that subject, there are many commercial sprays in the supermarket for disinfecting everything from kitchen counters to entire bathrooms—but they are *not* meant to end up on our food. They contain alkyl dimethylbenzy ammonium chloride, a powerful catalyst that greatly accelerates the decomposition of esters and amides, which are major components of all living organisms from microbes to people. In high enough doses this chemical will kill us, but it is present in commercial disinfecting sprays at a concentration of only 0.2 percent. Nevertheless, disinfecting sprays and wipes should not be used on surfaces such as cutting boards that will come in contact with foods.

Oh, yes, the definitions. A verminophobe is a person who is excessively afraid of germs; a mysophobe is a person who is afraid of dirt or contamination; a toxiphobe is a person who is afraid of being poisoned; and a sitophobe is a person who is afraid of food or eating, probably because he or she is already a mysophobe or toxiphobe.

For a list of other phobias, go to www.phobialist.com, unless you're a logizomechanophobe, in which case you will probably never know what logizomechanophobia is.

THE FOODIE'S FICTIONARY: Swiss chard—burnt cheese

A YUKON GOLD RUST

Yukon Gold potatoes are my favorites, but it seems
impossible to buy any that don't have rusty-
looking grayish-purplish marks in the flesh.
After I cut out these dark marks, the potatoes are
only fit for mashing. I have yet to find potatoes
that don't require major surgery. What is the
purple-gray mark, and why does this seem to
occur in Yukon Gold and not in other potatoes?

. . . .

Yukon Golds, along with cabbage, onions, and yellow rice, get their yellow color from chemicals called anthoxanthins. Anthoxanthins react with traces of metals such as iron and aluminum, which turn them blue-gray. A carbon steel knife can have that effect, so it's best to cut and slice these vegetables with stainless-steel knives. Other varieties of potatoes contain smaller amounts of anthoxanthins and don't stain as easily.

Storage at high temperatures can also turn anthoxanthins dark. So if some of the potatoes are already stained upon purchase, seek out a market that stores its supply at cooler temperatures.

Speaking of anthoxanthins (now there's a segue you won't see every day), carrots contain small amounts of anthoxanthins, the colors of which can depend on the presence or absence of metal ions (charged metal atoms) such as iron and aluminum. People who bake carrot cakes in cast-iron or aluminum pans are sometimes startled to find that the carrots have turned green.

As in the case of the Yukon Golds, the reaction product of a carrot anthoxanthin with iron or aluminum can well be blue. And guess what blue plus the carrot's yellow makes? Green!

Spanish Mashed Potatoes

When garlic is sizzled in olive oil, the intensity of the garlic is toned down while the oil is flavored. To make this recipe for a crowd, use this formula: For each 2 cups mashed potatoes, add 2 to 4 tablespoons extra-virgin olive oil, 2 sauteed cloves garlic, $\frac{1}{2}$ teaspoon coarse salt, $\frac{1}{2}$ teaspoon smoked sweet Spanish paprika (pimentón), $\frac{1}{4}$ teaspoon ground cumin, $\frac{1}{8}$ teaspoon cayenne pepper, 2 slices bacon, and 1 scallion. Leftover mashed potatoes are wonderful warmed up the next day as potato pancakes with a fried egg on the side. Serve with Sherry-Browned Chicken with Garlic (p. 32).

---

4 **large russet baking potatoes or 4 Yukon Gold or all-purpose potatoes, enough to make about 4 cups mashed potatoes**

$\frac{1}{4}$ **cup extra-virgin olive oil, or more to taste**

4 **cloves garlic**

4 **slices bacon**

1 **teaspoon coarse salt**

1 **teaspoon smoked sweet Spanish paprika (*pimentón*)**

$\frac{1}{2}$ **teaspoon ground cumin**

$\frac{1}{4}$ **teaspoon cayenne pepper**

2 **scallions, both white and green parts, thinly sliced**

---

1. Make the mashed potatoes: If using russet potatoes, place a rack in the middle of the oven. Preheat the oven to 400°F. Prick the potatoes with a fork, place on the rack, and bake for 1 hour, or until tender when poked with a knife. If using Yukon Gold or all-purpose potatoes, peel them, cut into 1-inch chunks, and simmer in salted water for 12 to 15 minutes, or until barely fork-tender. When the baked potatoes are done, remove from the oven, cut them in half lengthwise, and scoop the flesh out into a pot. When the simmered potatoes are done, drain and leave in the pot.

2. While the potatoes are cooking, pour the olive oil into a small skillet and add the chopped garlic. Cook over medium-low heat until the garlic sizzles and begins to take on faint color. Remove from the heat before it browns.

3. In a medium skillet, fry the bacon over low heat until done and crisp. Chop the slices into ¼-inch bits.

4. Add the olive oil and garlic, salt, paprika, cumin, and cayenne pepper to the hot potatoes. Mash the potatoes coarsely using a potato masher (see p. 207). Taste for seasoning.

5. Pile the mashed potatoes into a warmed serving dish. (Or scoop the mashed potatoes back into the potato shells.) Top with the bacon and scallions.

MAKES 4 SERVINGS

A RHUBARB OVER RHUBARB

A biologist friend tells me that rhubarb is poisonous. But I argue that that can't be true because I've been eating rhubarb pie for years and am still kicking. Who's right?

. . . .

Both of you.

All parts of the rhubarb plant (*Rheum rhaponticum*) contain various amounts of oxalic acid and its chemical progeny, oxalate salts, ranging from 0.1 to 1.4 percent. That's largely what gives rhubarb its prodigious pucker power, which must be tamed with sugar in the pie. Oxalic acid and oxalates are indeed poisonous.

During World War I, when fresh vegetables were in short supply in Britain, there were reported cases of people suffering oxalic acid poisoning from eating rhubarb leaves, which contain the largest concentration of oxalic acid anywhere in the plant. But inasmuch as you are still capable of arguing with your biologist friend, it should be obvious that the stalks, which are what you've been eating in your pies, contain much less oxalic acid than the leaves. Moreover, while there is no doubt that oxalic acid is poisonous, there is some doubt that it's the oxalic acid alone that poisons rhubarb-leaf eaters.

"Poisonous" is a relative notion, of course; it's purely a matter of amount. Cabbage, spinach, beet tops, potatoes, and peas also contain small amounts of oxalic acid, and the amounts in rhubarb stalks, although higher, are likewise considered harmless. As for rhubarb leaves with their much higher concentration of oxalic acid, you'd still have to eat about 10 pounds of them to reach the so-called LD_{50}: the lethal dose for 50 percent of human subjects.

So keep eating rhubarb stalks. And thank you! The more you eat, the less there will be for me. I hate it.

THE FOODIE'S FICTIONARY: Pie—3.1415927 . . .

Rhubarb Coulis

Rhubarb is not a fruit, although some people think of it that way because they make fruitlike pies out of it. It comes into season early and is often paired "half and half" with strawberries in pies and other desserts. Used here as a sauce, its tartness is a good foil for sweet desserts such as cheesecake (p. 71). In shopping, look for the deepest pink stalks.

1 pound rhubarb (about 6 stalks, each 12 inches long)

1 cup sugar

$^{1}/_{4}$ cup water

1. Cut the rhubarb into ½-inch pieces. You will have about 4 cups.

2. Place the rhubarb, sugar, and water in a medium saucepan over medium-low heat. Cover and cook gently for about 20 minutes, or until just tender and juicy. The mixture will get very watery as it cooks.

3. Let the mixture cool, and transfer 1 cup of it to a blender or food processor, purée it, and then pour it into a jar. Repeat with the remainder, 1 cup at a time. When all of the rhubarb has been puréed, store the jar in the refrigerator until ready to use. The coulis keeps for about 1 week.

MAKES ABOUT 2 CUPS

WHAT BLUTO NEVER KNEW

*I often read that a particular fruit or vegetable
contains certain minerals—iron, potassium, etc.
Since many of these fruits and vegetables can be
grown almost anywhere, that must mean that all
soils, including my back yard, must contain at
least trace amounts of these minerals. Is that
really true? What would happen if I planted
spinach ("rich in iron") in soil that contained no
iron? Would the spinach refuse to grow? Or
would it grow but be deficient in iron,
contradicting what the nutrition tables say?*

. . . .

First of all, if you check the "USDA National Nutrient Database for
Standard Reference" (www.nal.usda.gov/fnic/foodcomp/Data/SR17/
sr17.html), you may be surprised to find that spinach does not contain an unusual amount of iron: it has less than most breakfast cereals, about a quarter as much as raw clams, and about the same as
canned pork and beans (not counting the can).

Here's how the spinach–iron connection got started.

Near the end of the nineteenth century, German scientists cor-
rectly found that the amount of iron in spinach is comparable to that
in meat: some 3 milligrams per 100 grams, or 30 parts per million.
But in the report of their findings somebody put the decimal point
(actually, in Europe, a comma) in the wrong place, making the yield
of iron appear to be ten times as great. The error was corrected some
forty years later, but not before Popeye decided to adopt spinach as
his power food. After all, iron is strong, right? If Bluto only knew that
Popeye's cans of spinach were a bluff!

The final irony (pun intended) in all this is that whatever iron
spinach does contain is not readily absorbed by the body because

spinach also contains a small amount (1 percent) of oxalic acid, which ties up the iron into an insoluble form, ferrous oxalate. So only a fraction of spinach's modest amount of iron is available for our metabolism.

What if you did plant spinach in your back yard and there wasn't enough iron in the soil? That's really very unlikely, because iron is needed by plants in only trace amounts and iron is a widely distributed element, constituting about 5 percent of Earth's crust. Hypothetically, though, without any iron at all your spinach would grow, but it would show symptoms of a nutritional deficiency, just as you would if you were deficient in a vitamin. The leaves would be a sickly yellow instead of green, because plants use iron in synthesizing chlorophyll.

PLANTS IN GENERAL are made up almost entirely of compounds of carbon, hydrogen, and oxygen—compounds that chemists refer to as organic, with no relation to the word used to designate foods that conform to the USDA's National Organic [Foods] Program. Minerals, on the other hand, are the seventeen inorganic chemical elements that are essential nutrients for plants. Agricultural soils must contain all of them, either inherently or added as fertilizer.

Six of these seventeen elements, the so-called *macronutrients*—potassium, nitrogen, phosphorus, sulfur, magnesium, and calcium—are required by plants in rather large amounts. Without any one of them, plants would grow abnormally or not at all. The other eleven essential elements—iron, manganese, zinc, copper, molybdenum, cobalt, nickel, sodium, boron, chlorine, and silicon—are called *micronutrients* because they are needed by plants in only trace amounts. The distribution of these elements around the Earth is more spotty, and that's one way in which dissimilarities might arise among otherwise identical crops.

When we say that a certain element is present in the soil for a plant to absorb and utilize, that doesn't mean that the element is present in its elemental form—that is, as free atoms, not combined into compounds with other elements. They are indeed present as compounds. The iron, for example, isn't present as metal; it is present as compounds with oxygen and other elements (that is, in an *oxidized* form).

Nevertheless, and quite surprisingly, when you see "reduced iron" among the ingredients of a breakfast cereal, it is actually present as tiny particles of metallic iron! (*Reduced* is the chemical opposite of *oxidized*.) You won't have to stay away from magnets after breakfast, however, because the finely divided particles dissolve promptly in the hydrochloric acid in your stomach.

THE TEAR FACTOR

*I've read so many hints about how to cut onions
without crying, but none of them seems to work. Is
there some trick that I can use, short of always
buying sweet or "no tears" onions, which don't
have the same pizzazz as ordinary ones?*

. . . .

What makes *me* cry is all the misinformation going around about
onions, primarily about what causes the eye irritation and how sweet
onions differ from ordinary ones.

The tear-producing chemical (the *lachrymator*) in onions is not
pyruvic acid, as has too often been stated in print. Nor does pyruvic
acid "come from sulfur in the soil," as has also been frequently
asserted, because pyruvic acid contains no sulfur. Nor does the
lachrymator consist of sulfonic or sulfurous acid or any of the other
often-blamed chemicals. Indeed, it is not an acid at all. It is a sulfur-
containing compound called thiopropanal sulfoxide, a.k.a. thiopro-
pionaldehyde-s-oxide, which I shall henceforth refer to as *compound
T*, for tear gas.

While knowledge of that fact isn't going to change your life, the
record has long been in need of being set straight. So there.

Many people apparently think that there is a single chemical in
onions that both irritates our eyes and gives us the flavor effect of
pungency, a hot, sharp, and stinging sensation in the mouth. But
these two effects are largely due to different compounds. Compound
T is not primarily responsible for the onion's pungency, as is commonly stated in the popular food literature. Nor are the most pungent
onions necessarily the most notorious tearjerkers.

Here is an oversimplified account of the complex chemical reactions that take place when you cut an onion.

Neither the tear gas compound T nor the pungency compounds

exist as such in the uncut onion. They are formed when the cells are broken open by cutting or chewing, at which time the enzyme alliinase (A) and a group of compounds known as S-alk(en)yl cysteine sulfoxides (S), which until then had been isolated from each other in different parts of the onion's cells, are liberated. They then react with each other to form the tear gas: $A + S \rightarrow T$.

A different set of alliinase-activated reactions produces a mixture of ammonia, pyruvic acid, and unstable sulfenic acids. The sulfenic acids react further to form a number of flavor and pungency compounds, primarily alkylthiosulfinates.

The amount of pyruvic acid formed in the last two reactions is generally used as an index of pungency, but only because it is stable and easy to measure in the laboratory. *It is not itself responsible for the pungency of onions.*

And now for a few of what Dave Letterman might call "stupid onion tricks," measures that are often claimed to prevent tears while cutting onions. After reading my parenthetical comments, you can decide how much sense the tricks make.

- Cut the stem end off before the root end. (Any onion with half an IQ will remember the cutting order and behave accordingly.)
- Let a stream of cold water run in the sink while you do the cutting. (When the onion vapors see the water they will rush toward the sink to drown, even if it's halfway across the room.)
- Clamp a wooden match between your teeth. (You'll never notice your eyes stinging if you bite on the match head.)
- Keep a piece of bread in your mouth. (And make sure to chew it ostentatiously, so the onion will know it's there.)
- Wear contact lenses to protect your corneas.
- If you wear contact lenses, remove them because the irritating vapors can get behind them, preventing the tears from washing them out.

• Cut or chop your onions under water. You may either fill the sink with water and do your cutting beneath the surface, or put on your scuba gear and take the job to the swimming pool. (These methods should work, except for the little problem of the onion pieces floating away before you can collect them.)

But seriously, folks, here's the most practical and effective method of all (fanfare, please, Maestro): Chill the onions in the refrigerator for a couple of hours before cutting. This slows down the chemical reaction that produces the tear gas and lowers its vapor pressure (its tendency to float around).

Best of all, just learn how to dice an onion as quickly and efficiently as the chefs do, and there won't be time for the irritating vapors to bother your eyes very much. Several cookbooks illustrate the technique. And remember that using a very sharp knife will break fewer cells and produce less tear gas.

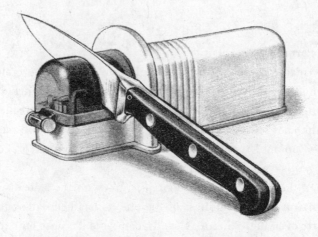

An effective, inexpensive knife sharpener made by Fiskars of Finland. The ingeniously angled abrasive wheels remove a minimal amount of metal. Available by the name "ASPEKT" at IKEA.

And speaking of sharp knives, everyone swears by his or her pet sharpening device, sometimes to the point that swearing can actually occur when two chefs defend their favorite methods. But I have found that a fancy, expensive sharpener isn't at all necessary. The inexpensive device shown in the illustration on the preceding page does an excellent job, especially if you follow it with a few swipes on a "sharpening steel," which straightens out any microscopically wavy edge left by the sharpener.

THE FOODIE'S FICTIONARY: Leek—a hole in the bucket

GEORGIA ON MY MIND

Why are Vidalia onions so much sweeter than other onions?

. . . .

*T*erroir.

Permit me to explain.

Vidalias aren't unique in their mildness. There are several brands of mild onions grown in other parts of the country, including the Maui, Walla Walla, Texas 1015, and OSO. Note that I have called them "mild," not "sweet." They don't necessarily contain more sugar than other onions; they simply contain lesser amounts of both the pungent-tasting and tear-producing compounds.

In the case of Vidalia, Georgia, a town on the state's southern coastal plain, the mildness of the onions has been attributed to a dearth of sulfur in the area's sandy loam soils. Because both the pungency chemicals and the tear-producing chemicals are compounds of sulfur (see p. 125), sulfur-deprived plants are presumably able to manufacture less of them.

Regardless of soil, weather, and cultivation conditions, any plant is the species and variety it is because the genes in its seeds tell it to manufacture precisely the proper proteins, enzymes, and hormones, and nothing a farmer can do will change that. Vidalia onions, for example, are all of the variety called yellow granex.

But that's heredity, and as everyone knows, an organism's characteristics are shaped by both heredity and environment. A multitude of environmental factors, such as the amounts of various nutrients in the soil; the soil's texture and drainage; its micro-flora and -fauna; its proportions of sand, rock, and clay; the land's slope; the growing temperatures; the amounts of rain, wind, and sun—in sum, a plant's entire micro-milieu, short of the phase of the moon at planting time—can lead to subtle differences in the ultimate fruit or vegetable. (That's no joke about the phase of the moon. Vintners who practice so-called biodynamic winemaking reportedly wait until the moon has waned before removing the sediment from their wines. They believe that inasmuch as the full moon draws up the tides, it would obviously draw the sediment upward and keep it from settling. What could be more logical?)

French winemakers have lumped all of these variables and imponderables (usually excluding the phases of the moon), along with a healthy measure of Gallic shrug and a *soupçon* of mysticism, into the concept of *terroir*, which is now modishly being applied to virtually all fruits and vegetables. But there is nothing profound about *terroir*, which literally refers to an agricultural region or territory. It is merely a summation of all the peculiarities of a particular local growing environment. And anyone who has traveled in France knows that on the other side of every hill or around every bend may be lurking a very different microclimate.

Let us return now to Vidalia, Georgia, where the Vidalia Onion is a registered trademark of the Georgia Department of Agriculture and where a state law decrees the characteristics the onions must have in order to wear that jealously guarded label. A vigorous marketing campaign encouraging us to "eat 'em like an apple" (but why would we want to, may I ask?) undoubtedly plays a role in gilding the onion, so to speak. And no one can deny that economics and politics are central ingredients in the onion's reputation. Quite a few lawsuits have been fought along the lines of "My onion is more Vidalia than your onion."

Clearly, not every acre of farmland within the officially sanctioned and virtually sanctified twenty-county Vidalia Onion region of southeastern Georgia can contain exactly the same amount of sulfur in the soil. Thus, sulfur cannot be the only factor. Lacking credible scientific evidence, I'm willing to chalk it all up to a *je ne sais quoi* factor. In other words, I believe in *terroirism*.

THE FOODIE'S FICTIONARY:

Bain marie—Mary needs a bath

IT'S BITTER BEING GREEN

At times, I find a cucumber that is bitter. Why?
Does the compound that causes the bitterness have
any health implications? Could it be dangerous?

. . . .

Cucumbers have been cultivated for thousands of years, and like many food plants, they have been improved by cross-breeding to accentuate the better and eliminate the bitter.

Old recipes often include a de-bittering step, such as soaking the slices in salt water. (I doubt that that works anyway.) But modern varieties are rarely bitter except in the skin, which can be peeled off.

Part of the flavor of cucumbers is due to slightly bitter compounds called cucurbitacins. But when a cucumber has had a hard life back on the plant, such as a long spell of hot, dry weather or a battle with insects or disease, the amount of cucurbitacins builds up defensively in the flesh as well as in the skin. The bitterness is Nature's way of saying, "Don't eat me or you'll be sorry." Alkaloids, for example, a class of mostly toxic chemicals found in plants, all have a bitter taste. But the amount of cucurbitacin you're likely to find in a cucumber certainly won't kill you. If you come upon a bitter cuke, chalk it up to the luck of the draw and move on to some others that may have had a less stressful youth back on the farm.

Today's rarely bitter cucumbers are often sliced and salted, not to remove bitterness but to crisp them up. Sprinkle salt on sliced cucumbers in a bowl, top them with a layer of ice cubes, and put them in the refrigerator for an hour or so. The salt will draw water from between the fruit's cells, firming up their structure. Wash the excess salt off before using.

While a coating of solid salt will draw water out of cucumber slices and crisp them, soaking them in salt water has the opposite effect: they will soak up water and become softer, or wilted. That's because osmosis draws water from a less salty environment into a saltier one. When the cucumber cells are in contact with solid salt, some of its water will be drawn out. But when they are in contact with a rather dilute salt solution, some of the solution's water will be drawn into the cells. (For further details, see "Osmosis," p. 188.)

Cucumber skins aren't completely impermeable to moisture, so the fruit will eventually dry out and shrivel if not protected by a moisture-proof coating. Cuke moguls therefore spray their product with an FDA-approved, edible wax to prolong their produce-counter lifetimes. The smaller, warty-skinned pickling cucumbers are not waxed because in pickling it is essential that the pickling liquor penetrate the vegetable. So-called English cucumbers, being long and thin with consequently large surface areas, must be protected by more than a wax coating and are usually wrapped in plastic film.

THE FOODIE'S FICTIONARY:
Arugula—the sound of a Model T's horn

SPILLED MILK

What is it about soy milk that makes it boil over?
One of my recipes requires cooking the soy milk.
I found I was able to accomplish this without
having it boil over as long as I only simmered it.
What is the chemistry behind this?

. . . .

I have often wondered how they milk those little soybeans, haven't you?

Sorry. Soy milk is made by soaking, boiling, grinding, and pressing the liquid out of soybeans. The liquid is called "milk" because it is white, but it bears as little relationship to cow's milk as does milk of magnesia.

Soy milk is a tempting alternative to cow's milk because it is higher in protein, lower in fat (and calcium), and free of cholesterol and lactose, which millions of lactose-intolerant people are incapable of digesting properly. When fortified with calcium and vitamins, it can be used as infant formula for the estimated 7 percent of babies in the United States who cannot digest cow's milk.

Nevertheless, soy milk is far from a substitute for natural milk, either in flavor or in many culinary applications. For one thing, the soybean-crushing process releases an enzyme, lipoxygenase, that catalyzes the oxidation of the beans' unsaturated fatty acids into unpleasant-tasting compounds. While that doesn't seem to bother Asian consumers, the enzyme must be deactivated for most Western palates by heating the "milk" to a temperature near its boiling point for 15 to 20 minutes.

Which takes us back to the stove.

Plants contain various sugar-related chemicals called glycosides that serve a wide range of functions. Some of the glycosides in soybeans are called saponins (from the Latin *sapo*, meaning soap) because they foam up into suds when boiled. They are the source of your boiling-over problem. But heat destroys the saponins, so a period of gentle heating will slowly eliminate the foaming tendency. That's why you can get away with simmering soy milk but not with boiling it, unless you simmer it first.

THE FOODIE'S FICTIONARY:

Lactose—a congenital foot deformity

Not-Very-Indian Pudding

Imagine soft polenta that tastes like gingerbread. That's Indian pudding.

The eighteenth-century New England colonists referred to the New World's maize as "Indian corn," and a pudding containing cornmeal eventually became known as Indian pudding. Of course, Native Americans didn't have soybeans, and neither did the colonists, but vanilla soy milk is an effective stand-in for the milk used in recipes for one kind of Indian pudding.

When ice cream is melted and stirred into the pudding, it is just as good as, and maybe better than, the milk or light cream that is usually called for in recipes for Indian pudding. The recipe is also delicious made with cow's milk and cow's-milk ice cream. The leftover pudding will thicken overnight, and it is delicious cold or hot. Try it for breakfast.

---

4 **cups (1 quart) vanilla soy milk**

$^1/_3$ **cup yellow cornmeal**

1 **tablespoon unsalted butter**

$^1/_2$ **cup dark molasses**

1 **teaspoon ground cinnamon**

$^1/_2$ **teaspoon ground ginger**

$^1/_2$ **teaspoon salt**

$^1/_2$ **cup vanilla soy ice cream, melted**

Vanilla soy ice cream for serving

---

1. Place a rack in the lower part of the oven. Preheat the oven to 300°F. In a small bowl, mix 1 cup of the soy milk with the cornmeal. Let stand.

2. In a medium saucepan, slowly heat 2 cups of the soy milk over medium-high heat until bubbles form around the edge of the pan. Gradually stir the cornmeal mixture into the hot soy milk. Reduce the heat to medium and cook, stirring, for 10 minutes. The mixture will be thin.

3. Add the remaining 1 cup soy milk and the butter, molasses, cinnamon, ginger, and salt, and stir just until the butter is melted. The mixture will be thin.

4. Turn the pudding into an ungreased 1½-quart casserole. Bake, uncovered, for 2 hours. The pudding will have a slightly dark film on the top.

5. Remove the pudding from the oven. Stir in the melted ice cream, combining it thoroughly until the pudding is smooth. Return the pudding to the oven and bake, uncovered, for 30 minutes longer.

6. Let the pudding cool on a wire rack for 2 hours. It will thicken as it cools, and a light skin will form. Just before serving, stir in the skin, then spoon the pudding into dessert dishes and serve slightly warm with a scoop of vanilla soy ice cream.

MAKES 8 OR MORE SERVINGS

ODE TO TOFU

There seem to be a dozen forms of tofu in my
supermarket. I know that tofu is made from
soybeans, but how do they make so many kinds?

. . . .

They begin by curdling soy milk, and then they manipulate the curds in different ways.

A variety of acids, enzymes, bacteria, and salts are able to coagulate the proteins in soy milk, that is, to unwind their long, twisted molecules, allowing them to rebind (*cross-link*) to one another like rungs in ladders, forming a tightly tangled, solid network that separates out from the liquid. As in coagulated real milk, the proteins form curds, from which the tofu is made.

Real milk is usually curdled by rennet, a stomach-lining membrane in the fourth stomach of an unweaned calf, and containing the protein-digesting enzyme rennin, or chymosin. (Makes you wonder how *that* little technique was discovered, eh? But see below.) The rest of the animal presumably ends up as "milk-fed veal." The curds are then fermented by molds or bacteria, aged and ripened into cheese.

(If only apocryphally, the story of rennet's discovery goes back to biblical times, when wine, milk, and other essential liquid foods were carried in containers made from the cleaned stomachs of calves or sheep. Perhaps a less than meticulously cleaned calf's stomach was used to carry milk on a trek across the desert, whereupon some residual rennin coagulated it into curds. Then, with the help of ambient bacteria they fermented, and *voilà!*—cheese.)

Soy milk, on the other hand, is generally curdled by acids or salts rather than by rennin. The Japanese have traditionally used *nigari*, the bitter, salty non-sodium-chloride residue (mostly magnesium chloride) left over from the evaporation of seawater in making sea salt. Today, calcium sulfate is most often used. The curds are then pressed into blocks called tofu.

Purists insist that tofu isn't "bean curd," as it is often called in English. The curd itself is called *oboro* in Japanese; it isn't tofu until it has been pressed so that the whey—the liquid that was left behind when the curdling took place—is squeezed out.

Various degrees of pressure and duration of pressing make tofu cakes of various consistencies from soft to firm and extra-firm. Little cubes of soft tofu can be tossed in salads, whereas the firmer, stronger forms will withstand deep-frying. Tofu is the modeling clay of cooking; it can be mashed, blended, formed, or cut into shapes and sizes to conform to almost any kind of dish, from salad dressings and sauces to sautés, stir-fries, and deep-fries. And it has the almost magical quality of absorbing the flavors of whatever it is cooked with.

Unlike cheese, which has already been attacked by voracious bacteria and/or molds and ripened often beyond olfactory appeal, tofu is a delicate, perishable product. It is sold vacuum-packed, or soaking in plastic containers of water, or in aseptic packages, or in bulk.

"Silken tofu," a smooth, custardy tofu, is manufactured by a method more like making yogurt than making cheese. Instead of coagulating the soy milk and draining off the whey, makers of silken tofu add a chemical called glucono-delta-lactone (GDL), obtained by the action of an enzyme (*glucose oxidase*) on glucose. The mixture is then packaged in its retail containers and heated mildly at 175 to 195°F (79 to 91°C) for about an hour. During that time the GDL spontaneously turns (*hydrolyzes*) into gluconic acid, which thickens the proteins into a homogeneous gel, with no separation of whey. It can be eaten with a spoon, like yogurt or custard.

All tofu should be refrigerated and used within a week. If it is kept in water, the water should be changed daily. It can be frozen, but the texture upon thawing will be chewier because freezing tightens up the proteins and squeezes out more whey. When it thaws, the tofu has a spongelike texture that enhances its ability to soak up flavorful liquids if cooked with other foods.

THE FOODIE'S FICTIONARY:

Soybean—Spanish for "I am a bean."

I GO, YOU GO, WE ALL GO FOR MISO

I love the flavor of the miso soup I've had in
Japanese restaurants, but I don't know what
miso is. Can I buy some and experiment
with it at home?

. . . .

Absolutely. Miso, known as "fermented soybean paste" in English, is one of the most versatile products you can find in Japanese and Korean markets. It's sold either by itself, to be used in home cooking, or already incorporated into soups, salad dressings, and sauces.

Like soy milk and tofu, miso begins with soaked, steamed, and ground or chopped soybeans. A certain mold, known as *Aspergillus oryzae* in Latin, *koji* in Japanese, and "a certain mold" in English, is added to the heavily salted soybeans, either by themselves or mixed with rice, barley, or chickpeas. (The Japanese use the same mold to make sake.) Traditionally, the fermentation is allowed to proceed for two or three years, until the desired intensity of flavor and color is achieved. Today, the process may be hurried by heating and other accelerating techniques. The role of the salt is to prevent the mixture from spoilage by less friendly microorganisms while the *Aspergillus*, which doesn't mind salt, works away at it.

There are dozens of kinds of miso, ranging in flavor from salty to sweet to salty-and-sweet, in color from ivory to coffee to dark brown, and in texture from smooth and creamy to lumpy. American chefs are having a field day experimenting with them, and you can, too. Try *shiro*, a light miso, or *aka*, a darker, heartier version.

Once you discover miso, it won't be a stranger on the shelf. Because of its intense flavor it needs to be balanced with other ingredients. Add it to a vinaigrette and serve with asparagus, artichokes, or a tossed garden salad. Or make miso soup by stirring a spoonful or two of the paste into vegetable broth and adding *udon* noodles.

Miso-Glazed Black Bass

The most common type of miso found in American markets is a thick paste that looks like crunchy peanut butter and comes in a range of colors, from beige to very dark brown. This salty, richly flavored condiment perks up the flavor of soups and marinades.

Because it is so thick, miso must always be blended with a bit of liquid before being added to a dish. Miso is available in most supermarkets and in Asian groceries. Any shade of light-colored miso will work fine in this recipe.

Tommy Klauber, owner-chef of Pattigeorge Restaurant on Florida's Longboat Key, serves this dish to rave reviews. Because he always has lobster on hand (doesn't everybody?), he uses lobster consommé as his poaching liquid. We'll use mirin and sake. You will need to marinate the fish for at least 2 hours or even overnight before broiling it. Have the vegetable garnish ready before you begin to cook the fish.

MARINADE:

6 tablespoons white or yellow miso

$^1/_3$ cup sugar

$^1/_4$ cup mirin (Japanese sweet rice cooking wine)

$^1/_4$ cup sake

4 black sea bass or black cod fillets, each about 6 ounces and $^3/_4$ to 1 inch thick)

GARNISH:

1 tablespoon peanut oil

$^1/_2$ teaspoon toasted sesame oil

1 cup each julienned carrot, fennel, and sweet red pepper

POACHING LIQUID:

1 cup water

3 tablespoons mirin

2 tablespoons sake

1. Make the marinade: In a small bowl, whisk together the miso, sugar, mirin, and sake until smooth. Transfer the mixture to a 1-quart zipper-top plastic bag. Add the fish fillets, turning them to coat, seal the bag, and refrigerate for 2 to 4 hours or up to overnight.

2. Make the garnish: In a large skillet, combine the peanut oil and sesame oil over low heat. Add the carrot, fennel, and sweet red pepper and cook for about 5 minutes, or until softened but not browned. Set aside.

3. Bring the fish and marinade to room temperature. Preheat the broiler.

4. Remove the fish fillets from the marinade. Place them, along with any marinade that clings to them, in a 9-inch pie pan or small baking pan with sides. Do not crowd the pan. Discard the remaining marinade.

5. Make the poaching liquid: Measure the water in a microwave-safe measuring pitcher and stir in the mirin and sake. Heat in the microwave for 1 minute. Pour enough poaching liquid into the pan to come about one-third up the sides of the fillets, about ¼ inch. This steams the fish a bit while allowing the top of the fillets to brown lightly under the broiler.

6. Broil for 5 to 6 minutes, or just until opaque in the center. For the most succulent results, the fish should be barely done in the center, and moist.

7. Serve the fish in warmed, wide, shallow bowls. Spoon some of the cooking liquid, about ¼ cup per serving, into each bowl. Garnish with the softened julienned vegetables, arranged alongside the fillets.

MAKES 4 SERVINGS

LEGGO MY LEGUME

In high school biology, I learned that legumes are
plants like alfalfa and beans that "fix" nitrogen
gas by taking it out of the air and putting it into
the soil so that plants can use it. But from
experience I also know that legumes like beans are
responsible for another kind of gas: what happens
to us after we eat them. Is there any "fix" for
avoiding these unpleasant consequences?

. . . .

Well, one thing you can do is to cut down on the amount of alfalfa in
your diet. But giving up all those other legumes, including peas,
peanuts, lentils, and the dozens of kinds of beans, would be too much
to ask. It's just one of those many times in life when we have to balance the benefits against the risks.

Leguminous plants are those that produce their seeds in pods.
Nutritionally, legumes (as the seeds are called) are high in protein
and contain many, but not all, of the essential amino acids. The problem is that they also contain certain complex carbohydrates (raffinose oligosaccharides, among others) that humans unfortunately lack
the enzyme to digest. I say "unfortunately" because those carbohydrates pass straight through the stomach and small intestine to the
lower bowel, where bacteria feed on them, producing various gases—
odorless carbon dioxide, hydrogen, and methane, seasoned with
highly odorous hydrogen sulfide and other sulfur-containing compounds called mercaptans. These gases, finding themselves already
in our nether regions, depart the body via the nearest exit.

Unfortunately (again), none of several recommendations for cir-
cumventing these ventings has been proven to be dependably effective, including rinsing the beans several times before cooking, or
cooking them along with any one of a variety of herbs, such as epa-

zote, that supposedly reduce the gas. And perhaps on the theory that the best defense is a good offense, some people say that the more beans you eat on a regular basis, as is done in countries where beans are a staple, the less your social reputation will be sullied.

Because both beans and people vary so much, it would be difficult to carry out the controlled scientific experiments that would be necessary to determine the efficacy of these strategies. One would have to measure the bean inputs of a large number of people under various conditions and measure the volumes of their gaseous outputs. I, as one scientist, shall not volunteer to do that experiment. Nevertheless, as is the case with many folk practices that lack scientific substantiation, people believe what they want to believe. And who's to say no?

One defense against your chemical weapons of mass eruption is Beano or one of the other commercial products that supply the digestive enzyme (alpha-galactosidase) our systems lack.

Another measure that apparently works in many people is swallowing capsules of charcoal, which adsorbs gas in the intestine. (Yes, that's *adsorb* with a *d*, not *absorb* with a *b*. The gas molecules diffuse into the extensive interior surfaces of the highly porous charcoal grains and adhere there. That adherence phenomenon is called adsorption.)

Both Beano and charcoal capsules are available without prescription. They're worth a try in an emergency, such as when you've had bean burritos for breakfast before church.

In the end (if you'll pardon the metaphor), there's really not much you can do beyond letting nature take its course and saying, "Who, me?"

AS THE key element in amino acids, the building blocks of proteins, nitrogen is a necessary component of all living things, both plant and animal. On Earth, there is a virtually unlimited supply of nitrogen gas molecules (N_2) in the atmosphere; air is about 80 percent nitrogen. But the bond between those two nitrogen atoms in N_2 is very strong, and the energy of photosynthesis isn't great enough to enable plants to break them apart and make proteins out of them.

In a remarkable case of symbiosis, leguminous plants and certain soil bacteria named *Rhizobium* have struck a deal that benefits them both. The bacteria produce an enzyme that lowers the energy necessary to break the $N \equiv N$ bond, freeing the nitrogen atoms for conversion into ammonia, NH_3, and nitrates. Most nitrates are soluble in water and can percolate down into the soil where the plant roots can absorb them. Ammonia also dissolves in soil moisture to form ammonium salts. The plants can use both nitrates and ammonium salts as raw materials in their protein factories. (One very nitrogen-rich fertilizer is ammonium nitrate NH_4NO_3.)

In the wild, these so-called nitrogen-fixing bacteria contribute only about 5 pounds of nitrogen per acre per year. But in a field crop of leguminous plants, they can produce several hundred pounds of nitrogen per acre per year.

Here's how the bacteria and the plants work together. When *Rhizobium* bacteria invade the roots of a leguminous plant, it responds by forming nodules, little sanctuaries loaded with bacteria vittles (sugar-rich juices). There, the bacteria can go on a feeding binge, making ammonium salts and nitrates in the process.

A typical bean plant may produce fewer than a hundred nodules, but a soybean plant may have several hundred, and a peanut plant may have a thousand or more of these miniature fertilizer factories.

SOAK IT TO ME

*My grandmother told my mother and my mother
told me: Always add a pinch of baking soda to the
water you soak your dried garbanzos in. Of
course, mothers never tell us why. So, why?*

. . . .

Always do what your mother says. When I was a kid my mother told
me (really!) that if I wore my rubber rain boots in the movies it would
ruin my eyes. I forgot to take them off once, and today I have to wear
glasses.

But seriously, your mother's dictum is somewhat more rational.
Garbanzos, the Spanish name for what Italians call *ceci* and we call
chickpeas, are often sold in dried form—hard, tough-skinned beans
that are notoriously difficult to soften. In many South Asian, Middle
Eastern, and Mediterranean countries, one of which your grandmother may have come from, it has long been the custom to soak dried
garbanzos at least overnight before cooking them. It was also found
that a bit of baking soda shortened the soaking and cooking time.

We now know that alkalis such as bicarbonate of soda attack the
fibrous cellulose skins and make them more permeable to water.
Various alkalis (lye, potassium carbonate, lime) are used in other
cultures to remove the cellulosic hulls from corn kernels in order to
make such foods as hominy and *masa harina*, the dough used to make
tortillas. (See "Tortilla tips," p. 230.) We also know that a pinch of
baking soda is particularly helpful if the beans are being soaked or
cooked in hard water, because bicarbonate removes the calcium and
magnesium in the water, which otherwise could form hard, insoluble
compounds in and between the beans' cell walls and make the beans
less susceptible to hydration. Too much baking soda, however, will
soften the beans too much and spoil their texture, not to mention
contributing a soapy, salty flavor.

But is it really necessary to soak dried garbanzos or other dried legumes in water before cooking them? Drying, which obviously predates canning by many centuries, is simply a way of preserving beans and other legumes for storage. It is still used for convenience in packaging and ensures a long shelf life. These days, however, you can buy many types of beans in cans, already cooked and soft.

Almost as much has been written—and argued—about soaking dried beans as about the 2000 presidential election, and in my opinion just as futilely. To soak or not to soak just doesn't have a simple answer.

The original reason for soaking was undoubtedly that it reduced the cooking time and therefore conserved valuable fuel. Today, most of us don't have to chop wood for cooking, and the small amount of gas or electricity saved by soaking matters little in our prodigal society. Inasmuch as soaking dried legumes has the same major objective as cooking them—making them soft and chewable—it's mostly a matter of how you want to split that chore between a preliminary soak and a hot-water simmer. The three relevant factors are size, temperature, and time.

- **Size:** Tiny lentils and small peas, especially split peas, have large surface areas compared with their weights or volumes (that is, they have a high surface-to-volume ratio), so water is offered abundant entryways into their interior. Since they hydrate quickly during cooking, there is little reason to give them a cold-water head start.

    Relatively bowling-ball-sized garbanzos, on the other hand, have a smaller surface-to-volume ratio, and the water has farther to go to penetrate into their centers. For these virtually impregnable seeds, a preliminary soak in cold water may well cut the cooking time down to a finite number of hours.
- **Temperature:** The diffusion of water into dried seeds occurs more rapidly at an elevated temperature. Thus, an hour of

simmering at the boiling point is much more productive than an hour of soaking in cold water. By comparing likely diffusion rates, I estimate that an hour of simmering accomplishes as much hydration as 3 hours of cold soaking. So if it would take 5 hours of simmering to bring dried garbanzos to a toothsome texture, you could do it in only 4 hours of simmering if you first soaked them for 3 hours.

• **Time:** How much time you have available is a consideration, as is what *kind* of time—attended (simmering) or unattended (soaking). It's tempting to do a lot of soaking because you can do it while you sleep, but trading off too much simmering for soaking can adversely affect the flavor of the finished dish. You want enough cooking time to allow the softened beans to absorb and release flavors from and to whatever other ingredients are keeping them company in the pot.

Oceans of ink and tons of hot air have been spilled over such questions as whether soaking affects the ultimate texture of the beans; whether to salt the beans (if at all) before or after simmering; whether soaking beans removes nutrients and flavors or removes gas-forming oligosaccharides. In the former case you would want to retain the soaking water, while in the latter case you would want to discard it. Research appears to show that small amounts of both oligosaccharides and thiamine (vitamin B_1) are extracted into the soaking water, reducing both nutrition and emission. You can't win.

But cooking beans is neither rocket surgery nor brain science (or something like that). Over the centuries, many different traditional means of dealing with beans have evolved in different cultures, without much scientific justification. So just do 'em the way your own ethnic background decrees.

And if it makes you feel righteous to "honor thy mother," by all means go ahead and soak 'em just because she told you to.

Chapter Four

Above the Fruited Plain

....

O N T H E P A G E S of his published works, William Shakespeare used the words *fruit* or *fruits* 122 times. On the pages of the King James Bible, the words *fruit* or *fruits* appear 361 times. On the ethereal pages of today's World Wide Web, the words pop up more than 20 million times.

In metaphor, we speak of an action that produces positive or profitable results as being "fruitful" or "bearing fruit," while an unsuccessful endeavor is said to be "fruitless."

What is it that so fascinates us about fruits?

The word itself comes from the Latin *fructus*, meaning enjoyment, an apparent allusion to the sweetness of a ripe fruit. Besides honey, no other source of sweetness was known outside of Asia and the South Pacific islands, where sugar cane originated, until post-biblical times.

There may be a deeper reason for the allure of fruits. Botany defines a fruit as the mature ovary of a flowering plant, its purpose being to contain, to nurture, and ultimately to disperse the plant's seeds. The fruit is thus the ultimate goal of the plant's existence, a tangible expression of its intent to procreate. A fruit is a symbol of life, hope, and aspiration.

But what, really, is a fruit? That's not an easy question to answer. Classifying the structural parts of the 270,000 known plant species into a small number of categories is a daunting task. But with their penchant for classifying things according to subtleties of form and function, most botanists divide fruits into three basic types, depending on how the flower's ovary develops into the fruit: *simple* fruits, *aggregate* fruits, and *multiple* fruits. Other classifications do exist. If you ask any two botanists, you may well hear three different classification schemes. However, we'll stick to triaging our fruits into *simple*, *aggregate*, and *multiple*. And don't be surprised at seeing some foods that you never thought of as fruits at all, or even some whose classification as fruits might seem a bit nutty. (All nuts are fruits, and so are peanuts, although they're not nuts.)

- A ***simple fruit*** develops from a single ovary of a single flower, and may be either fleshy or dry.

Among the *fleshy simple fruits* are the so-called berries and the drupes. The berries include the avocado, bell pepper, blueberry, grape, grapefruit, orange, and even the tomato and banana. (Yes, according to botanists, bananas are berries. Bananaberry pie, anyone?) The drupes, in which the inner layer (the *endocarp*) of the ovary's wall (the *pericarp*) has hardened into a pit or stone, are also known as stone fruits. They include the apricot, cherry, coconut, olive, peach, plum, and even the cacao pods from which we remove the seeds to make chocolate.

Among the *dry simple fruits* are the legumes (beans, peas, peanuts), the nuts (acorns, hazelnuts, walnuts), and the grains (corn, rice, wheat). Yes, grains are fruits. But they play such a central role in the human diet that I devote a separate chapter (Chapter 5) to them.

- An ***aggregate fruit***, such as the blackberry or the raspberry, develops from a single flower with many ovaries, making a mass of small drupes resembling a tight bunch of tiny

grapes. (Botanically speaking, blackberries and raspberries are not berries like, for example, bananas. Sheesh!)
• A *multiple fruit*, such as the pineapple, develops from the ovaries of many flowers growing in a cluster.

But where, oh where, is your favorite and mine, the strawberry? And where is that doctor-deterring apple? By now you will accept calmly the statement that strawberries are not berries. Nor are they simple, aggregate, or multiple fruits. They, along with the so-called pomes (apples and pears), are *accessory fruits*, fruits that develop from parts of the plant other than the ovary. Happily, I shall not attempt to describe their botanical configurations.

Enough botany! On to gastronomy!

THE FOODIE'S FICTIONARY:
Avocado— a nineteenth-century Italian physicist who discovered Avocado's number

THIS HORMONE IS A REAL GAS!

When I read in my newspaper's food section what's new and abundant in the produce markets, I buy these things but often don't know what to do with them after I get them home. How do I know which fruits are ripe and may quickly deteriorate, and which ones will improve if I keep them a while before eating?

. . . .

It's not easy. The chemical changes that take place in ripening fruits are quite complex, with different fruits differing mainly in the timing of those reactions.

For every type of fruit, there comes a time when the ripening reactions reach their peak, after which senescence (deterioration) sets in, ultimately leading to decay. That's Nature's dust-to-dust plan, and the bell tolls as well for thee and me.

Your problem is to know exactly when that peak of ripeness occurs. That's when the fruit will have a good color (green will have changed to yellow-orange or red-blue), a soft texture, and the best flavor, because acids will have decreased, sugars will have increased (except in lemons and limes), and various flavorful and aromatic substances will have been produced.

But hitting that moment of maximum ripeness can be like timing the stock market. For one thing, you don't get to make your selection in the store until some time after the fruit has been picked, and you don't really know how ripe it was at that time or what has happened to it since. It's like buying a stock based on last week's price.

Avocados don't begin to ripen until after they're picked, so don't be afraid to buy them rock-hard. But most other fruits reach their best eating qualities when fully ripened on the plant and ready to fall. That's Nature's get-'em-while-they're-hot plan to entice animals into eating them and spreading their indigestible seeds.

Many fruits, such as commercial tomatoes, strawberries, and especially bananas, are deliberately picked unripe so as to better withstand the rigors of shipping. Others (peaches, plums, melons) can be picked, shipped, and sold in an almost ripe condition, with a firm flesh that will slowly soften.

The most useful distinction to be aware of is that some fruits can continue to ripen after being picked, and some can't. If they can't, there's nothing you can do about it after you get them home; you have to buy them in an already perfectly ripe condition (good luck, if there's not a farmers' market handy) and refrigerate them to keep them that way, because low temperatures slow down the senescence reactions.

Fruits that continue to ripen after picking are another story. If they're bought in an unripe condition, there is something you can do at home to move them along: You expose them to a gaseous plant hormone called ethylene, a.k.a. ethene, $H_2C=CH_2$, that speeds up the ripening process. We don't usually think of a gas as being a hormone, but ethylene qualifies because, like other hormones, it is effective in tiny amounts of less than one part per million.

Where do you get the ethylene? The fruits themselves provide it. Many fruits undergo a burst of ethylene gas at just about the time they reach optimum ripeness and before senescence sets in. These fruits are called *climacteric* fruits, because their rates of ethylene production climax and then decline. (If you think you see a parallel with the decrease in female hormones at menopause, also referred to as climacteric, you're right on target.)

If a climacteric fruit is not yet ripe, it can be egged on toward ripeness by ethylene from another ethylene-emitting fruit, or even by its own emitted ethylene (if prevented from drifting away), which will stimulate it to make even more ethylene. In chemical lingo, this kind of self-stimulated reaction is said to be *autocatalytic*.

Fruits that don't exhibit a rise and fall in ethylene production during ripening, the so-called *nonclimacteric* fruits, are less affected by exposure to the gas. So all you have to know is which fruits are climacteric, and then you can gas them with ethylene to hasten their ripening. You get the ethylene from climacteric fruits that are still in the ethylene-producing stage.

Here's what you do. First, check Table 2 on page 153 to see which category your fruit belongs to. If it's in the nonclimacteric list, it may soften a little and lose its green color, but it won't get any riper before it starts heading downhill. Refrigerate it to preserve what ripeness there is.

But if it's in the climacteric list, leave it at room temperature; refrigerating it would slow down its ripening. If you want to speed things up, place a couple of the fruits without crowding into a paper bag with a few holes punched in it. That will trap some, but not all, of the ethylene that the fruits are emitting and hasten their ripening. Ethylene is slightly lighter than air, so some of it will escape through the holes in the bag. That's fine, because all it takes is as little as one part of ethylene per million parts of air to do the job. Don't use a plastic bag; the ethylene concentration and moisture may build up inside and nudge the fruit over the hill from ripe to spoiled. Remember that increased ripeness doesn't necessarily mean increased sweetness. Fruits will soften and perhaps intensify in fragrance, but among the most common climacteric fruits only apples, bananas, mangos, and pears will become sweeter as they continue to ripen off the plant.

If you're really in a hurry, put a world-class ethylene producer— an apple, banana, or passion fruit (the champ)—in the bag along with your climacteric fruit. Be sure to check the bag's contents every 10 to 12 hours or so, or you may be surprised to find rotted fruit inside.

"One rotten apple can spoil the whole barrel" may be a bit of an exaggeration, but if the baddie is still in its stage of copious ethylene emission it can certainly speed its brethren toward their ultimate demise. Especially if the bad apple is at the bottom of the barrel, its lighter-than-air ethylene may wash over all the other apples as it rises.

How, then, do apple growers prevent tens of thousands of boxes of apples harvested in September from overripening before they are shipped to market in January or later? For one thing, they refrigerate the apples at 31 to 36°F (-0.6 to 2.2°C) to slow down the ripening reactions. (Do the same at home to keep your apples at their peak.) But more important, the growers control the amounts of oxygen and carbon dioxide in the refrigerated rooms, because in addition to giving off ethylene, apples "breathe in" oxygen and "breathe out" carbon dioxide. This "breathing," more properly called respiration, continues in all fruits and vegetables after they are picked. It can be inhibited by low temperatures and also by reducing the amount of oxygen and increasing the amount of carbon dioxide in the storage room (which you are quick to recognize would also inhibit human respiration). In the apple industry, this is called controlled atmosphere (or CA) storage.

Table 2. Fruits that don't ripen after picking and fruits that do

DON'T RIPEN AFTER PICKING (nonclimacteric)	CONTINUE TO RIPEN AFTER PICKING (climacteric)
cherry	apple
citrus fruits (orange, lemon, lime, grapefruit)	apricot
	avocado
cucumber	banana
grape	blueberry
pineapple	fig
pomegranate	guava
soft berries (blackberry, raspberry, strawberry)	honeydew
	kiwifruit
watermelon	mango
	muskmelon (inaccurately called cantaloupe in the U.S.)
	nectarine
	papaya
	passion fruit
	peach
	pear
	persimmon
	plantain
	plum
	quince
	tomato

Poached Italian Prune Plums

Raw Italian prune plums are dusky purple and bland, with a mere hint of sweetness that won't improve much on standing at room temperature. But when poached in sugar syrup, they rev up their color and flavor, becoming crimson and tart-sweet. Look for them in the market from late summer through early fall. Poached prune plums are both delicious and beautiful served either plain or with vanilla ice cream.

1 **pound Italian prune plums**

1 **cup sugar**

1 **cup water**

1 **small cinnamon stick, about 2 inches long**

1 **teaspoon vanilla extract**

1. Wash the plums and halve them, but do not peel. Remove the pits.

2. In a large saucepan, combine the sugar, water, and cinnamon stick and bring to a boil over medium heat. Cook for about 5 minutes, stirring often, until the sugar dissolves and a light syrup forms.

3. Add the plum halves, reduce the heat to low, and poach gently, spooning the liquid over the plums occasionally and turning them once during the cooking, for 3 to 4 minutes, or until tender. Stir in the vanilla.

4. Serve the plums warm or cool with their syrup.

MAKES ABOUT 8 SERVINGS

SMASHED BUT SWEET

*Why do the brown, bruised parts of fruits often
taste sweeter than the other parts?*

. . . .

Think about this: If you smashed all the bottles of chemicals in a
chemistry lab with a baseball bat, you wouldn't be surprised at any
unusual chemical reactions that occured as their spilled contents ran
together on the floor, would you?

Well, plants are made up of remarkably packaged, exquisitely
organized little "bottles of chemicals" called cells. When physical
damage is done to a fruit, the cells are broken open and the chemicals
that were previously isolated from one another in different parts of
the cells spill out and mix.

When you bruise or cut into an apple, pear, or avocado, for example, the damaged flesh soon turns brown from the action of oxidizing
enzymes called polyphenol oxidases, which are released from their
captivity as soon as the cell walls are broken. These enzymes act upon
the fruit's phenols, a large group of antioxidant compounds responsible for flavor, color, and many other characteristics of our edible
plants, sending them along a chemical path leading to a variety of
large molecules (polymers), many of which are brown in color.

This so-called enzymatic browning—to distinguish it from both
caramelization and Maillard browning (see pp. 296–97)—can be mini-
mized by deactivating the enzymes with heat (in other words, cook
those apples promptly) or with an acid. Lemon and lime juices are the
most acidic substances in our kitchens, more acidic than vinegar.

Instead of destroying the oxidation-encouraging enzyme, we can
cut off the oxygen to the cells, for example by covering the cut surface
of the fruit with plastic wrap. Or we could treat it with any of a variety
of chemical compounds that inhibit oxidation, such as sulfur diox-

ide, ascorbic acid (vitamin C), or citric acid in the form of (again) lemon juice.

In some fruits, the enzyme-driven browning reactions do produce sweet sugars. But in others, including apples, sour acids or bitter flavors are produced.

So don't physically abuse your fruits in an effort to make them sweeter. Uninjured fruits always look and taste best.

ATOMIC BANANAS

Banana for banana, does a sweeter one have
more calories than a dull-tasting one? As they
ripen, they definitely do get sweeter, but can
they produce more calories just by sitting around,
or is that creating energy?

. . . .

You answered your own question. Yes, that would be creating calories, and calories are energy. Energy can come only from other forms of energy (heat, mechanical, electrical, and so on) or from matter via $E = mc^2$. If a banana knew how to convert matter into energy, as uranium does, we could make atomic "B-bombs" out of them.

I can guess what you're thinking, though. More sugar, more calories, right? But where is that sugar coming from? As the fruit ripens, starches are being broken down into sugars, and both starch and sugar—in fact, all digestible carbohydrates—give us the same 4 calories of energy per gram when we metabolize them. It's a calorie-for-calorie wash. It doesn't matter whether the sugar molecules are still tied together as starch molecules or free as a bird.

So you can't run a power plant on ripening bananas unless you set fire to an awful lot of them—not an easy job because their flesh is 75 percent water. Even if dried first, they would burn to release only 400 calories per pound of original banana. Compare that with a pound of coal, which burns to release 3,000 calories, or a pound of uranium, which can release 21 million calories.

The only way bananas could solve an energy problem would be for a tired athlete to carbo-load by eating a whole bunch of them at 27 grams of carbohydrate per banana.

THE SECOND BANANA

I bought some big, green bananas in a Latin American grocery store and put them on my kitchen windowsill to ripen. When they eventually turned yellow, I tried to eat one, but it was tough and tasted like chalk. What kind of bananas were they?

. . . .

They weren't bananas; they were plantains, tropical fruits closely related to bananas—both members of the genus *Musa*—but much starchier and containing much less sugar when ripe. They're also known as cooking bananas, which is a clear tip-off that they're not meant to be eaten raw.

Plantains are a staple in Africa and especially in Latin America, where they are known as *plátanos* in Spanish. In Puerto Rico, for example, *plátanos* are made into a variety of crunchy appetizers, including *tostones* (round slices of green plantain, flattened, fried, and garlic-salted) and *arañitas* or "little spiders" (fried, ragged pancakes of shredded plantain). Soft, ripe plantains, called *amarillos* ("yellows") are baked with butter, brown sugar, and cinnamon in a Caribbean version of Bananas Foster. (See following recipe.)

And by the way, the old windowsill-ripening ploy is sill-y. It was originally intended as a dependably sunny spot, but picked fruits don't need sunlight to ripen.

Bananas Byczewski

When your bananas are beginning to look like Chiquita's worst nightmare and there's no time to make banana bread, the fix is easy. Make sautéed Bananas, a simple but widely unappreciated dessert.

If that's not fancy enough for you, make the pride of New Orleans, Bananas Foster. Its banana liqueur enhances the fruit's flavor.

In 1951, as the story goes, Owen Brennan, owner of the still-famous Brennan's Restaurant in New Orleans, was asked to come up with a new dessert for a magazine feature story on the restaurant. His chef, Paul Blangé, created Bananas Foster, which today is perhaps even more famous than the restaurant.

But who was Foster? Richard Foster was a friend and good customer of Brennan's, and Brennan named the dish after him. There is no truth to the rumor that Mr. Brennan's even closer friend, Flawiusz Byczewski, committed suicide after losing out on the naming rights. Nevertheless, we have named our version of this dessert in his honor.

- **2 tablespoons ($^1/_4$ stick) unsalted butter**
- **$^1/_4$ cup honey**
- **$^1/_4$ teaspoon freshly grated nutmeg**
- **$^1/_4$ teaspoon ground ginger**
- **2 tablespoons banana liqueur, optional**
- **Freshly squeezed lemon juice to taste**
- **4 firm, ripe bananas, peeled and cut lengthwise into quarters**
- **Vanilla or butter pecan ice cream for serving**
- **$^1/_4$ cup dark rum**

---

1. In a 12-inch skillet, melt the butter over low heat. Add the honey, nutmeg, and ginger and stir until the honey liquefies and the ingredients are well blended. Add the banana liqueur, bring to a boil, and simmer for 2 minutes. (The recipe may be made ahead to this point. Reheat the sauce before continuing.)
2. Taste the sauce. If it is too sweet for your taste, squeeze in a few drops of lemon juice.

3. Add the banana pieces to the simmering sauce. Cook them, basting and turning, for about 3 minutes, or until they begin to soften. Do not overcook.

4. Meanwhile, place scoops of ice cream into each of 4 bowls or soup plates.

5. Pour the rum into a microwave-safe container such as a glass measuring cup and warm it for about 30 seconds on high. Pour the rum over the bananas, stand back, and ignite the vapors with a match.

6. When the flames have subsided, lift the bananas out of the pan and arrange them around the ice cream. Spoon the warm sauce generously over the top of the ice cream and serve immediately.

MAKES 4 SERVINGS

THAT'S OIL, FOLKS

*Can you comment on the chemical similarity
between edible oils (olive, sunflower, etc.) and
inedible oils used as lubricants? Is there some
chemical quality that makes a substance an "oil"?*

. . . .

Only the fact that they are liquids whose molecules don't stick together very strongly, so they can slide easily past one another. That's what makes them slippery. But chemically speaking, these two kinds of oils are quite different. And thereby hangs an embarrassing tale.

A few decades ago I was teaching graduate-level chemistry in Spanish (what chutzpah!) at a university in Venezuela, utilizing the vestiges of my high school Spanish augmented by a few sojourns in Mexico and a six-month residence in Puerto Rico. One day in class I was puzzled by the ripple of smirks that swept the room whenever I referred to the product of Venezuela's petroleum industry as *aceite*, which my dictionary had told me was Spanish for oil. A sympathetic student eventually took me aside and explained that *aceite* refers only to edible oils, most commonly the oil obtained from olives, or *aceitunas*. The word I should have been using was *petróleo*. I had inadvertantly been talking about Venezuelans pumping olive oil out of the ground! In the United States we use the same word, *oil*, for both. (I was partly vindicated years later by an understanding Spaniard, who pointed out that as soon as crude petroleum is refined into motor oil or machine oil, it is indeed referred to as *aceite*. At least in Spain.)

Petroleum is a mishmash of hundreds of hydrocarbons—compounds of nothing but carbon and hydrogen—which can be separated by distillation or broken down ("cracked") and refined into hundreds of products from gasoline to Vaseline, not to mention the thousands of synthetic petrochemicals that chemists can create once they get their hands on the raw material.

Hydrocarbons play only minor roles in living things. In fact, it might be said that petroleum consists of once-living plant and animal matter that has had all the life squeezed out of it. Petroleum-derived oils are therefore inert as far as our food metabolism is concerned; they are indigestible. A dose of mineral oil, a highly purified petroleum product, for example, passes straight through the body unchanged, lubricating the entire digestive tract along the way and acting as a laxative.

Although the edible oils that we obtain from plants do contain small amounts of hydrocarbons, they are predominantly triglycerides. Triglyceride molecules are largely similar to hydrocarbon molecules, but in addition to the long chains of carbon and hydrogen atoms, each of the triglyceride molecules also contains six oxygen atoms at one end. And changing the components or structure of a molecule even slightly can make a huge difference in its chemical and physiological properties.

Along with proteins and carbohydrates, triglycerides in the form of either liquid oils or solid fats make up the vital triumvirate of food components. Triglycerides are broken down in our bodies to produce energy, but in excessive amounts they are converted into what are known indecorously as love handles and spare tires.

The 1.4 billion gallons of salad and cooking oils that we consume each year in the United States (that's 33 million petroleum barrels' worth) must be processed before they are pure enough and acceptable to our finicky palates. Here are some of the typical cosmetic treatments that vegetable oil may suffer before it lands on your grocery shelf labeled "all-natural" and "100 percent pure":

- First, most of the oil may be squeezed ("expressed" or "expelled" or "expeller-pressed") out of the seeds by machines called expellers, which can handle as much as 30 tons of sunflower seeds, for example, in a single day. Expellers are screw-driven presses that use friction and pressure to squeeze the oil out of the seeds. The friction can heat the mass of oil and pulp to temperatures of 140 to 210°F (60 to 99°C), although water-cooled expellers are also used to make the "cold-pressed" oils that are preferred by "natural-food" and raw-food enthusiasts.
- More often, the oil is dissolved out of (extracted from) the ground-up seeds into hexane, a volatile hydrocarbon liquid that dissolves the oil and is later evaporated off by being heated to 212°F (100°C). Since hexane boils at only 156°F (69°C), there should be virtually none left in the finished oil, although traces of up to 25 parts per million can often be detected. That's why health-food stores brag about selling "expeller-pressed" and "cold-pressed" oils that have never been in contact with hexane. They're more expensive, however, because their supply is limited; hexane extraction gets a lot more oil out of the seeds than pressing does.
- The crude pressed or extracted oil may then be degummed by the addition of a small amount of water and/or citric

acid, which precipitates certain gummy chemicals called phosphatides.

• Next, the oil is treated with an alkali (usually sodium hydroxide, or lye), which removes any remaining phosphatides, proteins, and mucilaginous compounds and, most important, neutralizes any free fatty acids, which have unpleasant flavors. The reaction of the alkali with the fatty acids produces soap (yes, soap), which is removed by a later washing with hot water.

• If the oil has an undesirable color it is then bleached, not by Clorox, but by finely divided clays or activated charcoal, which adsorb molecules of pigmented impurities.

• If there are any remaining unpleasant odors, the oil is deodorized by steam distillation under vacuum. The vacuum (actually, just a low air pressure) lowers the boiling point of water and hence the temperature of the steam, so that the oil isn't subjected to a damagingly high temperature. This process also removes any residual pesticides and other chemicals that may have been used on the oil-bearing plants.

• Finally, an oil may be "fractionated," "dewaxed," or "winterized" by being cooled and having any fat fractions that freeze filtered off, so that the oil won't get cloudy if stored in a cool location. Note that if you keep your expensive extra-virgin olive oil in the refrigerator to delay rancidity—some experts may disagree, but I believe this does no harm—and it turns cloudy, there is nothing wrong with it. The oil will clear up as the solidified fat components melt again when restored to room temperature.

Is all this processing bad for us? You can call it processing or you can call it purification. "Processing" is a bad word these days in some circles, where any intervention by humans or their technology between nature and nourishment is considered unnatural and probably unsafe. But in the case of seed oils such as sunflower, safflower, canola, and peanut, the pressed or extracted crude oils contain many impurities that would affect the flavor, color, and cooking properties if not removed. These include seed fragments, pesticide residues, trace metals, phosphorus, wax, free fatty acids, chlorophyll, carotenoids, and other pigments and odors. If machinery and chemistry weren't being used to purify our vegetable oils, I doubt that we would find them palatable or in most cases even edible.

In short, "refined" means "purified." So what's bad about that?

But note that olive oil is a unique case. Coming as it does from the flesh, rather than the seeds, of the fruit, it's pure fruit juice that can be consumed just as it comes from the press. Some of the best extra-virgin olive oils, in fact, are bottled without even being filtered.

THE FOODIE'S FICTIONARY: Palm oil—a bribe

Beignets Soufflés

Virtually any cooking oil can be used for deep-frying, a wonderful cooking method for crisping and browning the outer surfaces of foods while leaving them moist and succulent inside.

The first time Bob realized that deep-frying could be used for desserts and pastries other than doughnuts was as a (relatively) young man visiting friends in Belgium and being treated to fruit beignets—inch-or-so chunks of fruit (almost any kind) dipped in a flour-and-beer batter (ah, that Belgian beer!), deep-fried, and dusted with confectioners' sugar just before serving.

This is the deep-fried dessert to make if you have no fear of frying but a fear of yeast dough. *Pâte à choux*, or cream-puff dough, is one of the easiest, most risk-free doughs in the pastry cook's repertoire. But instead of being dropped onto a baking sheet to make cream puffs, this soft dough is dropped into hot fat, where it swells, puffs, and browns.

To serve, pour a pool of fresh or bottled fruit syrup onto a dessert plate and top it with three sugared beignets.

$^1/_2$ **cup water**

4 **tablespoons ($^1/_2$ stick) unsalted butter, at room temperature**

Pinch of salt

$^1/_2$ **cup all-purpose flour**

2 **large eggs, at room temperature**

$^1/_8$ **teaspoon orange oil or 1 tablespoon dark rum, optional**

Vegetable oil for deep-frying

Confectioners' sugar for dusting

---

1. Combine the water, butter, and salt in a medium saucepan and bring to a boil. Remove from the heat and add the flour all at once. Stir vigorously until the mixture leaves the sides of the pan and forms a ball around the spoon. (If a ball does not form almost immediately, place the saucepan over low heat and beat briskly for a few seconds.) Let the dough cool slightly.

2. Add the eggs one at a time, beating vigorously until the paste is smooth and glossy before adding the second egg. Add the optional flavoring and beat again.

3. Add the oil to a wok, heavy skillet, or deep fryer to a depth of about 1½ inches. Heat the oil to 365°F. It's a good idea to fry just 1 beignet at first to determine the approximate cooking time, so drop in a tablespoon of dough and fry it before you proceed with frying the rest.

4. Working in batches, drop the dough by tablespoons into the hot oil. Fry, turning as needed, until browned on all sides and the center is cooked through, about 2 minutes per side. Drain on paper towels.

5. Serve hot, dusted with confectioners' sugar.

MAKES ABOUT 20 GOLF BALL–SIZED BEIGNETS

VARIATION: BAKED BEIGNETS SOUFFLÉS

If you have a fear of frying, you can bake beignets using the same dough.

Preheat the oven to 375°F. Place large rounded tablespoons of the dough on an ungreased cookie sheet, spacing them 2 inches apart. Bake for 30 minutes, or until the puffs are golden. When the puffs are cool enough to handle, carefully slice off the tops, their lids, and scoop out the unbaked dough at the centers. Let cool on a wire rack.

To serve, fill with ice cream, sweetened whipped cream, or vanilla pudding. Replace the lids and dust the puffs with confectioners' sugar before serving.

MAKES ABOUT FOURTEEN 2-INCH PUFFS

TRANS FATS TRANS-LATED

*I'm confused about trans fats. I recently read that
hydrogenated, partially hydrogenated, and
fractionated oils are considered trans fats. I then
bought a tub margarine from our local Whole
Foods Market which advertised that it contained
no trans fats. However, on closer inspection of the
label, I noticed that it contained fractionated oil.
So . . . here are my questions. Are fractionated oils
considered to be trans fats? What is the difference
between fractionated and hydrogenated oil? And
what does the "partially" add to the mix?*

. . . .

There is a lot of confusion surrounding trans fatty acids or "trans
fats." And may I say, if you will accept the compliment, that your
degree of confusion is one of the most thorough that I have seen.

The public's concern about trans fatty acids was heightened on
July 11, 2003, when the FDA issued its final rule on the labeling of
foods containing trans fatty acids, to wit: "In this final rule and given
the current state of scientific knowledge, the FDA is requiring the
mandatory declaration in the nutrition label of the amount of trans
fatty acids present in foods, including dietary supplements." (Note
that this new labeling is both "required" and "mandatory." I wouldn't
be surprised if it were also compulsory and obligatory.) The rule was
scheduled to become effective on January 1, 2006, some thirteen
years after the Center for Science in the Public Interest first blew the
whistle on the dangers of trans fatty acids. It's good to know that our
government agencies are on their toes.

Today, one can hardly walk down the street without hearing people asking one another, "What the heck *is* a trans fatty acid, anyway?"
That's why I'm here.

Being a mere Ph.D., not an M.D. ("not a *real* doctor," as an aunt of mine used to point out at every opportunity), I don't consider it my shtick to go into the health consequences of ingesting trans fatty acids, except to say that trans fatty acids appear to raise your total blood cholesterol level, raise your LDL or bad cholesterol level, lower your HDL or good cholesterol level, contribute to obesity and diabetes, and according to O.J. are the *real* killers of his ex-wife.

No, just kidding about O.J.

Trans fatty acids (I'll call them "trans FA's" from here on) don't occur naturally, except for small amounts in a few plants such as pomegranates, cabbage, and peas and making up about 3 to 5 percent of the fatty acids in the meat and milk of ruminants: cows, sheep, and goats. They are created in much larger amounts during the artificial hydrogenation of vegetable oils to make them more solid, most often to convert liquid soybean oil into manageably spreadable margarines. In fact, trans FA's are in every food that says "partially hydrogenated vegetable [or the name of a specific vegetable] oil" in the list of ingredients on the label. And you can assume that virtually everything on the snack-food shelves of your local convenience store is loaded with trans FA's.

Understanding trans FA's requires digesting a bit of chemistry. I have set this information aside in "Kinky molecules" on page 169. You may think of it as what the textbooks call Further Reading, which of course nobody reads. Read it or not; it's your call.

A no-trans tip

The softer a margarine is, the less it has been hydrogenated and the less trans fatty acid it will contain. But I don't like soft, almost liquid margarines; I like them to have some firmness for spreading on my toast. So I buy a soft, no-trans-fat margarine (according to the label) and keep it in the freezer, where it firms up to a perfect spreading consistency.

With or without the FDA's required, mandatory, compulsory, and obligatory labeling, how can you tell where all the trans FA's are hiding? You're not going to like this, but partially hydrogenated fats carrying their burden of trans FA's lurk in virtually everything you love to eat: margarine, commercial cakes and cookies, doughnuts, potato chips, crackers, popcorn, nondairy creamers, whipped toppings, gravy mixes, cake mixes, frozen French fries and pizzas, fish sticks, and virtually all commercially fried foods.

Restaurants that brag about using only "pure vegetable oil" don't tell you that it may contain as much as 40 percent trans FA's. Peek into the kitchen and you may see that before it was melted it was delivered as a semisolid, like Crisco. That's the tip-off that it has been hydrogenated—had hydrogen gas forced into it at a high temperature and pressure. (Unless that bucket of white fat is lard, which is another whole story.) To make matters worse, trans FA's are formed in small amounts at the high temperatures of frying, so you may even be producing them yourself at home.

There is, however, a ray of hope. The amount of trans FA's formed in the hydrogenation of oils depends on the temperature, the hydrogen gas pressure, the length of exposure, and many other factors. Now that the pressure is on from the feds, you can bet your Twinkie that packaged-food manufacturers have been scrambling to find ways of attaining the desired physical characteristics in their fats with the minimum production of trans FA's. They want to earn the right to put the coveted phrase "Contains no trans fatty acids" or "Contains no trans fats" on their labels.

But note that "no trans fatty acids" on a label doesn't mean NO trans fatty acids. According to FDA labeling regulations, it means less than 0.5 gram per serving. Insisting that there not be a single molecule of trans fatty acid in a food would be both unrealistic and unenforceable. There has to be some upper-limit definition of "none."

Oh, and about fractionated oils: Not to worry. Fractionation has nothing to do with trans FA's. All it does is remove some of the more saturated, higher-melting fats to keep the product from thickening or freezing when stored in a cool place.

A **MOLECULE** of any fat (a *triglyceride*) contains three fatty acid molecules attached to a glycerol (glycerin) base. The three fatty acids can be any combination of saturated, monounsaturated, or polyunsaturated. The health consequences of any given fat are purely those of the fatty acids (I'll call them FA's from here on) it contains.

The FA parts consist almost entirely of long chains of carbon atoms with hydrogen atoms sticking out like hairs on a caterpillar. In a molecule of a saturated FA, every carbon atom in the chain carries two hydrogen atoms, so the chains look like this: $-CH_2-CH_2-CH_2-CH_2-$, etc. (C represents a carbon atom, H represents a hydrogen atom, and — represents a chemical bond between carbon atoms.)

But in an unsaturated FA, there are occasional locations where two adjacent carbon atoms have only one hydrogen atom apiece, and the chain looks like this: $-CH_2-CH=CH-CH_2-$, etc. The two middle carbon atoms have squandered twice as much of their available bonding power just between themselves, with none left over for grabbing another two hydrogen atoms. That kind of connection between carbon atoms is called a double bond, indicated by $=$. If there is one such location in a FA molecule, it is said to be monounsaturated; two or more make it a polyunsaturated FA.

Wherever a double bond occurs in an unsaturated FA, it makes a kink or bend in the otherwise straight chain. Kinky molecules can't pack together as closely as straight molecules can, so the molecules are looser and an unsaturated fat tends to be a runny liquid rather than a firm, compact solid.

But even more significant than the physical properties of the fat is the fact that in most biological processes the exact shapes of molecules can be enormously important. As we metabolize them, it is primarily their different shapes that make kinky, unsaturated FA molecules more healthful than straight, saturated ones.

Food manufacturers want to convert unsaturated liquid fats into semisolid, consumer-friendly fats. So by applying high hydrogen gas pressure and heat—up to 150 psi (10 atmospheres) and 430°F (220°C)—they force two more hydrogen atoms into the double bonds. That is, they *hydrogenate* the unsaturated FA's to make them more saturated. But if they were to saturate every double bond in a polyunsaturated FA, it would become so hard that it would be as inedible as candle wax.

That's why liquid vegetable oils are only partially hydrogenated—that is, only a fraction of their double bonds are filled in with hydrogen atoms. Moreover, the hydrogenation process is inherently inefficient, so complete hydrogenation would be difficult to achieve anyway.

But here's where the trans FA's come in. During the course of hydrogenation, some of the double bonds evade the addition of two more hydrogen atoms by skipping off to another part of the chain. (The double bond *migrates*.) In the process, their original two hydrogen atoms, circled in the illustrations, which

cis

trans

may have been on the same side of the double bond—in a *cis configuration*—are likely to flip to opposite sides—into a *trans* configuration. This hydrogen-atom-flipping can take place even without double-bond migration, because the trans form is inherently more stable than the cis form. (*Cis*, pronounced "sis," and *trans* are from the Latin, meaning "on this side" and "across," respectively.)

So what if the hydrogen atoms *do* switch from the cis to the trans positions? Well, the two different resulting molecules (the two so-called *isomers*) have the same number of atoms of each kind, but they have different shapes. The cis molecules retain the original kinky shape of a normal unsaturated FA. But the newly formed trans molecules are straighter, more resembling a saturated FA.

And that's the problem. We all know that saturated FA's are cholesterol-boosting villains, and so then are the similarly shaped trans FA's. The body treats them as a type of saturated FA, with all its negative health implications—and more.

Note that trans FA's still have some double bonds, so they are included as unsaturated FA's in the Nutrition Facts charts on food labels. By the time you read this, however, the FDA may be requiring the amounts of trans FA's to be stated separately.

WHEN GOOD FATS GO BAD

*I've been reading and hearing a lot of buzz lately
about how easily most vegetable oils become rancid
and the possible harm that can cause. From what
I understand, oils become rancid, or oxidized,
when exposed to heat or oxygen or light, creating
free radicals that wreak havoc in the body. How
can I avoid oxidized oils?*

. . . .

*R*ancid is a sort of catchall word that comes from the Latin *rancidus*,
meaning rank or stinky. The word has no explicit chemical meaning.
It is used loosely to mean bad-smelling and -tasting, most often in
reference to over-the-hill fats. There are several things you can do to
avoid fat rancidity. But first, let's sort out the concepts in your question, because oxidation is only one of the ways in which fats can spoil.

Fats and oils can become rancid either by reacting with oxygen
(*oxidative rancidity*) or by reacting with water (*hydrolytic rancidity*).
Also, when oils are heated to high temperatures, as in deep-frying,
they can change chemically in other wicked ways.

Here, then, is a highly condensed version of "Fats Gone Wild."

• **Oxidative rancidity:** This happens primarily to fats containing unsaturated fatty acids. Helped along by heat, light, trace
metals, or certain enzymes, unsaturated fatty acids react
with oxygen in the air, producing highly reactive peroxides
and free radicals that, as you say, can wreak havoc in our
bodies. (See "Those home-wrecking radicals," p. 175.)

Whether the free radicals in rancid oils persist long enough to be
harmful when the oil is ingested is debatable. But many of the stable

end-products of the free-radical-driven reactions are bad-smelling chemicals called aldehydes and ketones, so rancid oils are unpleasant to ingest at the very least.

Many vegetable oils contain natural antioxidants—free-radical killers—called *tocopherols*; if they didn't, they wouldn't stay fresh as long as they do. Animal fats, on the other hand, which contain mostly saturated fatty acids, are not as susceptible to oxidative rancidity. That's why lard, for example, can be kept nearly forever without going rancid.

To foil oxidative rancidity, then, you should protect your vegetable oils from the oxygen, heat, and light that spark the free-radical reactions. Keep the bottle tightly sealed in a cool, dark place. Even refrigerating your oils isn't a bad idea if you don't use them very often. Because every oil is a mixture of fats with different freezing (solidification) temperatures, some of them may freeze in the fridge, but they will liquefy again on warming

- **Hydrolytic rancidity:** This is caused by *hydrolysis*: the reaction of a fat with water, whether the fat is saturated or unsaturated. The reaction is helped along by heat or by enzymes called lipases.

When water reacts with a fat, the fat molecule splits into its glycerol portion and its fatty acid portions. Free fatty acids generally smell pretty bad, especially the lightweight (small-molecule) ones that can float off easily into the air toward our noses. The predominant bad-smelling, small-molecule fatty acid in rancid butter is butyric acid, whose other common habitat is unwashed armpits.

Butter is ideal prey for both oxidative and hydrolytic rancidity: oxidative because 32 percent of its fatty acids are unsaturated, and hydrolytic because it contains about 18 percent water, distributed in the form of microscopic droplets throughout the matrix of fat. Defensive tactics against rancidity in butter must therefore include protection from both oxygen and heat, inasmuch as heat accelerates both types of rancidity. These considerations dictate both airtight wrapping and refrigeration.

- **Rancidity from deep-frying:** When a piece of food is plunged into very hot fat, the water on its surface—and all foods contain water—can react with the fat to hydrolyze it, freeing its fatty acids. As the fat is used and perhaps reused, the free fatty acids build up, negatively affecting its flavor and that of anything fried in it.

But that isn't the worst of it. When the fatty acids are split off from a fat molecule, what remains is the glycerol portion of the molecule. Upon further heating, the glycerol decomposes into a highly irritating, acrid gas aptly named *acrolein*. At about the same time, the fatty acids decompose, producing smoke. The longer the fat is heated, the more free fatty acids it will contain and the more likely it will be to smoke at progressively lower temperatures. Another thing that happens to long-used deep-frying oil is polymerization: the free fatty acids combine to form large molecules that darken and thicken the oil until it is almost syrupy.

The moral of the frying story is that to minimize the production of foul-tasting fatty acids, lung-clogging smoke, eye-watering acrolein, and other possibly carcinogenic compounds, use your deep-frying oil only once or at most twice. I dispose of mine by pouring it into an empty food can, freezing it, and discarding it with my solid garbage.

Sidebar Science: *Those home-wrecking radicals*

ELECTRONS, not unlike people, have a strong compulsion to pair up. A free radical is an atom or group of atoms that contains one or more unpaired electrons; that is, one or more of its electrons is missing a partner. (The etymology of "free radical" in the chemical, rather than the political, sense is convoluted and unhelpful.)

Given the slightest opportunity, a free radical will steal an electron from another molecule whose electrons are happily paired—like a predatory bachelor breaking up a marriage. That second molecule is now an unpaired-electron free radical itself, and will in turn steal an electron from a third molecule, and so on through a long chain of hundreds or thousands of partner-swapping reactions that, in our bodies, can disrupt the normal chemistry of our cells by changing the structures of molecules.

Free-radical chain reactions are quenched by chemicals called antioxidants, molecules that donate electrons to the pair-hungry free radicals, thereby quenching their spousal cravings. (The antioxidant may thereby become an electron-shy free radical itself, but not as destructive or "radical" a one as the one it quenched.)

Electron-donating antioxidants include the food additives BHA (butylated hydroxyanisol) and BHT (butylated hydroxytoluene), as well as vitamins A, C, and E.

IS LIGHT ALL RIGHT?

Other than the difference in calories, how does
light olive oil differ from "regular"?

. . . .

Whoa there! Light olive oil does not contain fewer calories than other olive oils or, for that matter, any edible oils. As far as calories are concerned, an oil is an oil, all oils are fats, and all fats give us approximately 9 calories of energy per gram.

The word *light* (or the nonword *lite*) is thrown around by food manufacturers to mean anything they want it to mean, including virtually nothing. In the case of olive oil, however, all you have to do is look at the bottle and you know that in this case it means light in color, and almost certainly in flavor.

We use vegetable oils in the kitchen mainly for sautéing, frying, and dressing salads. These functions are primarily physical rather than chemical in nature. In frying, for example, oil acts as an inert liquid that allows us to cook foods very quickly at a temperature much higher than that of boiling water. On salads, oil helps the dressing to stick; it "cuts" the acid; it carries other flavors, such as those of garlic and herbs; and it imparts unctuousness—a smooth, flowing mouth feel. These qualities are all largely physical, not chemical, and any relatively flavorless oil such as canola or corn oil can do those jobs.

Perhaps without realizing it, then, we may be tempted to think of kitchen oils in purely mechanical rather than flavor-related terms. As a result, many Americans prefer oils that are relatively tasteless— in fact, the blander the better—and colorless (or at most pale yellow). The olive oil producers oblige those customers by making a decolorized and deodorized version. They decolorize the oil, which is often not of top quality to begin with, by adsorbing the colored substances onto a fine clay, and they deodorize it (odor being a big part of flavor) by treating with high-pressure steam, in much the same way in which seed oils are refined. (See "That's oil, folks," p. 159.)

But that's really a shame, because natural olive oils, ranging in color from yellow to gray-green, possess a remarkable diversity of rich flavors and aromas that cooks prize for various culinary uses. Unlike most other kitchen oils, olive oil contributes its own flavor to whatever is cooked in it or dressed with it. It is a flavor ingredient in itself, not just a medium for carrying other flavors. That's why most Mediterranean cooking, which uses olive oil almost exclusively, is so flavorful. (The garlic also helps.)

The flavors of olive oils, like those of wines, vary with the country of origin, the variety of fruit (there are some fifty different species in general cultivation), the local soil and climate, how the groves are cultivated, when the olives are harvested, and how they are processed. The predominant flavor notes in olive oils include fruity, green, fatty, grassy, sweet, bitter, and astringent.

The chemistry of olive oils can be discussed from at least two standpoints: what are they made of in general, and what are their flavor and aroma compounds in particular? I won't burden you with the polysyllabic names or formulas of all these chemicals, but I do want to point out a few of the ones that are of particular relevance to the qualities we value most highly in olive oils.

In view of the wide variation in olive oils, no exact analyses of their fatty acids can be stated, despite the supposedly exact figures quoted in many food publications. The oleic acid content, for example, can range anywhere from 55 to 83 percent. Nevertheless, some average values, not to be taken too literally, are shown in Table 3. Not listed are about a dozen other fatty acids that are present in minor amounts.

When olives are crushed to express their oil, they release enzymes (*lipoxygenases*) that oxidize some of the polyunsaturated fatty acids to produce a wide variety of volatile aromatic compounds, including aldehydes, esters, and alcohols. More than one hundred volatile compounds have been identified in the olives' aromas alone, and chemists know the details of how most of them are formed.

The acidities of olive oils—that is, the percentages of free oleic acid molecules broken off from fat molecules—have been much dis-

Table 3. Average fatty acid composition of olive oils

NAME	SATURATION*	%
Oleic	Monounsaturated (18:1)	75.5
Palmitic	Saturated (16:0)	11.5
Linoleic	Polyunsaturated (18:2)	7.5
Stearic	Saturated (18:0)	2.5
Palmitoleic	Monounsaturated (16:1)	1.5
γ-Linolenic	Polyunsaturated (18:3)	1.0
Arachidic	Saturated (20:0)	0.5

* See "Fatty acid chains," on page 181.

cussed. Acidity is easy to measure, and quality-control examiners have long used the degree of acidity, along with several other characteristics, as a gauge of quality. Supposedly, the more free acid, the harsher the flavor and the lower the quality. In the fall of 2003, the European Union reduced the maximum permitted acidity of EU-produced extra-virgin olive oils from 1.0 to 0.8 percent. Nevertheless, it has recently been shown that acidity and flavor quality are not necessarily directly related to each other.

According to regulations of the EU and the International Olive Oil Council, here are the characteristics of the several grades of olive oil, in order of decreasing quality.

- **Extra-virgin olive oil** is virgin olive oil (see following grade) that meets strict composition and flavor characteristics. It's the top o' the heap. Obtained from perfect olives that have been crushed as soon as possible after harvest (their flavor deteriorates quickly) and processed without the use of heat or steam, extra-virgin oil exhibits the ideal flavor

and aroma of its variety. It must contain less than 0.8 percent of free fatty acids. Extra-virgin oils are sometimes
called "cold-pressed," but that term is being phased out as
pointless; olive oil presses don't need to be cooled and are
rarely, if ever, heated.

• **Virgin olive oil** must contain 100 percent olive oil from
olives of one or more varieties. It must be obtained only by
pressing, washing, decanting, centrifuging, and filtering,
or certain other processes that do not alter its natural state.
No additives, colorants, flavorings, or any other foreign
matter may be added.

• **Pure olive oil or 100% olive oil** is virgin olive oil that has
been blended with *refined* olive oil: oil that has been further
processed with steam to remove off flavors and acids. But it
still contains nothing but olive-derived ingredients.

• **Light or extra-light olive oil** is typically a blend of virgin and
highly refined oils, most of whose colors, off flavors, and
(for that matter) "on flavors" have been removed.

• **Pomace oil:** The oft-quoted statement that extra-virgin oils
come from the "first pressing" of the olives is baloney.
Olives are pressed only once. But more oil may later be
extracted from the pressed pulp, skins, and stones (the
pomace), which still contains some 4 to 10 percent oil. It
can be extracted by a combination of pressure, heat, and
chemical solvents, yielding what is called pomace oil, the
bottom of the barrel in quality. You won't even find it in
most grocery stores.

Which brings us back to your question. (Remember your question?) By the time olive oil has been filtered, purified, decolorized,
and practically de-olived to make light olive oil, most of its most flavorful, aromatic, and healthful compounds are gone. So rather than
using an oil that has been stripped of its olive-ness, be a sport and
experiment with the wide variety of olive oils on the market until you

find your one or two favorites. Choose based on one and only one criterion: what you like.

Some chefs and cooks believe it's a waste of a good drinking wine to use it in cooking. Others say that if it's not good enough to drink, it's not good enough to cook with. Similarly, conflicting advice abounds on whether a good, extra-virgin olive oil is wasted by using it to sauté or fry. Except for deep-frying, I prefer extra-virgin oil, both in cooking and on the table. For deep-frying in olive oil (Americans don't do that very much, but Spaniards do), I use a good virgin oil. If you do too, try to find out from a specialty store or from the brand's website the name of the predominant variety of olives that went into the oil. Spanish *picual* oil is reputed to be exceptionally stable at high frying temperatures.

Keep your olive oil ever within reach—but not too near the stove. Heat deteriorates all cooking oils and olive oil in particular, because its high percentage of unsaturated fatty acids is more susceptible to oxidation than are the saturated fatty acids of many other vegetable oils.

Like heat, light too is an enemy of olive and other vegetable oils. That's why most olive oil bottles are green or smoky colored. You've read a million times (including a few pages ago in this book) that you should keep oils in "a cool, dark place," but there's no need to go overboard. "Cool and dark" doesn't mean inside a refrigerator whose door is never opened lest its interior light go on.

"Cool" is a relative term, best interpreted as "not warm." Nor does "dark" mean pitch-black. The high-energy ultraviolet rays in sunlight are what do the damage, so by all means keep your oil out of direct sunshine. Incandescent lighting doesn't contain enough ultraviolet light to worry about, unless your kitchen is as bright as an operating theater. Fluorescent fixtures, however, do emit a substantial amount of ultraviolet light and should not be too near your oil-dispensing station.

THE FOODIE'S FICTIONARY:
Carotene—an adolescent carrot

Sidebar Science: *Fatty acid chains*

THE NUMBERS in parentheses in the middle column of Table 3 on page 178 are shorthand for the molecular structures of the fatty acids. The first number (16, 18, 20) is the number of carbon atoms in the molecule's chain. The number following the colon is the number of double bonds (see "Kinky molecules," p. 169) in the molecule; o indicates a saturated molecule, 1 indicates a monounsaturated molecule, and 2 or higher indicates a polyunsaturated molecule. For example, the monounsaturated FA molecule oleic acid (18:1), stretched out, would look like this, where O indicates an oxygen atom:

$$CH_3 - CH_2 - CH_2 - CH_2 - CH_2 - CH_2 - CH_2 - CH_2 -$$
$$CH = CH - CH_2 - CH_2 - CH_2 - CH_2 - CH_2 - CH_2 - CH_2 - C - OH.$$
$$\|$$
$$O$$

Note in Table 3 that almost 80 percent of the fatty acids in olive oil are monounsaturated and almost 10 percent are polyunsaturated. This high level of unsaturation has been linked to the healthful effects of olive oil. However, bear in mind the wide variation in types of olive oils. The percentage of saturated fatty acids in olive oils can range from 8 to 26, monounsaturated from 53 to 87, and polyunsaturated from 3 to 22.

Besides fats, olive oils contain other healthful chemicals in small amounts. Among the antioxidants are polyphenols; tocopherols, including vitamin E; and beta carotene, which manufactures vitamin A in the body.

The good-fat, bad-fat follies have been in continual ferment for the past few decades, so I won't venture out onto any limbs that may crack off before you read this. Nevertheless, at this writing, it's safe to say that saturated and trans fatty acids (see p. 169) are the bad guys, while unsaturated (mainly monounsaturated) fatty acids are the good guys. Stay tuned.

Citrus Brioche Loaf

May the brioche police forgive me, but this loaf is made with olive oil instead of butter. It is scented with the zest of orange and lemon and bakes up airy and flavorful.

Many recipes for brioche call for double risings of the dough and a rest overnight in the refrigerator. This version is quick and easy to mix in the food processor with no overnight rise. It can also be stirred together conventionally in a large bowl. It is not kneaded. Bake the brioche in a loaf pan if you want even slices, or use a fluted pan to give the classic brioche shape. Serve plain or toasted with sweet butter and jam, such as the Strawberry Preserves on page 190. Day-old brioche makes excellent French toast or bread pudding.

$1^1/_2$ teaspoons active dry yeast

3 tablespoons warm whole milk

$^1/_4$ cup sugar

2 cups all-purpose flour

3 large eggs, at room temperature

Grated zest of 1 orange

Grated zest of 1 lemon

$^3/_4$ teaspoon salt

6 tablespoons mild (not "light") extra-virgin olive oil

---

1. Lightly oil a 9-by-3-inch loaf pan or a 4 ½-cup fluted brioche mold, or spray with nonstick cooking spray.

2. Sprinkle the yeast over the bottom of a food processor work bowl and add the warm milk along with a small pinch of the sugar, ⅓ cup of the flour, and 1 egg. Pulse 8 to 10 times, or until the mixture, or starter, is creamy. Scrape down the sides of the work bowl.

3. Put the remaining flour on top of this starter, but do not mix it in. Cover the work bowl with the top of the food processor. Allow the mixture to stand until you can see that the starter has begun to foam and that the yeast is activated. Depending on the conditions in your kitchen, it can take from 15 minutes to 1 hour.

4. Add the remaining 2 eggs, the remaining sugar, the salt, and the orange and lemon zests to the work bowl of the processor. Turn the machine on and whirl for 10 to 15 seconds, or until the dough comes together to form a ball. Leave the machine on, and pour the olive oil in a fine stream through the feed tube. The stream should be fine enough so that the ball will not lose its shape as you pour. The movement of the ball of dough around the edge of the work bowl will incorporate the oil into the dough. The dough is fairly forgiving. It will be sticky, wet, and creamy.

5. Spoon and scrape the dough into the loaf pan or brioche mold. The pan will be about one-third full. Although a topknot is traditional on individual brioches, it gets in the way of slicing on a larger loaf such as this one. I prefer to leave it off.

6. Allow the dough to rise almost to the top of the pan. Depending on the temperature of the kitchen, this can take from 1 to 2 hours. The risen, leavened dough will be very light and about three times its original volume. Preheat the oven to 375°F about 15 minutes before the dough is ready.

7. Bake the brioche for about 30 minutes, or until golden brown.

8. Remove the loaf from the oven. Allow to rest in the pan on a wire rack for 5 minutes, then turn out onto the rack and let cool completely before slicing.

MAKES 1 LOAF

Substituting olive oil for butter in baking

Olive oil can be substituted for butter in many breads and desserts. But because butter is only about 80 percent fat, you must use less olive oil. No other modifications are necessary. Here's how to substitute. (Some of the amounts have been rounded off but are accurate enough in light of the fact that butter varies in its water content.)

BUTTER	OLIVE OIL
1 teaspoon (1/6 oz.)	3/4 teaspoon
1 tablespoon (1/2 oz.)	2 1/4 teaspoons
2 tablespoons (1 oz.)	1 1/2 tablespoons
1/4 cup (2 oz.)	3 tablespoons
1/3 cup (2.7 oz.)	1/4 cup
1/2 cup (4 oz.)	1/4 cup plus 2 tablespoons
2/3 cup (5.3 oz.)	1/2 cup
3/4 cup (6 oz.)	1/2 cup plus 1 tablespoon
1 cup (8 oz.)	3/4 cup

Source: Bertolli Lucca

OLIVE-GREEN, OR OLIVE-BLACK?

For years I had been told that olives are green or black depending on when they were picked. Then a friend who had lived in California told me that they were picked at the same time but processed in different ways. Which is true?

. . . .

Living in California doesn't make a person an expert, except perhaps in surrealistic politics. But just as in politics, there is some truth in both your positions.

Olives are unusual sources of oil, in that almost all other vegetable oils reside in the fruits' seeds, whereas in olives the oil is in the flesh.

As olives ripen, their colors change from straw-colored to green, purple, and, finally, black. The transformation from green to black takes place over a period of about 3 to 4 months. So you win the first round; olives may be picked at any one of these stages (except when they are straw-colored), depending on their destiny, whether for oil or for eating at the table. ("May olives be eaten with the fingers?" "No, the fingers should be eaten separately."—Henry Morgan.) Purplish olives generally produce better-quality oil than fully ripe black ones.

But your victory may be as hollow as a pitted olive, because some "black" or "ripe" California olives are picked at the purple stage and then blackened by treatment with alkali, air, or iron compounds (see below) to produce what are called "black-ripe" olives.

The olives on a tree don't all ripen at the same time, so there is always a mixture of stages to be harvested. Perhaps the biggest problem faced by olive growers is deciding exactly when to harvest for the best yield of the best stage of ripeness for the olives' intended purpose. Over the years, different countries and regions have developed and maintained their traditional harvesting practices, which contribute to the different flavor characteristics of, for example, Greek and Italian oils and even oils from different regions of Italy.

Historically—and by that I mean for thousands, not hundreds, of years—olives have been harvested by hand, either individually plucked or by means of a sort of comb known as a *pettine* (which is Italian for, well, "comb") that is raked along the branches. Alternatively, workers may simply beat the branches with poles to dislodge the fruit. Hand-harvesting is still widely used today, although in Spain, the world's largest producer of olive oil (a lot of olive oil labeled "Italian" is shipped from Spain and bottled in Italy), I saw heavy, tractor-like machines clamp strangleholds on tree trunks and shake the bejeebers out of them, the ripest and less tenacious olives falling into nets placed on the ground around the tree.

For table use, all olives must be processed in some way; you can't snack on them right off the tree because they contain a bitter phenolic compound called oleuropein. It must be removed either by microbial fermentation or by soaking in a strongly alkaline solution such as sodium hydroxide (lye).

In California, semi-ripe, greenish-purple olives are soaked in a series of lye solutions of diminishing concentrations, being rinsed and aerated after each soak. This treatment, aided in some cases by the addition of ferrous gluconate, an iron compound, turns the olives thoroughly black, after which they are canned.

So round two must go to your California friend, who may have been referring to this blackening process which, like many California customs, is not practiced anywhere else in the world. In Greece and Turkey, though, they do use a similar process to make fully ripe blackish olives dead black.

OSMOSIS IS A TWO-WAY STREET

I tried making strawberry preserves by boiling the
berries first, figuring I could add the sugar later.
But all I got was mush. What went wrong?

. . . .

Osmosis went wrong. It went in the wrong direction.

Whenever two water solutions containing different amounts of sugar (for example) are on opposite sides of a plant's cell wall, water molecules will move spontaneously through the cell wall in the direction of the more concentrated (stronger) solution, making it less concentrated—diluting it. That's osmosis.

When you cooked the berries in plain water without any sugar, water molecules moved into the cells, where some dissolved sugars already existed, until the cells could hold no more water and burst.

Ruptured cells, having lost their crisp cellular structure, are mushy cells.

On the other hand, when you cook a fruit in water with lots of sugar—more sugar than exists inside the cells—water molecules move *out of* the cells into the external sugar solution. The cells will shrink like deflated balloons, but they won't burst and their cell walls will still be more or less intact, retaining their toothsome texture. The berries therefore won't be softened as much by cooking in sugared water as they would be in plain water.

Sugar also has a strengthening effect on the fruit's cells even when they're deflated, because it reacts with the proteins in the cell walls.

In Nature, osmosis moves water from a solution of low concentration (of sugar, salt, etc.) through a cell wall or other kind of membrane, into a solution of higher concentration on the other side, thereby diluting or watering down the more concentrated solution. (See "Osmosis" on the following page.) But food producers often want to make a solution *more* concentrated; that is, to remove water from it—the exact opposite of what osmosis would do.

To accomplish this, they reverse the osmosis process by forcing water out of the concentrated solution, through a membrane, and into a more dilute solution. The process, called reverse osmosis, can require a substantial amount of pressure—as high as 1,000 pounds per square inch—to counteract the natural *osmotic pressure* and reverse the natural direction of water flow.

For example, the watery whey from cheese making was once considered a waste product and, when discarded, an environmental pollutant. But today, through reverse osmosis, the water is removed and the protein is sold to food manufacturers as the "whey powder" or "milk protein concentrate" that you see in the lists of ingredients in processed foods.

Reverse osmosis is also used to purify water. In this case, the pure water "squeezed out" of the impure water is, of course, the desired product.

Sidebar Science: *Osmosis*

IN A SOLUTION of sugar in water, there are both sugar molecules and water molecules. If there aren't many sugar molecules (that is, if the solution is *dilute*), the water molecules can freely bombard the walls of their container without much interference from the sugar. If those walls happen to be the walls of a plant cell, which are somewhat permeable to water, many of those water molecules will succeed in passing through to the other side. On the other hand, if a sugar solution is strong (*concentrated*), the sugar molecules will interfere severely, and not as many water molecules will succeed in penetrating the cell wall.

So if we have a dilute solution on one side of a cell wall and a concentrated solution on the other, more water molecules will be flowing from the dilute side to the concentrated side than

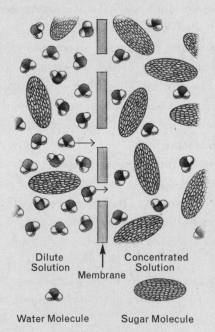

Dilute Solution

Concentrated Solution

Membrane

Water Molecule

Sugar Molecule

A dilute sugar solution (left side of the water-permeable membrane) and a more concentrated sugar solution (right side of membrane). Because there are relatively more water molecules in the dilute solution (left) than in the concentrated one (right), there is a net tendency (*osmotic pressure*) for water molecules to move though the membrane from the dilute solution into the more concentrated solution (from left to right).*

in the opposite direction, as if there were a net amount of pressure (*osmotic pressure*) forcing them in that direction. They will continue flowing that way until the concentrated solution has been watered down (*diluted*) to the same dilution as the dilute solution.

* For simplicity, I have portrayed the membrane as if it has holes big enough for water molecules to fit through, but not big enough for sugar molecules to pass. In reality, the mechanisms by which animal and plant membranes selectively permit water, but not other kinds of molecules, to pass through are more complicated and in many cases not completely understood.

Strawberry Preserves

In much of the country, locally grown strawberries can be found in farmers' markets for only a few weeks in late spring. Make the most of this window. Select small, firm but ripe berries in perfect condition. In this method, standing periods alternating with short cooking times yield a preserve with deep red color and fresh flavor.

In making preserves, jams, and jellies, the proportions of the three primary ingredients, fruit pectin, sugar, and acid (lemon juice), are crucial. The gel is formed by the action of the acid on the pectin, so too little pectin or acid will prevent gel formation and you'll have syrup instead. Too little sugar will make a tough jelly, while too much sugar will make a weak one. Simply put, the ingredients must be measured carefully. That's why in this recipe the sugar and berries are weighed, rather than measured by bulk.

I usually start this recipe in the late afternoon and finish it up the next morning. Do not double the recipe, because the longer cooking time will break down the berries' pectin and prevent gelling.

About $2^1/_4$ pounds strawberries

2 pounds (5 cups) sugar

$^1/_4$ cup freshly squeezed lemon juice

---

1. Wash and hull the strawberries. Keep smaller berries whole, but slice larger ones in half.

2. Weigh out 2 pounds strawberries and place them in a large stainless-steel saucepan or heavy preserving kettle. (I use an enameled cast-iron Le Creuset Dutch oven.) Add the sugar and, using a rubber spatula, gently mix it with the strawberries. Let stand for 4 hours, stirring occasionally.

3. Place over medium heat, bring to a boil, add the lemon juice, and cook rapidly for 12 minutes. Cover and let stand in a cool place overnight.

4. In the morning, bring the berry mixture to a boil over high heat, then turn down the heat to low. Remove the berries with a slotted spoon, draining them thoroughly, and spoon them into sterilized half-pint jelly jars, filling

them only halfway. Thorough draining is important, because too much liquid in the jars at this stage will thin the jelly.

5. Bring the syrup remaining in the pan to a boil and cook until thickened or until it registers 224°F (107°C) on a candy thermometer. To test if the syrup is ready, dip a soup spoon into the syrup and hold it horizontally over the pan; the syrup should fall from the spoon's surface in "sheets."

6. Pour the hot syrup over the berries to fill within ½ inch of the rim. Wipe the rims clean and seal with rubber-rimmed self-sealing tops and metal ring bands. As each jar is filled and sealed, turn it upside down. Allow it to cool in that position.

MAKES SIX HALF-PINTS

BOBBING FOR PUMPKINS

I'm planning a party on Halloween at which there will be bobbing for apples. Must I buy a certain kind, or do all apples float?

. . . .

Although most apples will float, they can vary somewhat in their aquatic stabilities. Buy samples of a few varieties several days before the party and test them. Then go back to the store and load up on the best floaters. Asking your guests to bob for apples that sink to the bottom would severely compromise your reputation as a caring host.

There is no easy way to predict whether an object will float or sink in water. You just have to try it. On *The Late Show with David Letterman*, a pair of attractive models drop various objects into a tank of water after Dave and sidekick Paul Shaffer have speculated about whether they will sink or float. Inspired by your question, but unfortunately unable to recruit the models, I decided to play "Will It Float?" on my own.

I went to the supermarket and, to the dismay of the cashier, purchased one each of a variety of fruits and vegetables. ("What's this?" she often inquired. I answered "Rutabaga" each time, and she was apparently satisfied.) Back home, I filled the kitchen sink with water and, humming my own rendition of Shaffer's fanfare, dropped them one by one into the water and recorded the results in my laboratory notebook.

Here, then, revealed for the first time in the annals of gastronomic science, are the results of my research. Floaters: apple, banana, lemon, onion, orange, parsnip, Bartlett pear, pomegranate, rutabaga (barely), sweet potato (barely), zucchini. Sinkers: avocado (barely), mango, Bosc pear (barely), potato, cherry tomato.

Almost all of my experimental subjects had difficulty making up their minds as to whether they wanted to sink or float. That's understandable, because they are all made mostly of water. According to the USDA's National Nutrient Database for Standard Reference (2003), the edible portions—the flesh—of my subjects range from 73 percent to 95 percent water. They would therefore tend to stay pretty much suspended. In fact, as indicated above, several of them just barely floated or sank.

Note that the USDA's figures are averages, and my supermarket samples were random individuals. Different varieties and samples of apples and (as I found out) pears may give different results. All in all, though, the odds are good that you'll find floating apples to bob for.

All of this made me think about the role of density in cooking. Density is a measure of how heavy a substance is for its bulk or volume. It can be expressed as a number of pounds per cubic foot.

Do you remember Archimedes, who jumped out of his bathtub and ran naked and dripping through the streets of Syracuse shouting "Eureka!" (which is Greek for "Who stole my towel")? Well, Archimedes discovered the principle that governs whether an object will sink or float in a fluid.

Once, when he was a little kid in school, Archimedes' principal ... no, let's start over.

Archimedes' Principle states that "a body immersed in a fluid is buoyed up by a force equal to the weight of the fluid displaced." That statement may be the way we "learned" it in school, but it's about as illuminating as a firefly wearing an overcoat. How many of us (including our teachers) really understood it? I confess that I never did until I figured it out for myself while fully clothed and dry. Here it is, in a one-paragraph nutshell.

Let's say we're bobbing for pumpkins. We'll completely submerge a 15-inch-diameter pumpkin, which has a volume of one cubic foot, into a big tub of water. One cubic foot of water now has to get out of the way to make room for the pumpkin. That displaced water is necessarily pushed upward—there's no place else for it to go—so the water level rises. But the water now has a pumpkin-sized hollow in it, and the displaced water wants to flow back down, as is its gravitational habit, and fill it. The only way it can do that is to push the pumpkin back up out of the hollow with whatever force or weight it can muster; for a cubic foot of water, that amount of weight is about 60 pounds. If the one-cubic-foot pumpkin should happen to weigh, say, only 50 pounds, it will be pushed up (buoyed up) by that extra 10 pounds of force from the water. That is, it will float. If that one-cubic-foot pumpkin should happen to weigh 70 pounds, however, it would overcome the 60 pounds of buoyancy and sink.

Conclusion: If an object's density is less than that of water (which is actually 62.4 pounds per cubic foot), it will float; if its density is greater than that of water, it will sink. (In reality, a 15-inch-diameter pumpkin weighs about 40 pounds and would float.)

What does that mean to us in the kitchen? Here are a couple of examples.

Gnocchi, ravioli, and pierogi will sink at first when you put them into boiling water because they are more dense than the water. But as their starch granules swell in the hot water, their density decreases until they are less dense than water, whereupon they inform you that they are cooked by floating to the surface.

Note that the density of an object can decrease either by the object's losing weight or by its expanding in volume. When a human object gains both weight and volume, his or her density decreases, because fat is less dense than muscle. Draw your own conclusion.

Another example: In making beignets, or "doughnut holes," we drop spoonfuls of dough into deep, hot fat. The dough ball is less dense than the oil and therefore floats. But as the portion below the surface browns in the hot oil, it loses water in the form of steam and becomes even less dense. The bottom of the ball is now less dense than the top, and it may actually capsize like a top-heavy boat and proceed to brown its other side.

The first time I saw this phenomenon I was as surprised as if I had seen a pancake flip itself over when its first side was done.

THE FOODIE'S FICTIONARY: Rutabaga—an early, unsuccessful competitor of the Studebaker

WHICH CIDER YOU ON?

Would you please explain the difference between apple juice, natural-style apple juice, and apple cider? Are they nutritionally identical? Do they have to be pasteurized?

. . . .

It depends on where you live. In this country, *apple juice* and *apple cider* are often used interchangeably, referring simply to the liquid that runs out of pressed apples. But in most other countries, *cider* means apple juice that has been allowed to ferment and produce alcohol, just as grape juice ferments to produce wine. We Americans would call fermented apple juice "hard" cider, as distinguished from unfermented, alcohol-free "sweet" cider. To sidestep this ambiguity, we'll adopt the international nomenclature: if it's unfermented it's apple juice, if it's fermented it's cider.

The word *cider* and its variations are ancient, originally meaning any intoxicating beverage made from fruit. Because all fruits contain fermentable starches and sugars, and because all you have to do to ferment them is leave them lying around so that airborne yeasts can fall on them, the world's cultures have come up with a most remarkable variety of alcoholic beverages.

Apple juice may be bottled while still cloudy from suspended particles of fruit, or it may be filtered to clarify it. It's just a matter of preference. As on most food labels, the word *natural* on a juice label can mean anything the bottler wants it to mean. But in the case of apple juice, it might be intended to mean unfiltered.

There is no federal requirement that apple juice be pasteurized, but many brands are routinely heat-treated to keep them from fermenting. If they haven't been heat-treated, the labels must say "Keep refrigerated," so the absence of that warning is your assurance that the juice has been pasteurized. Unpasteurized apple juice left in the refrigerator will become fizzy within a couple of weeks, indicating fermentation. It's not wise to drink it, though, because the strain(s) of bacteria doing the fermenting are unknown, and the fizz means that they are feasting on sugar, producing carbon dioxide and alcohol, and multiplying like—well, like bacteria. In the reproduction department, rabbits can't hold a candle to bacteria. (Just a figure of speech. Try very hard *not* to picture a rabbit holding up a candle to a petri dish of bacteria. Whoops! You failed, didn't you?)

Regarding nutrition, some apple juices, especially the pasteurized ones, are likely to have been fortified with vitamin C. Check the label to see.

BACCHANALIAN BEES

Can you straighten out the various alcoholic
apple beverages? I've heard of hard cider,
apple wine, apple brandy, and applejack.
Or are they all the same?

. . . .

They differ mainly in the ingenious methods that have been invented to arrive at their percentages of alcohol.

Apple juice can be allowed to ferment naturally by just leaving it around in the open and letting airborne yeast cells fall into it. These microscopic, single-celled plants feed on the fruit sugars, converting them to ethyl (grain) alcohol. It doesn't take many yeast cells to start the ball rolling, because the more they feed the more they reproduce, growing into voracious sugar-eating machines in a couple of days. But when all the sugar is consumed, the feeding frenzy ends; the alcohol concentration is about 5 percent, about equivalent to beer. That's *hard cider*, as opposed to—well, "soft" or nonalcoholic cider, which is really just apple juice.

We humans don't have a monopoly on intoxication. I used to have an apple tree that dropped its apples onto my driveway every fall. The apples would break open and release their juices, which would soon ferment. Bees would be attracted, sip the sweet alcoholic juice, become intoxicated, and roll around in delirium on the ground. I had lots of fun watching this apian bacchanal, but I was kept busy calling cabs to take them home to the hive. (*Don't drink and fly!*)

In the cider-producing regions of England, France, and Spain—the south of England, the north of France, and the Asturias region of northern Spain—where apple trees thrive and grapevines don't do very well, ciders are often drunk or used in marinating and cooking instead of wines. The characteristics of different ciders can vary as much as those of different wines. Like wines, ciders can be matched with foods based on their acidity, dryness, and fruitiness, qualities that arise from the specific varieties of apples the cider was made from and how it was fermented.

The dryness of a cider is the extent to which the apples' sugars have been fermented to alcohol; the driest ciders have had all their sugars used up. The very dry Spanish *sidra* of Asturias, for example, is a particularly good stand-in for dry white wine in virtually all its applications.

A sparkling or effervescent cider, like sparkling wine, has been bottled before fermentation is complete. A highly regarded example of this is the French-style cider (*cidre*), either sparkling or still, with its alcohol content limited to 2 to 5 percent by arresting the fermentation process, either by pasteurization or by the addition of sulfur dioxide.

Very early in the game, humans figured out what was happening to fermenting apple juice and wanted to boost the alcohol content to fuel their paeans to Dionysus. They added more sugar to feed the yeast, eventually also allowing the juice to absorb tannins from the insides of wooden barrels for complexity and depth of flavor. The alcohol content was in this way boosted to between 10 and 12 percent, comparable to that of grape wines. We have now made *apple wine*.

Want still (pun intended) higher alcohol content? Distill the apple wine, just as some wineries distill their grape wine to make brandy. That is, boil the liquid and cool the hot vapors to condense them back to a liquid. Because alcohol evaporates more readily than water does, the vapors and hence the condensed liquid (brandy) will be richer in alcohol than the original liquid (wine) was.

Laird & Company, the biggest producer of apple brandy, distills cider until it is 80 percent alcohol (160 proof), cuts it with water to about 65 percent (130 proof), and ages it in charred oak barrels. It comes out as *apple brandy*. At bottling time it is adjusted so that the alcohol content is 40 or 50 percent (80 or 100 proof) and labeled *applejack*, although strictly speaking it is still a brandy, according to the U.S. Alcohol and Tobacco Tax and Trade Bureau.

The French apple brandy Calvados, a product of the eponymous *département* 14 in Normandy, is similarly made by distilling apple wine twice: first to achieve an alcoholic content of 28 to 30 percent and again to reach 72 percent, after which it is "cut" to a more drinkable 40 to 43 percent (80 to 86 proof).

The word *brandy* comes from the Dutch *brandewijn*, meaning burnt (actually, distilled) wine. In France, brandy is known as *eau de vie*, or water of life. I guess it's a matter of priorities.

Sidebar Science: *Let'sh hear it for apple(hic!)jack!*

IN THE eighteenth century, American colonists in New England came up with an ingenious way of boosting the alcohol content of apple wine without the complicated apparatus of a still. They just left barrels of the wine out in the cold New England winter, where the surfaces froze. But water freezes at 32°F (0°C), while ethyl alcohol won't freeze until the temperature gets down to −179°F (−117°C). So the surface ice was relatively pure water. The wily New Englanders skimmed off the ice and discarded it, finding that the remaining liquid in the barrel had been enriched in both alcohol content and apple flavor. They called it *applejack*.

When the unwearied but thirsty colonists were lucky enough to have a run of 20-below-zero (−29°C) nights, the applejack would reach a 27 percent concentration of alcohol. That's 54 proof, which was perfectly adequate for warming the cockles (whatever they are) of their hearts until spring.

Cider Sauce

This sauce is equally at home with the flavors of a roasted pork loin or warm gingerbread. You can make it with either hard or "soft" cider. If you use the hard stuff, some of the alcohol will remain in the sauce.

1 cup apple cider or apple juice

$^1/_3$ cup firmly packed brown sugar

1 tablespoon unsalted butter

1 tablespoon freshly squeezed lemon juice

Pinch of ground cloves

1 tablespoon cornstarch

1 tablespoon water

1. In a 1-quart saucepan, combine the cider or juice, brown sugar, butter, lemon juice, and cloves. Place over medium heat and cook, stirring occasionally, until the mixture comes to a full boil. Boil for 3 minutes or until somewhat reduced.

2. In a small bowl, mix together the cornstarch and water. Stir the starch mixture into the hot cider mixture. Continue cooking, stirring constantly, for 1 to 2 minutes, or until the sauce has thickened. Serve warm.

MAKES 1 GENEROUS CUP

CASHEW! GESUNDHEIT!

I like to buy raw cashew nuts at a health-food
store. I sometimes pulverize them to make a tasty
milk. But my daughter came home from school
telling me that cashew nuts contain a highly
corrosive, toxic substance and that they must
never be eaten raw. Health food?!

. . . .

The succulent "fruits" of the tropical cashew tree *Anacardium occi-dentale*, often called cashew apples, are about the size and shape of a pear. They are not only edible but quite delicious. Since they are highly perishable, however, you won't find them very far from the trees. I was lucky enough to taste them when I lived in Venezuela, where they grow and are called *merey*.

A "cashew apple" on the tropical cashew tree, *Anacardium occidentale*.
The edible "apple" is known as *merey* in Venezuela, *cajueiro* in Brazil,
and *marañón* in most of the rest of Latin America. The cashew "nut"
(botanically, the fruit) is inside the lower, kidney-shaped appendage.

Attached to the "apple" at its lower end is the kidney-shaped nut (which, botanically speaking, is actually the fruit), encased in a double shell. Between the shells is a gummy phenolic resin containing the corrosive and poisonous chemicals anacardic acid and cardol, among others. If eaten, this resin would actually cause blisters in the mouth.

Obviously, the poisons must be removed before the nuts are safe to eat. This is accomplished by roasting the unshelled nuts in hot oil, which does two things: it drives off the resins, and it makes the shells brittle enough to crack by hand with a mallet, a method that continues to survive into the twenty-first century. Both the shells and the corrosive chemicals are long gone before you ever see them in the store.

The nuts are perfectly edible at this stage, and are sold as "raw cashews" in spite of the fact that they have already been cooked at 365 to 375°F (185 to 190°C). Commercially packaged cashews are usually roasted again at 325°F (163°C); this roasting softens them and enhances their color and buttery flavor.

Those raw-foods-only restaurants and other raw-food devotees who insist that food must never be allowed to exceed 118°F (48°C) make frequent use of "raw" cashew nuts and "raw" cashew butter in their creations. Either they're kidding themselves or they don't know that their nuts were roasted at a much higher temperature long before they saw them.

Chapter Five

For Amber Waves
of Grain

....

I T MAY seem strange that after two chapters on agricultural crops that supply us with our vegetables and fruits, I now turn to the cultivation of grass. And I don't mean what some readers might think.

Nor am I referring to the hundreds of square miles of home-encircling green carpet that we plant, water, fertilize, spray, manicure and trim, only to harvest the top inch time and time again and throw it away. (Futility, thy name is lawn.) And don't get me started on the wastefulness of golf courses, especially in the water-starved desert regions of our country.

No, by "grass" I'm referring to cereal grasses, the family of plants that, more than any other, feeds the world. Also called grains, cereal grasses supply us with the starchy, edible seeds we treasure: wheat, rice, rye, oats, barley, and corn. Not only do these six plants sustain most of the world's human population, but they feed the cattle and poultry who turn them into meat. Grains are the most ancient and still the most important of all food crops.

Wheat is probably the oldest. It is still a widely cultivated grain, with a worldwide annual production (in 2003) of 556 million metric tons. It is surpassed by rice, at 589 million metric tons, 90 percent of which is grown in Asia. But the world's champion is corn (maize), with 638 million tons being produced in 2003. All other grains (barley, rye, oats, and sorghum), known as coarse grains, total another 242 million metric tons worldwide. (Source: United Nations Food and Agriculture Organization, FAOSTAT.)

The most important nutritional feature of all grains is their starchiness. Starch is, of course, a carbohydrate, as are its building blocks, the sugars. So speaking chemically rather than agriculturally, this chapter might more broadly, if also more textbookily, be titled "Carbohydrates," whether from grains, legumes, or, in the case of honey, insects.

In that vein, allow me to set the stage with a Sidebar Science on carbohydrate chemistry which, as with all sidebars, may be scanned, skimmed, or skipped.

Sidebar Science: *A nano-course on carbohydrates*

THE MOLECULES of all carbohydrates—sugars and starches— are made up of anywhere from two to hundreds or even thousands of molecules of glucose, all joined together. As the number of glucose units per molecule increases from a few to dozens or hundreds, we cross the rather fuzzy borderline between sugars and starches.

• **Monosaccharides:** Its name derived from the Greek *mono*, meaning one or single, and *sakcharon*, meaning sugar, a monosaccharide is a basic "sugar unit" whose molecules cannot be broken down (by *hydrolysis*) into any simpler sugars. Monosaccharides are the smallest of carbohydrate molecules. The most common ones are glucose, fructose, and galactose. (See Table 4 on p. 206.)

Glucose is the ultimate, energy-giving breakdown product of all the carbohydrates we eat. It can go directly into the bloodstream.

• **Disaccharides:** Table sugar, sucrose, is a disaccharide ("two sugars"); its molecules are made up of one molecule each of glucose and fructose, the very sweet simple sugar found in fruits. When treated either with an acid or with the enzyme *invertase*, the sucrose molecule breaks down into a mixture of equal amounts of its glucose and fructose parts. The resulting mixture is called *invert sugar* and is, surprisingly, sweeter than sucrose itself because fructose is sweeter than sucrose.

This illustrates a fundamental principle of chemistry: A chemical compound (sucrose, for example) can have very different properties from a simple mixture of its components (a mixture of glucose and fructose, for example). The obligatory chemistry-textbook example is sodium chloride (table salt), which we eat with impunity despite its being composed of a metal that explodes in water (sodium) and a poisonous gas (chlorine).

Other disaccharides are lactose, found only in the milk of mammals, and maltose, formed when grains are malted—soaked in water until they sprout, such as in making beer and Scotch whisky from barley.

• **Oligosaccharides:** Oligosaccharides—the name comes from the Greek *oligos*, meaning few—are carbohydrate molecules made up of fewer than ten monosaccharide units, and are still generally referred to as sugars rather than starches. The three- and four-unit oligosaccharides raffinose and stachyose (note that the names of all sugars end in -ose) are present in beans but are not digestible by humans. Instead, bacteria in our intestines feed on them, showing their ingratitude by producing those gaseous consequences we associate with beans.

• **Polysaccharides:** Finally, there are polysaccharides ("many sugars"), also called complex carbohydrates or starches, whose molecules are made up of anywhere from about forty to thousands of glucose units. If the units are joined in long, rather straight chains, they are called amylose starches; if they are joined in a branching, bushy configuration, they are called amylopectin starches. Because of their different molecular

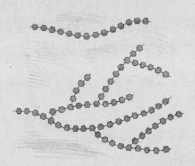

The two forms of starch molecules. Top: the linear structure of amylose. Bottom: the branched structure of amylopectin. Each hexagon represents one glucose unit.

shapes, they impart different properties to our starch-containing foods. Most plant starches are mixtures of both amylose and amylopectin.

Other polysaccharides whose names you may have seen on food ingredient labels are dextrins, which are rather large molecular chunks that break off from bigger polysaccharide molecules like dead branches from a tree, when the polysaccharides break down in water.

Too lazy to articulate a four-syllable word, many people today are talking about—and counting—the number of grams of "carbs" in their foods. Carbohydrates—uh, carbs—range upward in molecular size and complexity to thousands of glucose units. If the molecules are big enough, we can't digest them and they pass right through our alimentary canals without giving us any calories or nutrition. The smaller, digestible carbohydrate molecules—sugars and starches—are loosely referred to as "net carbs" in the proliferating literature of weight-loss dieting, because they're the ones that are metabolized to yield calories at the rate of 4 calories per gram.

Table 4. What sugars and starches are made of

NAME	ALTERNATE NAMES	WHAT MONOSACCHARIDE UNITS IT IS MADE OF	WHERE IT IS FOUND
MONOSACCHARIDES			
Glucose	Dextrose, blood sugar	---	Grapes, blood
Fructose	Fruit sugar	---	Fruits, honey
Galactose	---	---	Milk, brains
DISACCHARIDES			
Sucrose	Cane sugar, table sugar	One glucose + one fructose	Sugar cane, sugar beets, maple trees
Lactose	Milk sugar	One glucose + one galactose	Milk
Maltose	Malt sugar	Two glucoses	Germinating grains
POLYSACCHARIDES			
Cellulose	--	Many glucoses	All plants
Dextrin	--	Many glucoses	Grains
Starch	--	Many glucoses	Grains, potatoes

THE FOODIE'S FICTIONARY: Invert sugar—Whoops!
I knocked over the sugar bowl

M*A*S*H

Every time I make mashed potatoes I get different
results. Worst of all is when they turn out sticky
and gluey. What am I doing wrong?

. . . .

Mashed potatoes would seem to be the easiest thing in the world to make: just boil 'em and mash 'em, right? But potatoes are mostly starch, and a lot depends on how the starch behaves.

Potato flesh is made up of plant cells. Inside the cells are thousands of starch granules, little round packages in which the plant has stored the molecules of starch that it manufactured during photosynthesis. The starch inside the granules has a gelatinous consistency, so that the granules may be thought of as tiny sacks of glue.

When heated in a moist environment, the granules take on water

The OXO potato masher. When used with a straight up-and-down
motion, it extrudes the potato through its rectangular holes,
producing a coarse, non-gluey texture.

and swell until some of the sacks disintegrate, spilling their gummy contents. The granules lose their grainy structure and become *gelatinized*. (See "In a fog about pea soup" on the following page.)

But the game isn't lost yet. If the spilled gelatinous starch remains trapped within the potato's cells, your spuds are still okay because the potato's cell structure keeps them firm. But if you then smash the cells open, the gooey starch runs out and gums up the works.

The best masher, in my opinion, is the type that has square or rectangular holes in a flat plate. It extrudes the potato through the holes as a ricer does, rather than crushing it. When mashing, use an up-and-down motion; don't slide the masher sideways, which would squash open more starch grains. That's the trouble with those zigzag rod mashers; their round rods squish the potato sideways. And never use a food processor. It is notorious for making gluey potatoes because its sharp blades slash through the swollen starch grains, liberating lots of gluey gel.

Beyond all that, some potatoes are better for mashing than others. Small redskins are waxy and make a waxy mash. Best are the russets, or "Idaho baking potatoes," and Yukon Golds, whose cell structures give a nice, mealy texture. And the color of the Yukon

How to make mashed potatoes

Cut the potatoes into 1-inch pieces and precook for about 10 minutes at a simmer, not a full boil. That gives the starch grains a chance to swell without rupturing. Then drain the potatoes and let them cool. That allows the swollen starch granules to firm up.
When you're almost ready to mash, simmer the potatoes the rest of the way until they're barely tender, not mushy. Drain them very well and mash them with a potato masher or ricer. The firmed-up starch granules won't release their goo as easily as they would have without the precooking and cooling steps.

Golds (see p. 117) makes your guests think there's more butter in the mashed potatoes than there is.

IN A FOG ABOUT PEA SOUP

*Why is it that when I make split pea soup and
put the leftovers in the refrigerator, they set up
like cement? I then have to add a lot of water
and beat it into submission to make it thin
enough to eat with a spoon.*

. . . .

Before I answer your question, have you ever wondered why split pea soup has to be made from split peas, rather than whole ones? I know I have. After all, once they've been reduced to pottage, who cares whether they were originally intact spheres or, one must presume, had been carefully split in two at the factory by a tribe of elves wielding tiny machetes?

In truth, the split pea is a specific variety of pea whose proper name is field pea, originally native to southwestern Asia and one of the earliest crops cultivated by humans. They have a weak plane or layer that splits apart when the peas are dried. That easy-splitting phenomenon, also found in some minerals, is what mineralogists call cleavage. (Now get your mind back on what I'm talking about!)

All peas are varieties of *Pisum sativum*. The field pea is to be distinguished from the common garden pea, a.k.a. green pea or English pea, which is usually sold fresh and still in its pod, to be shelled by grandmothers seated at the hearth or, when fresh and young (the peas, not the grandmothers), to be eaten whole, pod and all. The French are particularly fond of their tiny young peas, which they have imaginatively named *petits pois*, or "little peas."

Your solidified soup phenomenon is not unique to peas; it is caused by the peas' abundance of starch, and exactly the same thing will happen in any starchy soup or sauce, such as a gravy that has been thickened with cornstarch or flour and subsequently refrigerated. They, too, will be unyieldingly thick and gelatinous after having been refrigerated.

Here's a simplified version of what's going on.

Under a low-power microscope, starch looks like a collection of translucent round or ovoid capsules of various sizes, called granules. Inside each granule are millions of invisibly small starch molecules, arranged in a relatively organized pattern.

As we heat a starch-bearing food in water, the starch granules become dispersed throughout the liquid, where they gradually absorb water and swell. The swollen granules then rub up against one another like too many overfed fish in too small a pond, and the entire mixture becomes more viscous, or thicker. Some of the granules may even burst and spill their contents, further thickening the soup or sauce into a sort of paste. This entire process is generally called gelatinization.

A dish containing gelatinized starch is just fine if you eat it while it's hot. The smooth, silky texture of a properly made flour- or starch-thickened white sauce, for example, is one of gastronomy's great pleasures.

But when the starchy leftovers are cooled in the refrigerator, two processes take place in succession: first, *gelation* (not gelatinization), and then *retrogradation*. (Note that gelatinization—becoming gelatin-like—took place upon heating, while gelation—formation of a gel—takes place upon subsequent cooling.)

In the first cooling stage, gelation, starch molecules inside the swollen granules slow down because of the falling temperature. (All molecular motion is slower at lower temperatures.) The starch molecules can then begin to mesh with one another and tangle together, forming a weblike structure that traps a lot of water. That kind of structure, a semisolid mass containing a large amount of locked-in liquid, is called a *gel*. As the gel continues to cool and more starch-to-starch bonds form and tighten the net, some previously trapped water may even be squeezed out, a phenomenon known as *syneresis*. The soup or sauce "weeps," and little beads of water can be seen on the surface.

After several hours of cooling and aging, the starch molecules are so tightly tangled with one another that they are no longer dispersible in water. If you add water to try to thin it out, the thick, gummy mass refuses to break up and return to its earlier consistency, because in their tangled gel form the starch molecules cannot unbond from one another to make room for the water and then swim freely into it. In short, the starch has *retrograded*—gone back—to an insoluble form. You can then try beating it into submission by adding water and whisking vigorously while heating, but it may never be as smooth as it was just after being cooked.

Don't despair. I'm told that the traditional Dutch pea soup (*erwten-soep*), also called *snert* (that's right, *snert*), is deliberately made a day ahead and refrigerated, so that when reheated, it will be thick enough to support a spoon standing straight up. When much of your country is below sea level, I guess you have to do *something* for fun.

DOGGIE-BAG RICE

Servings in Chinese restaurants are often too large
to finish, so I end up taking "doggie bags" home
for the refrigerator. But the rice always hardens
into tough, separated grains, a far cry from the
soft, sticky consistency it had in the restaurant.
I thought it might have been dehydrated, but
adding water just makes it mushy.
How can I restore its soft texture?

. . . .

I know what you mean. The waiter asks, "Do you want me to pack the rice also?" And you say, "Yes, please," while thinking, "Not really, but I paid for it, and I don't want him to think I lack respect for the soul food of his homeland." So there you are, two or three days later, wondering whether your conscience will allow you to throw it out.

Some dehydration does indeed take place in the fridge, as you can see from the fact that the top layer of rice is drier than the rest. But the main effect is that the starch in the rice has undergone a partial reversion (retrogradation) to the hard, water-insoluble state it was in before it was cooked. The same two processes—gelation and retrogradation—take place in the rice's starch as take place in pea soup and all starch-thickened gravies and sauces when the cooked foods are refrigerated. (See "In a fog about pea soup," p. 209.)

Replacing the water that was trapped during retrogradation isn't easy, but heating the rice in a very small amount of water may partially restore its soft texture. Personally, I don't try to restore leftover rice to softness. I make fried rice out of it.

HOW TO PLAY PICK-UP STICKS

I understand that Chinese rice is sticky, rather than in separate grains the way we Americans like it, so that it can be picked up with chopsticks (though not by me). Is it a special rice, or a special way of cooking it?

. . . .

It's the type of rice. Bear with me and I'll reveal an ancient Chinese secret—okay, a modern American one—for using chopsticks.

There are tens of thousands of varieties of rice known today, but in the interests of sanity we can divide them into three categories: short-grain (less than 5 millimeters long), medium-grain (from 5 to 6 millimeters long), and long-grain (6 to 7 millimeters long).

In recent years, several specialty rices have become popular in the United States. One is the traditional Italian arborio rice, a particularly absorptive medium-grain variety. It is rich in amylopectin starch (see the illustration on p. 205), the branched, bushy molecules of which trap and absorb water quite readily. Arborio rice will easily absorb three times its own volume of stock or broth, making it ideal for risotto. The choice rices for paella, which needn't be as sticky, are the medium-short, less-amylopectin-containing Valencia or *bomba* varieties.

Other exotic rice strains that have caught the American fancy are jasmine and basmati rice from Thailand and India, respectively. Jasmine rice is a long-grain white rice with a fragrant aroma. Basmati rice is also aromatic (the Hindi word *basmati* means fragrant), with a nutty flavor and aroma. Close genetic relatives of both these Asian varieties have been appropriated by growers in the United States, however, and the word *jasmine* or *basmati* on a package can no longer be depended upon to mean the genuine, imported product. (A Texas company named RiceTec even attempted to patent the name *basmati* in 1997, although most of its claims were disallowed when the Indian government made waves.) In the United Kingdom, however, the term "basmati rice" may be applied only to the long-grain aromatic rice grown in India and Pakistan.

Chinese and Japanese rice is short-grained and rich in the branched molecules of amylopectin starch, which make it sticky when cooked. American long-grain rice, on the other hand, is richer in the straight-chain molecules of amylose starches that don't trap as much water. It cooks up into fluffy, separate grains that after retrogradation (see p. 210) are easier than the Chinese variety to resoften with moist heat.

Now to your dexterity perplexity.

While East Asians are incredibly adept in using chopsticks to pick up their sticky rice, Westerners are often bamboozled when finding themselves forkless. To most of us, chopsticks are the *real* Chinese torture. Bamboo slivers under the fingernails are painful, yes, but at least you don't starve to death.

I'm one of those insufferable Western snobs who always use

chopsticks in Chinese and Japanese restaurants, claiming that the food "tastes better" that way. Even more insufferably, I bring along my own pair of ivory sticks. The simple truth, however, is that I just happen to possess the manual dexterity for handling chopsticks, and I like to show off.

Well, help is at hand, so to speak, for the rest of you. Never mind those how-to-hold-your-chopsticks instructions that are printed on the place mats but which might as well be in Chinese for all the help they give. There really is an easy way to eat Chinese and Japanese food with aplomb, or even without the plum.

The secret to chopstick *savoir faire* is a simple little rubber band. With it, you can transform those infernal wooden shafts into a tool that can be used efficiently by even the most digitally challenged klutz.

I would love to say that I discovered this secret while traveling through the Far East several years ago, but I didn't. On that trip I could only watch with amusement as my fellow Americans attempted more maneuvers than in Sun Tzu's *The Art of War* in an effort to convey perhaps every fifth morsel of food to the general vicinity of their oral cavities.

In China and Taiwan, I observed some of my desperate companions holding the sticks about an inch from the bottom, in the mistaken belief that less leverage would make them more controllable. (It doesn't.) In Japan, the chopsticks were often pointed, so stabbing quickly became the method of choice. And watching my fork-facile friends deal with wet noodles was more fun than SeaWorld.

I'll never know why the rubber-band trick didn't occur to me on that trip. I had to wait until a server in a Samurai Japanese Steak House, right here in the USA, showed me how to do it. (See "How to use chopsticks, though American," on the following page.)

THE FOODIE'S FICTIONARY: Paella—Spanish for "payola." There's something in it for everyone.

How to use chopsticks, though American

Remove the chopsticks from their paper wrapper through one end, leaving the wrapper intact. Flatten the wrapper and then roll it up until it resembles a miniature roll of paper towels. Hold the sticks parallel to each other, and insert the paper roll crosswise between them, about an inch or so from their top ends. Still holding the sticks together, wrap a rubber band around and around their top ends above the paper roll. Just before you run out of rubber band, take a turn or two around the protruding ends of the paper roll to keep it from slipping down the sticks. Now let go.

An easy way to use chopsticks.

Voilà! (or its Chinese equivalent). You now have a pair of spring-loaded tweezers that you can hold pretty much like a pencil. Just push the sticks together with your thumb and forefinger to grab any morsel you hanker for. When the food arrives within mouth range, release the pressure and the sticks will spring open, ready for their next trip to the plate.

The next time you go to a Chinese or Japanese restaurant, take along a rubber band. You'll really impress that snob (me?) at the next table.

ASK UNCLE BEN

*A recipe tells me to add parboiled rice to a
casserole. How does one make parboiled rice?*

. . . .

Parboil it.

Okay, seriously: Parboiling is boiling a food just enough to cook it
partially but not completely. Quixotically, the word comes from the
Latin *per bullire*, meaning to boil thoroughly, but in Middle English
per became *par* and was confused with *part* or *partial*. Thus, "thorough
boiling" came to mean its opposite, "partial boiling."

When you're cooking a casserole that contains rice along with
faster-cooking ingredients, the recipe may tell you to parboil the rice
first so that everything will be done at the same time.

As rice comes from the field, its grains are encased in an inedible, protective hull or husk, which is removed at the mill. Beneath the
husk is a thin layer of bran, which is left on for brown rice or removed
by abrasion to make white rice. The bran layer gives brown rice its
characteristic tan color and nutty flavor. Brown rice is chewier than
white rice and takes longer to cook.

Before the hulls are removed, rice is often treated with high-
pressure steam, a treatment that rice millers call parboiling. Besides
softening the hull, the steam forces nutrients from the bran into the
starchy white grains or endosperm, but it doesn't qualify as parboiling in the timesaving kitchen sense; the rice is still "raw" and may
even take more time to cook than non-parboiled rice.

By the way, in case you've also wondered what "converted" rice is,
it's Uncle Ben's trademark for factory-parboiled rice. "Quick" or
"instant" rice is rice that has been fully cooked and then dried, for
people who are *really* in a hurry.

THE FOODIE'S FICTIONARY:
Parboil—what a golfer does when his opponent makes par

FLOUR POWER

How does bleached flour differ from unbleached
flour? And why does unbleached flour cost more
than bleached flour? They're charging me extra
for not bleaching it?

. . . .

Wheat flour is naturally slightly yellowish because it contains
carotenoid pigments, natural yellow and orange compounds found in
many fruits, vegetables, and grains. (Carrots' famous orange color,
carotene, is the mother of them all.) But most people are less color-
tolerant than you and don't like their flour to be yellow. The major
exception is the semolina flour used in making pasta. Although it
contains even more carotenoid pigment than other wheat flours, it
isn't usually bleached. Pasta that is slightly yellow, with its implica-
tion of eggy richness, is more appealing than if it were dead white.

If given half a chance, though, flour bleaches itself. That is, as it
ages in contact with air, the pigments are oxidized and transformed
into colorless compounds. But aging requires storage time, and time
is money. That's why "unbleached"–meaning naturally self-bleached
during storage—flour costs more.

Flour millers can simulate the effects of aging by adding an oxidizing agent such as potassium bromate (in which case the flour is said
to be bromated), or chlorine dioxide, or benzoyl (BEN-zo-eel) peroxide. The bleaching of flour isn't mere cosmetics. Flour that has been
matured, either by natural aging or by being treated with oxidizing
agents, makes doughs that produce finer-grained, higher-volume
bread and a dough that bakers report as being more elastic during
kneading. That's because oxidation not only removes the yellow color
of flour but removes certain sulfur-containing chemicals (*thiols*) that
interfere with the formation of gluten, the sticky, elastic protein in
dough that traps gas bubbles and gives bread its light texture.

Some people are concerned about the intimidating names and properties of the bleaching chemicals. But after doing their jobs they are gone, having been chemically transformed into harmless substances. Chlorine dioxide is a gas that dissipates, so there is none of it left in the flour. And any excess of benzoyl peroxide would decompose in the heat of an oven.

After reacting with the carotenoids and thiols in the flour, the 50 or 75 parts per million of added potassium bromate turn into potassium bromide, a perfectly harmless salt. For most of the eighty-plus years of bakers' use of potassium bromate, no one was able to detect any residual excess bromate in baked goods. However, chemists today have such sensitive analytical methods—down to billionths of a gram in many cases—that extremely low levels of residual bromate can be detected in baked goods made with bromated flour. Analytical detection instruments are so sensitive these days that they can find traces of almost any given chemical in almost anything, a fact that much of the public doesn't understand. A finding that a certain food "contains toxic XYZ" often generates unfounded fears. But *everything* is toxic in large enough amounts and harmless in small enough amounts.

Nevertheless, because *high* levels of bromate have been found to cause cancers in rats, many consumers fear it, and the American baking industry, in consultation with the FDA, has voluntarily stopped using it. Canada and the United Kingdom have banned the chemical altogether.

Incidentally, the claim that the bleaching of flour destroys its vitamin E is true but empty, because wheat flour contains negligible amounts of vitamin E to begin with.

THE FOODIE'S FICTIONARY: Couscous—a couple of couses

ARISE AND COMBINE

*I have a recipe that calls for self-rising flour, but I
can't find any where I live. Can I make it myself?*

. . . .

Sure. Self-rising flour is flour that has some baking powder and salt
already mixed into it. Most of the bigger supermarkets carry it. But to
make it yourself, just add about 1¼ teaspoons of baking powder and ½
teaspoon of salt to each cup of all-purpose flour or cake flour and mix
well. A gently wielded whisk does the best mixing job.

PASSING THE BUCK

*What kind of wheat is buckwheat? Could I make
bread out of buckwheat flour?*

. . . .

No, for two reasons: buckwheat isn't wheat at all, and even if it
were, its flour couldn't make bread.

Buckwheat groats, known as *kasha* in eastern Europe and
sayraisin in France, are the seeds of the plant *Fagopyrum esculentum*,
which is not related to wheat or any other grassy cereal plant. The
generic word *groats* refers to hulled and cracked grains of any kind,
such as wheat, buckwheat, oats, or barley. When the grain happens to
be corn, *groats* morphs into *grits*.

The name *buckwheat* comes from the German and Dutch for
"beech wheat," because its edible seeds, shaped like tetrahedra
(pyramids with four equal, triangular sides), resemble beechnuts.
The seeds can be cracked down into groats or ground to flour and
added to wheat flour for making buckwheat pancakes. But buckwheat
flour isn't good for breadmaking because when wet it forms very little

gluten, the elastic protein that traps gas bubbles and gives bread its open structure and chewiness. Wet buckwheat flour is just barely sticky enough for the Japanese to make *soba* noodles out of it.

> **THE FOODIE'S FICTIONARY:**
>
> Gluten—a person who greedily eats too much

THE PASTA ROSTER

Is there any reason for using one shape of pasta rather than another, such as using flat linguine rather than round spaghetti? I would think that the shape with the greatest surface-to-volume ratio would absorb the most sauce and be most flavorful. So why do people use all of those other shapes?

. . . .

Surface-to-volume ratio? I'll bet you're an engineer.

For one thing, the almost limitless variety of pasta shapes provides both fun for the eye and differing sensations in the mouth. But there are also real differences in their compatibility with different sauces.

It's not a matter of the pasta absorbing sauce through its surface; pasta isn't that absorbent and sauces aren't that liquid. But some sauces adhere better than others and will stick to the pasta surface no matter what its shape. And, of course, the more surface area there is, the more sauce can stick.

Ultimately, however, it's a matter of how well the heap of pasta on the plate envelops and incorporates the sauce and how well the pasta will retain the sauce when it's twirled on a fork or, in the case of a small, compact shape, when it's picked up on a spoon. The overall result is dictated by both stickiness and mechanics.

Most sauces are chunky to some degree, and the spaces that the chunks must nestle into—the empty spaces within the pasta tangle—are very different for long pasta such as spaghetti and linguine, for tube pasta such as penne and rigatoni, and for special shapes such as *conchiglie* (seashells) and *farfalle* (bow ties). Obviously, a pile of fat spaghetti will have more empty spaces than a pile of thin spaghetti, which can nestle together more compactly.

One should therefore try to match the sauce to the pasta shape.

Fusilli (springs), for example, hold on to chunky sauces well; the larger tubes, such as rigatoni, are good with meat sauces; fettuccine goes well with sticky sauces that coat its flat, ribbon-like surface, such as in fettuccine Alfredo. Spaghetti is probably the most versatile shape, but when it is extra-thin, as in angel hair or *capellini*, it's best with thin, liquidy sauces that distribute themselves throughout the heap by capillary action. *Capellini* Alfredo would sit in the plate like a ball of mud.

Table 5 on the following page lists the pasta-and-sauce pairings recommended by the Barilla Alimentare S.p.A. pasta company of Parma, Italy, for a few of the shapes it distributes in the United States. For pictures of these shapes, along with everything else you could possibly want to know about pasta manufacture and technology, the website www.professionalpasta.it lists 822 shapes from *abissini* to *zituane*. Many of these, however, are aliases used in different parts of Italy.

But hey, the pasta police are greatly understaffed and underfunded, so you can probably get away with any cockamamie combination of shape and sauce that you enjoy.

Mangia!

THE FOODIE'S FICTIONARY:
Al dente—an Italian fender bender

Table 5. Some pasta shapes and their recommended sauces

PASTA SHAPE	PERFECT SAUCE MATCHES
Capellini/Angel Hair	Butter and cheese, butter with fresh aromatic herbs, fish sauce
Elbows	Salads, cheese (macaroni and cheese), oil-based sauces, butter, tomatoes, or vegetables
Fettuccine	White sauces, sauces combined with meat, vegetables, or cream and cheese
Linguine	Pesto, tomato pieces, oil-based sauces, fish sauces
Orzo	Soups, minestrone, or cream sauce with vegetables
Rigatoni	Sauces with meat, vegetables, sausage, or baked pasta molds
Rotini	Pasta salads, light tomato sauces, cream sauces, carbonara (egg and bacon)
Spaghetti	Tomato sauce with meatballs, tomato pieces, oil-based sauces, fish sauces
Ziti	Sauces with fresh tomatoes and vegetables, meat and fish sauces, spicy sauces

THE FOODIE'S FICTIONARY: Rigoletto—a type of pasta

PLEASE DON'T EAT THE MATTRESS

If I make a smoothie by blending fruit with
milk, yogurt, or whatever, are the positive
effects of the fiber eliminated by processing
the fruit in a blender?

. . . .

No. No matter how thoroughly pureed it is, the fiber is still effective.

In the dietary context, the word *fiber* is misleading because it conjures up images of eating coconut husks and mattress stuffing. But *dietary fiber* doesn't refer to a physical texture. It's a catchall term for the components of vegetable foods that humans don't have the enzymes for digesting, and that therefore have no energy value and pass through our digestive tracts unchanged (which is their major virtue). We used to call it bulk or roughage. Although it has no chemical or nutritive value, it is essential for physically moving everything we eat through the processing plant we call the alimentary canal.

Dietary fiber, found in fruits, vegetables, and grains but not in animal products, has been found to decrease the risk of certain disorders such as colon cancer, although that finding has been challenged. Nevertheless, fiber is one of the main reasons that eating fruits and vegetables is so important to health.

There are both water-soluble and water-insoluble fiber substances, and nutritionists recommend eating lots of both kinds. The soluble ones are mostly pectins and gums, found in fruits; they're what cause fruit jellies to gel. Tart apples, crab apples, sour plums, Concord grapes, quinces, gooseberries, red currants, and cranberries are especially high in pectin. The most common insoluble fibers are cellulose and lignin, the binder between the cellulose fibers that make up the structural framework of plants' cell walls.

Some termites can digest and utilize the energy inherent in cellulose and lignin, but we humans can't. On the other hand, termites are lousy at Scrabble.

THE FOODIE'S FICTIONARY:
Roughage—the opposite of smoothage

FIBER OPTIONS

I was reading the Nutrition Facts chart on my box of cereal. I thought that, by definition, fiber is indigestible and therefore has no calories. But this box shows fiber as carbohydrates. Can you sort this out?

. . . .

Dietary fiber is indeed completely or almost completely indigestible. In fact, as you point out, that's how it is defined: those parts of our foods that provide us with no vitamins, minerals, or even calories.

Chemically, the fiber compounds in plants are complex carbohydrates. They are therefore included in the total amounts of carbohydrates listed on the labels. Sometimes the chart will break the dietary fiber down into soluble and insoluble fiber, but they're both noncaloric anyway. The "other carbohydrates" listed are sugars, sugar alcohols (see p. 233), and—well, other carbohydrates, mostly starches. All the numbers should add up to the number of grams of "Total Carbohydrates."

The number of carbohydrate *calories*, however, comes only from the digestible carbohydrates: from the starches and sugars that you would expect. If you subtract the number of grams of fiber from the number of grams of total carbohydrates, you'll have the approximate number of grams of nutritional carbohydrates, which, at 4 calories per gram, should equal the number of carbohydrate calories in the chart.

I said "approximate" because there may be other carbohydrates hiding somewhere off the Nutrition Facts charts of many foods—the sugar alcohols, for example, which include glycerol, mannitol, sorbitol, inositol, and xylitol (in fact, anything in the ingredient list ending in -ol). They are present in relatively small amounts as sweeteners, but they are metabolized less completely than sugars and therefore contribute fewer calories.

THE GRITTY DETAILS

Can you straighten out for me all the corn products on the shelves of my supermarket? There are cornmeals labeled yellow or white, coarse or fine, and stone-ground or steel-cut, not to mention cornstarch or the hominy and grits that they like in the South. Which ones do I use for cornbread, for muffins, or for polenta—or does it matter?

. . . .

Yes, it matters, but mostly in terms of texture, not substance.

They're all made from that incredibly versatile and internationally esteemed New World grain called corn in the United States and maize—from the Caribbean Taíno Indian word *mahiz*—almost everywhere else.

A kernel of corn is a seed with essentially three parts. The tough, outer hull (the *pericarp*) is made mostly of indigestible cellulose. A body of starchy material (the *endosperm*) nourishes the seed when it sprouts (*germinates*). The life-transmitting embryo (the *germ*) in the middle of the seed is the part that will grow into a new plant when conditions are right for germination. It contains the seed's main energy supply in the form of oil.

Corn kernels can be processed in dozens of ways to produce an astounding variety of products. One main distinction hinges upon which parts of the kernels are retained. The starchy endosperm is always used, but the outer hull and/or the germ may or may not be removed. What is called cornstarch in the United States and corn flour in the United Kingdom is the dried and finely powdered endosperm alone.

Another main distinction among cornmeal products is the texture, that is, how coarsely or finely the dried kernels have been ground. But the names can be perplexing:

Flour, of course, is fine, not coarse,
>*While **meal** is much more coarse, of course.*
The meal called "Medium," of course,
>*Is coarse, but not as coarse as "Coarse."*
But if the label calls it "Fine,"
>*It's flour, not meal, I would opine.*

Historically, of course (*Editor to author: NOW CUT THAT OUT!*), dried corn kernels were pulverized between millstones in a waterwheel-powered mill down by the old mill stream. Stone-ground cornmeal, sometimes nostalgically but nonsensically called water-ground cornmeal, is available in many "health-food" stores. It is slightly more nutritious and flavorful than other cornmeals because it retains some of the hull or bran and some of the oil-containing germ. But because of the oil, it is perishable and cannot be stored at room temperature for very long without turning rancid. Refrigerated, it will keep for a couple of months.

Most modern cornmeal is produced by crushing the dried kernels between huge steel rollers, making grains that are more sharply shaped than in the stone-ground meals. The rolled product, referred to as steel-cut, contains only the starchy endosperm with very little hull or germ, and it therefore has a very long shelf life when kept in a cool, sealed container. If your supermarket's cornmeal isn't labeled stone-ground or water-ground, it's steel-cut. (To split a hair, steel-cut cornmeal isn't cut; it's steel-crushed.)

After the kernels' hulls and germs are removed either mechanically or chemically with lime or lye, the endosperm can be washed and dried, at which time it is known as hominy. Then it may be ground or crushed into rather coarse particles to form hominy grits. After their water is restored by boiling, hominy grits can be found on virtually every breakfast plate below the Mason-Dixon Line.

Which product to use for what? Southerners insist that their traditional cornbread be made from stone-ground white cornmeal, either coarse or medium depending on individual preference. Yankees aren't so fussy, and even go so far as to combine the cornmeal with wheat flour and sugar to make a more breadlike bread, because cornmeal doesn't contain the gluten that gives bread its elastic texture.

Polenta is generally made with yellow cornmeal of either coarse or fine grind, because the boiled cornmeal softens into a homogeneous mass anyway. And need I point out that yellow cornmeal is made from yellow corn and white cornmeal is made from white corn? (Apologies.)

THE FOODIE'S FICTIONARY: Hominy—an unknown number, as in "Hominy cooks does it take to spoil the broth?"

Polenta Two Ways

Some home cooks shy away from making polenta because the traditional Italian method (adding cornmeal to boiling water over direct heat with continual stirring) takes too much of the cook's attention. Your Italian grandmother may be shocked, but there are other ways to make polenta that are easier on the cook. You can make it in a double boiler or in the oven. When the polenta is ready, it will be thick and smooth, with no sign of grittiness.

DOUBLE-BOILER POLENTA:

4 cups water

1 teaspoon salt

1 cup yellow cornmeal, coarse or fine

Butter to taste

1. Bring 2½ cups of the water to a boil in the top part of a double boiler over direct heat. Add the salt.
2. In a medium bowl, mix the cornmeal with the remaining 1½ cups water. Add the mixture to the boiling water and stir well. Reduce the heat to medium and cook, stirring constantly, until the mixture boils.
3. Place the cornmeal mixture over boiling water in the bottom part of the double boiler. Cover and cook, stirring occasionally, for about 45 minutes, or until smooth and thick. Stir in butter to taste.

MAKES ABOUT 4 CUPS, OR 4 SERVINGS

BAKED POLENTA:

2 tablespoons olive oil

2 cups yellow cornmeal

$6^1/_2$ cups water

$1^1/_2$ teaspoons salt

1. Preheat the oven to 400°F. Grease a 9-by-13-inch baking pan.
2. In a large bowl, mix together the olive oil, cornmeal, water, and salt.

3. Transfer the mixture to the baking pan. Carefully place the pan in the oven. (It will want to slosh over.)

4. Bake uncovered for 45 minutes. With a fork or a wooden spoon, stir the polenta until evenly combined and smooth. Bake for 5 minutes longer, or until slightly puffy.

MAKES ABOUT 8 CUPS, OR 8 SERVINGS

VARIATIONS ON THE THEME

Polenta with Gorgonzola: Spoon soft, cooked polenta into a warmed serving dish. Make a well in the center and fill it with, say, 3 tablespoons unsalted butter and 3 ounces crumbled Gorgonzola cheese. Amounts will vary according to the amount of polenta you have made. Spoon some of the butter and cheese onto each serving of polenta.

Broiled Polenta Slices: Spoon soft, cooked polenta into a greased 9-inch square pan. Spread to make a layer about ½ inch thick. Chill. Turn the polenta out of the pan onto a work surface, and cut into squares or rectangles. Place the pieces on a greased cookie sheet. Brush with melted butter and broil, turning once, until browned and crisp on both sides.

Leftover Polenta: Spoon soft, cooked polenta into a greased loaf pan. Smooth the surface with a wooden spoon, cover with plastic wrap, and refrigerate. Cold polenta, sometimes called mush, is delicious for breakfast. Cut into slices, fry in butter or bacon fat, and top with maple syrup.

TORTILLA TIPS

*My local market sells two types of Mexican
tortillas: flour and corn. I assume that the flour
tortillas are made out of regular wheat flour. But
the corn tortillas are made out of masa harina,
which, I'm told, is a kind of flour made from
corn. Can you tell me how it's made? And why is
lime listed among the ingredients?*

. . . .

You're correct about the flour tortillas, which should rightly be called wheat flour tortillas, because there are many other kinds of flour made from a wide variety of grains, including barley, rye, and rice. But you'll rarely find flour tortillas south of the border. In Mexico tortillas are made from corn. Flour tortillas are a Tex-Mex invention.

The word *flour* evolved from *flower*, as used metaphorically to mean the best part of something, such as the flower of a plant or, in culinary use, the best part of a cereal grain. The supposedly inferior parts, the chaff and bran of the wheat berry and the hull of the corn kernel, have presumably been disposed of. To complicate matters, however, the literal translation of the Spanish *masa harina* is "flour dough," with no specification of the kind of flour. On corn tortillas you may also see the more explicit *harina de maíz*, which distinguishes corn flour from *harina de trigo*, or wheat flour.

Spanish class dismissed.

The cellulose hulls of corn kernels can be loosened and the germs released by being soaked in water containing an alkali. Acids can be powerful chemicals, but so can alkalis. One exceedingly strong alkali is sodium hydroxide ($NaOH$), also known as caustic soda or lye. It's so powerful that we use it to unclog drains—it actually dissolves hair and grease. (It turns the grease into soap, but that's in Chemistry 102.)

In Mexico, the corn kernels are treated with lime, which is much milder than lye but still strong enough to open the cellulose husks of the corn kernels and uncover the starchy endosperm. Lime has been used for this purpose for thousands of years in Mexico and Central America. The husked kernels are then washed, dried, and ground or pounded into *masa* (dough).

Small balls of the dough are flattened into very thin, almost perfect disks by the astoundingly dexterous hands of Mexican women, then baked on a hot griddle for 30 to 60 seconds on each side, and distributed still warm and fresh to lucky local Mexicans, who have never had to deal with the factory-produced, machine-rolled-and-stamped-out, imitations that we gringos must often settle for. The main problem with these commercial pretenders is that a fresh corn tortilla should contain about 40 percent moisture, which is almost impossible to maintain during the packaging, freezing, and shipping of the mechanized version.

Sidebar Science: *Lime in the limelight*

LIMESTONE, seashells, coral, chalk, marble, eggshells, pearls, stalactites, and stalagmites all consist mainly of a remarkably versatile and plentiful chemical compound called calcium carbonate ($CaCO_3$). It constitutes about 7 percent of our planet's crust, the 20-mile-or-so-thick top layer. When heated to 1520 to 1650°F (825 to 900°C), calcium carbonate decomposes into carbon dioxide gas (CO_2) and calcium oxide or lime (CaO). Lime has been used for centuries to make mortar, glass, and many other useful materials.

When lime is added to water, it forms calcium hydroxide, $Ca(OH)_2$, also known as limewater or slaked lime. It is quite alkaline, but not as much so as lye.

The Aztecs used an even more easily obtained alkaline material to treat their corn: wood ashes. All plant materials, including wood, contain potassium (it's the "potash" in fertilizers), and when they are burned, their ashes are rich in the alkaline chemical potassium carbonate.

The Aztecs didn't know all that, because Chemistry 101 wasn't scheduled to be taught for another five hundred years. We can only guess at why they started boiling their corn in water containing wood ashes.

HELLO, SUGAR!

I'm amazed at how many prepared foods list
sugar among their ingredients. Do the
manufacturers think the only way to make
something taste good is to make it sweet?

. . . .

The fact that everybody likes sugar certainly has a lot to do with its presence in so many processed foods. Some breakfast cereals, for example, will surprise you with their content of sugar, if you figure it out. To check your cereals (or other manufactured foods) for sugar content, look at the Nurtrition Facts table and divide the number of grams of sugars per serving by the number of grams of cereal (or other manufactured food) per serving and multiply by 100. You'll find, for example, that Kellogg's Raisin Bran is 30 percent sugar by weight and Multi-Bran Chex is 21 percent sugar.

Note that the Nutrition Facts table lists "sugars," in the plural. That means not only the sucrose from sugar cane (listed as "sugar" among the ingredients) but also sugars present naturally in the food, such as the lactose in milk, the fructose in fruit (such as the raisins in Raisin Bran), and the glucose, maltose, and fructose in any corn sweeteners that may be present. So in addition to sugar (sucrose), look for such ingredients as fructose, maltose, lactose, honey, corn syrup, high-fructose corn syrup, molasses, and fruit-juice concentrate. And note that "evaporated cane juice" is a sneaky euphemism used by "health-food" purveyors to avoid the dreaded s-word on their labels. Evaporated sugar-cane juice is, of course, nothing but sugar.

Then there are the sugar alcohols (*polyols*), which chemically speaking are not sugars, although they taste sweet. Glycerol (glycerin) is one. Their molecules have the characteristics of both sugars and alcohols. They contribute only about one-half to two-thirds as many calories as sugar, because they are converted only very slowly into glucose and may escape from the southern end of the alimentary canal before being fully metabolized. As a result, they can have a slight laxative effect if consumed in excessive quantities.

Because sugar alcohols don't cause tooth decay or a sudden increase in blood sugar, they are used mainly in sugar-free candies and chewing gums. You'll see them listed separately by name in the ingredient lists: sorbitol, xylitol, lactitol, mannitol, or maltitol. (Look for the suffix -itol.)

The sweet leaf of a South American shrub called stevia has been used for centuries by South Americans to sweeten their yerba maté. But the United States, Canada, and the European Union will not permit it to be added to foods, because although it is surely "natural," its safety has not been proved. (Ironically, however, it may be sold in "health-food" stores as a nutritional supplement.) While South America clearly hasn't been depopulated by stevia-sweetened drinks, the health authorities' reasoning goes that if stevia were permitted as a food additive in the United States and Canada, North Americans, addicted as they are to sweet soft drinks, might consume enormous quantities of it. And the effects of quaffing huge Slurpees and Big Gulps full of stevia have not been investigated.

Another sweetener used to some extent in the Middle Ages, but most enthusiastically by the Romans, was sugar of lead, a sweet-tasting but highly poisonous chemical known to chemists as lead acetate. The Romans used lead-lined cooking vessels to boil down crushed grapes and old wine that had partially soured. Soured (oxidized) wine contains acetic acid, and any freshman chemistry student will tell you that acetic acid plus lead metal will make lead acetate. All lead compounds are poisonous, but lead acetate is one of the few that are soluble in water—and wine. Thus, not only could over-the-hill wine be made sweet again, but sugar of lead could be produced for sweetening other beverages and foods. The oldest existing cookbook, De Re Coquinaria (On Cooking) by the first-century Roman gourmet Marcus Gavius Apicius, contains scores of recipes that include sugar of lead among the ingredients.

Lead poisoning is cumulative and causes a variety of maladies from gout to sterility and insanity. It was primarily the Roman patricians who could avail themselves of lead-sweetened wines and foods, and as a result they were the prime victims. For no lack of trying (he was quite a man with the ladies), Julius Caesar was able to sire only one (illegitimate) child. His successor, Caesar Augustus, was reportedly completely sterile, whether with spouse or concubine.

Today, good old-fashioned sugar—pure sucrose, whether from sugar cane or sugar beets—plays many roles in foods besides making them sweet. It makes breads, cookies, and other doughs more moist and tender; it stabilizes foams such as beaten egg whites; it acts as a carrier of other flavors, and it caramelizes when heated, making foods brown and giving them that unique sweet-sour-bitter caramel flavor. And it preserves foods—notably, when used in jams and other fruit preserves.

According to W. C. Fields, anyone who hates dogs and children can't be all bad. Sugar's not all bad either.

THE FOODIE'S FICTIONARY:
Molasses—the plural of molass

HI, HONEY!

*So many health foodies tout honey as the most
natural, healthful, and nutritious of all
sweeteners, certainly when compared with refined
sugar. But I understand that babies must not eat
it. Kind of contradictory, wouldn't you say?*

. . . .

I don't know what "most natural" means, unless somebody can give
me a good reason why sugar cane and sugar beets are somehow less
natural than honey. Perhaps because they are not produced by hairy
insects?

But chemically, there is quite a difference. Sugar cane and sugar
beets are loaded with sucrose, whereas honey's sugars are primarily
fructose (39 percent), glucose, (31 percent), and maltose (7 percent),
with only 1.5 percent sucrose. (See Table 4 on p. 206.) In addition,
4 percent of honey consists of other carbohydrates and small amounts
of minerals, vitamins, and enzymes. Most of the rest (17 percent) is
water, making honey a supersaturated solution of sugars. That is,
there is more sugar dissolved in the water than the water should ordinarily hold. That's why the excess sugar will "undissolve" slowly and
fall out as crystals (the honey becomes *granulated*) when stored for
long periods of time. It's mainly the glucose that initiates the crystallization process.

Actually, I love the crunchiness of granulated honey. Storing it
between 50 and 70°F (10 and 21°C) will hasten crystallization; higher
and lower temperatures discourage it. Take your choice.

Among its enzymes, honey contains *invertase*, which converts
sucrose to a mixture of glucose and fructose, or *invert sugar*. (See "A
nano-course on carbohydrates," p. 203.)

Another enzyme in honey is *amylase*, which breaks starch down
into smaller units. Honey also contains small amounts of all the B

vitamins and vitamin C, plus the minerals potassium, calcium, phosphorus, sodium, and traces of others.

The healthful reputation of honey is undoubtedly attributable to these minor constituents plus its content of flavonoid antioxidants. Medical history has credited honey with a variety of therapeutic and antibacterial qualities. Moreover, honey is much more interesting than ordinary sugar because it has an intriguing variety of flavors, depending on which local nectar bars the bees are in the habit of frequenting.

Unfortunately, as an anaerobic (oxygen-free) environment, honey is a good breeding ground for *Clostridium botulinum*, the bacterium that manufactures botulin toxin, a deadly poison. Bees may pick up *C. botulinum* spores while foraging (they are found in soil) and incorporate them into their honey. Human adults, with their fully developed immune systems and intestinal bacteria that destroy such spores, can handle a reasonable number of them, but babies under one year of age can't and may contract infantile botulism. It's a rare occurrence, but why take the chance? Feeding honey to your little Honey is just not worth it. And as one source put it, chances are your baby is already sweet enough.

THE FOODIE'S FICTIONARY:
Botulism—a morbid preoccupation with robots

Chapter Six

From Sea to
Shining Sea

. . . .

WITH A FEW minor exceptions, there are only two environments in which life can thrive on our planet: in air and in water. We *Homo sapiens* are one of millions of plant and animal species that thrive in our sea of air, the atmosphere, and there may be a similar or even greater number of still undiscovered species that thrive in the seas of water. And yet, few air-living species can live without water, and few water-living species (that we know of) can live without air, especially its oxygen and carbon dioxide.

But in the context of human food, that's where the symmetry ends. As an air-living species, we have exploited our environment, first by simply collecting the plants and animals that Nature provided, and later by growing our own preferred plants and breeding our own preferred animals. In the seas, however, we are still in the hunter-gatherer stage, venturing out onto the ocean's surface to collect what we can find. Only very recently have we begun to raise a few of our preferred species by aquaculture.

Among our preferred aquatic food species are many dozens of vertebrate fish and a variety of invertebrates, including mollusks (clams, oysters, mussels, scallops, squid, octopus) and crustaceans (lobsters, crabs, shrimp, crayfish).

This chapter is, in effect, a fishing expedition, in which we can hook or net and examine only a very small sampling of our favorite finfish, mollusks, and crustaceans.

THE FOODIE'S FICTIONARY:

Crappie—a species of sunfish, especially when not fresh

COLOR ME SALMON

As a chef with an avid interest in nutrition, I've been wondering: In light of all the controversy surrounding the dyes used in the feed of farm-raised salmon to give them their pink hues, has anyone thought about using lycopene, the red phytochemical in tomatoes with alleged antioxidant benefits, instead?

. . . .

I must duck your question for two reasons: (1) I don't know the answer, and (2) you're not going to drag me into the raging battle among salmon farmers, wild-salmon fishermen, and environmentalists. However, to muddle a few metaphors, I will walk a tightrope through the minefield and drop what pearls I can.

From decades-long experience, we consumers have expected our salmon to be a nice, orange-pink color. The muscle tissue of wild salmon ranges from deep red in the sockeye to pale pink in Chinook or king salmon. The colors come from the fish's diet of tiny shrimp-like crustaceans called krill that contain a pink carotenoid compound called *astaxanthin*. Wild (not lawn-dwelling) flamingoes are pink for the same reason.

Carotenoids are the chemical pigments largely responsible for the variety of beautiful colors in nature, both in plants and, via feeding, in many animals as well. There are over six hundred known carotenoids in flowers, fruits, vegetables, and birds.

Salmon raised in aquaculture pens do not have much access to the carotenoid pigments in krill, and are fed an artificial diet containing an added colorant: either astaxanthin itself or another FDA-approved carotenoid, canthaxanthin. (The latter, oddly enough, is also sold as a human skin-tanning drug.) Astaxanthin produces a somewhat redder hue (in salmon) than canthaxanthin, and salmon farmers can actually choose the shade they want in their fish by selecting their feed mixture from a color wheel.

On April 23, 2003, a Seattle law firm filed three class-action suits against the supermarket chains Kroger, Safeway, and Albertson's, claiming that all consumers who purchased farm-raised salmon over the preceding four years—not to mention the lawyers themselves—should be showered with literally millions of dollars because the stores failed to disclose the shocking fact that their salmon had been artificially colored. The families of those consumers who, we must presume, died of humiliation upon learning that they had eaten colored salmon certainly deserve to be compensated most generously, don't you think? Fortunately, the court didn't think so, and the suit was thrown out.

(Insert your favorite lawyer joke here.)

Less frivolous concerns about salmon farming are based upon such issues as whether the wild salmon population is endangered; whether fugitive farm fish will interbreed with wild stock, to the detriment of genetic diversity; whether crowded, net-caged salmon pollute their environment with parasites and disease; and whether their pens are contaminated with PCB's (*polychlorinated biphenyls*), any of about two hundred probably carcinogenic synthetic industrial chemicals that have not been manufactured since 1997 but that still show up in the environment.

And by the way, your suggestion of feeding salmon lycopene

instead of astaxanthin is probably impractical unless we could get salmon to eat tomatoes, in which lycopene is the predominant pigment. Might be worth a try.

Blistered Wild Salmon

When leading chefs cook wild salmon, they like to keep it simple. For best results, they caution, don't overwhelm the fish with exotic sauces and ingredients. Just season it and cook it until the center is barely opaque. This oven method is a favorite at our house. Bob loves the crisp skin and keeps reminding me that it contains all those healthful omega-3 fatty acids.

- 2 tablespoons olive oil
- 4 wild king salmon fillets, skin on, 6 to 8 ounces each
-    Salt and freshly ground pepper

1. Preheat the oven to 275°F.
2. Heat the olive oil in a large, ovenproof nonstick sauté pan. Add the fillets, skin side down. When the skin blisters, after about 1 minute, place the pan in the oven and roast for 8 to 12 minutes for medium-rare.
3. Remove the pan from the oven and place it over high heat for about 2 minutes, or until the skin crisps. Think undercooked and it will be perfect. Serve the salmon skin side up.

MAKES 4 SERVINGS

THE FOODIE'S FICTIONARY:
Poached salmon—salmon stolen from a fish farm

A TUNA TONER

I love sushi, especially the yellowfin nigiri. The raw tuna sometimes has different colors, however, ranging from pink to dark red. I never thought much about it, but I just saw a story in the newspaper saying that raw tuna is being treated with carbon monoxide to give it a bright red color, even if it isn't fresh. Isn't carbon monoxide lethal?

. . . .

Yes it is, under the right—that is, the wrong—circumstances. But not in the case of monoxide-treated tuna.

First, for the uninitiated, yellowfin tuna, which may be listed on the menu as *maguro*, the generic Japanese word for tuna, is not to be confused with yellowtail, a kind of amberjack, or with *toro*, the prized fatty belly of the bluefin tuna. *Nigiri* sushi is a filet of the raw fish on a pillow of vinegared rice.

Every year in the United States, several thousand people are treated in hospital emergency rooms for carbon monoxide poisoning. Some two hundred per year die from carbon monoxide given off by improperly vented gas-burning appliances such as furnaces, ranges, water heaters, and room heaters, while many others are killed by automobile engines running in enclosed spaces.

Carbon monoxide gas is particularly toxic because it goes from the lungs into the bloodstream, where it replaces the oxygen in the blood's oxyhemoglobin, destroying its ability to deliver oxygen to the body's cells. And the organs most likely to crash from oxygen starvation are the heart and brain.

All devices that burn carbon-based fuels, including gasoline-burning automobiles, gas-burning furnaces, kerosene-burning heaters, and even charcoal-burning hibachis, emit carbon monoxide because their fuels don't burn completely; the combustion process is inevitably inefficient. Instead of burning all the way to carbon dioxide, CO_2 (two oxygen atoms for every carbon atom), some of the carbon atoms in the fuel can't find that second oxygen atom and end up as carbon monoxide, CO. That's why these devices should never be operated in an enclosed space: the inevitable CO can build up to a lethal concentration.

Eating raw tuna that has been exposed to carbon monoxide gas is another matter entirely. In this case you're not breathing the gas, and for that matter you're not even eating it. Gases, of course, are ephemeral, and the carbon monoxide doesn't hang around on the fish after it has done its job of brightening its color. The FDA has declared carbon-monoxide-treated tuna to be GRAS—generally regarded as safe—because residual carbon monoxide on the fish is virtually absent.

But why should a food processor do such an outlandish thing as exposing fish to a poisonous gas? Well, follow the money. The red color of freshly cut tuna can change within a few days to an unappetizing brown. Consumers don't like brown fish and are willing to pay more for "fresher-looking" red. Hence, the cosmetic application of carbon monoxide "rouge."

Tuna flesh, like the flesh of many land animals, contains myoglobin, a pigmented protein that stores oxygen in the muscle tissue. Myoglobin changes color, however, depending among other things on how much oxygen is available to it. The dark, purplish-red color of freshly cut tuna is due to *deoxymyoglobin*, which in air changes first to bright red *oxymyoglobin* and then to brown *metmyoglobin*. Tuna purveyors must therefore rush their tuna from the boat to the sushi bar while it is still in the red *oxymyoglobin* stage.

Carbon monoxide thwarts these color changes by replacing the oxygen in the *oxymyoglobin* molecules (as it does in our blood's oxyhemoglobin molecules), converting them into a very stable complex: the watermelon-red *carboxymyoglobin*. The *oxymyoglobin* is thus derailed from being oxidized to brown *metmyoglobin*.

Tuna cosmetologists can of course buy their carbon monoxide gas in steel tanks, like many other gases. But there's a cheaper way to get it: by burning wood. Because of the incomplete combustion process described above, wood smoke contains carbon monoxide. The tiny particles that make smoke smoky can be filtered out along with the tarry chemicals that give smoke its flavor, leaving a mixture of gases— carbon dioxide, carbon monoxide, nitrogen, oxygen, and methane— called filtered smoke or tasteless smoke. It can be used instead of pure carbon monoxide to brighten the fish's color. The justification is made that tasteless smoke can be no more harmful than "whole smoke," traditionally used to make smoked fish and other meats. According to the FDA, however, foods treated with filtered smoke may not be labeled "smoked," because the expected smoked flavor isn't there.

The irony in all this is that the color of untreated tuna is *not* an indicator of its wholesomeness. Myoglobin's color changes take place long before the fish has begun to deteriorate. The association of bright color with freshness is all in the consumer's mind.

So is there anything wrong with carbon-monoxide-treated tuna? Not because of any presumed health hazard. But there will always be a few rascals who try to conceal over-the-hill fish by touching up its color, and that is an actionable offense according to the FDA. Moreover, research by the Food Science and Human Nutrition Department of the University of Florida has shown that dangerous time-induced spoilage can continue in monoxide-treated fish even though the color remains bright, perhaps luring unsuspecting diners to disaster like a gussied-up siren.

Because of the possibility of abuse by tuna suppliers, several countries prohibit carbon-monoxide-treated fish. Sushi-conscious Japan has outlawed it since 1997, while the European Union has begun to enforce its ban only since early 2004.

Your best resource as a consumer is, as usual, your confidence in your source. You shouldn't eat raw fish in any but the most trustworthy sushi establishments anyway, for reasons unrelated to carbon monoxide. If a given restaurant would never sell contaminated or spoiled fish under other circumstances, it would certainly never sell contaminated or spoiled fish that has been cosmetically enhanced. Fresh tuna has a clean flavor, relatively firm texture, and of course, no odor, no matter what its color. So if in doubt, just shut your eyes and let your mouth and nose be your guides.

And remember that yellowfin tuna varies in color from pink in smaller fish to deeper red in larger fish, so once again the color itself is no indication of freshness.

If your fish is a bright, unnatural-looking watermelon red, it has probably been treated with carbon monoxide or filtered smoke. But there is no known health hazard if the fish itself is fresh and clean.

CHEAPSKATE NO MORE

All my life, I've heard rumors that some scallops sold in fish markets aren't scallops at all, but have been punched out of skate wings or other kinds of fish. Any truth to that?

. . . .

I can't say that it's never been done, but I doubt that it has been done very often. And surely few of us would continue to patronize a fishmonger or restaurateur who had been found to try such a trick. At one time, skate was a low-priced fish caught accidentally (in the "by-catch") by fishermen in pursuit of more lucrative quarry. But no more. Skate isn't as cheap as it used to be, and the crime wouldn't pay as well as it used to.

An even better reason to doubt this urban legend is the fact that running through the middle of a skate wing is a thin sheet of plastic-like cartilage. A "scallop" with a layer of plastic in the middle wouldn't be very convincing. It's true that if the skate is big enough (the common skate can run up to 200 pounds), it can be filleted into two slabs, one above and one below the sheet of cartilage, and convincingly thick "scallops" could be punched out of each. But there are easier ways to make a dishonest buck.

(If you ever decide to go into scallop counterfeiting, beware of the tiny, almost microscopic barbs on the skate's skin. They don't sting, but they prickle annoyingly. And don't ask me how I know.)

Known as *raie* in France, the skate is indeed a kind of ray, a term that covers several families of flat, bottom-dwelling fish that, like sharks, have cartilage instead of bones. Rays (family Rajidae) range from the most-often-eaten European skate (*Raja batis*) to stingrays with poisonous tails and giant manta rays that can weigh up to 3,000 pounds. Rays' bodies are flattened out into ribbed, fanlike "wings" that undulate gracefully for locomotion. They are all edible, but some are not exactly gourmet fare.

Even if cookie-cutter cylinders of skate wing were to be passed off as scallops, they wouldn't fool anyone who has ever eaten skate, sometimes sold as raja fish. The flavors and meat colors are similar, but the texture is all wrong. The skate's toothsome, long-stranded texture is more like that of crabmeat than scallop. Be suspicious of any scallop that seems to come apart in strands or layers.

And by the way, those little hollow, rectangular, leathery black "mermaid's purses" that you see washed up on beaches or tangled in seaweed are the egg cases of skates, originally containing two large eggs and abandoned after the young 'uns have hatched.

THE FOODIE'S FICTIONARY:

Crab Louie—the husband of Nag Maggie

Sidebar Science: *Iced skates*

WITH SO much wing surface area exposed to the sea, rays would be at risk of having water extracted from their tissues into the saltier seawater by osmosis. As a defense against this potential dehydration, the rays' body fluids contain a large concentration of a highly soluble, nitrogen-containing chemical called urea, $CO(NH_2)_2$. (Yes, it was first discovered in urine, but it is made synthetically.) Urea breaks down into carbon dioxide and ammonia, so rays, even the freshest ones, tend to smell of ammonia, normally an indication of spoilage in other fish. The ammonia smell can be expunged by soaking the fish in any acid, such as lemon juice or vinegar, or by keeping it refrigerated—or better yet, on ice—until all the urea is gone.

EGGS, DRY-CLEANED AND PRESSED

My aunt came back from Sicily and brought me
some bottarga. I know it's bottarga because it says
so in big letters on the package, but the rest is in
Italian. (I didn't want to sound ungrateful by
asking, "What am I supposed to do with this?")
I know it's some kind of fish eggs, but it's
almost as hard as a rock. What is it,
and what can I do with it?

. . . .

I could tell you it's rockfish roe, but I won't.

Bottarga is dried, salted roe from either the Mediterranean tuna (*tonno* in Italian) or the gray mullet (*mugine*). *Bottarga di tonno* (also known as *uovo di tonno*, or tuna eggs) and *bottarga di mugine* are local specialties of Sicily and Sardinia, Italy's two large Mediterranean islands, and are valued as delicacies in the rest of Italy.

The roe sac is removed as soon as the female fish is caught. It is then washed; salted; pressed, traditionally between wooden planks or marble slabs; and dried, traditionally in the sun, for one or two months. It comes out looking like dark amber wooden boards, firm enough to be grated like Parmesan cheese. The salt helps the drying process by extracting water from the crushed eggs, which glue themselves together because of their albumen and fat.

Tuna bottarga has a bright, sharp salty flavor, whereas the mullet version is somewhat milder. The best thing to do with either is the simplest: make Sardinia's *spaghetti alla bottarga*. To a plate of cooked spaghetti, add extra-virgin olive oil, chopped garlic, parsley, and red pepper flakes. Toss, and grate some bottarga over the top before serving. Remember that bottarga is a condiment, quite salty and fishy, and a little goes a long way.

THE FOODIE'S FICTIONARY:
Grouper—a fish that hangs around starfish.

THE ACID TEST

*I've always wondered about seviche, the Latin
American seafood dish. Books say the fish is
"cooked" just by being marinated in lime juice.
Is it really "cooked," or is it still raw?*

. . . .

Virtually every mention of ceviche (seh-VEE-che; I'll use the Spanish spelling) by a food writer is accompanied by a gratuitous statement to the effect that lime juice does to protein what heat does to protein, and therefore the fish is essentially "cooked" by the lime juice.

Well, does "cooked" mean cooked, or doesn't it? And if the quotation marks are necessary, whom, pray tell, is everyone quoting? Apparently it's a vicious cycle, with everyone quoting everyone else. Let's just agree that "cooked" means subjected to heat, while "raw" generally means *not* cooked. So take your choice.

But before I serve up your mini-course in protein chemistry, here's a bit of an appetizer.

Ceviche is made from small pieces of any of several kinds of raw saltwater fish, or from scallops or other shellfish, or squid or octopus, all marinated in lime juice for several hours in the refrigerator, after which some oil, chopped onion and other vegetables, and spices are added and the mélange served cold. If the fish is fresh to begin with—and it absolutely must be—it is safe to marinate it for up to five or six hours; the lime's acidity (pH around 2.2) is strong enough to retard bacterial growth.

The citric acid in lime juice changes the proteins in fish by a process called *denaturation*. The normally twisted and folded protein molecules are unraveled or unfolded into less convoluted shapes. And the shapes of molecules, especially proteins, are responsible for most of their physical and chemical properties. In other words, they have lost their original natures: they have been denatured.

And yes, the heat of cooking also denatures proteins.

But besides acids and heat, a variety of other kinds of conditions can denature proteins. High concentrations of salts, including table salt—sodium chloride—can do it. Air can do it, as happens in the bubbles formed when cream is whipped. Even alkalis, the opposite of acids, and low temperatures, the opposite of heat, can do it, but less commonly. The analogy with cooking comes only from the fact that heat is the most familiar protein-denaturing agent in the kitchen.

Denaturing or unwinding protein molecules is no great trick, because the bonds that keep them twisted and folded aren't very strong. Evolution may supply a rationale for that fact: Over the eons, specific proteins have evolved to do specific jobs in specific living organisms, so they have no need to be stable under conditions vastly different from those that prevail in the organisms they serve. Animal muscle is normally only mildly acidic, while body temperatures are relatively low, especially in the case of sea creatures. Thus, meat and fish proteins can be destabilized when subjected to higher acidities and higher temperatures than those in the animal's muscles. That's why in making ceviche, fish protein can be denatured by an acid no stronger than lime juice, and even at refrigerator temperatures.

The different denaturing methods complement and enhance one another. For example, the stronger the acid a protein is subjected to, the lower the temperature at which it can be denatured by heat. That's why meat or fish bathed in a marinade containing lemon or lime juice (citric acid), vinegar (acetic acid), or wine (primarily tartaric and malic acids) will require less cooking time than an unmarinated sample. And if you want to explain that by saying the acid has partially "cooked" the meat, be my guest.

After the protein molecules in a food have been unraveled or unfolded by any of these denaturing environments, they may not stay that way. For one thing, if the conditions should change, they can re-ravel back into their original shapes or something similar. But usually this doesn't happen, because as they unfold or disrobe, so to speak, the protein molecules expose parts of themselves that previously had been concealed in the folds, and these parts can react with other chemicals in the vicinity that can change their shapes more or less permanently.

Or, the newly denuded sections can bond to one another, making so-called crosslinks that knit the molecules together into tighter structures. That's why when you either cook a piece of fish or soak it in lime juice to make ceviche, it develops a firmer texture. You'll notice also that it becomes more opaque, because light rays can't penetrate the tightly balled-up, crosslinked protein molecules. (The same thing happens to the proteins in an egg white; when cooked it turns from transparent to opaque white.) And under the right conditions, acidified, unfolded protein molecules will stick together and the protein will coagulate, as when cheese curds are formed when lactic acid denatures the casein in milk.

So why are acids so important in cooking? First of all, all our animal and vegetable foods are inherently either slightly acidic or neutral (neither acidic nor alkaline), and food chemistry, including the chemistry of cooking, is therefore very sensitive to even slight changes in acidity. The degree of acidity (expressed as a pH between 0 and 7) is critical to many of the chemical transformations that take place in cooking.

On the other hand, alkalinity (a pH between 7 and 14), the antithesis of acidity, plays virtually no role in cooking. Alkaline chemicals, being mostly unnatural in our foods, have generally deleterious effects on them and are rarely used in cooking. Nature has set the stage for that by making alkaline substances taste disagreeably bitter and soapy. All acids, on the other hand, add sourness—a very important element in our treasury of tastes.

But what about safety? Cooking temperatures will kill all bacteria and most spores, while the acid does so primarily on the surface of the food. Any parasites that may be lurking within the flesh can be killed by freezing or by the heat of cooking, but not by the acid.

Once again, however, if you're using fresh, inspected fish from a trustworthy supplier, your sushi, sashimi, and ceviche should be quite safe. Just don't buy your fish from that guy in the 1985 Chevy wagon by the side of the road.

| WILD, WILD MUSSELS |

I've enjoyed mussels many times in restaurants,
but the few times I tried cooking them at home
they were gritty and stringy. How should
I have cleaned them?

. . . .

You may have bought "wild" mussels, rather than cultivated or farm-raised mussels. The grit was probably sand, and the "strings" were remnants of their beards, which are routinely removed from the "domesticated" (tame?) ones before they reach the market.

Mussels don't burrow in the sand as clams do, cement their shells to each other as oysters do, or swim freely as scallops do. They anchor themselves to something stationary by means of a *byssus*, or beard—a clump of tough threads that they manufacture by extruding a liquid protein that hardens in seawater and sticks better than Super Glue to almost anything. In fact, scientists have been trying to reproduce it in the laboratory for possible use in gluing people back together after surgery.

Mussels are raised on underwater hanging hemp ropes in Spain, on bamboo poles in Thailand, on oak boards in France, on "long-lines" (Paul Bunyan–sized socks hanging from an underwater clothesline) in Sweden and Canada, and on shallow ocean bottoms in the Netherlands and Maine. In these environments they pick up little if any sand. Their beards are clipped by machine before they're sent to market, although you may still have to yank a few. Otherwise, culti-vated mussels need no cleaning beyond a cold-water rinse. Any whose shells gape open and don't close when tapped sharply with one of its brethren are dead, and should be discarded.

In the bottom-culture method used in Maine, wild, inch-long baby blue mussels are dredged from selected natural locations and sown by being scattered thinly onto leased beds where, not having to compete for food in the sea-floor jungle, they will grow to two to three inches in 18 to 24 months. In the wild, it might take them 7 to 8 years to reach that size. (If successful at evading ducks, crabs, starfish, and humans, mussels will live for 12 to 13 years, with some growing as old as 50.) Pampered and plump, cultivated mussels in the shell will be at least 25 percent meat by weight, whereas wild ones rarely exceed 15 percent.

Anchored as they are, mussels must depend for food on whatever the ocean currents bring them. Like clams and oysters, they feed by constantly taking in water and filtering out particles of plankton. A typical two-inch-long blue mussel may process 10 to 15 gallons of water per day. Unfortunately, its filtering system can also trap bacteria and other toxic microorganisms. That's why mussels from polluted waters are so dangerous; bacteria can pile up in a mussel like dirt in a vacuum-cleaner bag. Cultivated mussels are raised in carefully monitored waters.

There are seventeen known species of edible mussels in the world. The one that you'll see most often is the Atlantic blue mussel (it's actually blue-black), *Mytilus edulis*, which is raised mostly in the waters off Maine and Prince Edward Island, Canada. A similar species, *Mytilus troesselus*, is grown in the state of Washington. But from May through July, the blue mussels are likely to be devoting all their energies to spawning, which makes them weak and flabby and not good to eat.

Fortunately for mytilophiles, the Mediterranean mussel, *Mytilus galloprovincialis*, which is being cultivated on the West Coast, spawns in January and February, so it's good eatin' all summer. It is mild, sweet, plump, and big, ranging up to seven inches long and up to 60 percent meat at its peak.

Another kind of cultured mussel becoming more available in the United States is the greenshell, *Perna canaliculus* from New Zealand and *Perna viridisis* from Southeast Asia. The genus *Perna* has only one muscle, the adductor muscle, holding its shells together, while the genus *Mytilus* has two.

The greenshells, which measure three or four inches long, are edged with a startling emerald-green color, but the meat is the usual cream or orange color. (Male mussels are usually cream-colored; female mussels are more likely to be orange.) Because greenshell mussels are shipped frozen, you can find them year-round.

Even the blue mussels from Maine are now available year-round, because mussel beds in slightly different locations spawn at slightly different times, and the clever farmers can select the nonspawners for harvesting throughout the summer. You may now eat mussels in all months except those that have q's in their names.

Hot Wok Mussels

It doesn't get much easier than this. Chuck the mussels into a hot wok and shovel them around until they open and plump in their own juices. Period. They are perfect when dipped into a velvety sauce such as Smoky Garlic Mayonnaise. Serve these mussels as an appetizer or light supper, with crusty peasant bread for sopping up the flavorful juices.

---

2 pounds mussels, scrubbed and beards removed

Kosher or coarse sea salt

Freshly ground pepper

1 or 2 lemons, halved

Smoky Garlic Mayonnaise (p. 384)

---

1. Heat a large wok over high heat for about 2 minutes, or until very hot. Test the heat by flicking a few drops of water into the wok. If the drops head and dance across the surface, the pan is ready.

2. Discard any mussels that do not close when tapped. Add the remaining mussels to the hot wok all at once. Using a wok shovel or a large wooden or stainless-steel spoon, toss and turn the mussels for 4 or 5 minutes, or until they open and release their juices. Shovel and mix vigorously, so that all the mussels are exposed to the same amount of time on the bottom of the pile. The more noise you make with the shells clattering against the metal, the better. That appetizing sound is dear to the heart of every shellfish lover.

3. When all the mussels have opened and plumped—discard any that failed to open—sprinkle them with salt and pepper and divide them and their juices between 2 large bowls or 4 smaller bowls. Tuck a lemon half into each bowl, so that each person can squeeze juice over the mussels to taste. Spoon Smoky Garlic Mayonnaise into ramekins for dipping.

**MAKES 4 APPETIZER SERVINGS OR
2 MAIN-COURSE SERVINGS**

WELL, SHAVE ME WITH A CLAM!

Are razor clams good to eat?
And why are they called that?

. . . .

Yes, they're quite good to eat, breaded and fried, or made into fritters. They're harder to find here in the States than in many European countries.

They didn't get their name because their shells are sharp (which they are), but because the shells are shaped like an old-fashioned, curved-handled straight razor: two long, curved shells hinged together along the outer curve and with open ends through which the clam can poke out and do everything clams need to do.

Folklore has it that Native American men used to shave with the sharpened shells of a different species of clam, the quahog (*Mercenaria mercenaria*). The smooth, pearly lining (the *nacre*) of these clamshells often has beautiful purple patches, which were carved into tubular beads and used as wampum (money) in trade with Dutch and English settlers.

(The information in the preceding paragraph has nothing to do with razor clams and I provide it at no additional charge.)

In the United States, the common East Coast razor clam (*Ensis directus*) can be found up to 10 inches long. The Pacific Coast razor clam (*Siliqua patula*) is shorter and stubbier. Both kinds spend their lives in the sand or sandy mud around the low-tide zone of shallow bays, standing vertically with their foot pointing downward and their—well, other end (they have no head) pointing upward. Both ends protrude from the open-ended, tubular shell, so razor clams don't keep very well and must be cooked alive and fresh.

As in all clams, the "foot" isn't meant for walking; it's for digging. By extending its foot (sometimes called its digger) down into the mud, then thickening it at the bottom and trying to retract it up into the shell, the clam hauls itself downward in a perfect application of Newton's Third Law: For every upward pull there's a downward push (not Sir Isaac's exact words).

But just try to grab one and pull it out! The little devils can dig down faster than you can follow, and they can hold on so tightly that even if you do grab one, you may well break its fragile shell in the struggle to pull it from the mud. That's why you will find razor clams only very rarely at your local fishmonger's. It's a shame, because they are so good to eat.

On the other hand, my respects go out to any delicious species that has outwitted our attempts to decimate its population.

Ultimate Oven Paella

Paella might seem difficult to make, but it is really just a series of easy steps. This step-by-step method is for beginners. Later, you can experiment to your heart's content, because paella is not so much a dish as it is a rice-based concoction of local seafood and/or poultry and/or rabbit, depending on what part of Spain you're making it in. But more than anything, paella is all about the saffron-flavored rice.

Do all the advance cooking in a large, preferably black cast-iron skillet rather than in the paella pan. The skillet's idiosyncrasies will be familiar to you and therefore the pan more reliable. Also, the skillet fits better than an unwieldy paella pan on a stove-top burner. About a half hour before your guests arrive, turn on the oven, assemble the dish in the paella pan, and allow it to bake until the rice is cooked.

This recipe is designed for a 14- to 16-inch paella pan. Bob and I bought ours in Valencia, the home of seafood paella. Why that size? Because it was the biggest we could fit into our suitcase.

---

24 small clams

12 mussels

$1^1/_4$ pounds medium shrimp

5 to 6 cups chicken broth

A good pinch of saffron threads

$^1/_2$ pound chorizo sausage

6 to 8 chicken drumsticks, skin on

Salt and freshly ground pepper

About $^1/_3$ cup olive oil

1 large onion, finely chopped

1 sweet red pepper, finely chopped

1 sweet yellow pepper, finely chopped

6 cloves garlic, finely chopped

$^1/_2$ teaspoon paprika, preferably smoked sweet Spanish paprika (*pimentón*)

1 cup ripe cherry tomatoes, pierced with a knife

    1 **cup frozen peas, defrosted**

2 $^1/_2$ **cups Spanish short-grain rice, preferrably the _bomba_ variety**

      Lemon wedges for garnish

      Smoky Garlic Mayonnaise (p. 384) for serving

ADVANCE PREPARATION:

1. Discard any clams that do not close when tapped. Scrub the remainder under running water. Discard any mussels that do not close when tapped. Scrub the remainder under running water. Place them together in a bowl and refrigerate. Peel the shrimp, reserving the shells, then devein (remove the black vein down the back). Place in another bowl and refrigerate.

2. To enhance the flavor of the broth, place the reserved shrimp shells in a sauté pan with a little olive oil. Cook over medium-high heat for about 8 minutes, or until they turn red. Add 1½ cups of the chicken broth to the pan and let it simmer quietly for about 5 minutes. Strain the broth into a glass measure. Discard the shells.

3. Crush enough of the saffron between 2 spoons or with your fingers to yield ½ teaspoon crushed. Add it, along with a few whole saffron threads, to the hot broth to steep. Add enough additional chicken broth to make 5 cups. Place 1 cup additional plain broth off to the side. You may or may not need some of it.

4. Cut the chorizo into 4-inch lengths and simmer in water for 15 minutes. Let cool and slice into ¼-inch-thick slices. Set aside.

5. Rinse the chicken pieces and pat dry. Sprinkle all over with salt and pepper. Place a heavy cast-iron skillet or paella pan over high heat and add the olive oil. It should just film the bottom of the pan. When hot, add the chicken and brown for about 15 minutes on all sides. The chicken should be barely over half cooked. Transfer the chicken to a plate, leaving the oil behind in the pan, and set aside.

6. Add the onion and sweet peppers to the oil remaining in the pan and sauté over medium-low heat for about 10 minutes, or until the vegetables are softened but not browned. Add the garlic and paprika and cook for another 2 minutes, but do not let the garlic brown. Add the cherry tomatoes and cook for 2 minutes longer. Set the vegetables (this is called the *sofrito*) aside to cool.

FINISH THE DISH:

1. About 35 minutes before serving, place a rack in the lowest position in the oven. Preheat the oven to 400°F.

2. Place the *sofrito* in a 16-inch paella pan, spreading it out. Distribute the rice over the vegetables and stir to coat with the oil in the pan.

3. Bring the 5 cups broth to a boil in a saucepan. Place the paella pan on the stovetop over medium-high heat. Pour the boiling broth over the rice and vegetables. Bring to a boil, reduce the heat to low, and simmer, without stirring, for 10 minutes.

4. Turn off the heat. Add the sausage slices, pushing them into the rice. Add the shrimp. Add the clams and mussels, hinge side down.

5. If there is room, add the chicken pieces. If not, place the drumsticks in a shallow baking dish and bake them on the top oven shelf while the paella is on the bottom shelf.

6. Carefully place the paella in the oven and bake for 10 to 12 minutes. Check the dish. If the rice seems too dry, add some of the reserved broth. Do *not* stir the rice. When done, the mollusks will be open, the shrimp will be pink, and the rice should have a bit of a bite. If necessary, bake for 3 minutes longer.

7. Remove the paella from the oven. Scatter the defrosted peas over the surface. Cover the paella with a tea towel or foil and allow it to rest for 5 minutes. As it stands, the remaining liquid will be absorbed and the rice will become tender. This is a very important step.

8. Garnish with lemon wedges. Place the paella in its pan in the center of the table and allow guests to help themselves. Pass the chicken legs, if you didn't fit them in the paella pan, and pass the garlic mayonnaise.

MAKES 6 TO 8 SERVINGS

ALL THOSE WHO LOVE
SCALLOPS, SAY "EYE!"

*A seafood place told me that according to an FDA
regulation all sea scallops are treated with a
chemical dip to prolong shelf life. I'm surprised
that the FDA would mandate a process that
has no impact on safety but only keeps the
scallops fresher longer. What's the scoop? Is
there such a regulation? And maybe you could
enlighten me about "diver," "dry," and
"processed" scallops while you're at it.*

. . . .

First of all, don't go back to the "seafood place" that told you the
FDA requires them to soak their scallops. That's baloney. But before
I tell you why, let's see what all those scallopian adjectives mean.

A scallop is a lump of white seafood shaped like a marshmallow,
right? Wrong. We might as well say that a cow is a steak. "Scallop" is
the name of a remarkable critter that we almost never see whole.
Fishermen shuck most of them at sea as soon as they're dredged from
the bottom, throwing away all but that big, pale muscle that ends up
in our markets. That's the scallop's adductor muscle, which it uses to
close its hinged pair of shells that are shaped like Shell Oil signs.
Other bivalve (two-shell) mollusks, including clams, oysters, cockles, and most mussels, have pairs of adductor muscles, but scallops
have only that single, huge Schwarzeneggish one.

Americans generally disdain the rest of the animal, but it is all
edible (except for the shells, of course). Try it raw on the half shell if
you ever get the chance. A whole, raw scallop is sweeter than a clam
and without the oyster's sulfurous tang. But be sure it's absolutely
fresh—no more than a day or so out of clean, certified waters. Scallops spoil quickly—even faster than most other kinds of shellfish—

because their shells don't fit together tightly. Most other bivalves can be shipped around the country tightly "clammed up," still alive and fresh. But scallops die soon after being taken out of the water, and, gaping as they do, they're an open invitation to spoilage bacteria.

The two major species of scallops sold in the United States are loosely referred to as *sea scallops* and *bay scallops*. American sea scallops (mostly *Placopecten magellanicus*) are the bigger ones, averaging about 20 to 30 meats per pound. They're about an inch or more high and taken from shells that may be 8 to 12 inches across. Bay scallops (*Argopecten irradians*) are smaller in both muscle (less than an inch high) and shell (2 to 3 inches); they average about 60 to 90 per pound and are found closer to shore. The really tiny scallops you occasionally see in the market, at more than about 70 per pound, are calico scallops (*Argopecten gibbus*). Many fishmongers ignore the niceties of biology and geography, applying the names *sea* or *bay* based on size—or whim—alone.

The very large so-called *diver scallops* (10 or fewer per pound) have supposedly been hand-harvested by scuba divers rather than dredged from the sea bottom. Because of their impressive size, relative scarcity, and consequent high price, you'll find them only at expensive restaurants. But don't swallow the scuba story hook, line, and sinker. There's nothing to prevent a restaurant from calling any large scallop a diver, if it so chooses.

Using their big adductor muscles, scallops in the wild can clap their shells together forcefully, shooting themselves through the water by jet propulsion to escape a predatory fish or starfish. (It's a jungle down there.) They can even aim their spurts of water to propel themselves in almost any direction, although most often "forward" by jetting water straight out the hinge end.

You think that's wild? Wait'll you hear this. Many scallops have blue eyes. No kidding. They're the only bivalves that have eyes at all, much less baby blues. If you peek in between the shells of a scallop, you'll see two rows of fifty or more tiny eye dots, staring back at you from the critter's front edge, or mantle. While a scallop can't exactly read the bottom line on an eye chart, it can distinguish changes in light intensity, and that's a good enough warning that it's time to scoot away from any stranger that darkens its door.

One of my most exciting experiences (I know: You'll think I need to get a life) was wading among live scallops in the shallows off Cape Cod and watching each one jet away the instant my shadow fell upon him and her. (Note to editor: That's him *and* her, not him *or* her; most scallops are hermaphrodites.) In Europe, the female red roe is saved and served along with the adductor muscle, covered with a cream sauce, topped with browned bread crumbs, and called *coquilles St. Jacques*.

Scallop muscles have a tendency to dry out and lose weight, decreasing their per-pound value in the marketplace. So wholesalers, and even the fishing boat crews themselves during a long trip, may soak them in fresh water or in a solution of sodium tripolyphosphate (STP) to keep them hydrated. Because scallop meat is naturally saturated with salty seawater, osmosis will force water into it from the less salty soaking liquid. The STP helps the scallop to retain that water. Soaked scallop meats are called "wet" or processed scallops to distinguish them from unsoaked or "dry" scallops.

Processed scallops that have been loaded with water will be excessively heavy and should rightfully be sold at a lower price per pound. (Consumers, take note.) Processed or "wet" scallops will be almost pure white (the phosphate acts also as a bleach) rather than their natural ivory, creamy, or pinkish color, and they will be resting in a milky, sticky liquid that makes them tend to clump together. They're a disaster to sauté, because they'll release their excess water into the pan and steam instead of browning.

The role of the FDA? It monitors the water content of scallop products. Back home in the sea, scallops are 75 percent to 80 percent water. If a commercial product contains more than 80 percent water, the FDA requires that it be labeled an "x% Water-Added Scallop

Product" and, if applicable, "Processed with Sodium Tripolyphosphate." Scallops containing more than 84 percent water may not be sold at all. So much for that "The FDA made me do it" cop-out.

The problem is that these FDA-mandated labels are affixed to the wholesale buckets and you may never see them in the retail market. So buy your scallops only from a fishmonger whom you trust not to sell wet scallops at dry-scallop prices. Why pay $7 to $14 a pound, depending on size and season, for water?

CRUSTACEAN CAMOUFLAGE

When I buy raw shrimp, sometimes they're gray and sometimes they're pink, almost as if they'd been cooked. Are the pink ones somehow less fresh?

. . . .

No, they're just different species. Some are pinker and some are grayer, even when they're still gamboling about on the ocean floor. But all of their shells turn bright pink when cooked. That color is in the shells all along, but it is masked by darker colors that break down when heated.

At least in the case of domestic Atlantic shrimp, the shallow-water ones are more or less sand-colored for maximum camouflage against the sandy bottom. In deep water, where the prevailing light has a bluish cast, they can afford to be pink, because reddish pigments don't reflect much blue light and therefore don't show up.

Unless you live near the shrimp-boat docks, all the shrimp that you buy were almost certainly frozen fresh from the boat or even when still on the boat, and shipped to market in that condition. At the market, they thaw out batches of shrimp to put in the display case. Like a lot of other seafood, however, shrimp begins to spoil quickly after being thawed. Fortunately, you carry with you at all times an exquisitely sensitive instrument for detecting spoilage: your nose.

Any odor at all, other than that of a fresh ocean breeze, is your cue to buy something else for dinner. So don't be afraid to ask to smell a sample of the shrimp up close before you make your purchase.

(Once, I almost got my head handed to me by an indignant fish-monger on the waterfront in Marseilles when I picked up a squid and sniffed it. I hadn't realized that I was dealing with the fisherman himself, straight off the boat. How much fresher could it be?)

SHRIMP SHRIMP

What does the "scampi" mean in "shrimp scampi"?

. . . .

It sounds like a way of preparing shrimp, and in a way it is. But in a way it isn't.

Scampi is the Italian name for a species of large prawns known also as Dublin Bay prawns. And what is a prawn? Strictly speaking, it's a crustacean more closely related to a lobster than to a shrimp. But the name depends on where you live.

There are literally millions of species of animals in the sea, including twenty-six thousand known varieties of crustaceans. A lot of these critters look pretty much alike, and the same species may be known by many different names around the world. What we call a shrimp over here may be called a prawn over there. And it often is. Or vice versa. Or maybe not. (I hope that's clear.)

In Europe and most other parts of the world, a prawn is a specific variety of large (up to 9 inches long) crustacean with long antennae and skinny, lobster-like front claws. It is not a shrimp because shrimp have no claws. Instead, prawns are very similar to what we call crayfish or crawfish in the United States (or, in Louisiana, "mud bugs"). The prawns from Ireland's Dublin Bay are reputedly top o' the heap, *begorrah*!

On a French menu, the word *crevette* can go either way: as a *crevette rose*, it's a prawn, while as a *crevette grise*, it's a small, brown shrimp. (Yes, *grise* means gray in French; go figure.) Except, of course, when the chef calls a prawn a *langoustine*, which he or she may do whenever he or she feels like it. Prawns probably became *langoustines* in France when Spanish prawns, or *langostinos*, crossed the Pyrenees. (Not by themselves.)

In our freewheeling United States, alas, any large shrimp might be called a prawn, depending on how hard the chef wants to impress you. If the shrimp are not at least "jumbo" in size (around 20 or fewer to the pound), however, it's particularly stretching to refer to them as prawns. The only thing you can be pretty sure of is that the critters in "shrimp scampi" on most American menus aren't either scampi or prawns; they're whatever plain old shrimp the restaurant has at hand.

Be that as it may, chefs in Venice enjoy covering their scampi with fresh bread crumbs and broiling them in a garlicky butter sauce. Thus, when an American restaurant does that to their shrimp, they call the dish "shrimp scampi" which, when you come right down to it, means "shrimp shrimp."

That reminds me of when my daughter, Leslie, and I were strapped for something to cook for dinner and came home from the market with, among other things, some good-looking eggplants, known in most places outside North America as *aubergines*. We scooped out the pulp, did a few things to it that I vaguely remember as involving garlic, olive oil, and bread crumbs, stuffed the mixture back in the skins, baked them, and christened the dish "eggplant aubergine."

Redundancy raises its ugly head. Again.

Scampi Scampi

Shrimp scampi (or in Italian, *scampi scampi*) is a popular dish in Italian American restaurants, perhaps more so than in Italy. Top the garlicky shrimp with crisp, buttered bread crumbs for crunch. You can make your own, but I prefer to use the extra-crunchy Japanese bread crumbs called *panko*. Many non-Japanese markets carry *panko* these days.

CRUMB TOPPING:

- 1 tablespoon unsalted butter
- $^1/_4$ cup coarse, dried bread crumbs, preferably *panko*

SHRIMP:

- 3 tablespoons unsalted butter
- 1 tablespoon extra-virgin olive oil
- 1 pound shrimp, peeled, with tails removed, and deveined
- 4 large cloves garlic, sliced
- Kosher salt
- Freshly ground pepper
- $^1/_4$ cup dry white wine
- 2 tablespoons chopped fresh flat-leaf parsley
- 2 tablespoons freshly squeezed lemon juice

Lemon wedges for garnish

---

1. Make the crumb topping: Heat a small sauté pan over medium heat. Add the butter. When it is hot, add the bread crumbs and stir until they become tan. Immediately remove the pan from the heat and set aside.

2. Make the shrimp: Heat a large sauté pan over high heat, and add the butter and olive oil. When the mixture is sizzling, add the shrimp and sauté, tossing constantly, for 1 minute. Add the garlic and sauté for about 1 minute longer, or until the shrimp turn opaque and pink. Do not let the garlic brown. Season to taste with salt and pepper.

3. Reduce the heat to medium and add the wine. Bring to a boil, then reduce

the heat to low and simmer for 2 minutes. Remove the pan from the heat. Sprinkle the shrimp with the parsley and drizzle with the lemon juice, then toss to coat.

4. Divide the shrimp among individual-serving casserole dishes and top with the crisp bread crumbs. Serve right away. Pass the lemon wedges for added spritzing.

MAKES 4 APPETIZER SERVINGS OR
2 GENEROUS MAIN-COURSE SERVINGS

Chapter Seven

A Carnival
for Carnivores

....

FORTY-SIX BILLION pounds of beef, veal, lamb, and pork, plus 36 billion pounds of poultry, are consumed each year in the United States.

According to USDA statistics for the year 2001, the average American consumed 68.2 pounds of beef; 51.6 pounds of pork; 1.8 pounds of veal, lamb, and mutton; 77.8 pounds of chicken; and 17.9 pounds of turkey, all in terms of trimmed weight at the retail counter. That's a total of more than 200 pounds of meat for every man, woman, girl, boy, and baby in the country, even counting vegetarians.

Does that make you feel full?

Technically, the word *meat* includes the flesh, or muscle tissue, of any animal, including fish and shellfish. But we went fishing in the preceding chapter and will stick with two- and four-legged creatures in this one—that is, poultry and "red" meat, respectively.

Okay, the pork producers want us to call pork the "other white meat" because it isn't as red as beef or lamb. The reason is that pigs are lazy. (Nobody ever tried to fall asleep by counting pigs jumping over a fence.) Because they are congenitally inactive, their muscles contain very little of the red, oxygen-storing compound called myoglobin (see "How now, brown cowburger?" on p. 275) that other animals stockpile in their muscles for sudden energy demands.

Along with muscles for movement and locomotion, most animals have bones for support and internal organs for sustaining the processes of life. So besides meat per se, we'll talk a bit in this chapter about using bones in stocks, and we'll delve briefly into the edible but largely unappreciated (in this country) innards.

Differences among the world's cultures are reflected in their attitudes toward meat—what meats are eaten, and how, and when. In the United States, our red meats come almost exclusively from three mammals: cows, sheep (lambs), and pigs. We may read with fascination and various degrees of dismay about cultures in which other mammals are eaten (including goats, rabbits, camels, horses, whales, and dogs), not to mention amphibians and reptiles (frogs, lizards, alligators, and snakes), or even insects (grasshoppers and grubs).

But at the same time, other cultures may feel repugnance toward at least two of our three favorite meats: beef is forbidden to Hindus, and pork is forbidden to Jews and Muslims. Much of the Catholic world eschews all meats on Fridays, while vegetarians reject them at all times—or, in the current vernacular, 24/7/52.

Nevertheless, meat is valued as the "center of the plate" on tables around the world, with regularity in wealthy countries and whenever possible in poorer ones. Cultures based on raising livestock for their renewable resources, milk and wool, cannot generally afford to kill their "golden calves" for the sake of a hamburger.

Let's take a highly abbreviated look at the structure of meat and what happens when we cook it.

A mammalian muscle is made up of (surprise!) muscle cells, also known as muscle fibers. These long, skinny cells contain several nuclei apiece, and are packed together in parallel bundles inside an elastic husk (a *sarcolemma*), like a bundle of uncooked spaghetti inside a garden hose. These fiber-filled "hoses," still largely parallel to one another, are stacked together like a pile of logs to make up the muscle proper. That's why meat has a fibrous texture, or "grain."

Muscle tissue is made largely of protein. In a sirloin steak, for example, 57 percent of the dry weight is protein and, depending on how the steak is trimmed, about 41 percent is fat. The tiniest filaments within the muscle cells, called *myofilaments*, contain the actual protein molecules, which are mostly *actin* and *myosin*. When set off by chemical and electrical "move" signals from the nervous system, these protein molecules bond (*cross-bridge*) with one another to form tighter, shorter protein molecules, thereby making the myofilaments, and hence the whole muscle, contract.

But now, into the kitchen.

When we cook meat, the primary effect is that the protein molecules become *denatured* or reconfigured. That is, upon agitation by the heat, their convoluted structures unwind and then, generally, clump together by forming cohesive bonds. Known as *coagulation*, this clumping has several effects.

For one thing, the coagulation scrambles the neatly lined-up bundles of fibers in the muscle tissue, making the structures more tangled, random, and rigid. Second, the tighter structure of the reconfigured proteins squeezes out juices (muscle is 65 to 75 percent water) and dries out the meat. Thus, a steak becomes both tough and dry if cooked too long. Moderate cooking, however, has many virtues: it tenderizes meat, improves its flavor, improves its appearance, and makes it safer by killing microorganisms.

Now it's time to eat. Meat is a valuable source of high-quality protein containing essential amino acids, and fats containing valuable fatty acids. That's not to mention its abundance of iron and vitamins A and B. So grab that steak knife and let's dig in.

WHEN MEAT MEETS MACHINE

I'm an inveterate food label reader. In the past,
I used to see "mechanically separated chicken" or
"mechanically separated beef" on franks and
other manufactured meat products. I wondered
about it at the time, but now that I want to ask
about it I can't find it on labels. What is (or was)
mechanically separated meat, and why
don't they do it anymore?

. . . .

The Food Safety and Inspection Service (FSIS) of the USDA won't let them. It's a reaction to "mad cow" disease.

Mechanically separated meat is meat that has been separated from the bone by a machine, rather than by knife-brandishing humans. The first time I saw the words *mechanically separated beef* on a label I said to myself, "Well, what did you expect, Dummy?" (I hate it when I talk to myself disrespectfully like that.) "Did you think all the meat we buy is cut by blood-spattered slaughterhouse workers hacking meat off the carcasses, much as our prehistoric ancestors did after a successful mastodon hunt?"

Truth be told, yes. That is indeed the way most of the job is done. But these days, machines supplement those blood-spattered slaughterhouse workers by removing the remaining meat from the bones after the humans have done their best with their knives.

Although most of us would rather not think about it very much, meat begins with slaughtering at a packing plant, which might better be called a hacking plant. (The euphemism "packing" originated in colonial times, when pork was salted and packed in barrels for shipping overseas.) As soon as the animal has been killed and its blood drained out—procedures that the meat industry delicately refers to as "immobilization" and "exsanguination," respectively—what had previously been skeletal muscle has officially become meat. (Skeletal muscle is muscle attached to the skeleton rather than the muscular parts of the circulatory system, such as the heart.) But a carcass is not all meat; it contains internal organs, bones, cartilage, tendons, ligaments, fat, and skin, all of which need to be excised during the subsequent stages of "disassembly." That job is done mostly by saws and sharp knives, hand-wielded by packing-house workers.

After the carcass is split into two "sides" by a power saw, workers with knives cut it into eight so called *primal cuts*: chuck, rib, short loin, sirloin, round, brisket and shank, short plate, and flank. The primal cuts may then be packed and shipped as is or reduced to smaller cuts (*subprimals*) or even down to display-case cuts, depending on how much subsequent butchering, if any, the buyer wants to do at the retail level. In either case, there is still a lot of unrecovered meat left in the trimmings, and that's where the machines come in. They can separate almost all of the remaining meat from the bones.

There are two types of so-called meat recovery machines, depending on whether the bones are first crushed: the mechanically separated meat (MSM) systems, used since the 1970s, and the newer advanced meat recovery (AMR) systems.

In MSM machines, the bones are first ground or crushed, after which the soft tissues (muscle and fat) are forced at high pressure through a kind of sieve, separating them from the bone fragments, cartilage, ligaments, and tendons. What comes out is in the form of a paste or batter that can be thrown directly into the mixing vat for hot dogs, sausages, hamburgers, pizza toppings, taco fillings, and similar manufactured meat products, which have to be labeled as containing "mechanically separated meat."

In the more modern AMR machines, the bones are not crushed. They enter the machine whole and emerge essentially intact after the meat has been scraped, shaved, pushed, or pulled off in small pieces. The USDA allows this meat to be labeled simply as "meat." It may contain tiny pieces of bone the size of grains of table salt. This bone contributes most of the calcium listed in the Nutrition Facts tables on many processed meat products that you wouldn't expect to contain much calcium.

As a result of the outbreak of mad cow disease, or BSE (*bovine spongiform encephalopathy*), in the 1980s in Britain and subsequent incidents in North America, the USDA since March 3, 2003, has required the routine sampling and inspection of AMR-produced beef for the presence of any spinal cord or brain tissue. That's where the disease-transmitting prions (PREE-ons) are located in sick animals. Prions are rather mystifying proteinaceous particles. They have no DNA or genes with which to replicate themselves and are therefore not alive, but they can cause disease in animals and humans. They can't be inactivated by extreme conditions such as acids or heat that normally affect the nucleic acids in microbes and viruses. In humans, the mad-cow-transmitted disease is called Creutzfeldt-Jakob (KROYTS-felt YOK-ob) Disease, or CJD.

On December 30, 2003, the USDA announced that (a) all central nervous system parts (such as nerve cells along the vertebrae), not just brain and spinal cord tissue, must be absent in AMR meats, and (b) the use of mechanically separated meat (MSM) in human food is prohibited, because it is more likely to contain fragments of central nervous system tissue.

And that's why you no longer see the MSM words on labels.

Of course, the machines enable the meatpackers to sell more meat, and that's why they use them. But on its website (http://www .amif.org/FactSheetAdvancedMeatRecovery.pdf), the American Meat Institute explains the virtues of using the machines: "Hand trimming requires repetitive cuts with a knife, which can result in repetitive motion injuries to employees. Reducing hand trimming [by using AMR] protects employees."

It's nice to know that the meatpacking companies are so concerned about their employees' hands.

While you're perusing labels in the meat case, you may see some hot dogs labeled as containing "variety meats." This is a euphemism for any or all of the animals' non-skeletal-muscle parts: hearts, brains (except beef brains), large intestines (chitterlings or chit-lins), spleens (melts), pancreas and thymus glands (sweetbreads), kidneys, livers, lips, and tongues.

Other parts of animals that may find their way into wieners, sausages, and other mystery-meat products are blood, marrow, cheeks and other head trimmings, feet (trotters), tails (oxtails), stomachs (hog maw), lungs (lights), small intestines (sausage casings), skins (pork rinds), stomach linings (tripe), and testicles (fries, prairie oysters, or mountain oysters). Notice how the number of euphemisms multi-plies along with the indecorousness of the organs.

As my father once told me when I was a little boy, "They use every part of the pig but the grunts." For years I wondered which part of the pig was its gruntz.

Isn't that offal?

HOW NOW, BROWN COWBURGER?

My supermarket has a sign at the meat case assuring us shoppers that if we open a package of ground beef and find that the meat on the outside, visible through the plastic wrapping, is red while the meat on the inside is brown, there is nothing to worry about. They go on to say that once the hamburger is formed, all of the meat will return to its red color. Why does that interior meat turn brown? And why does it return to its red color, if in fact it does?

. . . .

I wrote briefly about this topic beneath the same corny heading in a previous book, *What Einstein Told His Cook: Kitchen Science Explained*. But I continue to receive letters from worried purchasers of prison-pallor hamburger meat. So permit me to address this question again, but in more detail than I did before.

The brown-meat syndrome has been a concern of consumers ever since the neighborhood butcher, who ground the meat before our very eyes, went the way of his sawdust-covered floors. In today's supermarkets, the meat is ground somewhere "in the back," or even at another location, and then packed into plastic trays and covered with plastic film. In some markets, it may languish in the cooler for a day or two, then sit even longer in your refrigerator before you get around to opening it and discovering that the inner meat is an unappetizing gray-brown.

Are they spraying the top meat with some sort of red dye? No. Is the brownish meat spoiled? No, not unless it smells bad, which indicates either spoilage by microbes or that the fat is becoming rancid. So brownish meat is okay to eat unless it smells bad.

The chemistry of meat color—any meat—is a bit complicated, and what we call "red meat" could give a chameleon a run for its money. But in a nutshell, the color of meat depends largely on the relative amounts of three colored proteins, just as when an artist mixes three pigments on the palette to achieve a desired hue. The three proteins are *deoxymyoglobin*, the deep purplish-red color of freshly cut beef; *oxymyoglobin*, a bright pinkish-red; and *metmyoglobin*, a grayish-brown color. (There are other forms of myoglobin, but these are the main ones.)

These three pigmented chemicals are in dynamic equilibrium with one another, meaning that they are all interconvertible. Their relative amounts at any given time depend on the availability of oxygen, enzymes, and antioxidants. But none of these three colored compounds has any effect on flavor or wholesomeness. It's purely a matter of cosmetics.

Pork and veal don't contain much myoglobin in any form, but beef contains much more, and the markets struggle to keep it for as long as possible in the consumer-friendly, bright-red oxymyoglobin form. But how?

First of all, there must be oxygen available to convert the fresh meat's purple deoxymyoglobin into either red oxymyoglobin or brown metmyoglobin. Which of these two will predominate depends mainly on the amount of oxygen available to the meat. When there is virtually no oxygen at all, as in vacuum packaging, the meat retains its purple deoxymyoglobin color. You'd think that would solve the brown-meat problem, but unfortunately, consumers don't like purple; they want red. Vacuum packaging therefore has only limited uses in retail sales of fresh (not cured) meats.

When only small amounts of oxygen are available to the meat, brown metmyoglobin is the chemically favored form. That's why the surface of beef exposed to the open air may exhibit bright red oxymyoglobin, while the oxygen-deprived meat underneath will slowly turn brown. At most retail markets, meat is packaged in rigid plastic trays overwrapped with an oxygen-permeable plastic film, usually polyvinyl chloride. The surface gets plenty of oxygen and is nice and red, but the oxygen can diffuse only so far down. The deeper you go, the browner the meat is.

And by the way, have you noticed those juice soaked absorbent pads beneath the meat in some of those trays? They're not just mattresses to keep the meat comfy. They're there to absorb wetness, known in butcherese as *weep* or *purge*. Obviously, it consists of juices that have "wept" out of the meat while standing, carrying along some of its water-soluble proteins and nutrients and thereby compromising its flavor and nutritional value. You don't want that. So choose packages whose mattresses are dry, not red with juices. A dry mattress means that the juices are still in the meat, where you want them.

There is some truth to your supermarket's claim that the brown interior meat will turn red again when exposed to air at room temperature (refrigeration slows the transformation down). The metmyoglobin may indeed react with oxygen and revert to oxymyoglobin, but that's a slow and incomplete process, even if you spread the meat out in a thin layer for maximum oxygen contact—and that's obviously not a good idea on sanitation grounds. Remember, though, that you're going to make the meat even browner when you cook it, so why bother? The heat of cooking not only browns the meat by Maillard reactions (see pp. 296–97) but encourages the conversion of oxymyoglobin to metmyoglobin.

A second major factor in the red-to-brown conversion of beef is that both the deoxymyoglobin and oxymyoglobin proteins contain a lone iron atom buried deep within each of their large, globular molecules. The iron atom is normally in what chemists call the reduced, or *ferrous*, form. But if the iron atom is changed into its oxidized, or *ferric*, form, the protein molecules lose their purple or red colors and turn brown. Antioxidant enzymes in the meat normally keep this change from happening, but if the meat is stored too long, even at refrigerator temperatures, the enzymes' activity diminishes and browning is facilitated.

This "old-age" browning, often accompanied by an off flavor, is what people think of when they see meat that isn't red. But as we've seen, browning can come also from a harmless deficiency of oxygen in fresh meat. The meat isn't really bad until bacteria get hold of it, in which case it will probably also have an off odor. So let your nose be your umbrella. (No offense, Cyrano.)

When bacteria do take up residence on the meat's surface either before, during, or after it has been ground, other browning—and decaying—reactions take place. Spoilage bacteria not only can turn red oxymyoglobin into brown metmyoglobin, but they can then turn the metmyoglobin into green choleglobin and sulfmyoglobin. And you already know that when you see green, your feet should beat a fleet retreat from the meat. Morever, in producing sulfmyoglobin from metmyoglobin the bacteria release hydrogen sulfide, a notoriously smelly gas.

If you're a suspicious type, poke a hole in the meat package as soon as you leave the market. Take a sniff through the hole while you can still storm back into the market in high dudgeon. (Is there a low dudgeon?)

A quality market will watch its ground-beef supply lines carefully, grinding and putting out just enough to keep up with sales. That way, it will always be oxymyoglobin-red at the time of sale. If the meat is allowed to begin losing its bright red color, shoppers tend to reject it even if it is not old-age brownness but merely lack-of-oxygen brownness. The retailer still has to mark it down in order to move it. That can be a boon to savvy or budget-conscious consumers.

The meat industry, of course, wants to minimize these color-related losses of revenue. One oft-used preemptive tactic has been to feed the cattle vitamin E, an antioxidant, before sending them off to meet their maker. Antioxidants prevent the iron atoms in the myoglobin molecules from becoming oxidized to the ferric form.

But the industry has yet to work out what is to them a vexing economic problem: The feedlot operators have to bear the cost of the vitamin E–laced feed, while it's the retailers who benefit from increased sales. In my opinion that's just too bad, and I refuse to lose any sleep over it. The way things have been going, it will probably be solved when a single, huge agribusiness conglomerate owns everything from the cattle ranch to the meat cases in your supermarket. From cradle to beyond the grave, so to speak.

Or, in an alternative universe, small, local meat farmers will increase in number, so that all our meat will *be* fresh and *look* fresh, without having been shipped thousands of miles and having its colors manipulated at the marketplace.

We can dream, can't we?

THE FOODIE'S FICTIONARY: Myoglobin—not youroglobin

PIGS IS PIGS

I like to try new products and bought a plastic-
wrapped package labeled "Souse" in my
neighborhood market. The package didn't include
even the simplest cooking instructions, nor could I
find any recipes in any of my dozen-plus cookbooks.
So I sliced it, coated it with cornmeal, and tried to
brown it in a frying pan, as I do scrapple. The
result was grease soup. What went wrong?

. . . .

Just because souse and scrapple have funny names and come in refrigerated rectangular blocks doesn't mean they're related, except for their porcine parentage.

Scrapple, often called Philadelphia Scrapple, is a Pennsylvania Dutch concoction of cooked pork scraps and trimmings (no gruntz) called *puddin'*, mixed with cornmeal mush, a.k.a. polenta, and spices. Refrigerated, it forms a fatty cake that can be sliced and fried for breakfast. The English, as Pennsylvania Dutch people call the rest of us, make a similar product that they call, ironically, by the German name *ponhaus*.

Souse, on the other hand, is—are you ready?—pickled, spiced, and seasoned scraps from boiled pigs' heads, feet, and ears. No cornmeal binding; it's held together by the gelatin that forms when the pieces are cooked. When you put yours into the frying pan, it was like trying to fry Jell-O.

Also known as head cheese, souse is meant to be eaten cold (if at all). It is related to the Italian *sopressata*, which is made by boiling a de-brained pig's head until the meat and tongue fall apart, where-upon they are cut into small pieces, seasoned and spiced, put into a cloth bag, and pressed (*sopressata* in Italian) into sausage form.

In this country, scrapple and souse are not commonly sold in upscale, "gourmet" meat markets, where the clientele may be more partial to such politically correct and trendy delicacies as free-range salami, roast suckling duck, and grass-fed trout. All to be garnished, of course, with stuffed chives. (Think about it.)

RAINBOWS ON RYE

Can you tell me what that weird, rainbow-y sheen is that I see on roast beef, corned beef, and pastrami? Is my fear of it irrational, or if I can manage to get past the appearance, is it safe to eat? I haven't eaten a deli beef sandwich in years.

. . . .

Shame on you. There's nothing better than a New York–style, kosher, thin-sliced, fat-laden corned beef sandwich on rye. But the diet pendulum has a habit of swinging back and forth, so depending on whether it's fat or carbohydrates that happens to be in the doghouse when you read this, there will be those who advise you to order your sandwich either without the meat or without the bread.

Now, about your multicolored meat: That iridescent or rainbow appearance that sliced meats sometimes take on is not a coating of nefarious mold or rot. It is merely an optical effect. You may find it on both cured meats such as ham or corned beef and uncured meats such as roast beef and pork. It's caused by the slicing process.

Meat, or animal muscle, is made up of *myofilaments*, tiny strands of protein. They are bound together in parallel bundles to form myofibrils, which in turn are bundled together to form the fibers that make up whole muscle. When a very sharp knife or slicing machine cuts the myofilaments crosswise at a certain angle, their severed tips, which are comparable in size to the wavelengths of light, can play optical tricks. One theory has it that the translucent tips bend (*refract*) the light waves into two different directions. This optical effect is called *birefringence* or *double refraction*. The two refracted waves then interfere with each other on their way to your eye and break up into their component rainbow colors.

Or, the iridescence on a meat surface may be caused by *diffraction*, the breaking up of light by the pattern of closely spaced myofibril ends, as in a so-called diffraction grating. In either case, the colors you see are dominated by green because the human eye is most sensitive to that color.

It's all perfectly harmless.

A COLORFUL CURE

Why do cured meats such as ham, corned beef, and hot dogs have that bright pink color?

. . . .

"**C**uring" meat means treating it to keep it from spoiling, thereby preserving it for future use. (Interesting that the "cure" prevents, rather than treats, the problem.) Ancient methods of curing meat include smoking, drying, and salting. When refrigeration and mechanical packaging came along, these flavor-intensive methods became unnecessary and experimentation with chemical curing began.

Meats cured with pure salt (sodium chloride, NaCl) tend to turn an unappetizing brownish-gray color. But about a hundred years ago it was found that if saltpeter (potassium nitrate, KNO_3) was added to the salt, the meat turned a nice, rosy pink. Today, we know that the potassium nitrate was being reduced to potassium nitrite (KNO_2) by microorganisms on the meat and that it's the nitrite that does the job. So potassium or sodium nitrite is now added to the curing salt directly, and saltpeter is rarely used. Nitrites give the meat a tangy flavor and an appetizing color, owing to the reaction of nitrite with myoglobin to form *nitric oxide myoglobin*. They also fight rancidity and the development of off odors and off flavors during storage.

But the most important function of nitrites is to inhibit the growth of pathogenic bacteria such as *Staphylococcus aureus* and *Clostridium botulinum*, the bacteria that cause botulism.

There's only one hitch in this rosy (literally) picture: Not only does nitrite kill botulin bacteria, but in doses of about 20 milligrams per kilogram of body weight it can kill humans as well. Fortunately, much of the nitrite added during curing is decomposed by cooking.

The USDA limits the amount of residual nitrite in any finished meat product, cooked or raw, to a maximum of 70 parts per million. At that level, a 150-pound person would have to eat 43 pounds of the product at one sitting to get a lethal dose of nitrite. That's a lot of bologna.

The bad news is that nitrites in cured meats can react with amines from the amino acids in heated meat protein to form chemical compounds called *nitrosamines*, many of which have been shown to cause cancers in experimental animals and are likely to be carcinogenic in humans as well. Bacon is a special case, because the high temperatures at which it is cooked are particularly conducive to nitrosamine formation. For that reason the USDA permits less nitrite to be used in curing bacon than in curing other meats.

Small amounts of nitrosamines occur naturally in some of our foods, such as fish. Moreover, bacteria in our mouths can change nitrate, which is present in many vegetables, to nitrite, which can then act upon the amines in the vegetables' proteins to form nitrosamines. Nitrosamines can also be formed by the action of the highly acidic juices in our stomachs upon a wide variety of amine-containing foods. Small amounts of nitrosamines can also be found in beer and tobacco.

All this may sound frightening, but don't give up on cured meats as a way of avoiding nitrites and nitrosamines. In our society we can't always eat fresh meat; some meat products must be cured before being distributed widely. Their small and carefully regulated nitrite content is a winning tradeoff against the risk of botulin poisoning.

On the other hand, it might be prudent not to tempt the nitrosamine gods by smoking a couple of packs of cigarettes while consuming 43 pounds of cured sausages and washing it down with a few gallons of beer.

In other words, stay away from Oktoberfest.

THE FOODIE'S FICTIONARY:

Knockwurst—a really bad knock-knock joke

Sidebar Science: *Blushing bologna*

NITRITES ACCOMPLISH their meat-curing magic by first being themselves transformed into (*reduced* to) nitric oxide (NO), a process that takes place only slowly by the action of natural antioxidants (also known as *reducing agents*) in the meat. The nitric oxide then bonds to myoglobin, the main pigment in red meat, to form nitric oxide myoglobin, which has an even brighter red color. Upon cooking or hot smoking, the nitric oxide myoglobin turns into nitrosylhemochromogen (sorry about all those syllables), which is the final pinkish color typical of all cured meats.

To speed up the development of color, meat processors add a reducing agent such as sodium erythorbate, a form of (an *isomer* of) the sodium salt of ascorbic acid, or vitamin C. You'll see sodium erythorbate or erythorbic acid listed as an ingredient on the labels of many cured meat products such as ham, bologna, sausages, hot dogs, and bacon.

The reducing agents used in curing have a second color-enhancing effect. Myoglobin in meats can exist in variously colored forms, ranging from purple to bright red to brown. (See "How now, brown cowburger?" on p. 275.) Reducing agents change the brown forms to red by changing the iron atoms in the myoglobin molecules from one form (the *ferric oxidation state*) to another (the *ferrous oxidation state*). That slight change in the iron atoms is enough to change the color of the myoglobin molecules from brown to a blushing red.

GO SOAK YOUR . . . STEAK

I am a cooking teacher and cookbook author,
but I have a question: Why do some recipes
say to marinate meat for only one or two hours?
For example, I have a pork in orange juice,
a chicken in rum sauce, and a lamb in beer.
It is easier for me (being on the run) to marinate
them overnight or all day.

. . . .

As you know, marinating—from the Latin *mare*, meaning sea—is the soaking of meat, poultry, or fish in a liquid concoction prior to cooking it, in an effort to improve either its flavor or its tenderness. But for a number of reasons, there can be no set rules for marinating. The amount of soaking time depends on the type and acidity of the marinade and the size, shape, and texture of the meat, among other things.

Ever since a sea nymph named Thetis dipped her son Achilles into the River Styx to make him invulnerable, the concept of a curative or restorative bath has appealed to our human yearning for quick and easy remedies. Innumerable spas and mineral-bath establishments around the world profit from this yearning by soaking their customers, both literally and figuratively. The "therapeutic baths" may consist of mud, cucumber puree, or Japanese stone juice. The fact is that a good soak in a hot bath of whatever composition (within reason) just plain feels good, and the customer goes away happy.

Unfortunately, the sources of our illnesses most often lie deep within our bodies, and "curative" elixirs simply don't soak through our skins like ink into a blotter. (Remember blotters?) But that fact hasn't kept the manufacturers of countless salves, balms, and ointments from claiming that they provide "deep, penetrating pain relief" or something along those lines. The most they can do is irritate the skin, whereupon the local blood circulation increases in an attempt to ameliorate the irritation, and the skin area feels warm.

And while we're in the neighborhood of dubious treatments, let me note that magnetic fields do indeed penetrate people, but so what? The health claims for wraps and pads containing sewn-in magnets are, to stick to culinary terminology, pure bologna.

The point of this rant against quackery is that the soaking of meat, if you'll forgive my sacrilegious characterization of the human body, cannot have an effect much deeper than its surface. And the same goes for marinating beef, pork, chicken, and fish, although, granted, we don't marinate whole pigs, skin and all, the way we do people.

Marinades cannot infuse deeply enough into the meat, even without skin, to deposit flavor throughout its volume. Marinating is therefore primarily a surface phenomenon, the marinade's ingredients penetrating no deeper than several millimeters (less than a quarter of an inch), depending on such factors as the density and structure of the meat, its cut, age, thickness, and temperature. Fibrous or "stringy" meats such as flank steak, however, may offer capillary channels between the fibers for the marinade to travel through, especially when the meat is cut into small pieces across the grain at an acute angle. The angle magnifies the openings of the capillary paths, just as when you cut a drinking straw on the diagonal; the circular opening becomes an oval of larger area.

To test some of these ideas, I cut raw flank steak into $\frac{1}{2}$-inch by $\frac{1}{2}$-inch by 2-inch bars, with the grain running the long way. I cut the ends across the grain with a very sharp knife to open as many of the putative passages as possible without crushing their ends. I then soaked the pieces at room temperature for various periods of time up to an hour in a mock marinade consisting of water, vinegar, and green food coloring.

At the end of the marinating period, I removed the meat and cut very thin slices off their ends to see how deeply the green color had penetrated. In no case did it penetrate more than a couple of millimeters.

It certainly seems that the effects of marinades may be, like a spa's "curative" waters, merely skin-deep, although longer marinating times might achieve somewhat deeper penetration. My one experiment does not a theory make. As I have written more than once at the ends of my published research papers, "further research is necessary to establish whether these results are generally applicable to other systems." (Translation: "I need more funding.")

That having been said and done, marinating meats has a long history and will undoubtedly persist as long as people perceive value in it. It does indisputably flavor the meat's surface and affect its subsequent cooking. So I'll continue to discuss marinating with the caveat that one mustn't expect too much of it.

A flavoring marinade, as distinguished from a marinade intended to tenderize, may consist of a wide range of seasonings incorporated into a liquid or a mixture of liquids. Wine-based marinades are quite commonly used, often seasoned with herbs, spices, or other flavorings that one expects will remain on or in the meat and contribute to its flavor during cooking. The larger the surface area of a piece of meat, the more opportunity a marinade has to affect its flavor. Thus, marinating is more effective for meat that has been cut into thin slices or into small cubes, such as for kabobs, than for thick steaks. Beyond a certain optimal point, marinating for a longer period of time will not effect deeper penetration; it can only intensify the flavor on the outer portions of the meat.

Contrary to common belief, stabbing the meat with a fork to produce punctures as entryways for the marinade is not only futile but counterproductive. Puncture wounds close up almost immediately because of the elasticity of the meat. Moreover, their latent tracks may later open up as the cooking heat shrinks the meat, thus creating exit paths for juices. Slashing or scoring a thick piece of meat before marinating, however, can boost its flavor by exposing more surface area to the marinade.

Marinades meant to tenderize tough cuts of meat almost invariably contain an acid, because acids deconstruct (*denature*) the proteins in muscle tissue. But that's a slow process. Smaller cuts and shapes of fibrous meats will require less soaking time, but acidic marinades in general require longer times to tenderize meat than simply to flavor it.

The more acidic the marinade, the shorter its optimum tenderizing time will be. In order of increasing acidity, a marinade may contain yogurt, buttermilk, beer, tomato juice, wine, orange juice, vinegar, lemon juice, or lime juice. Tenderizing marinades usually also contain an oil, because meats that are tough tend to be lean and dry as well. (The "juiciness" of meat is due at least as much to fat as to water.) Prepared vinaigrette salad dressings can serve as a double-threat marinade, because their vinegar tenderizes while their oil and condiments improve juiciness and flavor.

But how long, O Lord? With all of these variables, there can be no universal recommendation for marinating times. To quote conventional wisdom, however, most fish flesh is tender and somewhat porous, requiring short marinating periods of only 10 to 15 minutes. Dense-fleshed fish such as tuna and salmon may require twice that amount of time. Chicken may require 2 to 4 hours if skinless and 6 hours or more with the skin on. Various cuts of beef and pork are usually marinated for anywhere from 4 to 8 hours, the latter period of time often being referred to as overnight. Leave it much longer than that and the acid in a marinade can reconfigure the meat's protein molecules into tighter, more compact shapes, making the surface tougher. So don't sleep too late. And don't expect miracles. Tenderness is achieved only by selecting tender cuts of meat or by long, slow, moist cooking.

All of this having been said, the first law of marinating is Follow the Recipe. Any recipe worth its salt and pepper, taken from a reliable publication, has been tested and retested until it came out just right. The marinating time is simply another ingredient, like an amount of chopped onion or garlic, and shouldn't be monkeyed with. (Except that in my opinion one can always add more garlic.)

The most convenient way to marinate meat—and for safety's sake it must be done in the refrigerator—is in a sealed zipper-top plastic bag after you squeeze out most of the air to maximize liquid-to-surface contact. If you want to use the marinade to baste with during subsequent grilling or to make a cooked sauce, set aside some of it for that purpose *before* you add the meat, because even in the best of households raw meat can harbor pathogenic bacteria. Discard the rest of the marinade after it has done its job on the meat.

THE FOODIE'S FICTIONARY: French dressing—*habillement*

Sidebar Science: *Don't be a sucker*

THERE ARE a number of vacuum gadgets on the market that purport to speed up marinating. Even some commercial meat processors use them. But they're pure deception.

You're supposed to put your meat into a sealed container and pump most of the air out with a small hand-operated or electric pump. The idea is that as the air is sucked out of the meat's pores and channels, they'll absorb the marinade more quickly—"in minutes, not hours."

I never really bought this idea.

Just think about it. Sucking the air out of channels in the meat would collapse them, not open them up. It's like attaching a vacuum pump to a garden hose. Moreover, because the degree of vacuum (the *air pressure*) is the same everywhere in the container—in the meat and in the space around it—there is no force that could induce the liquid to flow from one location to the other. It's like expecting water to flow through a hose without any force, such as gravitation or a pressure difference, propelling it.

What does the research say? L. L. Young and D. P. Smith of the USDA's Agricultural Research Service (*Poultry Science* 83:129–131, 2003), marinated 256 chicken half-breasts either with or without vacuum for 30 minutes. They found that the vacuum increased absorption of the marinade slightly (by about 10 percent, according to an earlier study by the same group), but that "the added marinade is lost prior to or during cooking." Their conclusion: "Under the conditions of this study, vacuum appears to offer no real advantage over marination without the vacuum."

I decided to run my own experiments to see if I could tell what was actually happening to the meat. Instead of buying a— no kidding—Rhyme of the Instant Marinator (haha) for $24.95 plus shipping, I built my own from a clear glass vinegar bottle and a VacuVin: a pump-and-stopper device for pumping air out of partially empty bottles of wine, presumably so the wine doesn't oxidize when kept for several days before being tapped again. (I haven't done tests to see if wine really does keep longer when the bottle is pumped out by the VacuVin, but I have my doubts. Nevertheless, it makes me feel sophisticated to use it.)

I put some mock marinade (water, vinegar, and green food coloring) into the bottle, added pieces of flank steak, inserted the VacuVin stopper, attached the hand pump, and pumped the air out. (It should be realized that a pump can reduce the amount of air in a container, but it cannot create an actual vacuum, i.e., a space with no air in it at all. All a pump can do is reduce the air pressure, producing a *partial vacuum*.)

As I pumped the air out, I was fascinated to see the pieces of meat float up to the surface of the marinade! Dozens of tiny bubbles had emerged from the meat as I pumped; they adhered to the meat's surfaces and carried it upward like so many miniature life preservers. (The bubbles were too small to overcome their surface-tension-induced adherence to the meat and rise independently to the surface.)

Aha, then! Air was being sucked out of the meat's pores and channels, collapsing them as I had predicted, rather than opening them up.

After five or more minutes of marinating in repeated tests, I let the air back in. The bubbles mostly disappeared, because the air pressure now exceeded the pressure inside the bubbles, and the meat pieces promptly sank.

But did they sink because they had lost their bubbles, or because they had become heavier by sucking some marinade into their evacuated channels like a squeezed sponge suddenly being released under water—and thereby accomplishing the marinating task after all?

I removed the meat from the marinade and shaved off thin slices with a razor blade. There was virtually no evidence of the green marinade inside the meat, although the connective tissue on its surface had been dyed.

So should you buy a vacuum marinator? No. Any slight amount of marinade absorption that may take place when you release the vacuum, regardless of how long the meat had been marinating, is likely to be lost when you cook it, as was found by the USDA researchers.

Don't be sucked in by a "vacuum marinator."

Marinated Skirt Steak Fajitas

Skirt steak, which is the diaphragm that separates the chest and abdominal cavities of the animal, has a rich, beefy flavor. It used to be hard to find, but since fajitas have become popular, the cut is readily available at the supermarket. The thinness and loose grain of this rather tough cut make it a good choice for marinating.

In Mexican slang, a *fajita* is a small "belly band," girdle, or cummerbund. Edible fajitas are so named because of how the meat and other ingredients are wrapped into a tortilla.

A pile of corn chips on the side and a bowl of warm black beans or cool black bean salad are good companions to this dish.

- 2 **tablespoons olive oil**
- 2 **tablespoons freshly squeezed lime juice**
- 2 **cloves garlic, coarsely chopped**
- 1 **jalapeño pepper, seeds and ribs removed, coarsely chopped**
- 2 **small or 1 large skirt steak, about 2 pounds total**
- 2 **large, mild onions, sliced**
- 12 **flour or corn tortillas, 8 inches in diameter**
-   **Coarse salt and freshly ground pepper**
-   **Guacamole for serving**
-   **Salsa for serving**

---

1. In a mini–food processor or blender, combine the olive oil, lime juice, garlic, and jalapeño. Whirl until smooth and puréed. Place the steaks in a nonreactive dish or zipper-top plastic bag. Spread the mixture on both sides of the steak. Cover or seal closed and marinate in the refrigerator for at least 2 hours and up to 8 hours. Return to room temperature before cooking.

2. Preheat the grill or broiler. Preheat the oven to 300°F.

3. Broil or grill the onion slices and keep warm in the oven. Wrap the tortillas in a slightly dampened tea towel, put in a pie pan or on a cookie sheet, and place in the oven to warm and steam.

4. Grill or broil the steak, turning once, for about 5 minutes per side, or less, for

medium-rare. Transfer it to a cutting board and allow the meat to rest for at least 5 minutes.

5. Holding the knife at an angle to the cutting board, cut the meat across the grain into thin slices. Season the slices with coarse salt and pepper. (Coarse salt adds a nice crunch to the meat.)

6. Guests can build fajitas to their own liking. Holding a tortilla in one hand, add strips of meat, a helping of grilled onions, and a few spoons each of guacamole and salsa. Then roll the tortilla around the filling for a handheld meal.

MAKES 4 SERVINGS

PRAISING BRAISING

I'm familiar with almost all cooking methods, including boiling, simmering, steaming, roasting, baking, sautéing, frying, and grilling. Some of these methods use wet heat and some use dry heat. But I'm confused about braising, which seems to involve both wet and dry. Exactly what is braising, and what does it do that other methods don't do?

. . . .

Braising is a great vehicle for understanding both wet and dry cooking. Meat, poultry, shellfish, and vegetables are all grist for the braising mill, but I'll limit this discussion to meats.

I like to define braising as a two-step process: browning the meat to enhance its flavor, then simmering it for tenderness. The result can be a tender, juicy, and flavorful pot roast or fricassee. Without the initial browning, a unique set of flavors can be lost. Nevertheless, many food writers define braising as the moist-cooking step alone, including Crock-Pot and slow-cooker cooking. In these cases the meat is not initially browned because the equipment isn't designed to produce the necessary high, searing temperature. You could sear the meat in a skillet, which you then deglaze with some of the liquid to be added to the slow cooker. But that obviates one of the slow-cooker's advantages: no pan to clean.

Call it what you like. Include the browning step in the definition or not; many braising recipes skip it, with excellent results.

The noun *braise* in French means "glowing coals or embers," which were used traditionally for cooking over a brazier (and please make sure you pronounce that word with the accent on the first syllable) or for surrounding a heavy covered pot for the long, slow cooking of meats and vegetables, resulting in a carbonnade, *daube*, or stew. Today, we braise to conquer tough cuts of meat such as brisket, chuck, flank, round, and rump that would otherwise remain stubbornly tough and relatively un-infused with flavor.

Let's look at the browning step first.

The traditional Irish and Appalachian folk song has it that "black is the color of my true love's hair." But brown is the color of many of our true loved foods. We like our meats to be browned on their surfaces and our breads to display tan or lightly browned (often romanticized as "golden") crusts. Toast tastes better than untoasted bread; grilled steaks taste better than boiled beef. Heat-induced browning has long been used to add flavor to our foods. In the braising process, if we were to skip the initial browning step and merely simmer our meat and vegetables, we would lose much of the flavor of the final dish.

In Braising Stage One, we brown the meat by searing it on all sides in a small amount of hot oil in a heavy pot such as a Dutch oven, which we will later cover. During the searing, an intricate series of chemical reactions takes place, giving rise to the brown products. The reactions are called Maillard reactions, after Louis Camille Maillard (1878–1936), the French (obviously) chemist who characterized the initial step as being the reaction of a so-called reducing sugar, such as fructose, lactose, maltose, and glucose, with a protein.

Specifically, the initial Maillard reaction takes place between a certain part of the sugar molecule (its *carbonyl group*) and a certain part of the protein molecule (an *amino group* in one of its amino acids). After that first step, the Maillard process continues through a complex series of both consecutive and simultaneous chemical reactions, resulting in a hodgepodge of final compounds, many of which are dark-colored polymers and most of which are aromatic and flavorful. But some of them are bitter or, unfortunately, mutagenic—they increase the risk of inheritable genetic damage.

This is where our explanation of the Maillard reactions must come to a halt, as it does in other books not intended for professional food chemists. That's because the reactions are so complicated that chemists are still trying to isolate and identify the scores of transitional and final compounds involved. More than two hundred different chemical compounds have been isolated thus far in the products of Maillard reactions.

It would serve little purpose for me to escort you partway into the thicket of glycosylamines, deoxyosones, and Amadori rearrangements, and then leave you stranded in a sort of no-man's-land where the trail peters out. Most chemists (and I'll join them) simply cop out by referring to all the ultimately dark brown, nitrogen-containing compounds as *melanoidins*, from the Greek *melas*, meaning black or very dark.

Now, on to Braising Stage Two, wherein we add a small amount of liquid—such as stock, wine, cider, or beer—to the nicely browned meat and, if we're using them, the separately browned vegetables. Here's where braising departs from stewing; braising uses a small amount of liquid, whereas in stewing, the meat and vegetables are completely covered with liquid. As the meat simmers in the braising liquid, the water evaporates, condenses on the inside of the pot's cover, and drips back down, continuously basting the meat at a slightly-below-boiling temperature. This combination of heat and moisture converts one of the meat's major proteins, collagen, into a different form called gelatin.

Collagen makes up some 20 to 25 percent of all the protein in the mammalian body. It resides mainly in the connective tissue: the sheaths that surround the muscle fibers and the tough tendons and ligaments that tie the skeletal muscles to the bones. As its places of residence suggest, collagen is what makes meats tough. But when heated for a long time in a moist environment—just what we're doing in braising—collagen molecules undergo a change. Their triple-helical structure, looking like three braided strands of spaghetti, unwinds and breaks up into a number of small, random coils, like a bunch of tiny springs. These coils are molecules of gelatin. A much softer protein than collagen, gelatin has a prodigious ability to trap among its coils many times its own weight of water.

Evidence? The instructions on a box of regular Jell-O tell you to add two cups (237 grams) of water to only 8 grams of gelatin in the package (the rest is sugar). And yet all that water—thirty times the weight of the gelatin—is completely absorbed to form a semisolid gel when chilled.

Braising, then, captures the best of two worlds, turning out luscious Maillard-browned and -flavored, gelatin-tenderized dishes that can't be obtained in any other way.

The triple-helix structure of a collagen molecule. In the presence of heat and moisture, the strands unwind and break apart into coiled fragments, which are molecules of gelatin.

Sidebar Science: *Robert's rules of browning*

MUCH CONFUSION exists between Maillard browning and sugar browning or caramelization. Both a sugar molecule's carbonyl group and a protein molecule's amino group must be present if Maillard browning, also known as sugar-amine browning, is to take place. Heat accelerates the Maillard browning reactions, but they can take place at temperatures as low as 122°F (50°C). The reactions can even proceed slowly at room temperature, such as when foods turn brown from age.

In contradistinction, the browning of pure sugar or other carbohydrates at temperatures higher than about 250°F (120°C) —in the *absence* of an amino acid or other nitrogen-containing compound—takes place by a completely different set of complex chemical reactions, called *caramelization*. Many chefs seem to love the world *caramelize*, and use it indiscriminately to describe any food that turns brown upon being cooked. But meat, poultry, fish, vegetables, and other protein-containing foods do not caramelize. They simply *brown*. Not as fancy a word, perhaps, but accurate.

A third kind of food browning, *enzymatic browning*, is caused by enzymes in the food. The surface of a cut apple or pear turns brown because of the release of enzymes from the fruit's ruptured cells.

THE FOODIE'S FICTIONARY:
Collagen—a brand of canned chicken broth

Osso Buco

This is one of the best (and most delicious) illustrations of how collagen in the tough connective tissues in meat surrounding a bone turns into soft, smooth gelatin under the influence of moist heat.

Use your heaviest Dutch oven, preferably of enameled cast iron, to make this dish. When shopping, make sure that the bone of each piece of veal has a soft center full of marrow. Some bones do not. Give each diner a small, narrow knife (a lobster pick works in a pinch) to use for removing the creamy marrow. When spread on toast and sprinkled with salt and pepper, marrow is a treat. Serve the shanks with Baked Polenta (p. 228) and pass crusty peasant bread.

4 to 6   **meaty, bone-in veal shanks, each 8 to 12 ounces and about 2 inches thick**

        About $^1/_2$ cup all-purpose flour

        About 4 tablespoons olive oil

        Salt and freshly ground pepper

    1   **anchovy fillet**

    4   **cloves garlic, sliced**

    2   **small carrots, peeled and sliced**

    1   **onion, sliced**

    1   **celery stalk, diced**

  $^1/_2$ **cup dry white wine**

  $^1/_2$ **cup tomato purée**

GREMOLATA:

    2   **tablespoons chopped fresh parsley**

    1   **clove garlic, finely minced**

    1   **tablespoon grated lemon zest**

        Salt and freshly ground pepper

1. Preheat the oven to 325°F.
2. Coat the veal shanks with flour on both sides, shaking off any excess. Place a large, heavy Dutch oven over medium heat for 1 minute. Add 2 tablespoons

of the olive oil and 2 veal shanks and brown for 4 to 5 minutes on each side, seasoning them with salt and pepper as they brown. Do not crowd the pan. Remove them to a plate, add the remaining 2 veal shanks to the pot, and repeat. The browning for all 4 shanks will take a total of 15 to 20 minutes.

3. Add the remaining 2 tablespoons oil and the anchovy filet to the pot, mashing the anchovy into the oil. Add the garlic, carrots, onion, and celery, reduce the heat to medium-low, and cook the vegetables, stirring occasionally, for about 10 minutes, or until soft.

4. Add the veal shanks in a single layer, nestling them into the vegetables. Combine the wine and tomato purée in a small bowl, then pour the mixture over the meat and vegetables.

5. Cover the Dutch oven with a tight-fitting lid and place in the oven. Cook for 1½ to 2 hours, or until the meat is tender and falling off the bone and the juices are reduced. If the mixture starts to dry out during cooking, add a small amount of wine or water.

6. Make the *gremolata*: Just before serving, combine the parsley, garlic, and lemon zest in a small bowl.

7. When ready to serve, remove the meat to a warmed deep platter and cover to keep warm. Some cooks like to strain the sauce, but others prefer to keep the vegetables as they are, so strain it if you like. Stir the *gremolata* into the sauce and correct the seasoning with salt and pepper. Place the pot over medium heat and simmer for 2 minutes.

8. Pour the sauce over the meat. Serve right away.

MAKES 4 GENEROUS SERVINGS

Sidebar Science: *Why browning?*

WHEN WE brown our steaks in a skillet or on the grill, why aren't we "greening" or "redding" them?

First, let's remember that the color brown is simply an intense yellow. Thus, we're actually "intensely yellowing" our foods—that is, using heat to create high concentrations of yellow chemical compounds.

Okay, now why yellow? A substance appears yellow because it absorbs primarily blue light out of the all-color spectrum of sunlight—what we call "white light." Having had some of its blue removed, the light reflected back to our eyes is richer in its complementary color, yellow.

But why do our "browned" foods absorb mainly blue light? (Stick with me; we're getting closer.)

When a molecule absorbs a "piece" of visible light energy (a *photon*), it is the molecule's electrons that do the absorbing, in the process being promoted to a higher state of energy—being kicked upstairs, so to speak. The electrons in different molecules have different finicky preferences for the specific amounts of energy they will absorb—the specific numbers of stair steps that they are willing to be kicked up—and therefore the specific energies of light that they are willing and able to absorb. That's quantum theory.

The polymeric chemical compounds produced in the Maillard and caramelizing reactions are made up of very large molecules that hold on to their electrons rather tightly and that, as a consequence, can absorb primarily the higher-energy photons of light. The highest-energy light of all the colors that human eyes can see is blue, and when it is absorbed, the remaining light looks yellow—or, if it is more intense, brown.

STOCK OPTIONS

*Cookbooks tell me that when making a stock
I should always start with the bones and
vegetables in cold water, because cold water
brings out more flavor. That doesn't sound right
to me. Don't most substances dissolve better
in hot water than in cold?*

. . . .

Yes, they do. Just see how flavorful a stock you'd get by soaking the ingredients for hours in cold water, without ever simmering them. Or try making a cup of tea with cold water—in a respectable amount of time, that is.

On second thought, don't. You've heard of "natural," "environmentally friendly" sun tea? It's made by placing tea bags in cold water in a glass jar and placing the jar in direct sunlight to brew for several hours. Well, warm water—up to 175°F (79°C)—containing organic matter is a good breeding ground for bacteria. And of course, the "warm, gentle rays of the sun" add nothing to the brew except poetry. To be perfectly safe, always make your tea with water that's hotter than 195°F (91°C).

Cookbooks tell you how to make a stock, a concentrated water extraction of flavors from meat or fish bones and/or vegetables, but they rarely explain the reasons behind the steps. That's understandable, because the purpose of a cookbook is to help you do the job right. But it's easier to remember a procedure if it makes sense to you, rather than its being a mere series of "do this, don't do that" instructions. If you understand the reasons behind the instructions, as I hope this book will enable you to do, maybe next time you won't need the cookbook and can venture forth on your own.

Stocks are known as either "brown" stocks, in which the bones and perhaps the vegetables have been browned by being roasted in the oven before being put into the pot, or "white" stocks, which aren't really white, but merely not brown. Veal stocks are most often brown; chicken and vegetable stocks are usually white.

Dry-roasting the bones prior to simmering them adds a unique set of flavors to a stock because of the Maillard browning reactions: chemical reactions between the proteins and carbohydrates in the meaty and gristly hangers-on attached to the bones. (See pp. 296–97.) Without Maillard browning, those flavors would be absent from the stock. The other, "wet" flavors would still get a chance to develop as the water heats up and simmers.

Let's look at some of the reasons behind the customary instructions for making a stock.

• **Always start the bones and vegetables in cold water.** The statement that starting with cold water "extracts the most flavor" is very misleading. It's not that cold water extracts more flavor compounds than hot water does. It's that if you were to start by plunging the bones and vegetables directly into hot water, some of the flavorful proteins would be made more difficult to extract during the later simmering stage. Thus, you would ultimately wind up with more flavor by not starting with hot water.

Here's why.

When subjected to heat, proteins become reconfigured (*denatured*). That is, their curly-shaped molecules first unfold and then rebond into tighter, tangled structures. It's more difficult for water to extract flavorful molecules out of these coagulated structures than out of the proteins in their original forms. So to extract the most flavor into the water, we don't want the proteins to tighten up too soon.

If the bones and vegetables are started in cold water, the water-soluble proteins (some proteins are soluble in water; some aren't) will have ample time to dissolve in the water before being made insoluble and inaccessible by the denaturation process. Also, during this low-temperature stage some undesirable water-soluble impurities, such as those in blood, will have time to dissolve in the water, where they will later coagulate as the water becomes hot. (You know that to remove blood stains from fabrics you soak them in cold water, because hot water would "set" the stain by coagulating the proteins.)

During gradual heating from a cold start, these undesirable proteins coagulate slowly throughout the body of the liquid forming relatively large particles of gunk. Meanwhile, some of the fat on the bones will have been melting and rising to the water's surface. On its journey to the top, the oil will encounter the coagulated protein particles and coat them, acting as a sort of life vest to float them up to the surface as a greasy scum, which you can skim off.

On the other hand, in hot-from-the-start water, the impurity proteins would coagulate more rapidly, forming tinier particles of gunk that would neither settle out nor be captured by rising fat. They would stay suspended in the liquid, making it cloudy. (An exception to the cold-start procedure: Many chefs, for reasons of their own, prefer to add the vegetables only after the water is hot.)

- **Add only enough cold water to cover the bones.** Too much water would make a less flavorful stock; you want the extracted flavors to be well concentrated. Too little water, on the other hand, could leave some of the bones sticking out. Not only would their flavors be lost to the stock—water can extract flavors only from what is immersed in it—but the protruding bones could dry out, darken, and discolor the stock, a special concern if you're making a white stock. To keep the water at the right level, you have to replace any water lost by evaporation as the stock simmers.
- **Bring the water to a boil and then immediately turn down the heat to a simmer. Then simmer it; do not boil.** Why simmer a stock instead of boiling it? The main reason is that the agitation of a full boil would break down those clusters of fat-coated, coagulated protein gunk into such tiny particles that

they would evade your skimmer and once again you'd wind up with a cloudy stock.

Beef and veal stocks are simmered longest (6 to 8 hours) because their bones are relatively large and the flavor components are relatively inaccessible to the water. That's why the bones should be cut up into 3- to 4-inch pieces. Chicken stocks, containing smaller bones, are generally simmered for 3 to 4 hours, while fish and vegetable stocks are simmered for only 30 to 45 minutes. The objective is to extract as many good flavors as possible and to convert as much of the connective tissue's collagen into gelatin as you can, because gelatin gives the stock smoothness and body.

But certain flavor components begin to break down or become less desirable when a stock is cooked too long. (That's especially true of fish stocks, whose muscle proteins are less stable than those in land animals.) Restaurant chefs may let their stocks simmer for as long as 6 to 8 hours and then reduce them even further after removing the solids. But for smaller home quantities, 3 or 4 hours should do the job. These times are the best compromise between extracting the most gelatin and retaining the best flavor. Simmering for less time than that will generally produce a stock that is thinner and not as flavorful.

- **Skim the frothy scum off frequently.** As we've seen, the scum consists largely of insoluble, congealed proteins. It won't kill you, but it's unappetizing. If left in the water during cooking, the proteins will tighten up even further into gunky gray specks, many of which will stick to the inside of the pot at the water line, forming a kind of (excuse the metaphor) bathtub ring.

Do your skimming with a fine mesh or net skimmer, *not* with a spoon of any kind. A slotted spoon lets the scum fall right through, and a solid-bowl spoon removes not only the scum but also the float-

A fine-mesh stainless steel skimmer. Indispensable for removing "broth froth" without removing the flavorful layer of fat. Made by Calphalon.

ing layer of flavorful fat, which you will deal with later. The mesh on a skimmer is just the right size to capture the scum alone.

After the prescribed cooking time, scoop out the bones and vegetables (now's the time for your slotted spoon) and strain the remaining liquid through two or three layers of cheesecloth.

But, you ask, if you were eventually going to strain it, why all the fuss about preventing cloudiness? Because filtering through even several layers of cheesecloth doesn't remove the very tiny suspended particles (*colloids*) that can make liquids cloudy.

- **Cool the stock quickly.** A stock is just as yummy to bacteria as it is to humans. That is, it's a great culture medium. If allowed to cool slowly, it may spend too much time passing through the bacterial-growth-friendly temperature range of 40 to 140°F (4 to 60°C). (See also "Bacteria in suits of armor," p. 310.)

Restaurants have deep sinks with overflow pipes, in which running cold water circulates around huge pots of hot stock. At home, you can put your pot in a sink filled with cold water up to the level of the stock inside (any higher than that and the pot will float); stir the stock periodically and change the water as it warms up.

- **Refrigerate the strained, cooled liquid and remove the solidi-fied fat from its surface.** That's not only for the usual fat-phobic reasons, but because while solidifying, the fat will trap any of the oily flotsam that evaded your skimmer. (You'll see it clinging to the bottom of the cake of fat.) But fat is flavorful, so don't be ruthless. In the case of chicken stock, especially, you might want to allow some of the fat to remain.

Whatever you do, don't put any pot of hot stuff directly into the refrigerator. A large pot of liquid contains a lot of calories of heat that will warm up everything in there, encouraging spoilage. Either cool the whole pot as described above, or divide the contents into several small containers, seal them, and let them cool individually before placing them in the fridge. They will cool much faster than if you try to cool a whole potful, because there is more surface area for the cool air to make contact with.

Now freeze your stock in convenient portions to be used for boosting the flavor of soups, sauces, and such thirsty dishes as risotto.

Sidebar Science: *Simmering and quivering*

A POT is truly simmering when you can see only an occasional bubble breaking the surface. Bubbles are little pockets of water vapor, created at the bottom of the pot where the temperature is highest. They then rise, but most of them revert to liquid and collapse as they cool down on the way up, never reaching the surface. The only ones we consider "real bubbles" are those that make it all the way.

Several cookbooks attempt to define a simmer by stating specific water temperatures, often widely diverging ones, somewhere below 212°F (100°C). But the exact temperature of a simmering pot will depend on the characteristics of the burner, the pot, and its contents, not to mention the altitude of your kitchen and the weather. (At low barometric pressures, water boils at a lower temperature.) And if you're shooting for a specific simmering temperature, where are you supposed to measure the temperature of a stock? Near the bottom of the pot, where it's hottest, or somewhere higher up, where it's cooler?

So forget about trying to achieve a certain temperature and use the small number of occasional bubbles as your criterion for a proper simmer.

French cooks sometimes make a distinction between the simmering of soups or stews that contain solids, and the simmering of liquids such as water, milk, or thin sauces. In the former case, they use the verb *mijoter*, which is more or less equivalent to the English verb *simmer*. But when the entire surface of a pot of liquid is clearly visible to the cook, undisturbed by icebergs of meat and vegetables sticking up, there is a discernible pre-simmer or pre-bubble stage that the French call *frémir*, meaning to quiver or to tremble.

If you look closely at a pot of heating water as it approaches a simmer and before any bubbles break the surface, you will see the surface quiver—or, as some would have it, smile. The quiver is caused by *convection currents*, plumes of hot water rising through zones of cooler water, giving up some of their heat to the air when they reach the surface, and then, being a bit cooler than before, falling back down. The slight disturbances of the liquid's surface as these plumes reverse their direction creates a visible quivering effect.

An egg may be coddled or minimally cooked by *frémissement* (*frémir*-ing it) rather than by *mijotement* (*mijoter*-ing it), because it is completely submerged in the water. The average temperature of the cooking water will be slightly less than at a simmer.

BACTERIA IN SUITS OF ARMOR

Why all the cautions about cooling a soup or stock quickly to prevent the growth of dangerous bacteria? After all, the stuff has just been simmered for more than an hour. Wouldn't that have sterilized it, as long as I keep it covered while it cools so that new bacteria don't drop in for dinner?

. . . .

Unfortunately, no. Not all bacteria are killed at 212°F (100°C). Some of them can survive by protecting themselves within virtually invulnerable coatings. They're then called spores.

Most species of bacteria reproduce by binary fission, each organism splitting into two whole new organisms. That's why they can grow at exponential rates. Once they get started, bacteria can increase their numbers from, say, 5,000 to 10,000 to 20,000 to 40,000, and so on, doubling as often as every ten minutes, until they can reach as many as 10 billion in every milliliter (one-thirtieth of an ounce) of your soup or stock by the time they run out of nutrients.

But when conditions are not conducive to their growth, or are even out-and-out hostile, some species of bacteria (and fungi) can ride it out as spores—dormant and virtually indestructible forms. Protected by tough, horny suits of armor, the spores are capable of surviving such calamitous surroundings as boiling water, nutritional deprivation, dryness, freezing, ultraviolet light, corrosive chemicals, and even heavy-metal rock music. When conditions improve, such as when your stock cools to a comfortable growth temperature, the spores can transform themselves into whole new individuals that will resume reproduction in the normal way.

A common pathogenic genus of spore-forming bacteria found in soil, water, and the intestinal tracts of humans and animals is *Clostridium*, especially the species *C. perfringens*, which is a major cause of food poisoning, and the much rarer *C. botulinum*, which produces botulin toxin, one of the most potent poisons known. *Clostridium* bacteria don't need oxygen to live; in fact, they can't survive in air, so the interior of a pot of stock is a perfect growth environment for them.

To kill spores, temperatures significantly higher than 212°F (100°C) are needed. That's why medical and surgical equipment is sterilized in an autoclave, a sort of pressure cooker. Under higher pressures, water boils at higher temperatures. Pressure cookers and autoclaves are closed containers in which the steam pressure from boiling water builds up enough to raise the boiling temperature to about 250°F (141°C), high enough to kill most bacterial spores.

I have traveled in quite a few countries in which my American stomach was unaccustomed, and therefore vulnerable, to the local . . . shall we say, wee little beasties that can be found in food. I stuck as much as possible to deep-fried foods (which are often the best local snacks anyway), because oil at 350°F (177°C) will kill almost anything.

The inside of a food can is an excellent oxygen-free breeding place for *Clostridium* spores. That's why, after being filled and sealed, canned foods are sterilized by being heated in high-pressure steam kettles or cookers at temperatures of 240 to 250°F (116 to 141°C). If the sterilization isn't complete and live bacteria grow in the can, they produce hydrogen gas, which can cause the can to bulge. So if the end (the weakest part) of a food can bulges or buckles even slightly when you press on it, use the can to practice your shot-put into the nearest landfill.

A BONE-BENDING EXERCISE

I learned at my mother's knee to add a little acid—lemon juice, vinegar, or wine—to increase the amount of calcium that would come out of the bones when making a stock. Does it work?

. . . .

Yes, to a slight extent.

Bones are a combination of two kinds of substances: (1) soft, organic cells and proteins, which are partly extracted into the water during the simmering of a stock, and (2) a hard, inorganic mineral that doesn't dissolve appreciably or contribute any flavor. This mineral material in both bones and teeth is primarily a calcium phosphate compound called hydroxyapatite, which, as your dentist will hasten to inform you, is attacked by acids. (In the case of tooth decay, the acids are produced by bacteria.)

Unless the acid is very strong, it will take a long time to dissolve very much of the calcium phosphate in your soup bones. The small amounts of relatively weak acids in lemon juice, vinegar, or wine won't extract much calcium, even after hours of simmering.

But if you want to have some fun, try this: Immerse a cooked and well-cleaned chicken bone (the thigh bone works well) in a covered jar of undiluted vinegar and let it soak for four or five weeks. The vinegar's acid will dissolve enough of the hard hydroxyapatite so that mostly the soft, organic materials remain. You will then be able to startle your friends by bending a very flexible chicken bone.

Tell them it came from a rubber chicken.

WHY WINE?

Is the following assertion true? "Cooking with wine adds extra flavor to a dish because the alcohol dissolves and releases flavor components that are not dissolvable in water." I've seen this statement, or statements like it, in several places. But I'm a chemist, and it just doesn't sound right to me.

. . . .

Chefs I've spoken with accept this idea as quite reasonable, and indeed it does seem to make sense on the surface of it, because many substances do indeed dissolve in alcohol but not in water.

Nevertheless, the statement is false. The real reason we use wine in cooking is simply that a good wine contributes its flavor to the dish. It has nothing to do with dissolving flavor components.

Here's the catch: In a mixture of alcohol and water, such as wine, the alcohol doesn't act like pure alcohol and the water doesn't act like pure water. They act like a mixture of alcohol and water, and a mixture can have quite different properties from either of the pure liquids.

For example, if we mix equal amounts of alcohol and water, the mixture will be more than 2½ times as viscous ("thick") as either the pure alcohol or the pure water. The reason is that alcohol molecules and water molecules attract and stick to one another by forming so-called hydrogen bonds. They cannot flow as freely as the less hindered molecules can in either pure alcohol or pure water. The properties of the mixture, including what it can and cannot dissolve, vary as the percentage of alcohol varies. If a given substance dissolves in pure alcohol or pure water, that doesn't mean it will dissolve in any given mixture of alcohol and water.

Is all of this mere theory? No. I did an experiment to test it.

Annatto seeds, also known as *achiote* (ah-chee-OH-te), are the seeds of the tropical evergreen shrub *Bixa orellana*. They are coated with a paste-like oil containing an intense yellow-orange carotenoid pigment called bixin, which dissolves in oils and in alcohol but not in water. Annatto's bixin is an FDA-approved coloring for fatty foods such as butter, margarine, and process cheeses. In this experiment, I used the highly visible bixin to simulate an alcohol-soluble flavor component in a food.

I placed five annatto seeds into each of four small test tubes and added 15 milliliters (a tablespoon) of one of the following liquids to each tube: water, a chardonnay containing 13 percent alcohol, a vodka containing 40 percent alcohol (80 proof), and 95-percent-pure ethyl alcohol. I let the tubes stand at room temperature for several days, shaking occasionally.

Here are the results: Neither the water nor the wine showed any dissolved bixin color at all; the water remained colorless and the white wine remained, well, white-wine colored. The vodka turned mildly yellow from a small amount of dissolved bixin, while the 95-percent-pure alcohol turned intensely yellow.

Conclusion: Wine—even straight, undiluted wine—doesn't dissolve or "release" any alcohol-soluble bixin from the seeds. The alcohol concentration has to be high, some 40 percent or higher, to extract any appreciable amount of bixin. But such high alcohol concentrations never occur in cooking. Adding half a cup of vodka to a quart of sauce would produce a solution of only about 5 percent alcohol, even lower than the completely ineffective alcohol concentration in undiluted wine.

But that was at room temperature. What happens in the heat of cooking?

Although most substances are more soluble at higher temperatures, the facts of life regarding hydrogen bonding are still in effect. So while hot, pure alcohol will extract more alcohol-soluble components at higher temperatures, hot wine still won't. So the "wine extracts flavors" theory still doesn't hold water, so to speak.

Nevertheless, the alcohol in wine can contribute to flavor beyond the flavors inherent in the wine itself. During cooking, the alcohol can react chemically with acids in the food to form fragrant, fruity compounds called esters. You can demonstrate this by vigorously shaking some denatured ethyl alcohol (available in hardware and paint stores) with vinegar (acetic acid) in a tightly sealed bottle. After shaking for several minutes, open the bottle carefully and sniff; in addition to the odors of the alcohol and vinegar, you will detect a fruity note of ethyl acetate, one of the esters in the aroma of pineapple.

In the cooking pot, alcohol can react also with oxidizing substances to form aldehydes—compounds responsible for flavors such as almond, cinnamon and vanilla. Both the esters and the aldehydes are new flavors that were not present in the original ingredients. And contrary to widespread belief, the alcohol never "boils off" completely. It has plenty of time to take part in these chemical reactions during cooking.

So enjoy your *coq au vin* and *boeuf Bourguignonne*. The wine will add flavor in several ways, but don't expect it to "extract" or "release" any alcohol-soluble flavors from your food.

And now that I think of it, why must we extract flavor compounds from our food, anyway? If they're in there, they're in there, and we'll taste them when we chew, whether they are in the solids or the sauces.

Sidebar Science: *On solvents, solutes, and solvation*

FOR A SOLUBLE substance (a *solute*) to dissolve in a liquid such as alcohol (a *solvent*), the solvent's molecules must surround each solute molecule (*solvate* it) like a swarm of hungry piranhas and drag it out into the liquid. But if the alcohol is mixed with water, the hydrogen bonds between them hamper the alcohol molecules' ability to solvate the molecules of the solute. Thus, a mixture of alcohol in water cannot effectively dissolve what pure alcohol might be able to dissolve.

Moreover, the less alcohol there is in the water, the more its solvating prowess is weakened. For example, when you add half a cup of wine containing 12 percent alcohol to a quart of braising liquid, the alcohol concentration is reduced to 1.5 percent. The alcohol molecules are outnumbered by water molecules by nearly 200 to 1, so there just aren't enough of them to cluster around and solvate the solute molecules. Too many water molecules are getting in their way.

IT'S A GAS! OR IS IT?

I'm in the market for a backyard barbecue
grill and I'm trying to decide between gas
and charcoal. Everyone I ask has a different
opinion—that is, one of two opinions, and
they're all fanatical about their choice.
Do you have some objective advice?
....

I try not to get into politics or controversy in this book, but this issue is so critical, and the two candidates so contrasting, that I cannot resist asserting my position on this, the most contentiously debated concern of our time: "Which is better, charcoal or gas?" I hereby express my wholehearted endorsement of charcoal.

Caution: The opinions expressed below are inflammatory. Reader discretion is advised.

Grilling is hot these days. (Weak pun intended.) I have eleven grilling cookbooks on my bookshelves, but they all shrewdly gloss over two important points: that grilling and barbecuing are not the same thing, and that all fuels are not created equal.

Recognizing that almost no one understands the distinction between grilling and barbecuing, the cookbooks include both kinds of recipes in order to appeal to as many backyard Escoffiers as possible. And because an estimated 70 percent of all "barbecue grills" (a name that only compounds the confusion) in the United States are gas-fired, the authors stifle their unanimous but secret conviction (which they would admit only under oath) that charcoal is clearly superior to gas for grilling. An author cannot afford to lose a major segment of his or her potential readers, many of whom have shelled out big bucks for Brobdingnagian stainless steel, 18-wheeler gas grills equipped with everything but cruise control and a global positioning system.

In true grilling, the food is placed within several inches of a very hot—500 to 1000°F (260 to 540°C)—smoke-free fire and cooked quickly. Think of steaks, chops, hamburgers, kebabs, sausages, chicken parts, whole fish and shrimp, to name the most commonly grilled foods.

Barbecuing, on the other hand, consists of long (several hours), slow, relatively low-temperature cooking—300 to 350°F (about 150 to 180°C) or even lower—with the food confined in a pit or some sort of enclosure along with a (generally) smoky fire. Think of beef or pork ribs, pork shoulder, or brisket being slathered with top-secret sauces by men wearing cowboy hats. I'll stick to grilling here.

There are three kinds of fuels: lump charcoal, briquettes, and gas.

• **Lump charcoal:** If wood is heated in the absence of oxygen (a process called destructive distillation), it can't burn. Instead, it decomposes. First, its water is driven off. Then its carbohydrates (mainly cellulose and lignin) begin to break down into methyl alcohol (therefore known as wood alcohol), acetic acid, acetone, formaldehyde, and many other smokes and gases. Eventually, nothing is left but virtually pure carbon. That's lump charcoal.

For at least four thousand years, people have been making charcoal from wood for use as a cooking fuel. Contrary to an oft-repeated legend, charcoal was not invented by Henry Ford. Nor, I might add, did he invent wood or fire. (But see below.)

Today's commercial lump charcoal, still retaining the shapes of the wood chunks it was made from, burns hot and clean, with minimal amounts of smoke. It therefore earns my vote (and the secret ballots of most grilling experts) as the best possible fuel for grilling. There's no fuel like an old fuel.

• **Briquettes:** Briquettes—and I won't call them charcoal briquettes because they contain so much other stuff besides charcoal—were not invented by Henry Ford either. Fuel briquettes were invented and patented by one Orin F. Stafford, a professor at the University of Oregon. Then Ford, always looking to make a buck, jumped in and built a plant to manufacture briquettes on a grand scale, thereby turning the waste sawdust and wood scraps from his Model T plant into a profitable product.

Originally, briquettes were made from powdered charcoal, compressed and bound with starch. But today they're not that simple. According to a 2000 publication of the Kingsford Products Company, heir to the Ford Charcoal Company, their briquettes contain wood charcoal, mineral char (a soft, brown coal), mineral carbon (graphite), limestone (to produce that nice coating of white ash), starch (as binder), borax (helps release the briquettes from the molds), sawdust (for easier ignition) and sodium nitrate, which releases oxygen when heated and speeds the burn.

Personally, I would rather not have tar-laden coal, starch, borax, and sawdust burning beneath my steak.

- **Gas:** The fuel used in modern gas grills is either methane (natural gas, CH_4) or propane (C_3H_8), whose molecules are made of nothing but carbon atoms and hydrogen atoms. And that's the difference between charcoal (carbon) and gaseous fuels: the hydrogen atoms. While charcoal burns to produce only carbon dioxide (and some carbon monoxide), methane and propane produce both carbon dioxide and water vapor. Hold a transparent glass dish briefly above a gas flame and you'll see it fog up with condensed water.

Each molecule of burned propane produces four molecules of water. In a typical 40,000-Btu-per-hour gas grill, that translates to 1½ quarts of water being given off per hour. The bottom surface of the meat is thus being steamed, and its temperature cannot get as high as with dry-burning charcoal. No wonder you can't quite achieve that flavorful, seared brown crust that charcoal produces.

Case closed.

Grilling mavens distinguish between two techniques: direct grilling, where the meat is placed directly above a bed of charcoal, and indirect grilling, where the charcoal pile is off to one side.

In the direct method, the heat reaches the meat by both convection (rising hot air) and radiation (infrared rays). In the indirect method, since the meat isn't directly above the heat source, the heat reaches the meat predominantly by radiation. (The third heat transmission mechanism, conduction, doesn't play much of a role in grilling.) The meat therefore doesn't attain as high a temperature in the indirect method and cooks more slowly. If the cooking apparatus is covered, the rising hot air from the coals is trapped and circulates throughout the enclosure, making it into a sort of convection oven. Throw in a few chips of moistened hardwood and you can smoke the food at the same time.

Whoops! In that last paragraph I have slipped from grilling into barbecuing. That's easy to do, because the same equipment can be used for both, and few people—including the manufacturers of the equipment—bother to make the verbal distinction.

SMOKERS WELCOME

*My neighbors bought a smoker. It looks like a
big green egg about three feet high, standing on
its narrow end. They use it for cooking meats and
fish with smoke, and they have a collection of
several different woods that they say have
different flavors. How does wood smoke
cook and flavor food?*

. . . .

Not having been a termite in a previous life, I cannot comment on the flavors of the woods themselves. But when we burn them and, in effect, eat their smoke, I do have a few observations.

The proper name of your neighbors' big green egg is the Big Green Egg. It is one brand of *kamado*, a word derived from the traditional Japanese steamed rice cooker, the *mushikamado*, which in Japanese means, well, steamed rice cooker. A *mushikamado* is a hollow, egg-shaped, fired-clay urn, used by building a wood fire in the bottom and suspending a rice cooker from the lid. The rice not only cooks from the heat but acquires an interesting smoky flavor.

In the early 1960s, an enterprising American pilot named Richard Johnson discovered the *mushikamado* in Japan and decided that with a few modifications it could be used as an American backyard cooker and smoker. After more than forty years, his company, the Kamado Corp., still manufactures them in factories in Sacramento, California, and elsewhere. He owns the trademark Kamado, with a capital *K*, but the Big Green Egg people call their product a kamado with a lowercase *k*.

There are dozens of other kinds of smokers on the U.S. market, shaped like oil drums, rectangular iron boxes ("smoker ovens"), or you name it—anything that will collect the smoke from burning chunks or chips of hardwood inside an enclosure containing the food. Smoke fiends have been known to adapt everything from charcoal grills to old refrigerators.

Among everyone's favorite smoked foods are trout, salmon, beef brisket, pork shoulder, turkey, and even vegetables such as potatoes and tomatoes. The temperature is maintained somewhere between

The Big Green Egg, a device used for smoking, grilling, and barbecuing.
It is an adaptation of the Japanese *kamado*. (Courtesy of The Big Green Egg.)

125 and 220°F (52 and 104°C) for long, slow cooking, both to tenderize tough meats (except for fish, which cooks quickly) and to give the
smoke enough time to do its flavoring job. With some precautions,
foods can be smoked indoors also, either in the oven or in a special
range-top roasting pan designed for the purpose. (Turn off your
smoke detector and monitor the process carefully. And don't forget
to rearm the smoke detector when you're done.)

Note that we are talking here about so-called *hot smoking*. At 125
to 220°F (52 to 104°C), the foods are not only infused with smoke flavor but also cooked to some extent. Commercial smokehouses also
employ so-called *cold smoking* (see p. 354), where the temperature of
the food, such as bacon, is not allowed to exceed about 90 to 100°F
(32 to 38°C). Liquid smoke (see p. 353) is also often used.

One of the earliest cooking methods devised by humans was to
hang meat over a wood fire, burning in the bottom of a pit dug into
the ground. The intention was that the fire's heat would cook the
meat, but to twist an aphorism, where there's fire there's smoke, and
the effects of the smoke were inescapable. Important among these
effects—although it was not understood until modern times—is that
smoke acts as a preservative by killing decay-producing microorganisms. Eventually, the smoke itself became the desired instrument,
and smoking foods, most notably hams, to preserve them became a
worldwide practice.

Today, we have efficient distribution of foods from producer to
consumer, and long-term preservation isn't as important as it once
was. Moreover, we have refrigeration, which doesn't kill pathogenic
organisms but slows down their growth. So now we can smoke foods
at home just because we like the flavor. And, yes, different hard-
woods—alder, apple, cherry, hickory, maple, oak, and pecan—do impart
different flavors to the food via their smoke. After all, if the woods
were so chemically identical that they produced chemically identical
smoke, they wouldn't be different trees. Soft woods such as pine, fir,
and spruce are unsuitable for smoking food because they contain
too much sap and resin, which produce noxious, sooty smoke.

Now look at the blue flame on your gas cooktop or in your gas grill. The flame produces no smoke at all. That's because the gas is being fed enough oxygen to burn completely. It is all transformed—almost every molecule of it—into the invisible gaseous products carbon dioxide, carbon monoxide, and water vapor. But when wood or almost any other fuel burns, the burning reactions are rarely complete. Wood is solid, and its molecules don't all get a chance to mix freely with the oxygen in the air. The oxygen-starved fuel can't burn completely, and tiny particles of it, half-burned and still solid, are released into the maelstrom of flame and rise along with the gases as a black or gray cloud: smoke.

If we want the maximum amount of smoke from burning pieces of wood, then, we must partially starve it of oxygen. So we'll soak wood chips in water for an hour or so before heating them to their smoke point, at which time they will smolder away, infusing our food with flavors that can't be achieved in any other way.

And now for the bad news.

Along the way toward complete combustion—which, remember, wood fuel never achieves— hundreds of intermediate chemicals are formed and go up in the smoke. They include formaldehyde, formic acid, phenols, benzene, quinoline, and many other toxic chemicals, some of which are carcinogenic to boot. Among the worst actors are polycyclic aromatic hydrocarbons (PAH's), a class that includes the arch-carcinogen benzo[a]pyrene, B[a]P. The flat molecules of B[a]P can slip between the rungs of our DNA molecules' spiral ladder and, if you'll pardon the technical jargon, louse them up. That can lead to cancer. The popular and uniquely flavorful mesquite is a resinous wood whose smoke has been reported to be particularly rich in PAH's.

So what price flavor? The first time I had a steak cooked in Arizona over burning mesquite wood, I was, like, blown away, man! It was awesome! (That was for my younger readers.) I have not, however, persisted in a steady diet of mesquite-grilled steak (or any other kind of steak, for that matter), in spite of the fact that a risk is only a risk, not a certainty. But even if that steak doubled my minute risk of PAH-induced cancer, it was worth it.

On the basis of risk statistics, I ceased my daily ingestion of tobacco smoke more than twenty years ago. On the same basis, however, I see no reason to avoid an occasional hit of smoked salmon.

As Voltaire put it, "Moderation is the pleasure of the wise."

Sidebar Science: *The bricks and mortar of trees*

THE HUNDREDS of chemical compounds in wood smoke come from the burning of wood's two major structural components, lignin and cellulose. Lignin is a group of polymeric (large-molecule) chemical compounds that cement the cellulose walls of the plant cells together, as mortar cements bricks. Lignin thus increases the strength, hardness, and rigidity of wood. Without it, trees would be as droopy as a rubber telephone pole.

The primary flavor chemicals in wood smoke arise from the burning of lignin; they are the phenolic compounds syringol and guaiacol and their derivatives. The burning of the wood's cellulose, on the other hand, creates volatile compounds called cyclopentenolones, which add a sort of caramel note to the smoky flavor.

Chapter Eight

Spice Is the Variety of Life

. . . .

ATCH EACH of the following spices or condiments with the national cuisine that makes the most use of it. Answers are at the bottom of the page. No peeking.

1. Curry
2. Harissa
3. *Herbes de Provence*
4. *Ketjap manis*
5. Miso
6. *Mole*
7. Paprika
8. Pesto
9. *Pimentón*
10. Star anise

(a) China
(b) France
(c) Hungary
(d) India
(e) Indonesia
(f) Italy
(g) Japan
(h) Mexico
(i) Spain
(j) Tunisia

Your score of 7 or better has proven my point: The cuisines of various ethnic, national, and regional cultures can be characterized largely by the ways in which they use spices, herbs, and condiments.

Answers: 1-d, 2-j, 3-b, 4-e, 5-g, 6-h, 7-c, 8-f, 9-i, 10-a

Spices do indeed enhance the variety of culinary life around the world.

But what's the difference between a spice and an herb?

They can both be described as plant-derived food ingredients that yield large amounts of flavor from small amounts of substance. That operational nondistinction is really good enough in most situations, because knowing the characteristic flavors and uses of a spice or herb is far more important to the cook than knowing its botanical niceties. Nevertheless, there is a fairly reliable (though often muddied) technical distinction between herbs and spices.

The word *herb* comes from the Latin *herba*, meaning grass or green blades. To a botanist, *herb* is the term for all the soft, nonwoody parts of plants. In common usage, though, an herb (or in Britain a herb) is any leafy plant material used for its flavor, aroma, or reputed medicinal properties.

Herbs have historically been used not only in cooking but in mystical ceremonies and, allegedly, for healing. Today's flood of "herbal remedies" and supplements is only the latest incarnation of the age-old snake-oil industry. For some reason, many people believe that if it's "herbal" it's "natural" and therefore healthful. ("Here, Mr. Socrates, drink this cup of hemlock tea. It's an all-natural herbal supplement.")

The word *spice*, on the other hand, has no scientific standing; it's a catchall term for any plant material, usually excepting leaves, that adds strong aromas and flavors to foods. The word comes from the Latin *species*, meaning assorted merchandise, originally referring to the commercial goods imported from the Orient, of which spices were an important part. Spices may be roots, rhizomes, barks, seeds, fruits, or flowers, but most often they are seeds. Herbs are usually green and relatively mild, while spices can be brown, black, or red and have more pungent flavors.

Because most spices are native to tropical regions and herbs typically grow in temperate climates, cultural and linguistic differences often complicate the picture. For example, the cilantro plant and its herbal leaves are known by that Spanish name, but its seeds, called coriander in English, are a spice.

It would be nice to think that Nature created all those fragrant and flavorful botanical substances purely for our gastronomic delectation. But who do we *Homo sapiens* think we are, anyway? There must be some other evolutionary reason for plants' having developed the special chemicals in herbs and spices that so delight us. And there is.

Most plants depend for reproduction on pollination by bees and other insects, whom they must attract by some combination of physical and chemical devices. The perception of flower colors is the major physical enticement, but chemicals are just as important. Many plants have developed fragrant chemicals called *essential oils* (see "Quintessential but not essential," on p. 330) that are quite volatile, that is, that waft readily off into the air. (It may be noted in passing that flowers and perfumes are often a prelude to human reproduction as well.)

Other plants contain unpleasant-smelling or -tasting chemicals to repel foragers, and yet we humans find them pleasant when used in small amounts to flavor our foods.

Three families of plants provide the lion's share of our culinary herbs and spices.

- The mint family (Lamiaceae) provides us with basil, thyme, marjoram, rosemary, lavender, and catnip.
- The parsley family (Apiaceae) gives us anise, dill, coriander, caraway, cumin, poison hemlock (!), and such distinctively flavored vegetables as carrot, celery, parsnip, and fennel.
- The mustard family (Brassicaceae) includes radish, horseradish, and many vegetables such as broccoli, Brussels sprouts, cabbage, cauliflower, kale, kohlrabi, turnip, rape, and rutabaga, all of whose leaves have a peppery flavor, although they are not generally used as herbs.

In a class by itself is the genus *Capsicum*, included within the family Solanaceae. Capsicums are the spiciest of all spices. They are the fiery New World hot peppers that, as we shall see, are neither hot in the literal sense nor peppers.

Because there are more than a hundred herbs and spices used around the world to add zest to foods, all I can do here is fly low over the landscape and point out a few notable landmarks. But if there is anything—and I mean *anything*—you want to know about any herb or spice, go to http://www-ang.kfunigraz.ac.at/~katzer/engl/, a multilingual website operated with obvious passion by one Gernot Katzer at the University of Graz in Austria.

THE FOODIE'S FICTIONARY:

Celery—weekly or monthly wages

Spicy Chocolate Crinkle Monsters

Sugar and spice and everything nice—that's what these dramatic cookies are made of. They owe their appeal to their monstrous size, a hit of black pepper on the tongue, and an after-burn of cayenne. They look like the over-sized cookies that you see on bakery shelves or in coffee shops at outrageous prices. Commercial coarsely ground black pepper is okay to use instead of grinding it fresh, because of the consistent size of the commercial grind. Note that olive oil stands in for butter in the recipe. A spring-loaded ice cream scoop is ideal for portioning the cookie dough.

---

2 cups granulated sugar

$^3/_4$ cup mild olive oil

4 large eggs

2 teaspoons vanilla extract

$2^1/_3$ cups all-purpose flour

$^3/_4$ cups unsweetened cocoa powder, preferably Dutch process

2 teaspoons baking powder

2 teaspoons coarse black pepper

$^1/_2$ teaspoon salt

$^1/_2$ teaspoon ground allspice

$^1/_4$ teaspoon ground cinnamon

$^1/_8$ teaspoon cayenne pepper

About 1 cup confectioners' sugar

---

1. Preheat the oven to 350°F. Spray 2 cookie sheets with nonstick cooking spray.

2. In a large bowl, stir together the granulated sugar and olive oil. Whisk in the eggs and vanilla. In a medium bowl, stir together the flour, cocoa, baking powder, pepper, salt, and spices, mixing well to combine. Sifting is not necessary.

3. Add the dry ingredients to the egg mixture all at once and stir with a wooden spoon until no patches of the dry flour mixture are visible.

4. Place the confectioners sugar in a wide dish with shallow sides, like a soup plate. You will need this when you shape the cookies.

5. Note on shaping the cookies: To measure the volume of your ice cream scoop, fill it with water, then pour the water into a glass measure. It should measure ¼ cup. If you don't have a scoop, use a ¼-cup measuring cup to portion out the dough. Because there is oil in the recipe, the dough will not stick to your hands or utensils. To make a smaller cookie, shape the dough into balls the size of a large walnut.

6. To shape the first cookie, scoop out the dough with the ice cream scoop and release it onto the confectioners' sugar. Using 2 spoons or your fingers, roll the ball around in the sugar to coat well. Transfer the ball to the cookie sheet. Repeat with the rest of the dough, placing the balls 2 to 3 inches apart.

7. Bake for 12 to 15 minutes, or until the cookies have crinkled tops and are no longer soft to the touch. Remove from the oven and allow the cookies to rest on the cookie sheet on a wire rack for 2 minutes, then transfer them with a pancake turner to the rack to cool completely.

MAKES 16 LARGE COOKIES

QUINTESSENTIAL BUT NOT ESSENTIAL

I hear a lot about essential oils in everything from spices to skin moisturizers and aromatherapy products. What's essential about them? Are they like the essential amino acids we must have in our diets?

. . . .

No, not at all.

Essential oil is an unfortunate name. An essential oil is not necessarily an oil in the chemical sense, and may not even feel oily at all. Nor is it "essential" in the sense of being indispensable. Aromatherapy and cosmetic flacks take advantage of this misunderstanding by touting the essential oils in their products as if they were somehow imperatives for health and beauty. The adjective *essential* in the name means simply that the substance is the aromatic essence—the concentrated spirit, if you will—of the plant.

Essential oils can be obtained in pure form by steam distillation (boiling the crushed plant material in water and condensing the mixed oil and water vapors), or by extraction into cold fat (*enfleurage*), hot fat (maceration), or volatile organic solvents that can be evaporated away.

If an essential oil is to affect our senses as a flavor or fragrance, it must consist of small, light molecules (with molecular weights of less than about 300 or 400) that can float through the air and reach our noses. These airborne molecules can enter our upper nasal passages, either directly through the nose or through the back of the mouth when we eat the spice. In the upper nasal passages the molecules lock onto olfactory receptors, which fire nerve cells to generate a smell signal. These signals are interpreted in the cortex of the brain, along with taste signals received from our taste buds, to produce the overall sensation of what we call flavor. Although we habitually localize flavor in the mouth, anywhere between 70 and 85 percent of the flavor of our foods is contributed by our sense of smell.

Many essential oils are chemicals called *terpenes*, a class of unsaturated hydrocarbons. Some examples are menthol in oil of peppermint, limonene in orange and lemon oil, and zingerone, which (no kidding) puts the zing in ginger.

A funny coincidence? No. Our English name *ginger* comes to us via a tortuous path from *singivera* in Pali, the religious language of Buddhism, to the Greek *zingiberi*, the Latin *zingiber*, and the Old English *gingifer*. Hence its species name *Zingiber officinale* and the name of one of its main pungent components, zingerone. Our slang word *zing*, meaning zest, may have a consequential origin.

And before you ask, the distilled alcoholic beverage we call gin has an entirely different origin. Its name comes from its predominant flavoring agent, the juniper berry, called *genever* in Dutch. The beverage was invented "for medicinal purposes" (wink) by a seventeenth-century professor of medicine at the University of Leiden in Holland.

THE FOODIE'S FICTIONARY: Essential oil—WD-40

HOT, HOT, HOT!

I have always wondered about the words hot *and* spicy *with reference to the tastes of peppers and other spices. For example, why is black pepper "peppery," while chili peppers are "hot" and ginger is "spicy"? Are the chemicals that cause these sensations all the same?*

. . . .

No, those different sensory effects are caused by several different chemical compounds. (See Table 6, p. 336.)

It would be much neater if we had individual descriptive words for each of these sensations, because they are indeed all different. Instead, we apply the words *hot, peppery, spicy, pungent, piquant, biting, zingy,* and *sharp* almost indiscriminately to all. But black pepper, chili peppers, ginger, mustard, horseradish, and wasabi are all distinguishable from one another by their distinctive brands of what I'll generically call pungency, from the Latin *pungere*, meaning to prick or puncture.

The French *piquer* and the Spanish *picar*, meaning to prick or sting, give us the word *piquancy*, which is often used interchangeably with *pungency* but has the slightly broader connotation of an agreeable tartness or zest. A sauce, for example, may be piquant because of the pungent pepper it contains.

But "hot" spices give us much more than their "heat." Like all foods, they have their own complex flavors. Different hot chili peppers, which are so often characterized simply by their relative heats, contribute unique earthy, fruity, smoky, sweet, or flowery nuances to our dishes. Mexican cuisine excels at using different types of chili peppers in dishes that will benefit from their different flavor profiles.

Let's consider some of the "hot stuffs," one at a time.

Black pepper comes from the *Piper nigrum* plant, whose species name, suitably enough, is Latin for "black pepper." When the plant's berries are picked almost ripe and dried in the sun, enzymes turn them dark and they shrivel into our familiar black peppercorns, with their softly pungent flavor.

Green and white peppercorns are the same berry, but picked and processed differently. Green peppercorns are picked soft and unripe, then either dried or pickled in brine or vinegar, in which state they are often used instead of (and occasionally confused with) capers. White peppercorns are picked when ripe and red but then are allowed to ferment. Softened by the fermentation, the outer layer of skin can be washed off to expose the pale seed within. Alternatively, the outer skins of black peppercorns may be removed mechanically to uncover the white seed. After being dried, white peppercorns are somewhat less exciting than black ones, but they come in handy when you don't want to add black specks to a white sauce.

The pungent chemical in these true pepper berries is *piperine*, the main aromatic ingredient released when the peppercorns are cracked open. As this flavorful oil slowly evaporates, the cracked or ground pepper loses its pungency. That's why every recipe worth its salt and pepper specifies that the pepper be "freshly ground."

In quite another category, the fiery-hot "peppers" discovered in the New World by Columbus and other Spanish explorers (yes, I know he was Italian, but Spanish *pesetas* were footing the bill) are not real pepper because they are not from the *Piper nigrum* plant. They are members of the Solanaceae family of plants, specifically, varieties of *Capsicum annuum*. A cynic might suspect that the explorers named these fruits *pimiento* because real pepper (*pimienta* in Spanish) was such a valuable spice in Europe at the time that a little stretching of the truth might bring a better price back home. The explorers also called them *chile* and *ají* after their Aztec and Taíno Indian names, and the world has been confused about what to call them ever since.

Here's a quick rundown on this bewildering state of affairs.

In contemporary Spain, the capsicums are still called *pimientos*, while in Mexico they are still called *chiles*. But in other Latin American countries they are called *ají*, not to be confused with *ajo*, which is garlic. The British changed *chile* to *chilli*, while in the United States we spell it *chili*, reserving the word *pimiento* for another capsicum species, the sweet bell pepper, except that we sometimes spell pimiento *pimento*, not to be confused with *pimenta*, the tree from which we get allspice berries, which were so named because they taste like a combination of cloves, cinnamon, and nutmeg. (Got all that?)

The essential oils in chili peppers contain chemicals (*alkaloids*) called *capsaicin* (cap-SAY-uh-sin) and *dihydrocapsaicin* plus a few closely related compounds, all collectively known as *capsaicinoids*. These are the burning, pungent components of hot chili peppers. About 80 percent of the capsaicinoids reside in the placenta, the fleshy ribs that fasten the seeds to the walls, not in the seeds themselves, as is commonly believed. Because of the way the seeds are attached, cooks who habitually scrape away "the seeds" with a spoon or knife blade have unwittingly been removing the real culprits, the ribs.

Capsaicinoids are odorless and are not detected by our noses or taste buds; the true flavors of the various capsicum fruits are contributed by other chemicals, just as in nonpungent fruits. Instead of being tasted or smelled, the capsaicinoids stimulate nerve endings in our skins and mucous membranes, specifically those of the trigeminal nerve, which among other jobs conveys sensations of pain and heat to the brain from the face, mouth, and nose. Hence, our brains

persuade us to call these fruits "hot" and their pungency "heat," and
even to sweat when we eat them.

· How hot is a hot pepper? The various species of capsicums are
often listed in order of pungency, expressed in "Scoville units." Back
in 1912, Dr. Wilbur Scoville, an American pharmaceutical chemist,
devised his Scoville Organoleptic Test for measuring just how hot a
pepper tastes to a panel of tasters. He mixed the ground-up pepper
with sugar water and diluted it over and over again until the tasters
could no longer distinguish any pungency. (Homeopathic capsaicin,
anyone?) The number of times it had to be diluted is known as the
number of Scoville Units of heat for that pepper.

The species we call bell peppers or sweet red or green peppers
are capsicums that contain little if any capsaicin; they score zero on
the Scoville scale. At the other end of the spectrum, the heat of pure
capsaicin itself didn't disappear until a dilution factor of about 16
million. Mexican anchos registered 1,000 to 2,000, jalapeños 2,500
to 5,000, and cayenne 30,000 to 50,000. Habaneros, at 200,000 to
300,000, are the widely acclaimed champs, although that record has
recently been surpassed by the *Capsicum annuum var. aviculare* or
tepín, a tiny (quarter-inch) wild pepper found in the mountains of
northern Mexico. Scoville never saw one.

Note, however, that the same species of pepper can have different pungencies depending on growing conditions, so quoting exact
Scoville ratings and arguing about who can eat the hottest pepper—an
unfathomable point of pride among self-proclaimed chili-heads—is
pointless.

Moving on from peppers both real and misnamed, we find several other assertive spices whose blends of pungent chemicals in
their essential oils can kick our foods up a notch. (Apologies,
Emeril.) Table 6 shows which chemicals in several spices are primarily responsible for their pungency. You'll note that the most pungent ones are in the mustard family of plants, the Brassicaceae.

No need to memorize the names in Table 6; they won't be on the final. But notice how *isothiocyanates* are the main pungent chemicals of the mustard family. They are formed when the plants' seeds or roots are cut or crushed and the cells rupture, whereupon an enzyme in one part of the cells reacts with certain sulfur-containing compounds in another part to form the isothiocyanate. (*Thio-* in the name of a chemical compound indicates that its molecules contain one or more sulfur atoms.)

Allyl isothiocyanate is the very potent "hot stuff" in horseradish, mustard seed, and wasabi. It is also the primary component of mustard oil, which is used very sparingly in cooking, notably in some Chinese stir-fries.

Table 6. Where the heat comes from

	SPECIES NAME	PLANT FAMILY	PRIMARY PUNGENT CHEMICAL(S)
CLOVE	*Syzygium aromaticum*	**Myrtaceae (myrtle family)**	eugenol
DILL SEED	*Anethum graveolens*	**Apiaceae (parsley family)**	carvone (40 to 60%) and limonene (40%)
GINGER	*Zingiber officinale*	**Zingiberaceae (ginger family)**	zingerone and gingeroles
HORSE-RADISH	*Armoracia rusticana*	**Brassicaceae (mustard family)**	allyl isothiocyanate
MUSTARD SEED	*Brassica juncea (or Sinapis alba)*	**Brassicaceae (mustard family)**	allyl isothiocyanate and *p*-hydroxybenzyl isothiocyanate
RED RADISH	*Raphanus sativus*	**Brassicaceae (mustard family)**	4-methylthio-trans-3-butenyl-isothiocyanate
WASABI	*Wasabia japonica*	**Brassicaceae (mustard family)**	allyl isothiocyanate and sec-butyl isothiocyanate

Contrary to some scare stories that have made the rounds on the Internet, mustard oil has no chemical relationship whatsoever to the mustard gas—actually not a gas but an oily liquid sprayed as a mist— used by the Germans in World War I as a chemical weapon. It was called mustard gas only because of its sharp, acrid smell and because it irritates the skin like an old-fashioned mustard plaster. Of course, the irritation caused by mustard gas is infinitely worse: It kills rather than heals.

Mouths afire!

The capsaicinoids in hot peppers stimulate the same nerve endings in our mouths as heat does, but because they don't create actual heat, sipping cold water to "cool" an overenthusiastic mouthful is useless.

Capsaicin oils are not very soluble in water, although they do dissolve in alcohol. But—alas!—beer, at about 5 percent, doesn't contain enough alcohol to remove them from your burning tongue. Fortunately, however, tequila (at 40 percent alcohol or more) is better and is quite likely to be handy wherever too spicy foods are served.

Milk and sour cream are even better than tequila, because their protein molecules (mostly casein) are attracted to oils and drag them away, in much the same way as soap drags away oily dirt. But if you can't bear to swap your tequila for milk (¡Ay, carramba!), just chew a piece of bread or flour tortilla, which will abrade and absorb the oil from your tongue. And drink the beer anyway. Who needs an excuse?

Sidebar Science: *What's hot today?*

WILBUR SCOVILLE'S highly subjective method of determining pungency is gradually being replaced by more scientific methods. Using a technique known as high-performance liquid chromatography, or HPLC, chemists today can determine how much actual capsaicin and its relatives—dihydrocapsaicin, nordihydrocapsaicin, homocapsaicin, and homodihydrocapsaicin—a capsicum pepper contains. Capsaicin and dihydrocapsaicin together make up about 80 to 90 percent of the capsaicinoids in capsicum peppers. In pure form, Wilbur rated these two chemicals at 16 million Scoville units, while the other three scored a relatively wimpy 9,000 or so.

Chili Pepper Hash Browns

Chili peppers, even of the same variety, are not all created equal. Some of them may be quite hot, others relatively mild. If yours turns out to be mild and will not lend enough oomph to the dish, add a sprinkling of hot red pepper flakes to taste. This dish should be definitely spicy.

Preparation of the peppers and potatoes can be done in advance, allowing only about 12 minutes to finish the dish before serving. Try these hash browns alongside roasted chicken. In the unlikely event that you have leftovers, reheat the hash for breakfast for serving with a softly poached or over-easy fried egg.

---

2 large sweet potatoes, scrubbed but not peeled

1 tablespoon olive oil

1 tablespoon unsalted butter

1 small onion, finely diced (about $^1/_3$ cup)

$^1/_2$ small sweet red pepper, finely diced (about $^1/_2$ cup)

$^1/_2$ small sweet green pepper, finely diced (about $^1/_2$ cup)

$^1/_4$ cup chopped fresh chili pepper (ancho, serrano, poblano, or jalapeño), stemmed and seeded

Kosher salt

Red pepper flakes, optional

---

1. Bring a large saucepan of salted water to a boil. Add the whole sweet potatoes and simmer for 10 minutes; they will be quite firm. Drain. (Don't even think about cutting them in half or cooking any longer, or they will go to mush.)

2. When the potatoes are cool enough to handle, peel them, cut lengthwise into slabs, and then cut the slabs into ¼-inch dice. You should have roughly 3 cups.

3. In a large skillet, heat the olive oil and butter over medium heat. Add the onion and all the peppers and cook, stirring, for 1 to 2 minutes, or until softened. Add the sweet potatoes and cook, shaking the pan and flipping the

potatoes occasionally for about 10 minutes, or until they are nicely brown and tender.

4. Season to taste with kosher salt and, if necessary, red pepper flakes. Serve hot.

MAKES 4 SERVINGS

DON'T KISS ME!

I first encountered sopa de ajo (garlic soup) in Mexico, where it was served still simmering in an earthenware cazuela with a raw egg dropped into it just before serving. I was amazed—and still am, now that I make it myself—that the many cloves of garlic cook down to such a different, mild flavor, very unlike the flavors of raw or sautéed garlic. How does simmering garlic in water "tame" it so much?

. . . .

The same thing happens to garlic's no-kissin' cousin, the onion; French onion soup tastes nothing like raw or fried onions. It's all in the different chemical reactions that take place at room temperature, at the wet temperature of boiling water, and at the high and dry temperature of frying.

Raw garlic and onions have little or no aroma until cutting or chewing breaks open their cells. An enzyme and another preexisting chemical (a *precursor*) that had until then been isolated from each other can now meet and react chemically to produce the odorous and sharply flavored compounds we know too well.

But in hot water these seven-syllable chemicals (*alkylthiosul-*

fonates) change into other polysyllabic compounds: propyl and propenyl di- and tri-sulfides and thiophenes. These are among the compounds that give flavor to our garlic and onion soups.

And frying? Don't ask. Dozens of other chemicals are produced at the high temperatures involved, notably the many aromatic, flavorful, and bitter compounds created by the Maillard browning reactions. (See pp. 296–97.)

Let's look at what happens to onions as we subject them to more and more aggressive cooking techniques. Garlic behaves in very much the same way.

Dried, raw onions are made up of about 37 percent sugars and 8 percent proteins, so they brown predominantly by the Maillard, or sugar–amino acid, reactions. Yet virtually every chef refers to the browning of onions in a skillet as "caramelizing" them. Perhaps a reason for that can be found by examining the three different stages in the cooking of this uniquely flavored vegetable: sweating, goldenizing (I'll explain), and frying.

- **Sweating:** We sweat raw onions by placing them diced or sliced in a sauté pan with a little bit of butter or oil, covering the pan with a circle of parchment or waxed paper (or a cover), and cooking them slowly over very low heat. The heat vaporizes some of the water inside the onion's cells (onions are 89 percent water). The vapor pressure bursts them and releases their juices, in which the onions then simmer and steam. They turn soft and translucent (another consequence of the broken-down cell structure), but we stop cooking them before any browning takes place. The initial pungent flavor compounds will have been converted to the softer-flavored compounds we associate with onion soup.
- **Goldenizing:** If instead we cook the onions uncovered, the released cell juices will quickly boil off and the temperature will rise from around 212°F (100°C) to perhaps 300°F

(149°C), where the Maillard browning reactions proceed rapidly. The fact that some of the Maillard products are sweet is perhaps one reason that cooks are enticed into using the sugar word *caramelize* for this process. What they really mean, however, is taking the onions only to a soft, golden tan—the color of caramel candies—but stopping short of actually browning them.

In hopes of banishing the use of the word caramelizing for the gentle sautéing of onions, I hereby offer to the world the word *goldenizing*. I realize that *goldenize* has only three syllables to *caramelize*'s four (and for heaven's sake, people, it's CAR-a-mel-ize, not CARM-el-ize), but what it may lack in grandeur it more than makes up for in accurate imagery.

• **Frying:** If we continue cooking beyond that stage, Monsieur Maillard really goes to town and we wind up with honest-to-goodness fried onions, with their intense "browned" flavors.

So goldenize your onions to a pleasing russet hue and a mild, sweet flavor. But you're not caramelizing them unless you're one of those people who add a little bit of sugar to hasten the production of color.

May I never again hear or read about "caramelizing" onions or, for that matter, "caramelizing" any other foods that cook up brown. Except sugar.

Note: I know full well that I am fighting a losing battle. No matter what this chemist guy says, chefs will continue to talk about "caramelized" onions, "caramelized" grilled meats, "caramelized" *fond* in the bottom of a sauté pan, and "caramelized" anything else that turns brown when cooked. But I tried, and that makes me feel better. The Great Chemist in the Sky will bless me for it.

Sidebar Science: *How much garlic?*

WHEN THE CELLS of a garlic clove are broken open by slicing, crushing, or chewing, an enzyme (*alliinase*) in the cell vacuoles spills out and reacts with a precursor compound (*alliin*) in another part of the cell to form diallylthiosulfinate (*allicin*) and other thiosulfinates, which are the main odoriferous and flavor compounds. Until relatively recently—1993—it was thought that the odorous compounds were diallyl disulfide and other polysulfides, but it has been shown that these were merely the breakdown products of thiosulfinates, and were inadvertently created in the analytical laboratory by the high-temperature methods being used. (A scientific research principle: Always make sure that your analysis procedure isn't changing what you're trying to analyze.)

Thus, when garlic is cut into smaller and smaller pieces, or reduced even further by being crushed, more vacuoles are broken open, more alliinase enzyme is released, and more thiosulfinates are formed, producing a stronger aroma and flavor.

A similar sequence of events takes place in sliced and chopped onions, initiated by the same enzyme, alliinase, but producing somewhat different flavor and odor compounds. (See "The tear factor," p. 125).

So when a recipe specifies a paste from a garlic press, or slivers of cloves, or chopped garlic, pay attention; otherwise you may get more or less than you bargained for.

TRUE LOVE

*I absolutely adore garlic and use it in all its
forms: roasted whole heads or cloves, chopped,
minced, crushed, or pressed, depending on the dish
I'm making. But once in a while I'm stuck at the
last minute for a touch of garlic flavor in an
almost finished soup or stew or on Italian green
beans, so I sprinkle on a little garlic powder.
I know it's frowned upon by gourmets, but
emergencies are emergencies. What do you think?*

. . . .

I share your love of garlic. When my foodie wife, Marlene, and I first met for a blind coffee date, she didn't ask about my religion, politics, or income. Practically her first question was "What do you think of garlic?"

Without hesitation I replied, "Garlic is the closest thing we have to proof of the existence of God." And we have been cooking happily ever after.

First of all, garlic powder is not a good substitute for fresh garlic because in the process of being dried and powdered, garlic loses a great deal of its volatile flavors. But as you say, emergencies are emergencies. I won't tell anybody if you don't. (I use it on popcorn.)

Dried garlic was invented for the same reason as other dried spices and herbs: to preserve a perishable product. At the garlic-powder factories they first break the bulbs down into cloves, smash them, and blow away the papery skins. They then dry the naked cloves, remove any residual skin fragments, and powder the dried material. Much of our garlic powder comes from India and China, where both the raw garlic and the hand labor involved in processing it are relatively cheap.

But obviously, the fresh herb loses a lot of its "charm" in the process, so the dried and powdered product can't hold a candle to the fresh.

BOTULISM IN A BOTTLE?

I've heard warnings about garlic-infused oil,
but I never really got to the bottom of it.
My question for you is: Is there any validity to the
claims that garlic oil is dangerous?

....

We must be careful to distinguish between *garlic oil*, the intrinsic essential oil of the garlic plant, *Allium sativum*, and *garlic-infused oil*, an edible vegetable oil (usually olive oil) that has been flavored with garlic.

Pure garlic oil is indeed nasty stuff that is never ingested *per se*. One of its major ingredients is allyl trisulfide, a teaspoon of which in its pure form would kill half the people who swallowed it and burn the esophagus in the rest of them. But you could never eat enough garlic to come within miles of that amount, nor would anyone come within miles of you if you did.

When chemically pure garlic oil is required for nonfood purposes (it is an effective antibacterial, antifungal, and insecticide), it is obtained, as are most plant essential oils, by steam distillation, in which the crushed plant material is boiled in water. The resulting mixture of steam and vaporized oil is condensed, whereupon the water and the oil settle out as separate layers.

All right, then. So is garlic-infused olive or other vegetable oil dangerous? It depends on how you make it. If you add garlic cloves willy-nilly, unpeeled or peeled, whole or minced, to oil and let it stand for weeks at room temperature, yes, you're flirting with botulism.

The lethal *Clostridium botulinum* bacterium lives in the soil and in stream and lake sediments, among other places. It cannot flourish in extreme dryness or in air, but will thrive in a moist, airless (anaerobic) environment. And exactly those conditions can exist on the surface of a moist garlic clove smothered in oil.

Many references tell us that *C. botulinum* bacteria can be killed by being heated for 10 minutes at a temperature above 175°F (79°C) or that they can at least be inhibited by acidic media below pH 4.6. That's true of the active bacteria themselves, but their dormant spores, if present, can survive long periods of highly unfavorable environments such as air, dryness, and high temperatures. In fact, the 175-degree treatment may only "heat-shock" the spores into germinating more readily. The spores are not reliably killed until subjected to a temperature of 250°F (121°C) for several minutes, as is done in commercial canning. At home, that temperature can be reached in either an oven or a pressure cooker. But simple boiling or simmering will *not* do the job.

Executing the bacteria and their spores may be too little and too late, however, because it's not the bacteria themselves that are the potential killers; it's a neurotoxin they manufacture while multiplying. Botulinum toxin is one of the most powerful poisons known.

Virtually all references repeat the statement that the toxin is not destroyed by the heat of cooking. But that's a precautionary oversimplification. The toxin is actually unstable to heat, but it depends on what we mean by "cooking." Research by several groups of scientists in the 1970s showed that different amounts of toxin, different foods, different pH's, and different acids can affect the toxin-deactivation process differently. So it is indeed prudent to assume that you can't get rid of it by "cooking."

The symptoms of botulin poisoning were named *botulism* when a number of people died in Germany in the late eighteenth century after eating contaminated sausage; the Latin word for sausage is *botulus*. Botulism is a rare occurrence, with only ten to thirty outbreaks per year in the United States, so there is hardly a galloping botulism plague going on. But a head of garlic just *might* have some *C. botulinum* spores lurking under its skin, where they would lie protected from air until they found themselves in an airless medium, such as when submerged in a sea of oil. There, the spores *could* become active and launch a reproductive orgy, even at refrigerator temperatures. It's the better part of valor, therefore, not to tempt fate by making your own garlic-infused oil. Commercial garlic-infused oil products are usually acidified with vinegar to thwart bacterial growth. But acidifying a solid in an oil can be tricky, so it isn't recommended for home preparation of garlic-flavored oil.

Still want to make some? Adventurous types should make only a small amount from chopped garlic in olive oil, keep it refrigerated, and discard what isn't used after a week or two.

CURB THAT SPERB!

Sometimes a recipe will direct that a spice or herb
be added at the beginning of cooking, and
sometimes only near the end of a long simmer.
Does it really matter? If so, why?

. . . .

Yes, it matters.

The amount of flavor contributed by a spice or herb depends on the amount of essential oil it contains, not on the total amount or weight of the whole substance. Spices and herbs—instead of repeating "spice or herb" eleven more times in this section, may I call them generically "sperbs"? Thank you—sperbs that are powdered or ground give up their oils readily in the heat of cooking because their huge surface areas allow their essential oils to evaporate quickly. Thus, finely divided sperbs should be added near the end, rather than the beginning of cooking, lest all their essential oils evaporate and the kitchen smell better than the food tastes. Whole sperbs on the other hand, such as peppercorns and bay leaves, give up their essences slowly and are added at the beginning.

Because most essential oils are volatile, sperbs lose their effectiveness in storage as the oils slowly evaporate. So fresh sperbs are always more potent than stale ones. Even low levels of heat can slowly drive off the oils, so sperbs also should be stored in a cool location. Ground sperbs lose their strength by evaporation much faster than whole ones.

Nutmeg and black pepper, especially, should always be bought whole and ground on the spot when needed. Hot chili peppers, on the other hand, keep their heat even when dried and ground, because capsaicin, the "hot stuff" in them, is not very volatile. That's why you can't tell how hot a pepper is by smelling it.

You'd be surprised at how much of most sperbs' verve is lost over the period of a year or less, especially if ground. Sniff your sperbs; if you can recall that they smelled much more potent when new, replace them with fresh samples. It's a good idea to date the labels when you buy them. And check the vividness of their colors periodically. Green, leafy herbs such as tarragon and rosemary fade with age, as do red spices such as Cayenne pepper, paprika, and chili powder.

Some sperb fanatics (sperbivores?) go so far as to keep their sperbs in the freezer. I don't see why that shouldn't work.

THE FOODIE'S FICTIONARY:
Fennel—a device for pouring liquids into small containers

HOW MUCH IS THAT HERB
IN THE TEASPOON?

Many recipes call for fresh herbs, such as oregano,
thyme, parsley, and so on. But sometimes all I
have on hand is the dried herb. Is there a rule of
thumb for how much dried herb to use as a
substitute for the fresh?

. . . .

Unfortunately, there can be no dependable rule of thumb because herbs differ so much from one to another. But the following considerations may give you a few clues. Remember that it's not the amounts of fresh or dried vegetable matter that count in flavoring, but the amounts of essential oils they contain, because that's where the flavor is.

The leaves of herbaceous plants are 80 percent to 90 percent water by weight. At 80 percent water, 100 grams of leaf should contain 20 grams of dry matter, so the dried herb is five times more potent. In using this dried herb, then, you would use one-fifth the *weight* of the fresh herb. At 90 percent water, the fresh-to-dry factor is ten, so for that dried herb you would use one-tenth the weight of the fresh. All of this assumes, however, that the only thing lost in the drying process is water, and no volatile oils—and that's a rather shaky assumption.

The problem is that in the kitchen we generally measure herbs not by weight but by volume (teaspoons or tablespoons). Volume depends on the physical forms of the fresh and dried herbs—whole leaves, withered leaves, minced pieces, powder, and so on—and the volume ratios are therefore pretty unpredictable.

Thus, short of taking your herbs to a laboratory, having them analyzed for their percentages of essential oils, and then weighing them out, there can be no rule of thumb for how much volume of dried herb to use instead of the fresh form.

Nevertheless, if you have to substitute dried herb for fresh and can't spare the lab fees or the thirty-day wait for the essential oil analysis report to come back, try using somewhere between one-fourth and one-half as much of the dried herb as of the fresh kind. Of course, if you're substituting in the other direction, use between twice as much and four times as much of the fresh herb as of the dried one. In most cases, you won't be straying disastrously far from the Yellow Brick Road.

Okay, so I lied. That's a rule of thumb.

OLD SPICE

I'm surprised that most bottled spices and herbs in the supermarket are not labeled with a "best if used by" date. What is their average shelf life? Also, we leave them in our nonwinterized summer cottage that stays at or below freezing much of the year. Will they survive freezing temperatures?

. . . .

While there is no reliable average shelf life, checking them annually should serve your purpose. Bottled herbs and spices are thoroughly dried, and most spoilage bacteria can't live without water, so if the containers are tightly closed the herbs and spices should last indefinitely without actually spoiling. Also, things that are completely dry can't freeze; it's the water in foods that freezes. So the frigidity of your cabin is irrelevant as far as damage from freezing is concerned. In fact, low temperatures will extend their useful lives by slowing down the evaporaton of aromatic compounds.

Dried spices do lose their potency over time, however. In fresh, undried herbs, the essential oils are contained in a variety of locations within the leaves, such as in intercellular cavities, specialized oil cells, oil or resin ducts, glands, or hairs. But because the cell structure is broken down in the drying process, the essential oils are closer to the surface, from where they can more readily escape.

Do the sniff test the next time you leave for the season: Crumble a bit of each one between your fingers, and if it doesn't smell as strong as it did the preceding summer, make a note to bring a replacement on your return.

VOLKSWAGENS IN THE PANTRY

Bugs have invaded my cayenne pepper and are seemingly swimming blissfully around in the hot stuff. I couldn't believe my eyes! Did they invade my mace, paprika, or other milder spices? No! Just the cayenne. How do they suffer the hotness?

. . . .

It's just another case of biologically different strokes. Differences among animal species can be enormous. There's no reason to expect pests to behave like humans just because humans sometimes behave like pests.

The "heat" of cayenne and other hot peppers comes from chemicals called capsaicinoids (see p. 334). In humans and other mammals they irritate the mucous membranes of the mouth (and other mucous membranes at a later time, but we won't go there).

The "heat" sensation comes primarily from the stimulation of our trigeminal nerves, which also react to pain and heat. Although I'm not an entomological neurologist (is anybody?), I'd be willing to bet my jalepeño that insects don't have trigeminal nerves. On the other hand, their antennae react to stimuli that we humans can't even imagine, so let's not feel too superior in the sensory department.

There are quite a few species of insect that infest spices and other dried foods. By all means, immediately discard any spices that appear to be infested before the little devils spread throughout the kitchen— or the whole house. I once found some so-called cigarette beetles (*Lasioderna serricorne*) breeding in a package of imported crackers. It was a nightmare getting rid of them because they have wings, fly all over the house, and will eat almost anything, including, yes, tobacco. They're yellowish-brown, about three millimeters long, and look almost exactly like—believe it or not—Volkswagen beetles.

Many of our spices these days are irradiated before being shipped to kill insects and their eggs. But as a precaution I put all imported spices that I've bought into the freezer for three or four days. Freezing will kill cigarette beetle eggs but may have no effect on other species, so don't count on it.

The cigarette beetle, *Lasioderna serricorne*, a common pantry pest.
It feeds on dried tobacco, book bindings, and plant leaves. The larval
stages can feed on cereal products, fresh ginger, raisins, dates,
black pepper, dried fish, and seeds.

A BOTTLE OF SMOKE

The label on my bottle of barbecue sauce says it
contains "liquid smoke." Isn't that an oxymoron?

. . . .

Pardon me while I drink a glass of liquid ice, with cubes of solid water floating in it to keep it cold.

Ahh! That was refreshing. Now to your question.

While its name may be a bit nutty, liquid smoke is a legitimate and useful product. It adds a smoky flavor to foods without our having to go out and chop wood and build a fire and do all the rest of it.

Smoking is one of several ancient methods of curing or preserving foods, primarily meats and fish, by killing pathogenic microorganisms. Other long-used methods are drying (think jerky), salting (think *bacalao* or salt cod), and pickling (think . . . well, pickles). Drying works because bacteria can't grow without moisture, salting works because the salt draws water out of the bacteria's cells and dehydrates them, and pickling works because bacteria can't thrive in acidic environments such as vinegar. Smoking works because the smoke contains many bactericidal chemicals. Our ancestors discovered these methods empirically, of course, long before there was any knowledge of pathogenic microorganisms.

Wood smoke can be lethal not only to bacteria but, as all firefighters know, to humans as well—if there is enough of it. When we're exposed to only a little bit of it, however, we love its aroma (think fireplace on a winter's night) and its flavor (think smoked trout). But smoke is a mixture of hot gases and microscopic suspended particles, which are more difficult than a genie to capture and put into a bottle. So the food industry invented liquid smoke and not only uses it in prepared foods but bottles it and sells it for home use. You may be able to find liquid smoke in 4-ounce bottles under the brand name Colgin, in pecan, mesquite, hickory, and applewood flavors.

In a traditional smokehouse, meat is hung from the ceiling, and smoke from an outside fire of moist sawdust is blown in through ducts. In modern commercial smoking plants, the density of smoke, the temperature, and the humidity are all carefully controlled to produce specific effects.

Today, commercial smoking is done in either of two ways: cold smoking, in which the food isn't allowed to exceed 90 to 100°F (32 to 38°C), and hot smoking, in which the food can reach 200°F (93°C) or higher, and be partially cooked. Some processed meats are hot-smoked and are therefore considered to be cooked (bologna), while others are cold-smoked and sold raw (bacon). Smoked hams may or may not require further cooking; the labels will tell you.

Sausages are a real challenge to classify. The ground meat may be fresh or cured (with nitrites, for example); the filled casings may then be cooked or not, smoked or not, dried or not, and/or fermented or not. In a belt-and-suspenders precaution against bacterial contamination, frankfurters are usually cured, cooked, and smoked, while Italian salami is usually cured, fermented, and then dried. Fresh (uncooked) pork sausage, on the other hand, is neither cured nor smoked.

Vegetables can also be smoked, with mouth-watering results. In the village of La Vera in the Extremadura region of western Spain, I watched bright red *Capsicum annuum* (chili) peppers being simultaneously dried and smoked in long, low, two-level bungalows. The peppers were piled on wooden-slat platforms several feet above smoldering oak logs on the concrete floor below. The dried and smoked peppers were then ground to a velvety brick-red, paprika-like powder called *pimentón*, which has a smoky, sultry flavor. They make it in two varieties, *picante* ("sharp" or hot) and *dulce* ("sweet" or mild), depending on the "heat" of the pepper crop.

(A historical note: Although the New World's capsicum peppers found favor here and there in Europe after Columbus brought them back, it was the Hungarians who picked up the ball and ran with it. Still renowned today for their use of paprika, they reputedly adopted it when King Carlos V of Spain sent some *pimentón* to his sister, Queen Mary of Hungary, who thought it was great stuff and spread the word. Hungarian paprika doesn't have the rich, musky flavor of *pimentón*, however, because its peppers are dried without smoke.)

Inevitably, much of a commercial smokehouse's smoke eventually finds its way up the stack to pollute the atmosphere. And in today's environmentally conscious society, where there's smoke there's ire. Liquid smoke to the rescue!

To make it, one first generates real smoke by burning moist hardwood chips or sawdust. The moisture partially deprives the fire of oxygen to ensure maximum smokiness. The smoke is then blown at chilled condensers, where many of its chemical components (hundreds of different chemicals have been identified in wood smoke) condense to a brown liquid, which is then purified to remove undesirable—and toxic—components. What remains is usually mixed into acetic acid (vinegar) and can be added in that form to your barbecue sauce.

The FDA doesn't permit a food to be labeled "smoked" unless it has been exposed directly to real smoke from burning wood. Read the label on the package of your favorite hot dogs; some are only "smoke flavored" by having been sprayed with or dipped in liquid smoke.

Now, you have undoubtedly been unable to forget what I said earlier about smoke's having toxic components, and you're wondering whether liquid-smoke-flavored foods are safe. Well, what should I say?

Nightmare scenario: I say they're safe. You eat some and get a headache. An opportunistic lawyer tells you, "You have a case." He sues me and the food company, stuffs a jury box with migraine sufferers, and wins a $2 million settlement from the company plus $500 from my threadbare writer's pockets. He takes $1.5 million for himself and runs off after another ambulance, while after paying court costs you're left with the price of a bottle of aspirin.

So should I say that smoked foods are safe? Okay, I'll take the plunge.

Yes, the smoke chemicals in purified liquid smoke are safe in the small amounts you'll encounter in smoke-flavored foods. So sayeth the FDA. Sue them.

Real, gaseous smoke, however, can be quite another story. The decomposition of wood (and tobacco and grilled steaks and hamburgers) by intense heat, a process called *pyrolysis*, can produce highly carcinogenic 3,4-benzopyrene and other so-called polycyclic aromatics (PCA's). But none of these chemicals has been found in commercial, purified liquid-smoke products. On the other hand, liquid smoke, like its gaseous parent, contains bactericidal and antioxidant chemicals, such as formic acid and phenolics, that may even make a positive contribution to your health.

THE RIGHT STUFF

A friend who owns a Japanese restaurant told me
that the green paste you get in restaurants
(including his) isn't real wasabi, but only a green-
tinted horseradish. Was he making excuses?

. . . .

Nope, he was serving you the real scoop, if not the real stuff. I, too, have a friend who owns a Japanese restaurant, and he confided the same to me.

Most Americans who order sushi in a Japanese restaurant will recognize the condiments on the platter. One is a tangle of thin slices of pickled ginger, intended for palate-cleansing between bites, and the other is a glob of fiery green "wasabi." Genuine ginger, yes, but real wasabi, probably not. Most people outside of Japan have never tasted real wasabi.

So what *is* that ball of green paste on your plate at the local sushi bar? It's a blend of horseradish, mustard, cornstarch, and yellow and blue dyes, packaged as a dry powder to be made into a thick paste with water. Put more than a dab on your tongue and the incendiary stuff will clean your sinuses, make your eyes water, and nearly take your head off. The experience of real wasabi, on the other hand, is surprisingly refined.

True wasabi is a green-hued underground stem, or rhizome, known botanically as *Wasabia japonica* or *Eutrema japonica*, among other names. And it's not pretty. Long, stringy roots grow out of its sides, and even when cleaned up, it looks like a knobby sweet potato on a bad hair day. Wasabi is extremely hard to grow, requiring highly specialized conditions in icy waters, and there are only about five growers worldwide. It costs anywhere from $20 to $80 a pound wholesale and about $100 a pound retail. That's why it's rare to find the real thing outside of Japan.

But I was lucky enough to find some.

Andy Kikuyama, owner of KIKU, a Japanese restaurant in Pittsburgh, set up a taste comparison for Marlene and me. He placed two tiny saucers on the table. In the one on the left, a knob of the familiar bluish-green impostor. In the one on the right, a knob of pale yellowish-green, genuine wasabi. It was hard to tell them apart by their appearance.

With a chopstick, we picked up a tiny bit from the familiar mock wasabi in the left-hand dish and placed it on our tongues. The texture was a bit gritty and chalky, and the experience was one of intense heat, with no flavor to speak of.

Next, we tried the real thing. The texture was that of a finely grated vegetable. The taste was slightly nutty, slightly sweet. The heat was instant and bright, more of a brief kick than the long burn of chili peppers; it subsided into a very pleasant, mild vegetable flavor that even people normally averse to hot food might enjoy.

"Americans use much more 'wasabi' than the Japanese do. They seem to want punch, not subtlety," Andy says. "We keep both kinds in the restaurant, but we always serve the real wasabi with white sashimi—thin slices of raw fish eaten as is, usually yellowtail, snapper, and flounder. When there are many flavors in a dish, such as in cold soba noodles or intricate forms of sushi, we serve the horseradish type, because when mixed with soy sauce the subtlety of the real wasabi is wasted." He added that wasabi is never used in cooking because it loses its flavor when heated. (I explained that isothio-cyanates, the pungent chemicals in wasabi, are thermally unstable, but I'm not sure Marlene and Andy were listening.)

Until a few years ago, all true wasabi came from a small number of growers in Japan. But now an American company, Pacific Farms, in Florence, Oregon (http://www.freshwasabi.com), grows the real thing and markets it in paste form.

GRATE AND NOT SO GREAT

It is a tradition in our house for my husband to grate horseradish (the traditional bitter herb) for our Passover seder. He usually makes a lot, enduring burning eyes and sinuses to prepare that delightful condiment. However, the leftovers lose their potency and become quite mild after a couple of days. How can we keep it spicy and potent for the whole eight days of Passover, instead of shredding the root daily?

. . . .

The pungent and tear-producing (lachrymatory) compound in the essential oil of grated horseradish is *allyl isothiocyanate*, commonly known as mustard oil. (It's in black mustard seeds also.) It is created when the plant cells are cut apart by the grating, which releases an enzyme called myrosin and a compound called sinigrin. These two chemicals were previously isolated from each other in different parts of the cells, but when released together in the presence of water, they react to form the allyl isothiocyanate.

Once the oil has been produced, it begins to vaporize, releasing its strong vapors into the air. The vapor, however, is not very stable and dissipates after ten or twenty minutes.

Keep the excess grated material in a tightly sealed jar in the refrigerator, which will contain the vapors and slow down their release. Or try mixing the grated horseradish with chicken fat (technically known as *schmaltz*), another Passover staple. When refrigerated, the solidified fatty coating will seal in the pungent vapors.

Better yet, grate the horseradish into enough vinegar to dampen it, as the commercial producers do. The acid inhibits the allyl isothiocyanate-producing reaction by deactivating the myrosin enzyme on the surfaces of the shreds. Then when you chew the horseradish, you break open more cells, more enzyme is released, and the pungency will be born again, albeit not Christian.

Wasabi Guacamole

Even if you could lay your chopsticks on the real thing, it would be a shame to use real wasabi in this recipe, diluted as it would be by the other ingredients. So pick up some ordinary, freshly made "wasabi" paste and pickled ginger at any sushi bar or at a large supermarket. Powdered wasabi that can be reconstituted with water is available in cans. I have found that wasabi paste in plastic tubes varies in quality. Wasabi tends to lose its kick the longer it stands, so make the appetizer only an hour or so before serving. Serve the guacamole with deep-fried wonton or tortilla triangles as an appetizer with any menu with pan-Asian or Pacific rim accents.

1 large, ripe Hass avocado
Juice of 1 lime (about $1^1/_2$ tablespoons)
1 teaspoon wasabi paste
1 teaspoon minced pickled ginger, optional
1 small clove garlic, crushed and minced
Big pinch of kosher salt
1 scallion, both white and green parts, trimmed and minced
1 tablespoon chopped fresh cilantro

1. Halve the avocado lengthwise and remove the seed. With a paring knife, cut a grid pattern in the flesh of each half, down to the skin. Using a teaspoon, scoop out the diced flesh into a medium bowl. Add the lime juice.

2. Using a fork or pastry blender, mash the avocado, but leave it chunky. Add the wasabi paste, ginger, garlic, and salt. Mix until well combined. (Warning: Because wasabi and avocado are the same color, be sure to mix the ingredients well. A hit of pure wasabi paste would be an unwelcome surprise.)

3. Adjust the seasoning to your taste, adding more wasabi and salt if necessary, and stir in scallion and cilantro.

MAKES ABOUT 1 CUP

WHAT HAVE YOU BEEN SMOKING?

*I have a small electric coffee grinder that I use for
grinding dried spices such as mustard seed and
peppercorns. But I've noticed a strange occurrence.
After I ground some cloves, the grinder's plastic
hood was pitted and actually softened around
the edges. And now I can't wash the scent of the
cloves out. Do whole cloves have any
unusual corrosive properties?*

....

Yes, they do.

Cloves are probably the strongest of all aromatic spices, containing up to 20 percent of an intense, sweetly pungent essential oil.

Originating—appropriately enough—in the Spice Islands, now part
of Indonesia, they are the dried flower buds of the tropical evergreen
tree *Syzygium aromaticum*. Dried clove buds have a stem and a head, a
shape that gave them their name, *clove*, from the Latin *clavus*, "nail."
In the United States, they are most often seen protruding like spikes
from the surfaces of hams. (I hate it when I bite into one, don't you?)

Not surprisingly, cloves contain oil of cloves, the main chemical
ingredient of which is *eugenol*, known familiarly to chemists by its
nickname, 2-methoxy-4-(2-propenyl)phenol. You may at one time
have had it applied to a tooth by your dentist as an analgesic and
antiseptic.

Or, as I have done in Jakarta and on Bali, you may have smoked a
few Indonesian clove-flavored cigarettes. These cigarettes, called
kreteks, are filled with two parts tobacco and one part ground cloves.
Indonesia's passion for *kreteks* uses up approximately one-half of the
world's clove production.

Eugenol is a phenol, and phenols can have acidic and corrosive
properties. In your case, the eugenol invaded, dissolved, and soft-

ened the grinder's transparent plastic hood, which is probably made of polymethyl methacrylate, or Lucite. The aroma became permanently embedded therein.

I'm afraid you now own a dedicated clove grinder. Buy another coffee grinder for your less rapacious spices, and wash it out well after each use before you use it for coffee. Most other spices won't permanently flavor the grinder.

ON KOSHER PIGS

In Brittany, I saw salt containers made of pottery that are said to keep salt dry, even though they're open near the top so you can insert a measuring spoon or reach in with your fingers to take a pinch of salt. How do they work?

. . . .

This kind of container, common in France and England but also available in many stores in the United States, is called a salt pig. It is shaped like one of those wide-mouthed air intakes on ships that some people think are foghorns: squat, vertical cylinders bent into a right angle.

Salt pigs are made of pottery or terracotta that is not glazed on the inside and hence remains porous. The open pores provide a huge amount of surface area that can adsorb water vapor. The sea salts harvested in Brittany are particularly in need of this drying effect; they're often damp if they're not refined. That's because they contain small amounts of calcium chloride, which is *hygroscopic*— that is, it absorbs moisture from the air. Common American table salt contains a small amount of a drying agent, so that "when it rains, it pours."

And yes, you can keep kosher salt in a salt pig.

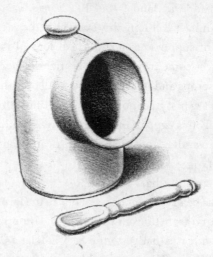

A pottery salt pig for storing and serving salt. The porous, unglazed interior surface adsorbs moisture and helps keep the salt dry.

I'LL TAKE VANILLA

A few years ago at "National Store X," a vial containing two vanilla beans cost $4.50. Now the price is $9.50. A few years ago in the same store, an 8-ounce bottle of Madagascar Bourbon Pure Vanilla Extract cost $11. Now the price is $20. With vanilla prices skyrocketing, many people are turning to Mexican vanilla. Is this product real or artificial? Based on its cheap price, I suspect it might be artificial.

. . . .

Your suspicions are well founded.

Real vanilla has always been expensive because wresting it from nature is a time- and labor-consuming enterprise and because it is grown in faraway lands. And like cacao, cashew nuts, and coffee beans, vanilla is a commodity subject to the vagaries of nature and to the laws of supply and demand. All four of these highly esteemed indulgences come from tropical latitudes, where storms periodically decimate crops and thus affect prices all over the world.

I can't explain economics (I sometimes think nobody can), but what I can do is explain the nature of real vanilla, how it differs from imitation vanilla, and what the Mexican products may or may not consist of.

First, real vanilla.

Vanilla beans are not beans. They're the fermented and dried seed pods (fruits) from one of two species of climbing-vine orchid plants, *Vanilla tahitensis*, native to the Pacific Islands, or *Vanilla planifolia*, native to Mexico. The Aztecs in Mexico were the first to marry vanilla's flavor with the seeds of another native plant, the one we now know as chocolate. (Talk about marriages made in heaven!) The Spanish conquistadors came up with the word *vainilla*, meaning "little scabbard, sheath, or pod," referring to the shape of the vanilla bean.

Today, about three-quarters of the world's vanilla production is of the Mexican *V. planifolia* variety but grown on the islands of Madagascar, the Comoros, and Réunion in the Indian Ocean. In the early nineteenth century these islands were under the rule of the Bourbon kings of France, and the vanilla from this region is still known as Bourbon vanilla. (No relation to you know what.)

When the vanilla orchid plant blooms, it produces only a few flowers at a time. Each flower opens in the morning, closes in the afternoon, and if not pollinated drops dead from the vine the following day. If it is to bear its valuable fruit it must be pollinated during the morning hours of its day of glory.

How, then, did vanilla plants manage to reproduce and survive for eons before humans came along and tried to cultivate them? Attempts to grow vanilla in parts of the world other than Mexico were unsuccessful for about three hundred years. Eventually it was discovered that a small bee of the genus *Melipona*, native only to Mexico, had been quietly doing the pollination job, as bees are wont to do. Today, almost all vanilla flowers in both Mexico and Madagascar are pollinated by human hands, using thin slivers of wood inserted precisely into each flower at precisely the right time. No bee was ever so meticulous. (Are you beginning to understand why vanilla is so expensive?)

When the vanilla pod reaches its maximum length of about 8 inches, it is harvested, dried in the sun for 10 to 30 days, and covered at night to sweat and ferment. Only then will the pods have developed their magnificent flavor and aroma.

Some 170 different chemicals have been identified in the aroma of vanilla, but most of it comes from the aromatic phenolic compound vanillin. Fortunately or unfortunately, humans can make vanillin much more efficiently than vanilla plants can. It can be synthesized from eugenol, the principal aromatic constituent of clove oil, or from guaiacol, a chemical found in tropical tree resins. Vanillin can also be made from lignin, a structural component of woody plants and a by-product of the manufacture of paper from wood pulp. But vanillin is no longer made that way in the United States or Canada because the process is environmentally unacceptable.

Synthetic vanillin is the main ingredient in artificial or "imitation" vanilla, which costs much less than real vanilla extract and is actually not too bad a substitute for the real thing, although it lacks the complexity of natural vanilla flavor. Synthetic vanillin used as a flavoring in packaged foods must be labeled as an artificial flavor. (But see "It's a natural—or is it?" on p. 422.)

Whole vanilla beans are sold in airtight containers to keep them from drying out and losing their flowery bouquet. They should be as dark and soft as a stick of licorice candy, not too hard or leathery. Most of the flavor resides in and around the thousands of almost microscopic seeds, which can be exposed by slitting the bean lengthwise. They can be scraped out with the tip of a knife and added to custards, sauces, and batters. But the seed-shorn pod still contains a lot of flavor. Bury it in a jar of sugar, tightly covered, and leave it for a couple of weeks. Use the vanilla-suffused sugar in, well, custards, sauces, and batters.

Vanilla extract is much more convenient to use than whole beans. In its inimitable bureaucratic style, the FDA defines Pure Vanilla Extract as "the solution in aqueous ethyl alcohol of the sapid and odorous principles extractable from vanilla beans." To be labeled as such it must have an alcohol content of at least 35 percent by volume (higher concentration of alcohol extracts more of vanilla's subtle flavor) and be made from no less than 13.35 ounces of vanilla beans per gallon. (Don't ask.) It may contain sugar and other ingredients such as glycerin or propylene glycol for smoothness, but if it contains added synthetic vanillin, it must be labeled Imitation Vanilla Flavoring.

And finally, the Mexican connection.

Mexico lost its world leadership in vanilla production when the revolution of 1910 destroyed most of its Gulf Coast vanilla plantations. But its reputation lingers on, and Mexican "vanilla extract" is widely available. But because labeling laws aren't enforced in Mexico as strictly as they are in the United States, Mexican "vanilla extract" may be a vanillin-based imitation flavoring.

Worse yet, some Mexican and Caribbean vanilla products might contain coumarin (1,2-benzopyrone), which is extracted from the beanlike seeds of the tonka tree, *Dipteryx odorata* (*cumaru* in Spanish). Coumarin has a strong vanilla-like aroma but is toxic; under the name warfarin it is used as rat poison because it thins the blood and the poisoned rats bleed to death internally. As the drug coumadin, it is used as an anticoagulant in the treatment of heart disease.

Coumarin was completely banned as a food additive by the FDA in 1954.

The bottom-line caveat is this: Be wary of Mexican and Caribbean "vanilla" liquids. At best, they may be imitation, made from synthetic vanillin, and at worst, they may contain coumarin. In theory, the FDA is supposed to block the import of coumarin-containing products, but coumarin has been found in some imports that slipped through.

Chapter Nine

Galley Gear

....

WHETHER CALLED a kitchen, galley, caboose, chuckwagon, or cookhouse, and whether situated in a home or restaurant, on a ship, freight train, or wagon train, or even outdoors wherever a shelter can be set up, it is a place dedicated to the vital task of preparing food for anyone from a sole diner to an army. Its barest essentials are a few pots of clay or metal, sources of heat and water, and perhaps a knife. All else is excess.

And in today's kitchens, boy, do we have excess!

We have refrigerators; gas, electric, and induction ranges; convection and microwave ovens; mixers; blenders; nonstick cookware; and—well, just look around your kitchen, you lucky dog. You've come a long way, baby.

But just as these tools have to be in proper shape to deal with a variety of foods, we have to know how to deal with the tools themselves. There is nothing more frustrating to a craftsman than having to repair a tool before being able to use it.

Does your dishwasher eat your aluminum utensils? Does your refrigerator exude an uninvited fragrance? Does your butter keeper spoil your butter? Does your oven cook a roast faster or slower than the recipe says? Do your pizzas come out flabby and your cakes goopy?

It's all in how you use your armamentarium of appliances, appa-
ratuses, equipment, tackle, gear, gadgets, and utensils. Treat them
with understanding and respect, for as Emerson wrote, "If you do not
use the tools, they use you."

Or, to paraphrase Thoreau, you become the tools of your tools.

THE FOODIE'S FICTIONARY:

Microwave—a baby's bye-bye gesture

IN SEARCH OF SMELLICULES

*I've always kept an open box of baking soda in
my refrigerator to absorb odors. But I've noticed
that there's now a new kind of baking soda box
in the supermarket that supposedly works even
better, even though the label says it contains
nothing but pure baking soda. How does
baking soda absorb odors, and how does
this new contraption do it better?*

. . . .

Like every other householder in this country, I have religiously kept
an open box of Arm & Hammer (is there any other kind?) baking
soda in my refrigerator, and I can testify that I have never smelled a
bad odor. It must also have worked to repel tigers, because not once
did I encounter a tiger in my house as long as that baking soda box
was in the fridge.

Is it possible that I never saw a tiger because I live so far from
India, or that I never smelled a foul odor in my refrigerator because
I'm such a fastidious fridgemeister? Nah! Not according to the Arm &
Hammer Division of Church & Dwight Co., Inc., and every domestic

maven in the U.S.A., who would staunchly maintain that the baking soda absorbed all the odors. (They make no claims about tigers.)

What hard evidence do we have that baking soda really works, at least for odors? None that I know of. But here's the theory.

Baking soda is pure sodium bicarbonate($NaHCO_3$), also known as bicarbonate of soda. It reacts with both acids and bases, that is, with both acidic and alkaline chemicals. (The bicarbonate ion is *amphoteric*.) But it is more than twenty times as effective in reacting with acids as with bases. And thereby hangs the odor-eating theory. Should a wandering molecule of a smelly acid alight upon a surface of baking soda, it will be neutralized, turned into a salt (shades of Lot's wife!), and trapped permanently. True enough. There is no arguing with the fact that baking soda will gobble up acids—if given the opportunity. But there's the rub, or rubs. How do we get the acid to come into contact with the baking soda, and why do we want to trap acids anyway?

First, why are acids the alleged stinkers? It goes back mostly to spoiled milk. In the old days of undependable refrigeration, and especially before pasteurization, milk quickly spoiled, not only by bacterial growth but by its butterfat breaking down into fatty acids, primarily butyric, caproic, and caprylic acids. Butyric acid is largely responsible for the odor of rancid butter, whereas caproic and caprylic acids are named after what they smell like: *caper* is Latin for goat. Get the drift?

So if you are in the habit of leaving month-old milk in the refrigerator for several weeks while you visit your time-share, many of the sour fatty acid molecules may indeed find their way to an open box of baking soda, fall in, and be neutralized.

But not all smelly molecules (smellicules?) that can pollute your refrigerator's air space are acids, or even bases (alkalis) for that matter; chemically speaking, they can be virtually anything. Claiming that baking soda absorbs "odors" generically is stretching the truth by a chemical mile.

Let's put it this way: An odor is a puff of gaseous molecules floating through the air to our noses. Each type of molecule has its unique chemical identity and its own unique set of reactions with other chemicals. No single chemical, sodium bicarbonate included, can claim to react with and deactivate any and all gaseous chemicals that happen to smell bad.

Even for acidic odors that are bicarbonate's main quarry, note that the landing pad for a smellicule on a box of baking soda is a mere 7 square inches (the box-top area) located at some random position within a 20-cubic-foot (35,000-cubic-inch) refrigerator air space. That's not a very efficient system for capturing smellicules. The box does not *attract* odors, as many people believe. It has no come-hither power, in spite of its toplessness.

The new "contraption" you saw is Arm & Hammer's creatively spelled Fridge-n-Freezer Flo-Thru Freshener, a standard one-pound box of baking soda with removable sides, intended to give gaseous molecules more access to the baking soda by "flo-ing thru" porous paper inner seals. That sounds like a great idea, but this box, "specially designed to expose more baking soda than any other package," uncovers only another 7 square inches of baking soda surface. And the air in the fridge doesn't "flo thru" the package anyway. There is no fan or other force blowing it into one side of the box and out the other. Nice advertising concept, though.

In short, as it says on Arm & Hammer's website, "Arm & Hammer Baking Soda's deodorization power is legendary!"

I agree. It's a legend.

What about the odor molecules that baking soda won't absorb? There is only one common substance that can gobble them all up indiscriminately: activated charcoal. It works not by trying to be a chemical for all seasons, but by using a physical stickiness that is essentially chemistry-blind. If gases find their way into its enormous interior network of microscopic pores, they stick by a phenomenon called adsorption, the adhesion of molecules to a surface by means of what chemists call van der Waals forces.

Charcoal is made by heating hardwood, nutshells, coconut husks, animal bones, or other carbon-containing materials in an oxygen-free environment, so that they don't actually burn, while substances other than carbon are driven off. It is then "activated" by being treated with very high temperature steam, a process that removes any remaining noncarbon substances and results in an extremely porous microstructure within the charcoal grains. A single gram (one twenty-eighth of an ounce) of activated charcoal may contain up to 2,000 square meters (18,000 square feet) of internal surface area.

You may be able to find activated charcoal (the best kind is made from coconut husks) in a drugstore, hardware store, appliance store, or pet shop. Spread it out on a baking pan with sides, and leave it in the offending fridge for a couple of days. Do *not* use charcoal briquettes; they contain coal, sawdust, and other substances, and their charcoal content wouldn't work anyway because it isn't powdered or activated.

In the end, there is only one sure-fire route to a sweet, odor-free refrigerator. Three words: prevention, prevention, prevention. Seal all your refrigerated food, especially "strong" foods such as onions, in airtight containers. Check frequently for signs of spoilage, round up the usual suspects, and throw them away. Wipe up spills promptly. Clean the fridge thoroughly. Yeah, I know, but do it more often.

Oh, you say there was a power outage while you were on vacation and all your refrigerated food spoiled and you could smell it all the way from the airport on your return? Poor soul. Neither baking soda nor charcoal will help, nor will cursing the power company. Make yourself a stiff drink, go to Louisiana State University's disaster information website http://www.lsuagcenter.com/Communications/pdfs_bak/pub2527Q.pdf, and follow the directions.

BUTTER KEEPERS DON'T

*Sticks of butter stored in a covered glass butter
dish in the butter-keeper compartment in the
door of our refrigerator develop a dark yellow,
slightly rancid-tasting skin. Is there
any way to prevent this?*

. . . .

You probably think you're doing everything right, don't you? Well, the worst place to keep butter is in a butter dish, and the worst place to keep the butter dish is in the "butter keeper" of your refrigerator.

Butter dishes were invented to facilitate serving, not preserving. Because they're not airtight, the butter's surface is exposed to air and can oxidize and become rancid.

Butter compartments should be banned. Many of them have little heaters inside to keep the butter at a slightly warmer temperature than the rest of the fridge to make it easier to spread. But the warmer temperature speeds up oxidation of the fat.

I keep my butter in the freezer compartment, tightly enveloped in plastic wrap. Yes, it's hard as a rock when I want to use it, but a sharp knife can whack off a piece that will warm up and soften rather quickly.

SAINTS (AND CHEMICALS) PRESERVE US!

*I've always wondered why some foods go bad so
quickly even if refrigerated, while others seem to
last forever without refrigeration. Things like
opened mustard and ketchup bottles can last for
weeks outside the refrigerator, and cheese, honey,
and peanut butter can survive at room
temperature for even longer. Is there any general
way to estimate how long a food will last?*

. . . .

Would that life were that simple! There can be no single rule that
covers all the foods we consume—an almost infinite number of com-
binations of thousands of different proteins, carbohydrates, fats, and
minerals that make up our omnivorous diet. "Going bad" can refer to
the effects of bacteria, molds, and yeasts; heat; oxidation from exposure to air; or enzymes in the foods themselves. Enzymes in fruits,
for example, are there specifically to hasten their ripening, matur-
ing, and ultimate decay.

One thing is inevitable, however: all foods will eventually spoil,
rot, decompose, disintegrate, crumble, putrefy, turn rancid, or
become just plain yucky. It's Nature's law, for dust they art and unto
dust shalt they return. Proteins will turn soft, squishy, putrid, and
green; carbohydrates will ferment and sour; fats will turn rancid.
Ketchup and mustard keep so long because they contain microbe-
inhibiting acid (vinegar), no fat, and no active enzymes.

In battling food spoilage, we humans have cooked our foods,
smoked them, dried them, acidified them, and salted or sugared
them—and, thanks largely to an American inventor named Clarence
Birdseye (yes, that was really his name), in recent decades we have
frozen them.

During a stint as a fur trader in Labrador, Birdseye watched the native people freeze fish and meats for later consumption. He noted that when frozen quickly in the winter instead of more slowly during the milder times, the food retained better texture, flavor, and color when thawed.

In 1925, Birdseye unveiled his "Quick Freeze Machine," and the frozen-food industry was off and running. Today, Birds Eye Foods bills itself as the nation's largest processor of frozen vegetables. And no, there never was a Mr. Jolly Greengiant.

Freezing preserves foods because the frozen water, a.k.a. ice, is unavailable for use by spoilage microorganisms, so they can't grow. Refrigeration, as distinguished from freezing, will slow their growth, but there are limits. At a typical home-refrigerator temperature, ten thousand bacteria can become ten billion in a few days.

Enter preservatives: chemicals added to prepared foods to extend their shelf lives—and the lives of us who eat them. Yes, preservatives are chemicals. And yes, they are also additives, because, obviously, they have been added. (So have salt, sugar, spices, vitamins, and so on.) Quite simply, without preservatives most of our foods would spoil. And yet we are continually wooed by food labels demurely hinting at their superiority with the phrase "Contains no additives or preservatives." Someday I'd like to see a label that adds "Will spoil almost as soon as you get it home."

What are these chemicals? They fall mostly into four categories.

- **Antimicrobials** inhibit the growth of bacteria, molds, and yeasts. They include the sulfur dioxide and sulfites used in fruits, fruit juices, vinegars, and wines; sorbic acid used in cheeses; calcium propionate and other propionates used to inhibit molds in bread and other baked goods; and sodium and other benzoates used to prevent fungal growth in beverages, fruit preserves, cheeses, pickles, and many other products. Benzoates occur naturally in cranberries, while propionates can be found in strawberries, apples, and cheeses.

- **Antioxidants** inhibit oxidation by air, which makes fats, especially unsaturated fats, turn rancid. They include sulfites (again), BHA (*butylated hydroxyanisole*), BHT (*butylated hydroxytoluene*), TBHQ (*tertiary butylated hydroquinone*), ascorbic acid (vitamin C), and propyl gallate. They're used in potato chips, nuts, cereals, and crackers.
- **Enzyme inhibitors** slow spoilage by enzyme-driven reactions in foods. Sulfites (again) inhibit enzymatic degradation reactions in fruits such as raisins and dried apricots. Acids, such as ascorbic acid and the citric acid in lemon juice, deactivate enzymes, including the enzyme phenolase, which makes apples and potatoes start turning brown as soon as they are cut.
- **Sequestrants,** also known as chelating agents, gobble up atoms of trace metals such as iron and copper that catalyze (accelerate) oxidation reactions and cause discoloration. The most widely used chelating agent is EDTA or *ethylene-diamine tetraacetic acid* (pronounced ETH-ill- een-DYE-a-meen- . . . oh, never mind). Other sequestrants are polyphosphates and citric acid.

Okay, so some of these chemical names are hard to pronounce. But contrary to the opinions of some, that doesn't make them evil. They're all added in tiny amounts regulated by the FDA, and nobody eats them by the spoonful.

Your alternative to eating foods containing preservatives is to visit the farm or farmers' market every day for fresh meat and produce. Also, make your own cream, preserves, pickles, cheese, wine, potato chips, cereals, and olive oil, being sure to consume them before they go bad.

And welcome to the eighteenth century.

NO NUKES

When we travel abroad and return to the United States, we're not allowed to bring home plants or foods for public health reasons. But aren't these items sterilized when they pass through the airport security X-ray machines?

. . . .

No. Airport security X-rays are not nearly intense enough to kill insects, parasites, and the like. The radiations used to sterilize and preserve foods are millions of times as intense.

BASICALLY, IT'S BASIC

I wonder why aluminum cookware and utensils become discolored and seemingly corroded in my dishwasher. An aluminum mesh strainer went particularly fast. Is this because there is an acid condition in the soap or water?

. . . .

No, it's not an acid. It's the chemical opposite of an acid: an alkali, known to chemists more accurately as a base.

Most dishwasher detergents for machines, as opposed to the dish-washing detergents for hand-washing dishes, contain the highly alkaline compound sodium carbonate, also known as good old-fashioned washing soda—*not* baking soda, which is sodium *bi*carbonate.

Alkaline chemicals are needed in the dishwasher because they gobble up grease, transforming it into soap. A soap is one of a class of chemical compounds formed by the action of an alkali on a fat. A detergent, on the other hand, is a more modern synthetic compound specifically designed to do soap's cleaning chores. That difference doesn't stop many people from calling all of today's household detergents "soaps" anyway.

But I digress.

We tend to think that if a chemical is attacking and dissolving a metal, it must be an acid. And that's generally true; a strong enough acid could devour a Humvee and spit out the tires. But aluminum is an unusual metal in that it is attacked by both acids and alkalis. (It is *amphoteric*.) So the alkaline sodium carbonate in the dishwasher detergent does indeed attack aluminum, at the very least eating deeply enough into the surface to make it dull and pewter-gray with aluminum compounds. For this reason most manufacturers of quality aluminum cookware advise against putting it in the dishwasher.

Worse yet, some dishwasher detergents contain potassium hydroxide or sodium hydroxide (lye), which are much stronger alkalis than sodium carbonate and will literally eat into your aluminum utensils. That's probably what converted your mesh strainer into a basketball hoop. If you still want to wash your aluminum cookware in the dishwasher, scan the labels of the dishwasher detergents in your supermarket and choose one that contains neither potassium or sodium hydroxide nor sodium carbonate. They do exist.

There's a second aluminum-damaging phenomenon going on in your dishwasher if the aluminum utensil happens to be touching another metal, which will most likely be stainless steel. Whenever any two different metals, in this case aluminum and what is essentially iron, are in contact while immersed in an electrically conducting liquid, an electrical (more properly, an *electrolytic*) reaction takes place that attacks one of the two metals, in this case the aluminum, corroding its surface and dulling it. So if you insist on washing an aluminum utensil in the dishwasher, make sure it isn't touching any other kind of metal.

Sidebar Science: *Stop, thief!*

FOR REASONS that are more elaborate than we want to get into here, iron atoms hold on to their electrons more tightly than aluminum atoms do. (Iron is said to be more *electronegative* than aluminum.) Thus, if the two metals happen to be in contact within an electrically conducting liquid (an *electrolyte*) such as dishwasher detergent dissolved in water, the iron atoms will actually steal electrons from the aluminum atoms. This transfer of electrons constitutes a flow of electric current, with the electrolyte completing the circuit.

The now-electron-deficient aluminum atoms (aluminum *cations*) want to regain their normal complement of electrons by reacting with something—anything—that has electrons to donate. The surface of the aluminum metal therefore reacts with negative ions (*anions*) in the solution, forming a dulling layer of an aluminum compound, most often aluminum oxide.

THE EMULSION COMPULSION

*I'm confused about emulsions. Some recipes tell me
I'm emulsifying certain ingredients, but all I can
see is that I'm merely blending them. Is there some
special trick I'm missing?*

. . . .

No, but I feel your pain. The word *emulsify* is too often misused as a synonym for *blend* or *thicken*. It is not. Restaurant menus love to call any thick sauce an emulsion. It is not. Chefs like to say they're emulsifying a sauce by using a *roux*. They're not.

Many substances, including flour, cornstarch, gelatin, pectin, okra, egg, and even pureed banana, will thicken a soup, custard, jam, gravy, or sauce. But when you use them you are not emulsifying anything. An emulsion is a very specific kind of mixture of two liquids that don't ordinarily mix, one suspended in the form of tiny droplets within the other.

The prototypical kitchen example of a true emulsion is mayonnaise, in which the mutual loathing between oil and water (the latter existing within the vinegar or lemon juice and egg white) has been overcome by two things: the brute force of being beaten together, and the action of a special chemical ingredient called an emulsifier. Only when this combination of physical and chemical powers is operating will oil and water mix and stay mixed in the form of a true emulsion.

As on that blind date we've all suffered through at one time or another, there are simply no attractive forces between a water molecule and an oil molecule. So even if you shake a bottle of vegetable oil and vinegar until they appear to have coalesced into a homogeneous whole, they will sooner or later, usually sooner, separate into two distinct layers. You will have failed to make a stable emulsion.

At most, you will have made a colloidal suspension, in which the oil has been broken down into such tiny microdroplets or globules that they are kept suspended in the vinegar by the constant bombardment of water molecules from all directions. But this marriage is doomed to failure. No matter how much muscle power you put into shaking your vinaigrette dressing, even with the assistance of a governor of California, the oil globules will eventually bump into one another and reunite into a coherent, separate layer. Again, no permanent emulsion.

We can foil the reunification of the oil globules by adding a secret ingredient called an emulsifying agent or an emulsifier. Emulsifiers are made of snakelike molecules that have long, oil-loving (*lipophilic*) tails and water-loving (*hydrophilic*) heads. Their lipophilic tails burrow into the oil globules, leaving their hydrophilic heads sticking out like thousands of cloves studding a ham. The "cloves" attract a cloak of water molecules because they contain positive and negative charges that pull on the water molecules' slightly negative and positive parts. (Water molecules are *dipoles*.) The resulting cloak of water molecules disguises the oil droplet as a water lover and prevents other oil droplets from attempting to unite with it. Because the emulsifier cloaks all the oil droplets in this way, they will not coalesce even if they bump into one another. They remain individually suspended. Now we have a true emulsion.

Where can we find those secret agents called emulsifiers? An excellent one is lecithin, a phosphorus-containing, fatlike chemical (a *phospholipid*) found in egg yolks. The phosphorus ends of its molecules are hydrophilic and their other ends are lipophilic. In mayonnaise, they emulsify the oil and vinegar into a permanently stable, homogeneous sauce.

Because we make mayonnaise from a small amount of vinegar or lemon juice (water) and a large amount—about eight times as much—

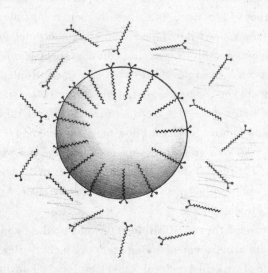

How emulsifier molecules make oil and water compatible. The zigzag, fat-loving (lipophilic) tails of the emulsifier molecules penetrate the oil globule, leaving their water-loving (hydrophilic) "eyes" sticking out, thereby giving the globule a water-loving surface.

of oil, it may be hard to believe that all that oil has been crowded into that small amount of water. Many people are thus led to believe that mayonnaise is a suspension of tiny water droplets in oil, rather than a suspension of tiny oil droplets in water. But in fact there are so many oil globules that they aren't actually suspended in the vinegar so much as coated with a very thin film of water, as in a bucket of wet peas, which tend to stick together because of the water's surface tension. That's why mayonnaise is so thick.

It is true, however, that a suspension of tiny water droplets in oil—the opposite of mayonnaise—is also classified as an emulsion. Butter and margarine, for example, are emulsions of water in oil.

When making mayonnaise with a whisk, we must dribble the oil into the acid-and-egg mixture very slowly to ensure that every added bit of oil is promptly reduced to colloidal-sized globules. If the oil drops are too big to remain suspended, they will coalesce while floating up to the top, where they will form a separate layer, defeating the entire purpose. After a while the oil can be added a little faster, because relatively large droplets will be quickly surrounded by millions of already emulsifier-coated colloidal globules that will "insulate" them from one another, keeping them apart temporarily until they themselves get whacked down to colloidal size.

When making mayonnaise in a blender, on the other hand, we can add a small amount of oil directly to the vinegar-and-egg mixture just before turning on the machine. The blender blades are much quicker than a whisk at chopping the oil globules down to colloidal size—so quick that the globules don't have time to coalesce.

Commercial dressings and other foods contain a wide variety of emulsifiers to keep their complex mixtures of carbohydrates, fats, proteins, and water together in a stable form. Some of the emulsifiers that you may see on ingredient labels are mono- and diglycerides, polyglycerol esters, propylene glycol esters, and sugar esters of fatty acids. And, of course, lecithin.

Foods are often thickened by substances such as gelatin, starches, and gums, including agar, acacia, xanthin, and carrageenan.

But thickeners aren't emulsifiers. Thickeners work by making the watery part so viscous that even relatively large oil droplets can't rise through it to coalesce into a layer.

Any old trick to keep a food homogeneous. Who wants to eat oily puddles mixed with globs of watery paste?

THE FOODIE'S FICTIONARY:

Hollandaise—Dutch Week at Epcot Center

Sidebar Science: *Mixing it up*

IN COOKING, we are continually mixing and blending ingredients. But there are several distinct kinds of mixtures. Emulsions are only one of them.

A combination of solid particles, such as salted and peppered flour or a blend of dried spices, is a simple physical mixture. But when liquids are involved, a mixture can take on any of several forms.

• **Solution:** The most homogeneous mixture of all is a *solution*, in which the individual molecules or ions (electrically charged atoms or groups of atoms) of one substance are dispersed intimately, molecule beside molecule, among those of the other. Examples are alcohol or sugar dissolved in water, where the alcohol or sugar molecules are intimately mixed in among the water molecules cheek by jowl—if they had cheeks and jowls. Another example is the tomato's red coloring compound, lycopene, when dissolved in an oil. (Notice how the fat in your tomato-containing recipes always turns red? The color is dissolved lycopene.)

• **Colloidal suspension:** Many other food mixtures are *colloids*, or *colloidal suspensions*, in which invisibly small but generally bigger-than-a-molecule particles of one substance (millionths to thousandths of an inch in size) are suspended throughout the other substance, which is most often a liquid. The particles are held in suspension against the pull of gravity because they are continually being bombarded from all sides by the molecules of the substance in which they are dispersed. The liquids within plant and animal cells are colloidal protein particles suspended in water-based solutions.

• **Emulsion:** An *emulsion* is similar to a colloidal suspension. In an emulsion, formed by the action of an emulsifying agent, slightly-larger-than-colloid-sized globules of one liquid are suspended in another liquid with which it wouldn't ordinarily mix. Mayonnaise and hollandaise sauce are the best-known examples in the kitchen.

Smoky Garlic Mayonnaise

Smoked Spanish paprika, *pimentón*, adds a subtle hint of wood fire to this garlic mayonnaise. It is a classic accompaniment to paella (p. 258), and is also good with Hot-Wok Mussels (p. 255). You can use it as a dip for raw vegetables, or serve it with steamed fish, especially with fresh cod. If the flavor is too intense, half olive oil and half peanut oil makes a delicious dressing.

For herb mayonnaise, add ½ cup minced fresh herbs (parsley, chives, chervil, tarragon) in place of the garlic in step 2. A blender does the best job of blending the herbs into the emulsion.

---

1 large egg

1 teaspoon smoked Spanish paprika (*pimentón*)

$^1/_2$ teaspoon dry mustard

$^1/_2$ teaspoon salt

2 tablespoons cider, sherry, or wine vinegar

1 cup mild extra-virgin olive oil

1 large clove garlic, coarsely chopped

---

1. Break the egg into the blender container. Add the *pimentón*, mustard, salt, and vinegar. Add ¼ cup of the oil. Cover the container and turn the motor on to low speed.

2. Immediately uncover and pour in the remaining oil in a fine, steady stream. Do not hurry. When all the oil has been incorporated, add the garlic (or the herbs, if using). Continue to blend for 1 minute, or until smooth.

3. Allow the mayonnaise to rest in the refrigerator for at least 1 hour before using, so the flavors will mellow and soften. Refrigerate for up to 4 days. Don't serve it cold, because chilling dulls the olive oil flavor.

MAKES ABOUT 1$^1/_4$ CUPS

HOME ON THE RANGE

*Oven temperatures are pretty easy to control; the
dials have actual temperature numbers on them.
But what about stovetops? I have a gas cooktop,
and the controls are marked "hi," "med," and "lo."
Two of them burn at higher Btu's than the other
two; "med" on them is hotter than "hi" on the
other two. I used to have an electric cooktop with
the same markings, but their cooking speeds were
completely different from my gas range. Are there
any industry standards for burner temperatures?*

. . . .

Unfortunately not. The only standard that I know of seems to be
that *high* is spelled "hi" and *low* is spelled "lo." In between "hi" and
"lo," my gas range has the digits 2 through 9, but the numbers indicate nothing whatsoever about temperature. The labels "hi" and "lo"
and the numbers 2 to 9 refer not to the temperature but the rate at
which the burner is generating heat.

There is a lot of confusion about the words *heat* and *temperature*
in the food world, so maybe it's "hi time" for me to give you the
"lodown."

First of all, heat and temperature are two different things. Heat is
a form of energy, distinct from gravitational energy, electrical
energy, energy of motion (*kinetic* energy), or nuclear energy. It is, in
fact, the ultimate form of energy into which all other forms eventually
degenerate. (See "The energy tax," p. 389.)

Cooking employs heat to cause physical and chemical changes
that we hope will improve the food's tenderness, digestibility, and
flavor. It should come as no surprise that when a food (or anything
else) absorbs heat, it gets "hotter," meaning that its temperature
rises. But what is temperature? It's nothing more than a convenient

number invented by humans (Mssrs. Fahrenheit and Celsius; see "Untangling F & C," p. 388) to indicate how much heat energy a substance contains. In cooking, specific changes take place when a food reaches specific temperatures, that is, when the food acquires enough heat relative to its size. You might say that temperature measures the concentration of heat in a substance.

So it's the temperature of the food, not the temperature of the gas flame or electric burner beneath the pot or pan, that matters to the cook. The burner is there only to pump heat into the food, no matter what its own temperature may be while doing it. We could place a white-hot poker beneath a frying pan, but it would be a terribly inefficient way to heat the food in the pan.

Then why do we say that one burner at a given setting is "hotter" than another? It's just loose talk; we don't really mean to imply that its temperature is higher. We mean only that that burner pumps out heat at a faster rate than the other one, thereby raising the food's temperature—and cooking it—faster. Instead of "hi" and "lo," then, we should really label the burner settings "fast" and "slow" (or, inevitably, "slo").

Different burners, whether gas or electric, do indeed pump out heat at different rates. We measure those rates in Btu's per hour. A *Btu*, or *British thermal unit*, is an amount of heat energy, just as a calorie is. (A nutritional calorie happens to be almost exactly equal to four Btu's.) But what's important about a cooktop burner is how many Btu's or calories it can pump out *per minute or per hour*. The number of Btu's pumped out per hour is a good indication of how fast a burner will heat and cook our food. A candle, for example, gives off a total of about 5,000 Btu's of heat over a period of a few hours, but that's hardly fast enough to cook with, because its Btu-per-hour rate is pathetic.

Most people, including appliance salesmen and cookbook authors, either are too lazy to say "Btu's per hour" or don't know the difference, so they (as you did in your question) speak simply of "Btu's" as if they were a measure of heating speed. But as Tony Soprano would say, wha'y'gon'do?

A home gas or electric range burner may put out between 9,000 and 15,000 Btu's per hour at their maximum settings. Check the literature that came with your range or contact its manufacturer to find out the ratings of your burners, and you'll know which ones are hotter (whoops! I mean faster).

In cooking, what ultimately counts is how fast the temperature of the food rises to its optimum cooking temperature and how steadily it will remain there at different burner settings. But alas, the burner's setting can be only a rough guide, because no matter what its Btu-per-hour rating, most of the heat it generates goes into heating up the kitchen.

Experience with a given cooktop will teach you approximately what each combination of burner and setting can accomplish. But good cooks simply keep an eye on what the food itself is doing, continually judging whether more or less heat is called for and adjusting the burner accordingly.

Life is tough.

Untangling F & C

In 1714 a German glassblower and amateur physicist named Gabriel Fahrenheit (1686–1736) made a gadget that would indicate how hot or cold an object was by how far up or down a thin column of mercury inside a glass tube would expand or contract as its temperature changed. To put numbers on it, he decided that there should be 180 "degrees" between the freezing point and the boiling point of water. Then he made up a batch of the coldest concoction he could create—a mixture of ice and ammonium chloride—and called its temperature zero. When he stuck his gadget into freezing water, the mercury went up 32 degrees higher than that. Since boiling water was to be 180 degrees higher than *that*, it came out to be 212. And that's how we got those crazy numbers, 32 and 212.

Six years after Fahrenheit himself cooled to room temperature, a Swedish astronomer named Anders Celsius (1701–1744) decided that it would be more convenient if there were only 100 "degrees" between the freezing and boiling points of water. So he set the freezing point at zero and the boiling point at 100. And that's how we got the Celsius scale of temperatures.

Every chance I get, I lobby for a little-known, simple method of conversion between Fahrenheit and Celsius temperatures. (And yes, it's in all my other books, and I'll keep doing it until everybody gets it right!) Forget those confusing formulas you learned in school. (Do you add—or is it subtract—32 before—or is it after—multiplying—or is it dividing—by 5/9? Or is it 9/5?)

My way is as easy as 1-2-3:

(1) Add 40 to the number you want to convert (either F or C).

(2) Multiply or divide the result by 1.8.

(3) Subtract 40.

That's it. All you have to remember is the fact that Fahrenheit temperatures are always bigger numbers than their Celsius equivalents, so you *multiply* by 1.8 to convert from C to F, and you *divide* by 1.8 to convert from F to C.

Example: 212°F + 40 = 252

252 ÷ 1.8 = 140

140 − 40 = 100°C

... and that's just what you expected it to be, right?

Sidebar Science: *The energy tax*

HEAT, THE energy we use in cooking, is the most universal form of energy. All other energy forms—chemical energy, energy of motion (*kinetic energy*), electrical energy, nuclear energy—eventually degenerate into heat, which you might say is a sort of energy of last resort. As chemical reactions give off energy, as moving things slow down, as a lamp converts electrical energy into light, as uranium atoms convert mass into radioactivity and heat, there can never be a 100 percent conversion. Inefficiency seems to be built into the universe. Some of the lost or converted energy must inevitably be "wasted" by being turned into heat. You might think of heat as a tax on the conversion of energy; it's like the fee charged by a money exchanger for converting one form of currency into another.

Most forms of energy can be well-behaved. For example, kinetic energy is well-behaved when a truck is moving in a straight line down a highway. Electrical energy is well-behaved when the movement of electrons is being controlled by a circuit. Nuclear energy comes from the *very* carefully controlled splitting of atoms. In contrast to all this, however, heat is a shockingly ill-behaved and disorderly form of energy, because it consists of the wild, random movement of atoms and molecules.

The science of *thermodynamics* has found that whenever a form of energy, such as the chemical energy in a truck's diesel fuel or in the uranium of a nuclear reactor, is being converted into another form, the disorderliness or randomness (the *entropy*) of the system must increase. That's the Second Law of Thermodynamics. The universe is inexorably winding down by losing energy and creating disorder. Chaos.

So whenever a form of energy is being used up or converted into another, some of a disorderly, more chaotic, higher-entropy form of energy must be produced. That's heat.

For further details, consult your friendly neighborhood thermodynamicist.

FOILING BROILING

I've been trying to get some answers to questions about oven broilers. They seem to be the most inconsistent of all kitchen equipment. I've moved several times and have had several broilers. One may sear a steak beautifully, while another steams it before it can get brown. How far from the heat should the food be? What about gas versus electric? Preheat or not? Door open or closed?

. . . .

You're right to be befuddled. Of the six basic methods of cooking, broiling is the hardest to control.

What are the six basic methods, you ask? They are (1) immersion in hot water or stock (boiling, poaching, stewing); (2) exposure to hot water vapor (steaming); (3) immersion in hot oil (deep-frying); (4) contact with hot metal (pan-frying, sautéing, searing, grilling); (5) exposure to hot air (baking, oven roasting); and (6) exposure to infrared radiation. That last-named method is what we call broiling. (Okay, add the absorption of microwaves to the list if you wish.)

Maybe you think you don't broil with infrared radiation. But the molecules of anything that's hot, such as the flame or heating element in a broiler, are emitting infrared radiation, a kind of electromagnetic energy that other molecules can absorb with the result that they become hot in turn. You can feel the warming of the molecules in your face when you walk by anything that's hot, such as a red-hot furnace or even a range burner that you forgot to turn off. So any cooking method that involves a source of heat—and what method doesn't? (okay, except microwaves)—is cooking the food at least partially by shooting infrared radiation at it.

Broiling cooks food almost entirely by infrared radiation. The heat source, whether a red-hot electric element or a line of gas flames, doesn't touch the food; it bathes it in intense infrared radiation, which is absorbed by the top surface of the food, heating it to 600 to 700°F (320 to 370°C) and searing and browning it quickly. Then, after you turn the food over, the same thing happens on the other side.

In electric ovens set on "broil," only the top heating element gets hot, and the food is placed close beneath it. In some gas ovens, the burner may be beneath the oven floor, doing double duty by also heating the oven, so the food to be broiled must be placed even below that, usually in a drawer-like arrangement.

But we all learned in school that heat rises, didn't we? So how come we can cook food *beneath* the source of heat? Well, pardon me, but heat doesn't rise. Heat from a hot object can flow up, down, or sideways. It will flow into any cooler object with which it happens to be in contact. What people mean when they say heat rises is that *hot air* rises. Heated air expands and becomes less dense, so it floats upward through the denser, cooler air like a bubble in water.

And while we're picking nits, what we usually call grilling—that is, placing food above red-hot charcoal or gas flames—can also be called broiling because it's not the rising hot air that cooks the food so much as the infrared radiation. Even so, largely because of the charcoal's smoke and the juices that drip down onto hot surfaces and vaporize, this kind of broiling imparts very different flavors to the food than "indoor" broiling does.

Broiling is a good cooking method for tender meats, poultry, and fish, because it's a dry, high-temperature, short-time method. Less tender meats generally need long, moist cooking to break down the collagen in their connective tissue. Beef steaks and other red meats are a natural for broiling, while pork, chicken, and fish have to be watched carefully to prevent their drying out.

The biggest question in broiling is how close the meat should be to the heating element or gas flames, because a small difference in distance can make a big difference in temperature. The right distance will depend on the type and thickness of the meat, on its fat content, and especially on the idiosyncrasies of the broiler itself. As you've noticed, your broiler isn't your mother's or your neighbor's broiler. They're all different. In general, though, the top surface of the meat should be 3 to 6 inches from the heat source, thin meat relatively closer and thick meat farther away so it can cook through before its surfaces char.

Should you leave the door open? Usually it's left open in electric ovens to prevent hot-air baking and to let the smoke out. In stove-bottom gas broilers, the drawer is kept closed because the flames consume the smoke, and leaving it open could make a greasy mess on your kitchen floor.

Should you preheat the oven? It's generally not necessary, although I've seen an almost equal number of "always preheat" and "never preheat" admonitions. The best advice—in fact the only good advice— is to follow carefully the directions in the broiling chart in the instruction manual that came with your oven. The manufacturers have spent a lot of time and effort to determine the best conditions for broiling various kinds of meat in their equipment. If you're one of those people who throw away instruction manuals, or if you can't find yours (have you looked in your kitchen's "everything else" drawer?), you can usually order a free replacement from the manufacturer.

Remember that the fat-catching broiler pan that came with your oven is an important part of the picture, so don't expect to get the same results with any old pan of perhaps a different size. When I use the recommended broiler pan, shelf height, lack of preheating, door ajar, and cooking time for broiling chicken in my electric oven, it comes out perfectly, even though it looks to me as if the chicken is much too close to the heating unit and the door is open too wide. It doesn't pay to second-guess manufacturers. They know their stuff best.

TWO TIMES ONE EQUALS 1.8

The instructions for my microwave oven tell me how long to reheat one serving of this or that. But sometimes I want to reheat two or more servings at the same time. To reheat x servings, should I set the timer for x times the number of minutes recommended for a single serving?

. . . .

No. Heating two servings of something takes less than twice the amount of time required for heating one.

Different foods absorb microwaves to different degrees. Water and fats absorb microwaves efficiently, while proteins and carbohydrates don't absorb much at all. That's why different foods require different amounts of time to heat or cook. Furthermore, the microwave generator (the *magnetron*) varies its output according to how big a "load" of absorbing material (a.k.a. food) is in the oven.

Here's a very rough way of looking at the problem. Let's say that your particular food absorbs—and turns into heat—a certain percentage of the magnetron's microwave output. But when there are two servings in the oven, neither one is being exposed to the magnetron's full output of microwaves; each gets only the un-absorbed "leftovers" from the other. So naturally it will take more time to heat two of them than to heat one. But how much more?

I'll spare you the arithmetic, but the way it works out is that if one of your servings absorbs, say, 40 percent of the microwaves that it is exposed to, then it will take only 25 percent more time to heat two portions than to heat one. This time increase won't always be 25 percent; it will be different for different foods that have different appetites for absorbing microwaves.

I tested these ideas with my own "smart" microwave oven, which has pre-programmed cycles for various common heating and cooking chores. For "Heating a Beverage," for example, the oven first asks me to press a button to tell it how much liquid I want to heat. It then begins its pre-programmed heating cycle for that amount. I timed the heating periods, and here's how long they lasted: for 0.5 cup, 30 seconds; for 1.0 cup, 50 seconds; for 1.5 cups, 70 seconds; for 2.0 cups, 90 seconds. You can see that the first half-cup requires 30 seconds but that each additional half-cup requires only 20 additional seconds. Two cups took only 1.8 times as much time (90 ÷ 50) as a single cup.

Another example: For "Baked Potatoes" (they're actually not being baked, but I'll let that go), the oven cooks one potato in 4½ minutes, and adds 3 minutes and 10 seconds for each additional potato. Putting it another way, two potatoes take only 1.7 times as long as a single potato; three potatoes take 2.4 times as long, and four potatoes take 3.1 times as long.

Lacking an omniscient oven that has pre-programmed cycles for every conceivable type and amount of food, all we can do is make an educated guess. For two servings, your first guess should be about one and three-quarters times the time required for a single serving. Doubling the time would be likely to overheat your food, perhaps making it splatter or dry out. It's best to be conservative, because you can always zap it a little longer.

Sidebar Science: *Say what?*

MICROWAVE OVENS are very complicated devices, truly understood only by their electrical-engineer designers. The analysis above, based on a constant percentage of microwave energy being absorbed by each portion, is oversimplified. But I didn't think you wanted to get involved in load impedances, cavity resonances, and loss constants. And neither did I, for the plain reason that I don't understand them.

NOTHING BEATS-A PIZZ-A

A new pizza restaurant opened recently in my area, with everything imported from Italy, from the furniture to the brick oven to Roberto, the owner, who actually earned a diploma in pizza-making in Naples. He attributes much of the superb quality of his pizzas to the brick oven. Also, some home cooks I know swear by their pizza stones for baking pizzas and crusty breads. Is there really something to these claims, and if so, what's so special about brick and stone?

. . . .

It's true. Dough, whether for pizza or for bread, baked on a stone surface such as the floor of a brick oven or one of those flat stoneware oven accessories called pizza stones, really does come out crisper and browner than if it were baked on a metal baking sheet or pan. If the oven walls are also stone or brick, so much the better. Early bakers *had* to build their ovens out of available natural materials such as stone and bricks made of clay. Today we bake our bread in "improved," technologically sophisticated ovens made of steel. And ironically, they don't do nearly as good a job.

Brick and stone have two properties that make them work so well: high heat capacity and high emissivity.

Heat capacity is a technical term meaning, well, the capacity to hold heat. If a substance has a high heat capacity, it can absorb a lot of heat without its temperature going up very much. That resistance to having its temperature changed cuts both ways: during heating and during cooling. Once the substance has had its temperature raised, it doesn't want to cool down any more than it wanted to heat up, so it retains its temperature for a relatively long time.

Stone and brick have higher heat capacities than metals. For the same thickness, an oven floor made of fire clay has twice the heat capacity of iron and two and a half times the heat capacity of copper. So once heated to the desired temperature (and that may take a long time), a clay floor holds its heat well, staying uniformly at that temperature and resisting temperature changes, such as when relatively cold dough is placed on it. Note also that the larger the mass of a material, the higher its capacity to hold heat, just as a bigger pitcher can hold more water. That's why massive brick ovens with thick floors and walls have always been valued for their baking prowess. On a smaller scale, that's also why a heavy frying pan "holds its heat" (that is, stays at a constant temperature) better than a thin one.

Brick, clay, and stone have a second, even more powerful advantage over metallic oven materials: their vastly superior *emissivities*.

Infrared (loosely called "heat") radiation in a hot oven is absorbed by the molecules of the materials it strikes, which then re-emit much of the radiation almost instantly. In some substances, notably metals, most of the absorbed radiation is dissipated before it can be re-emitted. Only a fraction of the absorbed radiation (16 percent in the case of a stainless-steel oven wall) is returned promptly to its environment: the air in the oven. (In techie talk, the *emissivity* of a stainless-steel surface is 0.16.) The rest of its heat stays in the oven wall and is wasted, as far as the food is concerned, except that it can slowly and inefficiently work its way back into the air.

Even at the same temperature, then, stone emits more infrared radiation than metal does. And because infrared radiation doesn't penetrate beyond the surfaces of materials, more infrared radiation striking the dough results in better browning and crisping of its surface.

So whether you're reheating a delivered pizza, making one from scratch, or baking a free-form loaf of bread, place it on a preheated pizza stone. If the stone is unglazed and therefore porous, it will have the additional advantage of absorbing the steam emitted from the bottom surface of the dough, keeping it dry for even more effective crisping.

Sidebar Science: *Heat capacity and emissivity*

• **Heat Capacity:** Let's take water as the most familiar example of a material that has a relatively high heat capacity.

When we heat water, we're pumping calories of heat into it; its temperature will therefore rise. Temperature is a measure of how fast the molecules are moving. Because water molecules stick quite tenaciously to one another (by *dipole-dipole attraction* and *hydrogen bonding*), it's relatively difficult to goose them into moving faster. We have to add a whole (nutritional) calorie of heat in order to raise the temperature of a kilogram (a liter) of water by a single degree Celsius. (That is, the *specific heat* of water is one kilocalorie per kilogram per degree C.) Conversely, when water cools, it has to lose a lot of heat—that same one nutritional calorie per kilogram—for its temperature to be reduced by a single Celsius degree.

A couple of consequences of these facts are that (1) it takes "forever" for a heated pot of water to come to a boil, and (2) a body of water, such as a large lake or an ocean, moderates the surrounding climate by refusing to heat up or cool down as easily as the land does.

• **Emissivity:** In any environment above absolute zero in temperature—and that includes *all* environments—there is infrared radiation flying through the space. When such radiation strikes a surface, the molecules in that surface absorb some of it. They exhibit the fact that they now contain more energy by moving more agitatedly: twisting, rotating, and tumbling like a hyperactive kindergarten class during a Ritalin shortage. Each kind of molecule has its own unique ways of rotating and tumbling, corresponding to the unique, characteristic sets of energies that it is capable of absorbing. (That is, different molecules have different *infrared absorption spectra*.)

After absorbing the radiant energy, the excited molecules

"calm down" by re-emitting some of it. Some kinds of molecules re-emit virtually all the energy they had absorbed, while others retain some, converting it into different forms of energy. A substance that re-emits 100 percent of the energy it absorbs is said to have an emissivity of 1.00. (In Techspeak, it behaves like a *black-body radiator*.)

In general, metals have very low emissivities because their loose electrons can soak up the energy like a sponge. Aluminum, for example, re-emits only 5 percent of the infrared radiation that strikes it; copper, only 2 percent. In contrast, materials such as stone and brick re-emit virtually all of the radiation they absorb: 90 percent for dark brick, 93 percent for marble, 97 percent for tile; that is, their emissivities are 0.90, 0.93, and 0.97, respectively. That's because the molecules in these substances are fixed rigidly in place, and can't retain the energy by oscillating and tumbling. In these materials, very little infrared energy is wasted; almost all of the infrared radiation that strikes these stonelike surfaces is re-emitted toward the food.

BAKING BY TOOTHPICK

Why do the directions on cake-mix boxes tell us to lower the oven temperature by 25°F if we're using a glass cake pan or dish instead of a metal one?

. . . .

Not all of the cake-mix boxes tell us that. In a perusal of the acres of cake-mix boxes on the shelves of my supermarket (in space consumption probably second only to breakfast cereals), I found, as expected, a wide variety of baking instructions, specifying a wide variety of baking times and temperatures for different pan sizes, shapes, and materials. And that's not even considering the plight of those unfortunates who live at high altitudes, who are exhorted to modify almost everything from the time and temperature to the amounts of flour and water.

The necessity of changing the time and temperature for various pan shapes and sizes is easy to explain. It's a matter of surface-to-volume ratio. That is, if the same volume of batter is spread out into a wide pan, exposing a large surface area to the oven's heat (a large ratio of surface to volume), such as in a sheet cake, it will cook faster than if it were poured into a bundt pan, which exposes relatively little surface area to the hot air.

Then there's the question of what the pan is made of. In my supermarket survey I found that for standard, shiny aluminum pans, almost all the mixes specify a preheated oven temperature of 350°F (177°C). For dark-colored pans, many of the boxes specify a lower temperature of 325°F (163°C). Several boxes specify 325°F for *glass* baking pans, but several also say 325°F for glass *or* metal pans, without mentioning dark-colored pans at all. And one devil-may-care box, bless its heart, says "350°F (any type pan)."

So what's a guy to do?

I am now going to violate the most fundamental principle of expository writing, if not of teaching, by admitting at the start that none of the recommendations matter in the end, and then asking you to bear with me while I explain the scientific reasons behind the recommendations.

- **The color of the pan:** A relatively shiny aluminum or stainless-steel cake pan obviously reflects visible light more than a dark-colored anodized one or a nonstick-coated one. Because all the light falling on an object must be either reflected or absorbed, that means that the dark surface is absorbing more light than the shiny one is. That extra absorbed light energy makes the dark-colored pan slightly warmer than the shiny one, even in a same-temperature oven. (To manage our body heat, we wear lighter-colored clothes in the summer and darker ones in the winter.)

But what light is there inside a dark oven, you ask? Infrared radiation, which many people refer to as infrared "light" even though it's invisible to the human eye. A dark surface absorbs more of this radiation than a light-colored or shiny surface does. That's particularly important because when an object absorbs infrared radiation it becomes warmer— significantly warmer than if it had absorbed visible light. Thus, a cake should cook faster in a dark pan than in a light one, and we are often advised to lower the oven temperature to compensate.

• **The material of which the pan is made:** A thin metal cake pan of any color conducts the oven's heat efficiently into the batter. But compared with metal, a glass pan is a very poor conductor of heat and is quite sluggish at transmitting its oven-given heat into its contents. Using a glass pan and given the choice of fast baking at a high temperature or slower baking at a lower temperature, we would choose the latter, because the oven's heat needs a longer time to penetrate through the glass to the batter. It's not a big effect, so a relatively small decrease in oven temperature or a small increase in baking time (which some cake-mix instructions specify) suffices.

And now, as promised, I repeat that none of this really matters. Home ovens don't work like the carefully calibrated equipment in the test kitchens of Betty Crocker or Duncan Hines. There, armies of lab-coated technicians painstakingly work out the best possible conditions for baking their mixes to ensure that the home cook garners accolades from his or her family and runs back to the store to purchase more. But in real life, home ovens may vary from their set temperatures by plus or minus 25°F (14°C) or even more, and the issue of 350 versus 325 degrees is in most cases moot.

So use whatever kind of pan you have, and by all means, turn your oven dial to the recommended number. But don't bet your cookies on it. After all the directives about pan material, oven temperature, and baking time, every cake-mix box that I've seen winds up admitting that the cake is done when, and only when, it *looks* done and a toothpick inserted into it comes out clean.

And that's the truth.

Sidebar Science: *How ovens cook*

WE SPEAK of oven temperature as the main variable that determines how fast a cake will bake or any food will cook. But although the temperature is of primary importance, it is only one factor. Even at exactly the same oven temperature, the amount of heat energy a food actually receives and absorbs may not be the same.

By "oven temperature," we mean the temperature of the air inside the enclosure, and that's what the temperature control device regulates. But once the air is heated to a certain temperature, there are still three ways in which the air's heat can be transmitted into the food: by conduction, by convection, and by radiation.

• **Conduction:** When two substances at different temperatures are in contact, such as hot oven air in contact with a food's surface, heat will flow from the higher-temperature air into the lower-temperature food by the process of conduction. Just as water always flows downhill if it can, heat will always try to flow "down-temperature" from high to low. The heat energy is conducted from the air to the food across their interface by direct molecular collisions. That is, the hot air molecules are moving faster than the cooler food molecules (that's actually the definition of temperature: it's the average motion energy—*kinetic* energy—of the molecules), and when they collide with the food's molecules they kick them up to a faster (hotter) speed, like a cue ball scattering a rack of billiard balls.

But conduction is very inefficient. Air molecules are separated from one another by interplanetary distances, relatively speaking, so the chances that a hot air molecule will collide with the surface of a cake pan or a roast are small. Heat conduction can be quite efficient between two solids in contact, such as your hand on a hot frying-pan handle, but not between hot air and anything else. You can put your hand in a 200°F (93°C) oven for several seconds without fear, because the rate of conduction of heat from the air into your skin is so extraordinarily slow. But don't try dipping your hand into 200°F water. Water is a much better conductor of heat because its molecules are much closer together than air's are.

And why are metals the best heat conductors of all?

In almost all other materials, the atomic electrons are parts of individual molecules. But in metals, the electrons belong, in effect, to all the atoms simultaneously. We can think of metal atoms as being embedded in a swarm or sea of shared electrons, like raisins in an electron pudding. When a metal comes in contact with the agitated molecules of a hot substance, it's the electron swarm that transfers the agitation—the heat—rapidly to all other parts of the metal. That's heat conduction.

In an oven, however, the other two heat transmission mechanisms, convection and radiation, are more important than conduction.

• **Convection:** Variable conditions inside the oven, such as inevitably uneven temperatures between one spot and another, make the air move, because hotter "pieces" of air rise, while cooler "pieces" fall, creating a kind of circulation that's called convection, or convection currents. This circulation boosts the efficiency of heat transfer between the air and the food, because it increases the amount of contact between the food and the hot air molecules in the enclosure. A convection oven enhances this effect by means of a fan that circulates the oven's internal air or some externally heated and blown-in hot air, leading to more efficient heat transfer and faster cooking. That's why it's good practice to lower the temperature by about 25°F (14°C) when using a convection oven rather than a standard one.

• **Radiation:** The third mechanism by which food becomes hot in an oven is by absorbing radiation. The oven's heating element or flame and its walls and floor are hot—they are what make the air hot—and hot things radiate infrared radiation. In fact, all materials at all temperatures are emitting some of their energy as infrared radiation. (See "Heat capacity and emissivity" on p. 398.)

For a given object, the hotter it is, the more infrared radiation it is emitting. When the infrared radiation coming from the hot oven walls and the hot air hits the food, the food molecules absorb it and move with increased energy. That is, they become hotter.

Infrared radiation isn't heat, as many books will tell you. It is electromagnetic radiation, like radio, radar, and microwaves, but of just the right wavelength to be absorbed by most kinds of molecules, which thereby become more energetic and hotter. I call infrared radiation "heat in transit," because it is emitted by hot matter and travels through space, yet it isn't transformed back into heat until it is absorbed by other matter.

OVEN RUBBER

*More and more, I'm seeing kitchen gadgets such as
spatulas and pastry brushes made of silicone.
What amazes me is the baking pans and muffin
"tins," which look and feel like rubber, but can
supposedly stand oven temperatures up to 500°F.
What's the secret?*

. . . .

The secret, as Julius Caesar might have said, is that all rubber is
divided into three parts. Or, in somewhat more modern language,
that which we call rubber by any other name would not bake as well.

I'll try again. There are three basic kinds of rubber, coming from
three different kinds of plants: natural rubber, which comes from
latex, the sap of the tropical tree *Hevea brasiliensis*; synthetic rubber,
which is made in a chemical plant; and silicone rubber, which comes
from, well, a different chemical plant. The last two were dreamed up
by chemists in attempts to duplicate some of natural rubber's unique
properties and improve upon others.

A synthetic rubber called neoprene was first marketed by DuPont
in 1931, and a wide variety of silicone rubbers have been manufactured by General Electric and Dow Corning since the 1940s. These
two man-made products inherited the silly name *rubber* from the
natural material, which was so christened by the English chemist and
clergyman Joseph Priestley in 1770, when he found that it would rub
out pencil marks, if not erase sins.

Unfortunately, in recent times the word *silicone* has been
implanted, so to speak, in the public's mind in but a single context:
cosmetic augmentation. But silicones are a remarkably versatile
family of chemical compounds with hundreds of uses. In culinary
applications, the French fiberglass-reinforced silicone baking-pan
liner called Silpat has been used in professional kitchens since it was

introduced in 1982. But silicones have only recently invaded the American home kitchen in many forms, all approved by the FDA for repeated contact with food. Today, the whole baking pan, not just its liner, is made of silicone.

Before I go any further, I must straighten out some terminology, because the words *silicone* and *silicon* are so often mistakenly interchanged.

Silicon (no *e*) is a chemical element, the second most abundant element on Earth (after oxygen). It is a rock-hard, brittle gray material that would make the world's worst cake pans, not to mention surgical implants. However, silicon the element is a semiconductor, and therefore immensely valuable in the form of "chips" or microprocessors in computers and hundreds of other electronic devices. That's why the high-tech region around San Jose, California, is called Silicon Valley. (It is to be carefully distinguished from Los Angeles, which has been dubbed Silicone Valley for reasons I need not explain.)

Silicones, on the other hand, are chemical compounds that, like the natural and synthetic rubbers, are polymers, meaning that their molecules consist of long chains of thousands of smaller molecules tied together. Silicone molecules have spines made of alternating atoms of silicon and oxygen, to which are attached various groups of carbon and hydrogen atoms. Depending on the lengths of the chains and the identities of the attached groups, silicones can range from liquids (used in brake fluids and water-repellent sprays) to gels (in breast implants) to greases (in lubricants and lipsticks) to elastomers, the rubber-like materials in Silly Putty, Superballs, refrigerator door gaskets, and, now, kitchenware.

Silicone bakeware has a remarkably useful set of properties. First of all, the material is inherently translucent, so a veritable kaleidoscope of bright colors can be incorporated into the products. (KitchenAid's line of muffin pans, loaf pans, and cake pans comes in red or blue.) Silicone pans can withstand high temperatures without melting (without their molecules flowing apart from one another) because the molecules are very long and tightly intertwined, like a plate of cold, leftover Spaghetti with Glue Sauce. That's also why you can take them directly from the oven to the freezer or vice versa without any fear of cracking; the molecules, while individually flexible, are so rigidly fixed in place that the material can't expand or contract very much with changes in temperature.

Silicones don't absorb microwaves, but like all microwave-safe utensils they can get hot in the microwave oven from contact with the heated food. Because silicones are chemically inert, the pans are dishwasher-safe; caustic detergents can't touch them. Also because of their nonreactivity, they are more or less nonstick; cakes and muffins release easily—most of the time—since you can flex the pans to pop them out. But don't try to use them as Jell-O or aspic molds; sitting the mold in a warm water bath won't release the gelatin because the silicone is a heat insulator.

Any disadvantages? Being electrical insulators (one of the most important properties of silicone rubbers in other applications), they are subject to static electricity and may collect dust in the pantry between uses. And their floppiness can be disquieting, for example when you're carrying a batter-filled pan to the oven. Carry the pan on a rimless baking sheet, using the sheet as a peel when inserting the pan into the oven.

Caveat emptor department: As with everything else, there are high and low qualities of silicone bakeware. Remember that "silicone" isn't a single chemical material. Dow Corning, for example, sells dozens of different silicone formulations with different properties, for fabricators to use in molding their commercial products. Some may not be as heat-resistant as others, so check the maximum temperature ratings on the labels. They can range from 450°F (232°C) up to 675°F (357°C) for silicone trivet pads.

SHAPE MATTERS

*Recipes are always telling us to roast something at
a certain temperature for a certain length of time.
But then they tell us to test it near the end to see
whether it's done, and in my experience it almost
never is. Shouldn't the recipe developer be able to
give me a more exact cooking time?*

. . . .

The quick and dirty answer is no; there are just too many uncontrolled variables.

The cruel fact of life is that when a recipe tells you to cook for "*x* hours at *y* degrees," it's only a guideline, an educated guess, a ballpark estimate. It's what worked most of the time—for the elves who tested the recipe, but there's no guarantee it will work for you. So, sorry, Virginia, but there is no Santa Claus. (I've been wanting to straighten that kid out for years.)

Except perhaps in a food research laboratory, there is no such thing as a standard roast on a standard rack in a standard pan at a standard position in a standard oven at a carefully regulated oven temperature. Each one of these factors can vary, producing different results even if all other things were equal. But as Wolke's Law of Pervasive Perversity says, "All other things are never equal."

You can't just go around saying that a beef or pork roast or a chicken or turkey should be cooked for so many minutes per pound at a certain temperature. Even if Wolke's Law didn't apply and you could magically control everything else, the one variable that you have no control over is the most important one: the shape of the roast. Not its weight but its *shape*: how much surface area it presents to the oven's heat. Heat can enter the meat only through its surface, so the more surface area a roast has for its weight, the faster it will cook.

Here's an example.

If we had two roasts of the same weight—that is, the same volume—one shaped like a cube and the other shaped like a sphere, the cubic roast would have 24 percent more surface area than the spherical one. That's just geometry. Work it out yourself if you get your kicks that way. For my part,

> *I never saw a cubic cow*
> *I never hope to see one.*
> *But I can tell you anyhow,*
> *It'll roast about 24 percent faster than a spherical one.*

Another example: Suppose we cut that cubic roast in half parallel to one face. Its surface area will then be increased by 33 percent. The two halves, then, should cook in roughly 33 percent less time than the whole one.

So again, dear, naïve little Virginia, no Santa Claus, or even a reasonably good fairy, exists who can weigh your irregularly shaped rib roasts or turkeys and tell you exactly how many minutes per pound to cook it, even if Wolke's Law were repealed.

TIME AND TEMPERATURE
WAIT FOR NO HAM

> *I want to roast a piece of meat in an oven for*
> *24 hours at 180°F (82°C). Would this use*
> *less gas or electric energy than roasting it*
> *for 3 hours at 375°F (191°C)? How about*
> *6 hours at 250°F (121°C)?*
>
> ....

This may sound like an odd question, but it was asked of me by the food authority and author Paula Wolfert when she was working on her book *The Slow Mediterranean Kitchen: Recipes for the Passionate Cook*.

Her concept was that long, slow cooking can produce tender, juicy, flavorful meats that higher-temperature cooking cannot match. And as usual, she's right, as the recipes in her book amply demonstrate (although none of them approaches 24 hours of cooking).

It has always been an oversimplification to say that cooking time and cooking temperature are inversely proportional to each other—that the same, or similar, results can be obtained in a short time at a high temperature as for a longer time at a lower temperature. That concept is woefully inadequate, except over a very limited range of times and temperatures, because cooking is not a matter of simply injecting a given number of calories of heat into a food. As the old jazz song would have it, "It ain't whatcha do, it's the way hotcha do it."

At the time of our discussion, the world was in one of its periodic energy crises, and Paula worried that long, low-temperature roasting might use more energy than shorter, higher-temperature roasting. Fascinated, I leapt at the challenge. Rather than taking the experimental approach, spending days in the kitchen after turning off all electrical devices in the house (it's amazing how many there are, if you count them) except my electric oven and recording the readings on the electric meter, I decided to take the theoretical approach and try to solve the problem mathematically. Here's what I came up with.

There are two energy-consuming stages in roasting meat: preheating the oven to the roasting temperature and maintaining that temperature during the roasting period.

It will obviously require more energy to preheat the oven to the higher of the two temperatures. (The actual difference in energy usage will depend on the characteristics of the individual oven.) But in either case the preheating time is short compared with the total roasting time, so we can probably neglect that difference. The difference in preheating times does, however, work in favor of less energy consumption by the low-temperature method.

During the roasting period, the oven will be persistently trying to cool down by losing heat to its surroundings. But whenever its temperature falls to a certain level, the oven's automatic temperature control feeds in gas or electrical energy to replenish the heat that was lost. Thus, over the entire roasting period, the total energy *input* should be equal to the total energy *lost* by cooling. I could then obtain the energy usage under the two roasting conditions by calculating the rates of energy loss by cooling. The average rate of cooling (in calories per hour or Btu's per hour) times the number of roasting hours should give me the total amount of energy used.

For my calculations I used Isaac Newton's Law of Cooling (yes, *that* Isaac Newton), which says that the rate of cooling of a hot body is proportional to the difference in temperature between the body and its surroundings. In this case, the "body" is the air inside the oven, and its surroundings are the air in the kitchen. (The intervening oven walls slow the transfer of heat but don't change the amount of heat that is ultimately transferred.)

Because all the heat-transfer parameters will differ from one case to the next, I can't calculate absolute amounts of energy loss. But from Newton's Law, I can calculate the *break-even time*: the number of slow-roasting hours at which the energy usage becomes equal to the energy usage in the fast-roasting method. If we slow-roast any longer than this, we will be using more energy than in the fast method.

Here are the results of my calculations. (Gluttons for mathematical detail may consult "(Warning: calculus ahead)" on p. 413.)

In Paula's first example, the energy break-even point for slow roasting at 180°F comes out to be about 9 hours. Thus, roasting for 24 hours at 180°F will use substantially more energy than roasting for 3 hours at 375°F. But 24 hours at 180°F is a rather extreme set of slow-roasting conditions anyway.

In Paula's second example, the energy break-even point for slow roasting at 250°F comes out to be about 5 hours, which is close enough to Paula's desired 6 hours. So go for it, Paula! The energy police will not break down your door.

What I've found, then, is that long, slow roasting need not use more energy than faster, higher-temperature roasting, provided that the slow roasting is not done at too low a temperature. Somewhere between 225 and 250°F (106 and 121°C) is probably the lowest practical limit. But if energy consumption isn't an issue, by all means pull out the stops and cook your roast at any temperature above about 165°F (74°C) which is hot enough to kill most surface germs. Or do as Paula recommends in *The Slow Mediterranean Kitchen*: Blast or sear the surface of the meat first to take care of any surface germs before you lower the oven to roasting temperature.

Sidebar Science: *(Warning: calculus ahead)*

TO COMPARE the fast (*f*) and slow (*s*) methods of roasting a particular piece of meat to a given state of doneness, we will compare the total amount of oven cooling during fast roasting for h_f hours at T_f degrees with the total amount of oven cooling during slow roasting for h_s hours at T_s degrees.

To obtain the number of slow-roasting hours at which the two energy consumptions are equal, we'll equate the two cooling rates and calculate h_s, the energy break-even time for slow roasting.

For this application, Newton's Law of Cooling can be written

$$-dT/dt = k(T - T_{room}),$$

where T is the oven temperature, t is time, and T_{room} is the room temperature. The constant k depends on the specific oven and is assumed to be the same under both roasting conditions.

If the temperature fluctuations in the oven are relatively small compared with the oven temperatures themselves, and if the successive cooling periods are relatively short compared with the numbers of hours of roasting, we can approximate the differential rate of cooling with a temperature difference divided by a cooling time. Moreover, I will assume that the total amounts of time spent in cooling-and-reheating cycles under both sets of conditions are at least comparable. This can be partially justified by considering that the slow, low-temperature roasting, even though lasting longer, will require fewer reheating cycles because of its slower cooling rate.

Using these assumptions, we obtain

$$h_s = h_f (T_f - T_{room}) / (T_s - T_{room}).$$

In words, the number of slow-roasting hours that consumes the same amount of energy as fast roasting is equal to the number of fast-roasting hours times the number of degrees above room temperature in the fast method, divided by the number of degrees above room temperature in the slow method. It doesn't matter whether the temperatures are in Fahrenheit or Celsius, because only differences in temperature are involved.

In Paula's examples, if the fast method roasts for 3 hours ($h_f = 3$) at a temperature $T_f = 375$, the energy break-even point h_s for slow roasting at temperature $T_s = 180$ comes out to be 8.6 hours, and the energy break-even point for slow roasting at temperature $T_s = 250$ comes out to be 5.1 hours.

I can't understand why Paula decided not to put these calculations in her book.

Low-temperature cooking delivers meltingly tender, rare meat. The lamb is first browned in a hot oven, then the temperature is reduced to 225°F. Roasting continues until the internal temperature of the meat reaches 130 to 135°F. The roast must rest before carving. The temperature will slowly rise to 135 to 140°F for a rare and juicy roast.

When carving, start at the shank end and slice perpendicular to the main bone. To obtain tender meat, always slice across the grain. Serve this Turkish-style lamb with the traditional Red Onion–Parsley Relish.

---

1 bone-in leg of lamb, 5 to 6 pounds

2 tablespoons pomegranate concentrate or molasses

$^1/_3$ cup water

$1^1/_2$ tablespoons extra-virgin olive oil

$^1/_2$ cup finely chopped onion

4 large cloves garlic, crushed

2 teaspoons tomato paste

1 teaspoon crushed red pepper flakes, preferably Aleppo or Turkish

Pinch of sugar

Salt and freshly ground black pepper

1 cup chicken or vegetable broth

1 to 2 tablespoons unsalted butter

Red Onion–Parsley Relish (recipe follows)

---

1. Five to 6 hours before you plan to serve the lamb, trim off the excess fat, leaving about a ¼-inch layer. In a large, deep bowl, dilute the pomegranate concentrate or molasses with the water. Stir in the olive oil, onion, garlic, tomato paste, red pepper, and sugar. Add the lamb and turn to coat. Let stand for no longer than 2 to 3 hours at room temperature, turning once or twice.

2. About 3 hours before serving, place a rack in the lower third of the oven. Preheat the oven to 450°F.

3. Set the lamb, fattiest side up, on a rack in an oiled shallow roasting pan. Season the lamb with plenty of salt and black pepper and set in the oven. Immediately reduce the oven temperature to 250°F. Roast the lamb, basting occasionally with the pan drippings, for 1¾ hours. Turn the roast over and continue roasting and basting for about 30 minutes longer, or until the lamb reaches an internal temperature of 130 to 135°F.

4. Remove the lamb to a carving board, cover loosely with foil, and let rest for 15 to 20 minutes. (During this time, the temperature will rise to 135 to 140°F.) Meanwhile, defat the pan juices. Add the broth, set the pan over medium heat, and stir to scrape up all the brown bits that cling to the bottom. Boil until reduced to napping consistency. Adjust the seasoning and keep hot.

5. Carve the lamb and serve with the sauce and the accompanying onion-parsley relish.

MAKES 6 TO 8 SERVINGS

Red Onion–Parsley Relish

2 red onions, thinly sliced

1 teaspoon coarse salt

¹/₂ cup chopped fresh flat-leaf parsley

1 teaspoon ground sumac*

Toss the red onions with the coarse salt. Rub the salt into the slices and let stand for 5 minutes. Rinse the onions under cold running water and drain thoroughly. Mix the onions with the parsley and sumac. Serve within 30 minutes.

MAKES ABOUT 1 CUP

*Sumac is a nonpoisonous red berry that gives a distinctive, tangy-lemony flavor to dishes. Purchase ground sumac from a spice specialty store. If you have a choice, choose the best-quality sumac, which comes from Jordan. Store in the freezer to maintain quality.

Chapter Ten

A Few Lagniappes for the Insatiable Inquiring Mind

. . . .

THE CUSTOM of giving someone "a little something extra" permeates all societies in one form or another.

In restaurants and taxis, we routinely pay, in the form of a tip, more than the bill requires. And for reasons I have never been able to fathom, employees of many corporations—but regretfully not of universities—are occasionally handed perks called bonuses. ("Oh, by the way, here's some extra money.")

In the days before supermarkets, a baker's dozen meant thirteen rolls instead of twelve, an 8.33 percent increase in the amount of goods for what a cynic might suspect was covered by a hidden 8.33 percent increase in price. It was a brilliant way of selling more rolls by taking advantage of the customer's ingrained concept of "a dozen" as a rigidly fixed unit. For if one bought a dozen and received thirteen, it was not just receiving thirteen instead of twelve; it was a dozen plus a "free" one. A faker's dozen, I call it. But it sure made the customers feel good.

Also making customers feel good is the habit in some restaurants of presenting a *lagniappe*, a small, unexpected treat that appears neither on the menu nor on the bill. (*Lagniappe* is the Creole spelling of the Spanish *la ñapa*, meaning . . . well, something extra.) Every time I am offered one in a restaurant, my cynicism vanishes in a flash and I think, "Oh, how nice!"

In that tradition (and because I couldn't find a better place to put them), I offer in this final chapter a few lagniappes for your insatiable inquiring mind: sundry items about language, cookery, and science with which to cap off the information feast that I hope you have been enjoying.

To borrow a famously ungrammatical slogan from Sara Lee, nobody doesn't like chocolate. So as we began our shared repast with something to drink, I will end it with two chocolate desserts that I hope will leave a pleasant, long-lasting aftertaste in your inquiring mind.

WATCH YOUR LANGUAGE

Dear Dr. Wolke: Can you please write something about the misuse of technical words in relation to foods? Your devoted reader, R. L. Wolke.

. . . .

I'll be glad to. Thanks for giving me an excuse to do so, because a discussion of language in a food-science book might otherwise appear to be out of place. But the English language is one of my most precious treasures, and I welcome the opportunity to reply to your request and set a few things straight.

I'm the kind of guy who upon being handed a menu in a restaurant scans it for spelling errors before beginning to think about the food. But even though the other day I actually saw "tuna tar tar" on a menu (honest!), this section won't be about spelling. Anybody can slipp up on that once in a while.

Well, maybe just one gripe about spelling. The word *restaurateur* does *not* have an *n* in it. In eighteenth-century France, before the word came into general use for the operator of an eating establishment, it referred to the proprietor of a stopping place along the road at which a traveler could rest his horse and perhaps score a meal, which might include an energy restorative, or *restaurant*, such as a bowl of rich broth. The soup chef or proprietor, often the same person, was afforded the honor of being called the *restaurateur*, the restorer.

Okay, one more spelling gripe. The name of the *shiitake* mushroom is spelled with two *i*'s. It does not begin with an Anglo Saxon four-letter word.

Now on to gripes about misused words. I am well aware that nothing I say here will change the world's misuse of the words that follow. But I must do my duty to the language I love by recording the following distinctions. Call this the Department of Lost Causes.

- **High heat.** Cooks often talk about "a higher heat" when they mean "a higher temperature." I can understand the convenience of saying, "Cook such-and-such over a high (or low) heat," meaning a high (or low) setting on the range dial, when the objective really is to produce a higher (or lower) temperature in the food. But please, folks. Butter melts at a low temperature, not at a low heat.

Here's the distinction between heat and temperature: A pot of hot soup may have a certain temperature—that is, it may contain a certain amount of heat per ounce. When you remove a spoonful of soup from the pot, the temperature of the soup in the spoon is the same as that of the soup remaining in the pot, but the spoon is holding a lot less heat because it contains a lot less soup.

• **Melting:** Have you ever heard a person protest when going out in the rain without an umbrella, "I won't melt"? And how many times have you heard that sugar melts in hot coffee? Wrong!

Melting is the conversion of a solid into a liquid caused by heat. And neither tea nor coffee is nearly hot enough to melt sugar. Every solid has its melting point, the temperature at which this solid-to-liquid transition takes place. Ice melts at 32°F (0°C), salt (sodium chloride) melts at 1474°F (801°C), and iron melts at 2800°F (1538°C). Sugar (sucrose) will melt if you put it in a saucepan and heat it to about 350°F (177°C), as you might do when making caramel, peanut brittle, or other candies. But it does not melt when you add it to hot water, which cannot exceed 212°F (100°C).

• **Dissolving:** What happens to sugar in coffee and to salt in your stew is not melting but dissolving, from the Latin *dissolvere*, meaning to come apart. The crystalline structures of solid sugar and salt do indeed disintegrate or come apart, the resulting submicroscopic fragments (molecules or ions) being liberated to swim freely around among the water molecules. In water, sugar and salt do not become molten lumps, as if liquefied by heat. They are present invisibly in dissolved form: "in solution."

Now don't write to tell me that *melt* is defined in your dictionary as "1. to change from a solid to a liquid state, generally by heat; and 2. to dissolve; disintegrate." Lexicographers compile dictionaries with the express purpose of reflecting the current use of our changing language, not of ordaining what is right and what is wrong. The latter responsibility must be borne by sticklers like me.

• **Leaching:** Whenever a nutrient or flavor component dissolves out of a food into the cooking water, odds are that it will be said to be "leached out." No, it is simply *dissolving* in the water. "Leaching" is a highly specific type of dissolving, and it doesn't often happen in cooking.

True leaching is a liquid passing through a porous solid and extracting soluble substances along the way. For example, when you pour hot water through a heap of coffee grounds in a cone filter, the water will leach out many water-soluble components as it passes through the grounds. Rain will leach minerals out of the soil as it filters downward. And an underground stream will leach calcium minerals from the rocks as it passes through their cracks. That's how hard water is made.

On the other hand, when you're simmering spinach in a pot of water, some of the vitamin C in the leaves may well dissolve in the water. But the water has simply extracted, or dissolved (not leached) the vitamin out of the spinach.

In brief, any old dissolving is not leaching.

• **Melding:** Similar to but distinct from melting is melding. Cookbooks tell us to combine ingredients— say, for a sauce, dip, or salad dressing—and then refrigerate them for several hours to let the flavors "meld." Well, do they?

Meld is what is known as a portmanteau word—a word invented by fusing two words. (Lewis Carroll's poem "Jabberwocky" in *Through the Looking Glass* is a masterpiece of portmanteauism: "'Twas brillig, and the slithy toves / Did gyre and gimble in the wabe . . .").

The word *meld* was melded (if I may say so) from the words *melt* and *weld*, and means to blend, merge, or unite—but *not* to melt. It could be used quite accurately as a synonym for *dissolve*, because dissolving is a true merging of one substance (the *solute*) into another (the *solvent*, which is usually water).

A computer search turned up 843,000 web pages on which *meld* is used, with more than 8,000 of them accompanied by the word *fla-*

vor. Example: "Cook for another few minutes until the flavors meld." (Does a bell ring when they're melded?)

Flavors can certainly change, and in many cases improve, upon standing or mixing. Everyone knows that a ragoût tastes better on the second day. And of course many wines mature with age.

But when we blend ingredient X with ingredient Y and detect the growth of a new flavor, it may be forever beyond our ability to identify chemical A in ingredient X that has reacted with chemical B in ingredient Y to produce the new product C with a new flavor. If we find empirically that the overall flavor improves, let's just make the most of it. Melding is probably as good a word as any. Although some romantically inclined food writers prefer to say that the flavors "marry."

Ultimately, the true blending and combining of the profusion of taste, smell, and texture senses that we experience when chewing a food takes place in the brain. Individual molecules of foods act upon our taste and smell receptors, which send messages to the cortex of the brain. There, the messages are combined with physical texture and mouth-feel signals from the nerves in our oral cavities to produce that consummate sensation of "Mmmm, good!"

That's true melding.

IT'S A NATURAL—OR IS IT?

Many packaged food products say "natural flavorings" in the list of ingredients, but when I consult the table of nutrients no specifics are given. What are they adding and why don't they have to say what it is? Is it salt, enzymes, or what? Natural is not the least bit enlightening as an adjective! My chemistry professor used to protest that everything on Earth is natural.

. . . .

This chemistry professor agrees. If it isn't natural, what would it be? Supernatural?

My dictionary lists fourteen meanings for the adjective *natural*, ranging from "not adopted" (for the parent of a child) to "neither sharped nor flatted" (for a musical note). So your confusion is perfectly . . . uh, natural.

Many consumers appear to believe that *natural* is a synonym for good or healthful, as opposed to anything made or processed by humans. But Nature hides many decidedly unfriendly chemicals in our foods. Many of the trace-amount chemicals responsible for the natural flavors of foods are so toxic in larger amounts that they would never be approved by the FDA as additives.

Consider also that the chemical amygdalin, a "natural" glycoside found in apricot and peach pits, reacts with an enzyme in the stomach to produce prussic acid (*hydrogen cyanide*), the lethal gas that has been used to execute convicted criminals. A close chemical derivative of amygdalin called Laetrile has been promoted as a cure for cancer by certain alternative-medicine clinics. The fact that the American Cancer Society has labeled Laetrile quackery hasn't stopped many Americans from traveling to Mexico for "treatment."

Prussic acid is also present in the cassava tuber, a.k.a. manioc, yucca, and tapioca root, which when grated has to be thoroughly washed to remove the poison before it is made into flour and other products. I have bought flat, eighteen-inch discs of crisp, dry yucca bread from children on the roads in Venezuela, hoping that the raw material had been adequately washed, and I have survived.

To control the rampant use of the word *natural* on the labels of food products, the FDA has come up with a definition, at least in the context of flavor additives. The ubiquitous *all-natural*, which manufacturers use to sell everything from cosmetics to toilet cleaners (heavens!—you wouldn't want an unnatural toilet cleaner, would you?) is not regulated and probably cannot be, because it can mean almost anything the manufacturer wants it to mean—including nothing at all.

The official FDA definition of natural flavoring is published in the Code of Federal Regulations (21CFR101.22) in the form of more than a hundred words that meticulously plug every conceivable loophole and that would put a permanent wave in the brains of most lawyers, even if they knew what "hydrolysate" and "enzymolysis" meant in the definition.

In simple terms, a natural flavor is defined as a substance extracted, distilled, or otherwise obtained from plant or animal matter, either directly from the matter itself or after it has been roasted, heated, or fermented. Note the inclusion of "animal matter" in this definition, a revelation that would shock vegetarians to their carrot roots and send those who adhere to the kosher segregation of meat from dairy products running to their rabbis for elucidation. But animals are just as natural as plants, are they not? Note also that a natural flavor does not have to come from the food it is flavoring. For example, a natural flavor chemical derived from chicken—which needn't necessarily taste like chicken—can be used to flavor a can of beef ravioli.

An artificial flavor, on the other hand, is defined straightforwardly by the FDA as any substance that does not fit the definition of a natural flavor. Ironically, such synthetic flavoring chemicals, though unabashedly unnatural, are acceptable in all restrictive diets from vegan to kosher, because they are neither animal nor vegetable. (You will search in vain for any philosophical or religious injunctions against 2,6-dimethylpyrazine, the prominent artificial-flavor chemical in chocolate.) Furthermore, most of the chemical compounds in both artificial and natural flavors are not recognized as food by our digestive systems and are not metabolized. That's why you won't find them listed in the Nutrition Facts chart; they are not nutrients and are at any rate present in only trace amounts.

Not often realized is the fact that all flavoring additives, natural or artificial, are made by humans. To make an artificial flavor, a flavor chemist (called a flavorist) in a laboratory has to select and blend the right chemical compounds in the right proportions to simulate a natural flavor. And to make a natural flavor, someone in another lab-oratory or factory has to extract and distill or concentrate the flavor compounds from the raw plant or animal materials.

An even less appreciated fact is that in many cases the man-made flavoring chemicals are identical to Nature's flavoring chemicals. For example, one of the primary flavor chemicals in bananas is isoamyl acetate, which can be made synthetically and used as a (rather poor) imitation of banana flavor.

Most natural flavors, however, are much more complex than that. Some thirty-seven different chemical compounds have been identi-fied in the flavor of mangoes, and more than eight hundred in the aroma of coffee. To imitate the effects of these natural flavors on the palate, a flavorist must blend a dozen or more chemicals, no single one of which hits the flavor nail directly on the head.

An interesting case is the vanilla bean, most of whose natural fla-vor comes from its 2 percent content of vanillin, known to chemists by its nickname, 4-hydroxy-3-methoxy benzaldehyde. If this and the other natural vanilla flavors are extracted into alcohol, the product may legally be labeled Pure Vanilla Extract, a "natural" flavoring. But if the product contains synthetic vanillin, which can be made by any of several processes, it must be labeled Imitation Vanilla Flavoring.

But get this: If the synthetic vanillin was made not by combining chemicals in a laboratory but by allowing bacteria to ferment ferulic acid, a chemical obtained from corn or rice, it may be labeled Natural Vanilla Flavor, because fermentation is a "natural" process. The vanillin obtained by the fermentation, however, is absolutely identi-cal to the vanillin made in the lab.

The bottom-line issue for cooks is "Does artificial vanilla flavor-ing taste as good as natural vanilla flavoring?" Well, in taste panels convened by Cook's Illustrated magazine over a period of several years, the imitation vanilla flavoring was actually preferred over the natural product. So there!

TRICKLE-DOWN ERGONOMICS

I have observed an interesting phenomenon with
milk and orange juice cartons. After I pour out the
"last" drops, I can always come back later and
pour out more liquid. What's going on?

. . . .

So you've noticed that, too, eh? It happens when you're "emptying" all sorts of containers, including cocktail shakers and wine bottles. I hadn't given it much thought, but you have inspired me to figure out what really *is* going on.

What's undoubtedly happening is that as you "empty" the container, some of the liquid encounters microscopic rough spots or non-wettable spots on the container's inside surface. These spots hold back small drops of the liquid, which remain stuck there as long as the container continues to be inverted. But when you return it to its upright position, the small drops can slide back down, because the path had been smooth up until they encountered those snags. So the drops do slide back down, joining their brethren at the bottom to form a pool. The pool is now heavier than any individual drop, so when you invert the container again the pool can steamroller right down past the rough spots.

I hope you are happier for understanding that. I know I am.

WANT S'MORE?

*I am curious about marshmallow. Ever since I
was a kid I've wondered how that sweet, puffy
substance with such an odd name and texture was
ever invented. Is it really old?*

. . . .

The modern version is only about a hundred years old, but it's a new take on a several-thousand-year-old treat.

The magical material we call marshmallow is named after the marsh mallow plant (*Althaea officinalis*), whose roots contain a sweet, gummy sap that has been used as a confection and for its supposed medicinal properties for some four thousand years.

In the late nineteenth century, when candy makers were unable to keep up with demand for the real thing, an imitation marshmallow was concocted from sugar, starch, and gelatin. Today, most marshmallow candies are made from corn syrup, sugar, modified starch, and gelatin. (Modified starch is starch that has been treated chemically or physically to improve its characteristics for manufacturing purposes, such as by making it able to mix with and thicken cold water.)

The most pleasurable characteristic of marshmallow is its uniquely soft, pillowy texture, unmatched by any other food. To make it, a hot ($240°F$ or $116°C$) mixture of corn syrup, sugar, water, and gelatin is whipped vigorously into a frothy foam until it is two to three times its original volume. Zillions of microscopic air bubbles remain trapped as the mixture cools and the gelatin sets. The result is a solid foam that is only 35 to 45 percent as dense as water.

Technically, a foam is a suspension of gas bubbles in a liquid. The bubbles are so tiny (they are of *colloidal* size) that they never rise to the surface; they stay suspended in the liquid. Often, as in the case of marshmallow, polystyrene foam (trademarked Styrofoam), and baked meringues, we still call it a foam after the liquid has solidified or dried. Foams can be stabilized—the air bubbles prevented from coalescing into bigger bubbles—by emulsifying agents such as soaps and certain proteins. In foods, we prefer the protein stabilizers: gelatin, the casein in whipped cream, and the albumins in egg-white meringues can all do the job.

The most familiar brands of marshmallow confections, Campfire and Jet-Puffed, are in the shape of small cylinders about an inch in diameter and an inch long. Why that shape? In marshmallow factories the liquid foam is piped through a long, one-inch-diameter tube as it cools, and the emerging rope is then chopped into approximately one-inch lengths. (In case anyone ever asks you, Campfires are an eighth of an inch wider and an eighth of an inch shorter than Jet-Puffed marshmallows.)

By measuring and weighing them carefully (okay, so I'm a nut), I have calculated (a) that Campfire marshmallows are 23 percent puffier (less dense) than Jet-Puffed, and (b) that the 90 million pounds of marshmallows consumed annually in the United States would make a single marshmallow 30 yards in diameter and as tall as the Washington Monument.

The texture of marshmallow can be controlled by adjusting the proportions of ingredients and the amount of whipping. It ranges from the semiliquid Marshmallow Fluff to the more elastic and chewier marshmallows that can stand up to being coated with chocolate. That's why chocolate-covered marshmallow candies are never as soft inside as you expect them to be.

You cannot have read this far without thinking about toasting marshmallows on a stick over a campfire, right? The fire's heat both melts the gelatin and caramelizes the sugar, producing a hot, caramel-flavored goo that yin-yangs your tongue with heat and sweet. But as in all cooking, there is a right way and a wrong way.

Wrong way: Hold the marshmallow just above the flames until it catches fire, and let it burn until it has a crisp, black crust. Don't be deterred by the fact that the crust is made of indigestible carbon laced with bitter-tasting and undoubtedly carcinogenic tars.

Right way: Wait until the fire has died down to glowing coals and then hold the marshmallow high over them, rotating it until it slowly develops a nice uniform tan color. (Patience, patience.) If it should catch fire, blow it out immediately, let it cool for a few seconds, and resume toasting.

In the Boy Scouts I learned to search out and cut a long green twig that wouldn't catch fire. Today, you can buy a package of 30-inch-long Smorstix that are, according to the Smorstix website (http://www.smorstix.com), "made of 100% untreated white birch without any additives, dirt or grime." With these, you can supposedly toast your marshmallows with a clear environmental conscience instead of "trampl[ing] the underbrush and damag[ing] trees and forests" (in Smorstix's words) during your search for a toasting stick.

Ah, for the simpler, politically incorrect days of my youth!

My female readers are likely to know why Smorstix were so named: for s'mores, the Girl Scouts' traditional campfire dessert made (according to the recipe in a 1927 Girl Scout manual) by inserting two toasted marshmallows between halves of a Hershey bar sandwiched between graham crackers. The hot, gooey marshmallow melts the chocolate, making even more goo.

For those who don't have access to a campfire, I (don't blame Marlene for it) have created Marshmallow Zaps, an indoor alternative to fire-roasted marshmallows.

Marshmallow Zaps

These marshmallow-caramel treats, crisp on the outside and soft on the inside, are not only a unique treat, but fun to watch while you're making them. Look, Ma, no hands!

---

6 large (not miniature) marshmallows
About 2 tablespoons confectioners' sugar

---

1. Arrange the marshmallows in a Stonehenge-style ring, placing them upright and well separated, on a microwave-safe dinner plate.

2. Zap the marshmallows in the microwave oven on high, watching through the window as they balloon to several times their size. Stop the oven when they have developed brown, volcano-like holes on top, after about 1½ minutes. (The time depends on the power of your microwave oven.)

3. Remove the plate carefully (it may be quite hot) and place it on the counter to cool completely, during which time the marshmallows will deflate and flatten.

4. Remove each Zap from the plate (it will be quite sticky), dip its bottom into confectioners' sugar, and place it on a serving dish or platter. It will be crisp as a meringue on the outside and chewy on the inside, with a layer of brown caramelized sugar in the middle as if it were an inside-out fire-roasted marshmallow.

They may not look pretty, but you'll sure want s'more.

Sidebar Science: *How the Zaps work*

IN THE interior of the marshmallow, the microwaves' energy converts water into steam, which first puffs up the marshmallow and then, when the gelatin's elasticity limit is exceeded, breaks its way out through a hole it punches in the top.

Meanwhile, the sugar begins to caramelize under the influence of the heat. Because dehydration is the first step in the complex series of chemical reactions involved in caramelization, it is the dehydrated interior sugar that caramelizes first. The outer parts of the marshmallow, still saturated with steam, would not caramelize unless they were heated longer than in the Zaps recipe. As the marshmallows cool, the steam condenses and the foam collapses.

FOOD OF THE GODS

Lately, many of the better food stores have been carrying a wide assortment of chocolate bars from different countries. Some of my friends are comparing and discussing their merits as if they were wines. Mostly, they talk about "percents," but percents of what? Also, I find the ingredient lists on the wrappers to be confusing. Can you help me sort these things out so I can be as snobbish as my friends?

. . . .

Americans seem to have discovered only a few years ago that "chocolate" doesn't have to mean Hershey bars and Whitman Samplers; they learned that serious chocolate bars, as distinguished from candy bars, could open a whole new world of flavors. There are now dozens of dark chocolate bars on the market from both American and foreign manufacturers. Among foodies, chocolate tastings threaten to replace wine tastings as entertaining and educational activities.

The ingredient lists on the wrappers can indeed be perplexing, because most of the ingredients go by a number of aliases. So let's look closely at what is in a serious bar of dark chocolate.

It all starts with cacao (ka-KAH-oh), not cocoa (KO-ko), beans. Cacao beans are the seeds of the fruit of the tropical tree *Theobroma cacao.* (*Theobroma* literally means "food of the gods," a name obviously chosen by a chocophile taxonomist.) The bitter cacao bean was enjoyed as a spice by the Mayans and Aztecs, but only after it made its way to Europe was it sweetened with sugar.

The percentage number on a bar's wrapper is the percentage of the bar's weight that actually came from the cacao bean. That is, it's the bar's content of honest-to-goodness cacao bean components. Natural cacao beans contain 54 percent fat by weight; the other 46 percent is hard, solid vegetable matter. Thus, the percentage number on the wrapper of a chocolate bar is the sum of its cacao fat (called cocoa butter in the United States) and its cacao solids.

The rest of a chocolate bar is almost entirely sugar, so a "75%" chocolate bar will contain about 25 percent sugar. Thus, the higher the percentage number on the wrapper, the less sweet, more bitter, and more complex the flavor. Minor ingredients, usually present at less than one percent, may include vanilla or vanillin (an artificial flavor) and lecithin, an emulsifier obtained from soybeans that enhances the chocolate's smoothness and creaminess.

Here, then, are the three major components of a quality chocolate bar, together with their aliases. My preferred names (and I wish the world would standardize upon them or their translations) are in boldface.

- **Chocolate liquor,** cacao, cacao mass, cacao paste, or cacao liquor: By any of these names, this is the "raw material" of chocolate: ground-up cacao beans. It is often referred to as a paste or liquor because the friction of grinding melts the dense fat, and what comes out of the grinding machine is a glistening brown paste. The percentage of chocolate liquor in a bar is the percentage of actual chocolate.

• **Cocoa butter** or cacao butter: The fat from the cacao bean. *Butter* is a more appealing word than *fat*, but don't let it fool you into thinking it comes from a cow. Not even a brown cow.

• **Cocoa**, cocoa solids, or cacao solids: The brown, solid parts of the cacao beans, ground to a powder.

That's it. Just three main players in the cast of characters: whole chocolate, its fatty part, and its solid part. If the cocoa butter and the cocoa solids are separated, they can be combined with sugar in various proportions to make a variety of different "chocolates."

"Unsweetened chocolate" or "baking chocolate" is simply chocolate liquor that has been poured into molds and solidified by cooling. The FDA requires that it contain between 50 percent and 58 percent fat, a leeway of 4 percent on either side of natural cacao beans' fat content of 54 percent.

In addition to its 54 percent content of fat, chocolate liquor contains about 17 percent carbohydrates, 11 percent protein, 6 percent tannins, and 1.5 percent theobromine, an alkaloid similar to caffeine and a mild stimulant. It also contains less than 1 percent of phenylethylamine, a somewhat stronger stimulant similar to amphetamine, known in certain quarters as "speed" or "uppers." Other minor ingredients of chocolate are polyphenols, antioxidants that counteract harmful free radicals; and anandamide, a close relative of tetrahydrocannabinol (THC), the active ingredient in marijuana. But note that the amounts of all these physiologically active and psychoactive chemicals are minuscule. Moreover, the "highs" they produce are short-lived and not very lofty.

Before a batch of molten chocolate is ready to be poured into bar molds, it is usually *conched*: kneaded and massaged in heated tanks for anywhere from two to six days while chemical changes take place, flavors develop, moisture and bad flavors such as acetic acid evaporate, and the sugar is reduced to smaller particles, leading to a smoother texture. (The word *conch* comes from the shell-shaped blades of the early conching machines.)

Chocolate factories can squeeze the fat out of whole cacao, thus separating the fat from the solids. The fat-free solids are commonly and quite properly called cocoa and are sold as such. The manufacturer often adds some of the separated fat to a chocolate-bar mix in order to adjust the smoothness and melting properties of the ultimate bar. Because this added cocoa butter changes the cacao's natural 54-to-46 ratio of fat to solids, it is listed separately as an additive in the list of ingredients. The percentage number on the wrapper includes this added fat.

Note that I have not included milk, milk solids, or nonfat milk among the ingredients because (and I know I'll get flak for this) I don't consider milk chocolate to be chocolate. It's just candy. Milk chocolate contains so much milk and sugar that its percentage of true cacao may be as low as 10 percent, the minimum required by the FDA for calling it "chocolate" on the label. Hershey's milk chocolate contains about 11 percent cacao. By contrast, a serious dark chocolate bar will contain anywhere from 65 to 85 percent cacao.

The smoothness of a chocolate bar—one result of how much fat it contains—is a matter of national preference. In continental Europe, people like their chocolate very smooth, containing sugar particles no bigger than 80 millionths of an inch (2 microns), while the British prefer slightly gritty chocolate containing 400-millionths-of-an-inch (10 micron) sugar particles. Almost nobody likes the grittiness of chocolate containing solid particles bigger than 600 millionths of an inch (15 microns).

In 2003, as a result of squabbling among Belgium, England, France, and Germany with anxious input from Switzerland, the European Union ruled that up to 5% of the cocoa butter in chocolate may be

replaced with other vegetable fats. That's why many of the best European dark chocolate bars brag about their high cacao content by print-
ing their percentage numbers in huge type on their wrappers.

If you're truly interested in upping your snob quotient, taste as
many serious dark chocolate bars as you can find (or afford; they're
not cheap). Use the percentage of chocolate liquor only as an initial
indicator of how sweet or bitter you like your chocolate. Then try a
variety of bars in that range to find your favorites in brittleness or
"snap," flavor, and mouth feel. Learn the cacao percentages and
countries of origin of a few bars, and at every opportunity, talk about
them in terms taken from a wine magazine (bouquet, fruit, finish,
and so on). Use the word *cacao* (not cocoa) as often as possible, and
you can be as good a chocolate snob as any of your friends.

MY CHOCOLATE HAD A SEIZURE AND I LOST MY TEMPER!

*As a pastry chef, I know all the techniques for
working with chocolate to prevent disasters such
as my chocolate's seizing or losing its temper, or
being too hard or too soft for molding or piping,
etc. From training and experience, I know all the
exact temperatures and so on, but I would like to
know more about how and why they work.*

. . . .

Chocolate is indeed a difficult material to work with, owing to its
complex composition, mostly its content of several different fats.

As it arrives in the kitchen from your purveyor in the form of
slabs or pastilles, it consists of microscopic particles of cocoa and
sugar distributed throughout a sea of solidified fat or cocoa butter.
It's the fat that's the main problem, because it consists of at least six
different chemical compounds—different fats that have different
crystallization temperatures—and you have to keep all but one of

them from crystallizing. It's a temperature juggling act called tempering. Table 7 shows what chocolatiers have to deal with.

In the table, the six different fats are listed, from bottom up, in order of increasing crystallization temperatures. What is a crystallization temperature? Consider the liquid called water. When we cool it down to 32°F (0°C), it crystallizes into what we call ice. But when we heat it above 32°F (0°C), the crystals melt into liquid. That magic temperature is both the *crystallization temperature* and the *melting temperature* of H_2O.

Similarly, the crystallization temperatures in the table are the approximate temperatures below which the fats crystallize into their own unique kinds of crystals and above which they melt into liquid. Of the six crystal forms (*polymorphs*), it is only number V that has exactly the properties we want in our chocolate: it's glossy and, when solid, crisp and snappy when bitten into. But it will still melt in our mouths because our body temperature of 98.6°F (37°C) is a few degrees higher than its crystallization (or melting) temperature of 94°F (34°C).

The problem is, how do we get rid of the other, less desirable crystal forms? First (see the graph on p. 438), we heat the chocolate to about 120°F (50°C), which melts all six forms. Then we cool it down to about 80°F (27°C), where forms IV and above will crystallize. And then we slowly raise the temperature to 90°F (32°C), which melts the crystals of form IV, leaving us with only forms V and VI in crystallized form. But since form VI requires days or weeks to crystallize, it doesn't. The result is that the only crystals remaining are those of the desirable form V. We have tempered our chocolate to achieve the ideal working characteristics for the pastry chef.

If, while you are working with the tempered chocolate, it loses its temper (along with you losing yours) by being heated or cooled too much, there is nothing to do but repeat the entire tempering cycle.

In cooking, rather than in decorating, with chocolate, there are a number of pitfalls, the most exasperating of which is seizing: the chocolate's suddenly turning from a smooth, viscous liquid into a

Table 7. The six crystal forms of cocoa butter

FORM	CRYSTALLIZATION TEMPERATURE	CHARACTERISTICS
VI	97°F (36°C)	Highest crystallization temperature Most stable Slow to form (weeks) Dense, hard
V	94°F (34°C)	Most desirable form Good gloss, snap
IV	82°F (28°C)	Intermediate characteristics
III	78°F (26°C)	Intermediate characteristics
II	70°F (21°C)	Intermediate characteristics
I	63°F (17°C)	Lowest crystallization temperature Least stable Less dense, more crumbly Soft, no snap

mess of grainy, muddy clumps. This can happen for several reasons, the most common of which is the effect of a small amount of water. But paradoxically, a large amount of water or watery liquid such as cream will not make the chocolate seize; the chocolate and the watery liquid will blend together like a dream.

Here's why.

Think of well-tempered chocolate as zillions of microscopic cocoa (and sugar, if it's semisweet) particles suspended in a sea of fat. Cocoa and sugar particles are not fat-loving (lipophilic); on the contrary, they are water-loving (hydrophilic). If even a few drops of

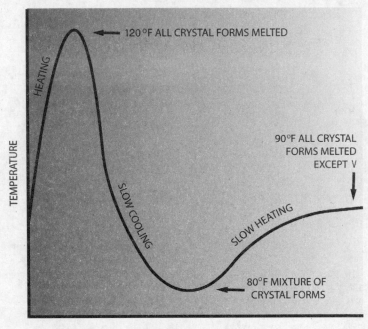

Tempering chocolate. The chocolate is first heated to 120°F (50°C) to melt all crystal forms, then slowly cooled to 80°F (27°C) and reheated to 90°F (32°C), so that all crystal forms are melted except the desired form V. (See Table 7.) (Temperatures are approximate.)

water are added, the water will be attracted to and will wet the particles, making them clump together into something like a mud ball. And a little bit of water can wet an awful lot of tiny particles, creeping between them in a thin film and holding them together by capillary attraction.

If stirred, virtually the entire pot of melted chocolate will then freeze into a thick mud—useless for making into smooth, glossy frostings and confections. That's why melted chocolate must be protected from contact with the tiniest amount of water, such as condensed steam from a double boiler. Many of today's pastry chefs melt their chocolate in a microwave oven to sidestep this danger.

But oddly enough, a *large amount* of watery liquid will not make the chocolate seize. If you have ever made a sand castle at the beach, you know that a little bit of water will cement the sand grains together into a mass that will hold its shape. But when a wave washes in, the *large* amount of water disintegrates the mass by separating the grains from one another.

That's why, in the recipe for ganache on page 443, you can add a whole cup of cream to the melted chocolate and it won't seize. The fact that heavy whipping cream is about 38 percent fat doesn't hurt.

Cake decorating 101

When decorating with melted chocolate by piping it onto a cake or a sheet of parchment for later stripping, you want it to set up hard, rather than remaining liquid and spreading out. Before you pipe it, deliberately induce it to seize slightly by adding water carefully, drop by drop while stirring, until it begins to thicken. When the right amount of water has been added, a piped test sample will harden quickly, especially if refrigerated for 3 to 5 minutes.

WHEN CHOCOLATE IS IN BLOOM

In a box of assorted chocolates I noticed that
only the candies covered with dark chocolate
acquired a white film after several months,
while the milk chocolates did not. I have
wondered what in the chemical composition
of the dark chocolate causes this.

....

After several months, you say? In my house, a box of chocolates is lucky to last a week.

The white film is called "bloom" and is caused by excessive or varying temperatures. You have committed the crime of chocolate abuse by not storing it properly.

The white film is not mold and is perfectly harmless, affecting only the chocolate's appearance and to some extent its texture. Milk chocolate typically consists of about 70 percent powdered milk and sugar, with only about 12 percent chocolate liquor, so it isn't as prone to bloom as is dark chocolate, which may contain as much as 75 percent.

There are three kinds of chocolate bloom: fat bloom, sugar bloom, and age bloom.

Fat bloom happens when under conditions of excessive warmth some of the liquid fat constituents migrate to the surface, where they form relatively large, light-reflecting crystals. Chocolate should never be stored at a temperature higher than 80°F (27°C); 63°F (17°C) is ideal.

Sugar bloom happens when the chocolate is wet or stored in high humidity, which dissolves some of the sugar out of the surface, where it remains as solid crystals when the water evaporates.

Age bloom happens to old chocolate, when the slow-forming fat crystals of form VI (see p. 437) have had a chance to develop. They form big, coarse crystals that disrupt the smooth texture of the chocolate to the extent that it may actually crumble. For example, if you drop a bar of chocolate behind the seat of your car and forget about it, discovering it only two years later when you're cleaning out the car before selling it, you will notice—oh, I can't go on! It's just too horrible to contemplate.

The best way to avoid chocolate bloom is to consume all chocolate as soon as it comes within reach. That's my method.

THE GRINCH WHO STOLE CHOCOLATE

In health-food stores I have seen chocolate bars
made out of carob, presumably to avoid the
fat and caffeine in ordinary chocolate.
What, exactly, is carob?

. . . .

Here we go, from the sublime to the ridiculous.

First of all, contrary to common belief, chocolate doesn't contain much caffeine at all. A square (one ounce) of unsweetened baking chocolate averages 23 milligrams of caffeine, while a cup of coffee might contain more than 100 milligrams. An ounce of unsweetened chocolate does contain 376 milligrams of theobromine, however, an alkaloid closely related to caffeine but a milder stimulant.

The leguminous carob tree (*Ceratonia siliqua*), also known since biblical times as the locust bean tree, grows in relatively arid, semi-tropical climates such as in California, Florida, and the eastern Mediterranean region. Its pods have been dubbed Saint John's bread because the Bible says that John the Baptist survived in the wilderness by eating "locusts and honey." In spite of the Bible's preoccupation elsewhere with locusts (the word appears twenty-nine times in the King James version), it is more likely that John munched on locust *beans* rather than on the insects.

Locust bean gum, which appears in many food ingredient lists, is a tasteless, mucilaginous polysaccharide thickener obtained from the carob's seeds. It is used to thicken frozen desserts, cultured dairy products, cream cheese, and other foods. It interacts with the other vegetable gums xanthin and carrageenan to form rigid gels, and is therefore rarely used alone.

So where does chocolate come in? The carob tree makes long, edible, seed-bearing pods that can be dried and ground into a powder. Because the powder is brown, sweet (it contains about 40 percent sugars), and virtually fat-free, someone got the not-so-bright idea of using it as a substitute for chocolate. Unfortunately, because it lacks chocolate's fat it has a sandy, gritty texture, not to mention an almost total absence of flavor.

Carob is the Grinch who stole chocolate. Fuhgeddaboudit.

WE HAVE ARRIVED at the last course in our feast of knowledge: our dessert. We'll conclude, then, with recipes for two sweet treats, a classic one and an off-beat one.

The classic one is a *ganache*, a blend of the two most luxuriant ingredients in our epicurean armamentarium: chocolate and whipping cream. In essence a marriage of two fats, cocoa butter and butterfat, ganache on a menu is not for the faint of *carte*. Rarely billed by its own name, it might be concealed as the frosting on a cake or the filling between its layers. Or it might be the center of a truffle. Wherever it appears, ganache is the definitive chocolate *crème*, and you know that when cream is spelled the French way, it's gotta be good.

Our offbeat concluding confection is a grilled chocolate sandwich. Yes, a sandwich. Bread and all. Any time you're in the mood for a soul-nourishing nosh, you can quickly whip up the cacao gods' answer to the grilled cheese sandwich.

I hate it when a restaurant server says, "Enjoy."

But enjoy!

Ganache

A ganache is a mixture of melted chocolate and heated heavy cream, blended together until very smooth. The relative amounts of the two ingredients may vary, but equal amounts give good results and are easy to remember. Ganache is often cooled and shaped into balls to form the soft centers for truffles. Here, lukewarm ganache is poured over a cake to make a smooth and luscious shiny glaze.

For a 1-layer 8- or 9-inch round cake, you will need about 1 cup ganache. Use the leftover ganache as a sauce for poached pears, ice cream, or other dessert. It will keep for up to 2 months in a well-covered container in the refrigerator—if you can keep from eating it with a spoon, that is.

---

8 ounces semisweet or bittersweet chocolate, finely chopped

1 cup heavy cream

---

1. Put the chopped chocolate in a medium heatproof bowl.

2. In a small saucepan, bring the cream to a boil. Pour the hot cream over the chocolate and whisk gently until the chocolate is completely melted and smooth. Allow to cool to warm.

3. Place a cool 8- or 9-inch cake layer on a rack over a baking sheet or a piece of foil. Pour the warm ganache over the cake and use a metal icing spatula to coax and spread it over the top of the cake and down the sides. Let the iced cake set for about 1 hour before serving.

MAKES 1^1/$_2$ CUPS

Grilled Chocolate Sandwich

This sandwich makes a surprising and delicious dessert, afternoon snack, or indulgent breakfast. It is a semi-incestuous marriage, if you will, of transatlantic cousins, the American grilled cheese sandwich with the French *pain au chocolat*. In the latter *pâtisserie* classic, *batons* of chocolate are wrapped in rectangles of flaky pastry.

Bob and I prefer dark chocolate, but you can make yours with milk chocolate if you wish.

---

2 teaspoons unsalted butter, at room temperature
2 slices plain white or sourdough bread, each
  about $^1/_2$ inch thick or less
1 ounce bittersweet chocolate, coarsely chopped

---

1. Spread 1 teaspoon softened butter on 1 side of each slice of bread. Place 1 slice, butter side down, in the center of a small, cold nonstick skillet. Carefully scatter the chocolate over the surface of the bread to within ¼ inch of the edge. Top with the other slice of bread, buttered side up, to make a sandwich.

2. Place the skillet over medium-high heat. Put a flat weight, such as a small plate, on top of the sandwich. Cook for 2 to 3 minutes, or until the bottom slice is lightly browned. The chocolate should be barely melted, not oozing out the sides. Turn the sandwich over and cook for about 2 minutes longer, or until the second side is browned.

3. Remove the sandwich to a plate, cut into quarters, and serve warm.

SERVES 1 OR 2 INDULGENTLY

PLEASE NOTE: *Nowhere in this book have I used the word* myriad.

INDEX

alkylthiosulfonates, 340–41
allicin, 343
alliin, 343
alliinase, 126
allyl isothiocyanate, 336, 358
allyl trisulfide, 345
alpha-galactosidase, 142
Althaea officinalis, 427
aluminum
    discoloration and corrosion in dish-
        washer, 376–78
    emissivity of, 399
American sea scallops, 262
amino groups, 297
ammonia, odor of, in fish, 347
Amontillados, 30
amphoteric substances, 369, 377
AMR (advanced meat recovery) systems,
    273–74
amygdalin, 423
amylase, in honey, 236
amylopectin starches, 204–5
anacardic acid, in cashews, 201
anandamide, in chocolate, 433
anchos, 335
angel hair pasta, 221, 222
angular momentum, 97
angular velocity, 97
anions, 14
annatto seeds, 314
anthocyanins, 13–14, 47, 109, 110
anthoxanthins, 109, 117
antimicrobials, as preservatives, 374
antioxidants, 175
    in cattle feed, 279
    in honey, 237
    as preservatives, 375
Apiadeae, 327
Apicus, Marcus Gavius, 234
apple(s), floating in water, 191–92
apple brandy, 197–98
apple cider, 194–95
applejack, 197, 198
apple juice, 194–95
    fermented, 195, 196–98
    filtering of, 195
    pasteurization of, 195
apple wine, 197
arborio rice, 212–13
Argopecten gibbus, 262
Argopecten irradians, 262
Arm & Hammer, 368, 370
ascorbic acid, as preservative, 375

Aspergillus oryzae, 138
astaxanthin, 240
ATB (Alcohol and Tobacco Tax and Trade
    Bureau), 36
Atlantic blue mussels, 253, 254
aubergines, 266
autocatalytic reactions, 151
avocados
    ripening of, 150
    wasabi guacamole, 360

BAC (blood alcohol concentration), 44–45
bacteria
    in buttermilk, 63
    in butter production, 83–84
    converting nitrate to nitrite, 283
    good and bad, 77
    meat spoilage and, 278
    multiplication of, 311
    nitrites to inhibit growth of, 283
    nitrogen-fixing, 143
    rotting of eggs by, 101
    spores formed by, 310–12, 346
    toxins produced by, 311
    warm water as breeding ground for, 303
    in yogurt production, 60–61, 62
    see also specific bacteria
baker's dozen, 417
bakeware
    oven temperature and, 400–401
    silicone, 405–8
baking
    of beignets soufflés, 165
    in brick ovens, 395–97
    pizza stones for, 395–97
    substituting olive oil for butter in, 184
    see also ovens; oven temperature
baking chocolate, 433
baking soda
    to keep refrigerator smelling fresh,
        368–71
    in vegetable cooking water, 112
    in water used to soak dried beans, 144
bananas
    plantains distinguished from, 157
    ripening of, calories and, 156–57
Bananas Byczewski, 158–59
Bananas Foster, 157, 158
B[a]P (benzo[a]pyrene), 323
barbecue sauce, Jack Daniel's rib-ticklin,'
    38
barbecuing, grilling differentiated from,
    317

Fahrenheit scale, conversion between
    Celsius scale and, 388–89
Fajitas, Skirt Steak, Marinated, 294–95
farfalle, 221
farm-raised salmon, dyes used in, 239–41
fat(s)
    in Brie cheese, 73–74
    in butter, 82–83
    cacao, 432, 433
    in chocolate, 432, 433, 434–35
    in cream, 52–59
    in cream cheese, 70
    hydrogenated, 168, 170
    in milk, 52–55
    in muscle tissue, 271
    removing from cooled stock, 308
    trans (trans fatty acids), 166–71
    see also butter; cocoa butter; olive oil;
        vegetable oils
fat bloom, on chocolate, 440
fat-free milk, 52, 55
fatty acids (FAs)
    chains of, 181
    in olive oil, 177–78
    saturated, 169, 171
    sugar esters of, 381
    trans, 166–71
    unsaturated, 169–70
FDA. *see* Food and Drug Administration
        (FDA)
ferric form of iron, 278
ferric oxidation state, 285
ferric sulfide, in eggs, 98–99
ferrous form of iron, 278
ferrous oxidation state, 285
ferrous sulfide, in eggs, 98–99
fertilized eggs, 90
fettuccine, 221, 222
fiber, dietary, 223–25
finishing sauces with butter, 82–83
Finos, 30
fish
    ammonia smell in, 347
    "cooked" in lime juice, 248–51
    Miso-Glazed Black Bass, 139–40
    raw, caution regarding, 244
    stock, 306
    see also specific types of fish
Fiskars knife sharpener, 127, 128
Fit Produce Wash, 114
flatulence, with legumes, 141–42
flavonoids, 109, 237
flavor(s)

added by wine, 315
of beer, 24–25
of butter, 84
of capsicums, 334–35
of cucumbers, 130–31
deep-frying oil and, 174
essential oils and, 331
of garlic, 340–42, 343
of mangoes, 425
melding of, 421–22
of olive oil, 177
of onions, 340–42
release by alcohol, 313–15
smoking foods and, 322–23, 324
of tea, 11
of yogurt, 61
flavoring
    artificial, 424–25
    natural, 424, 425
flavoring marinades, 288
Fleming, Alexander, 75
flour
    bleaching of, 217–18
    buckwheat, 219–20
    corn, 226
    self-rising, making, 219
    semolina, 217
    unbleached, 217
flour tortillas, 230
foams, 427–28
Food and Drug Administration (FDA)
    cheese categories of, 80–81
    definition of "natural" of, 423–24
    fat content in chocolate required by, 433
    labeling requirements for foods con-
        taining trans fatty acids and, 166
    Pure Vanilla Extract defined by, 366
    regulation of cheese production by,
        77–78
    silicone approval by, 407
food labels
    fiber on, 224
    "natural" on, 422–25
    natural on, 195
    sugars on, 233
foot, of clam, 256–57
Ford, Henry, 318
Ford Charcoal Company, 318
fortified wines, 30
Foster, Richard, 158
fractionation, of oils, 162, 168
free radicals, 175
freezing